THE ART IN PAINTING

PUBLICATIONS AUTHORED BY MEMBERS OF THE ART DEPARTMENT STAFF

THE ART IN PAINTING
Albert C. Barnes

THE AESTHETIC EXPERIENCE
Laurence Buermeyer

AN APPROACH TO ART
Mary Mullen

ART AND EDUCATION
Dewey, Barnes, Buermeyer, Mullen & de Mazia

ART AS EXPERIENCE
John Dewey

PRIMITIVE NEGRO SCULPTURE
Paul Guillaume & Thomas Munro

THE FRENCH PRIMITIVES AND THEIR FORMS
Albert C. Barnes & Violette de Mazia

THE ART OF RENOIR
Albert C. Barnes & Violette de Mazia

THE ART OF HENRI-MATISSE
Albert C. Barnes & Violette de Mazia

THE ART OF CÉZANNE
Albert C. Barnes & Violette de Mazia

THE BARNES FOUNDATION JOURNAL OF THE ART DEPARTMENT

VISTAS

Wall of Gallery, Barnes Foundation (254)

THE ART
IN PAINTING

Albert C. Barnes

ONE HUNDRED TWENTY-TWO ILLUSTRATIONS

THIRD EDITION, REVISED AND ENLARGED

FIFTH PRINTING

THE BARNES FOUNDATION PRESS

MERION STATION, PA.

TO

JOHN DEWEY

WHOSE CONCEPTIONS
OF EXPERIENCE, OF METHOD, OF EDUCATION,
INSPIRED THE WORK OF WHICH
THIS BOOK IS A PART

PREFACE TO THE THIRD EDITION

THE PURPOSE of this, the third edition of *The Art in Painting*, is to present the essentials of the increased knowledge and fuller experience gained during twelve years' constant use of the original volume as a guide in teaching and research. Not only has the material of the previous editions been reorganized and made better adapted for study and teaching, but practically every section of the book has been rewritten in the light of the accrued knowledge: the present volume contains a fresh study of each of the traditions of painting, of the individual artists discussed, and of the particular paintings analyzed in the Appendix. The illustrations include reproductions of sixty-two paintings which did not appear in the previous editions of the book. Incorporated also is the material of three extensive special researches carried out by the author and his colleagues and published in the form of monographs.* Special efforts were directed to present all the basic essentials of these researches and to merge them as an integral part of the form of this volume as a whole.

ALBERT C. BARNES.

MERION, PA., MARCH 1937.

* *The French Primitives and Their Forms*, Barnes and de Mazia, Barnes Foundation Press, 1931; *The Art of Henri-Matisse*, Barnes and de Mazia, Charles Scribner's Sons, 1933; *The Art of Renoir*, Barnes and de Mazia, Minton, Balch & Co., 1935.

PREFACE TO THE SECOND EDITION

WHEN the first edition of this work was published, it was intended to fill an urgent need for study in the galleries of Italy, France, England and the United States. This need has broadened and a similar need has made itself felt for analysis of the early German, Flemish, Dutch and French paintings. In this edition, these schools have been studied and their best and most representative pictures have been analyzed at first-hand. Also, much of the material on contemporary painters has been rewritten in order to coördinate better old and modern art as, chiefly, different versions of traditional forms. Many new illustrations have been added to facilitate this purpose.

The method of study described in this book is pursued in many American universities, colleges and schools, and in classes conducted in numerous public galleries, including the Louvre, Paris, and the Metropolitan Museum, New York. The increased demand, on both sides of the Atlantic, for a systematic and objective study, is encouraging as evidence of the rapid and universal growth of interest in plastic art.

ALBERT C. BARNES.

MERION, PA., January, 1928.

PREFACE TO THE FIRST EDITION

THIS book represents an effort to set forth briefly the salient features of a systematic study of both old and modern paintings which developed a method that has been in use for more than ten years.

At the Barnes Foundation, Merion, Pennsylvania, the plan is being further developed and applied in seminars, lectures, demonstrations and classes for teachers of art, painters, writers and non-professional people. The method comprises the observation of facts, reflection upon them, and the testing of the conclusions by their success in application. It stipulates that an understanding and appreciation of paintings is an experience that can come only from contact with the paintings themselves. It emphasizes the fact that the terms "understanding," "appreciation," "art," "interest," "experience," have precise meanings that are inseparable parts of the method. It offers something basically objective to replace the sentimentalism, the antiquarianism, sheltered under the cloak of academic prestige, which make futile the present courses in art in universities and colleges generally.

From the earliest times down to our own age, the traditions of painting, like those of science, have been in a constant state of evolution, and their determinants have always been the prevailing conditions of culture. The arid periods in history were characterized by slavish imitation of previous traditions which, in their own age, were living embodiments of human values. The aridity disappeared and the traditions were modified, when greater men recognized that the vitality of a custom consists precisely in its representing the spirit of its age. No tradition has ever persisted unchanged and no sound tradition has ever completely disappeared; these facts admit of no question in the history of painting. The traditions of previous ages have always been the foundation stones upon which new developments are based, even though that truth has been generally unrecognized at the time. Important creators have usually suffered grievous wrongs through the blindness of their contemporaries, and our own age is living up to that historical record. A person who professes to understand and appreciate Titian and Michelangelo and who fails to recognize the same traditions in the moderns, Renoir and Cézanne, is practicing self-deception. Similarly, an understanding of early Oriental art and of El Greco carries with it an appreciation of the contemporary work of Matisse and Picasso. These modern and contemporary painters have merely added contributions of their own, just as Titian and Michelangelo, El Greco and the Orientals, founded their work upon the traditions of their predecessors.

In this book an effort is made to trace in the history of painting the essential continuity of the great traditions and to show that the best of the modern painters use the same means, to the same general ends, as did the great Florentines, Venetians, Dutchmen and Spaniards. To show that continuity, it has been necessary to analyze the plastic forms of the principal painters from the dawn of the Italian Renaissance down to the present day. Historical data are treated as merely incidental: no attempt has been made to present a complete summary of the history of painting, although no important movement and no really first-class artist has been entirely left out of account in the general evaluations.

The summaries of characteristics of the work of the artists treated, and the analyses of the particular paintings mentioned, are compiled exclusively from my own observations recorded in notes made in front of the paintings themselves. The plan thus offers a method of approach, as well as a test of its value in the presence of objective facts.

It is not assumed that the conclusions reached with regard to particular paintings are the only ones compatible with the use of the method: any one of them is of course subject to revision. What is claimed is that the method gives results as objective as possible within any field of aesthetic experience and that it reduces to a minimum the rôle of merely personal and arbitrary preference. Preference will always remain, but its existence is consistent with a much higher degree of objective judgment than at present prevails. Our intention is to offer a type of analysis which should lead to the elimination of the prevailing habit of judging paintings by either academic rules or emotional irrelevancy. In other words, this book is an experiment in the adaptation to plastic art of the principles of scientific method. So far as I know, the plan as a whole is new. The technique, in its

PREFACE

general psychological and logical aspects, is derived from Dewey's monumental work in the development of scientific method. For the underlying principles of the psychology of aesthetics I owe much to Santayana and to my associate, Laurence Buermeyer. To Mr. Buermeyer and to Violette de Mazia I am indebted also for their fine services in bringing into orderly arrangement my scattered notes relating to the paintings in the galleries of Europe and in our own collection. My other associates, Mary Mullen, N. E. Mullen and L. V. Geiger, have also rendered much valuable service in connection with the book and the educational plan out of which it grew.

ALBERT C. BARNES.

MERION, PA., January, 1926.

CONTENTS

PAGE

PREFACE TO THE THIRD EDITION vii
PREFACE TO THE SECOND EDITION ix
PREFACE TO THE FIRST EDITION x

BOOK I

INTRODUCTION

CHAPTER   PAGE

I. THE PROBLEM OF APPRECIATION 3
II. THE ROOTS OF ART 8
III. EXPRESSION AND DECORATION 13
IV. THE ESTHETIC VALUES OF PAINTING 20
    I. ART AND SUBJECT-MATTER 20
    II. THE NATURE OF FORM 25
    III. FORM AND TECHNIQUE 28
    IV. PLASTIC AND OTHER VALUES 31
    V. FORM AND MATTER 38
    VI. QUALITY IN PAINTING 42
V. ART AND MYSTICISM 45
VI. SUMMARY 48

BOOK II

THE ELEMENTS OF PAINTING

PAGE

FOREWORD. THE RAW MATERIALS OF PAINTING 53
CHAPTER
I. PLASTIC FORM 55
II. PLASTIC FORM AND SUBJECT-MATTER 72
III. COLOR 82
IV. DRAWING 90
V. COMPOSITION 102

BOOK III

THE TRADITIONS OF PAINTING

CHAPTER   PAGE

I. THE DAWN OF MODERN PAINTING 111
II. THE FLORENTINE TRADITION 115

CONTENTS

CHAPTER   PAGE

III. The Sienese Tradition 141

IV. The Venetian Tradition 144

V. Rubens and Poussin 157

VI. The Important Spanish Painters 166

VII. The German Tradition 172

        General Characteristics of German Primitives 172

        The Bohemian School 173

        Painting in the Rhine Region 175

          Painting Previous to the Cologne School 175

          The Cologne School 176

          Rhine-Region Painting Contemporary to Cologne School 187

        Painting in Westphalia 188

        Painting in Hamburg Region 190

        Various Other Versions of the German Tradition . . . 191

VIII. The Flemish Tradition 199

IX. The Dutch Tradition 215

X. The French Primitives 230

XI. French Painting of the Eighteenth Century 250

XII. French Painting of the Nineteenth Century Prior to Impressionism 265

XIII. Portraiture 270

XIV. Landscape 278

Book IV

MODERN PAINTING

CHAPTER   PAGE

I. The Transition to Modern Painting 291

II. Impressionism 300

III. Manet 305

IV. Renoir 313

V. Cezanne 319

VI. Degas and Puvis de Chavannes 325

VII. The Post-Impressionists 328

VIII. American Painting 336

Book V

CONTEMPORARY PAINTING

CHAPTER   PAGE

I. The Transition to Contemporary Painting 351

II. Contemporary Painting 356

III. Matisse 359

IV. Picasso 369

V. Other Contemporaries 374

CONTENTS

APPENDIX

	PAGE
1. ANALYSES OF PAINTINGS	389
2. CATALOGUE DATA	479
INDEX	505

[xv]

LIST OF ILLUSTRATIONS

PAGE

BELLINI, GIOVANNI, "Allegory of Purgatory" (89) 80
    "Madonna of the Little Trees" (430) 426
Bohemian Master, end of fourteenth century, "Resurrection" (409) 183
BOTTICELLI, "Allegory of Spring" (90) 161
Byzantine Mosaics of the sixth century, "Empress Theodora Makes an
    Offering to Religion" (412) 117
    "Massimiliano" (detail) (413) 296
CARPACCIO, "Dream of St. Ursula" (431) 425
CASTAGNO, ANDREA DEL, "Last Supper" (77) 21
    (School) "Saint Eustachius" (79) 129
CEZANNE, "Bathers" (175) 332
    "Men Bathing" (175A) 295
    "Mount Ste. Victoire" (176) 404
    "Still-Life with Gray Jug" (178) 77
CHARDIN, "Child with Teetotum" (298) 254
CHIRICO, "Alexandros" (179) 381
    "Horses Near a Lake" (256) 402
CLAUDE LE LORRAIN, "Landscape" (180) 281
Cologne Master, beginning or middle of the fourteenth century,
    "Crucifixion and Four Scenes from the Life of Christ" (58) 182
CONSTABLE, "Salisbury Cathedral" (133) 282
COROT, "Landscape" (181) 281
    "Woman in Pink Blouse" (182) 255
COURBET, "Painter's Studio" (308) 256
DAUMIER, "Water Carrier" (183) 415
DEGAS, "Race Horses" (184) 312
DELACROIX, "Triumph of St. Michael" (185) 295
DEMUTH, "Negro Dancing" (186) 342
DÜRER, "Self-Portrait" (313) 273
Egyptian Sculpture, XVII Dynasty, 2000 B.C., "Figure" (188) . . 361
EYCK, JAN VAN, "Crucifixion" (35) 202
    "Jan Arnolfini and Jeanne de Chenany, his Wife" (134) . . 445
Flemish Master, fifteenth century, "Crucifixion" (189) . . . 203
Flemish Master, active c.1480, "Man's Portrait" (190) . . . 201
FRAGONARD, "Bathers" (316) 163
    "Music Lesson" (319) 474

LIST OF ILLUSTRATIONS

PAGE

French Master, fourteenth century, "Crucifixion" (191) 241
French Master, end of fourteenth or beginning of fifteenth century,
    "Entombment" (324) 243
French Master, active c.1400, "Scene in Temple" (195) 241
French Master, fifteenth century, "Altarpiece of St. Etienne" (110) 242
GAUGUIN, "Landscape: Haere Pape" (199) 329
GIORGIONE, "Concert in the Open Air" (330) 98
    "Two Prophets" (200) 149
GIOTTO, "Saint Francis Blessing the Birds" (20) 120
GLACKENS, "Race Track" (201) 331
GOGH, VAN, "Postman" (203) 296
GOYA, "Don Galos" (204) 276
GOYEN, VAN, "Seascape" (205) 223
GRECO, EL, "Annunciation" (206) 24
    "Vision of St. Hyacinth" (207) 58
Greek Pottery, 500 B.C., "Vase" (208) 57
Greek Sculpture, 400 B.C., "Figure of a Man" (209) 294
GRÜNEWALD, "Crucifixion" (55) 416
    "Entombment" (56) 416
Hindu-Persian Miniature, sixteenth-seventeenth century, "Interior
    with Figures" (211) 362
Hindu Scuplture, Kushan Empire, third-fourth century, "Fig-
    ure" (212) 364
HOLBEIN, THE YOUNGER, "Erasmus" (336) 184
HUBER, WOLF, "Man's Portrait" (213) 184
HUGO, JEAN, "Audierne" (214) 384
KANE, JOHN, "Farm" (215) 284
LEYDEN, LUCAS VAN, "Adoration of the Magi" (216) 204
LIPPI, FRA FILIPPO, "Virgin Adoring the Child" (98) 130
LOCHNER, "Madonna in the Garden of Roses" (69) 181
LONGHI, "Interior Scene" (217) 255
MANET, "Washerwoman" (218) 293
MASACCIO, "Adam and Eve Expelled from Paradise" (83) . . . 414
    "Tribute Money" (87) 118
MASTER FRANCKE, "Flight of St. Thomas of Canterbury" (120). . 183
MATISSE, "Joy of Life" (220) 100
    "Music Lesson" (221). 363
    "Reclining Nude" (222) 364
MICHELANGELO, "Original Sin and Expulsion from Eden" (421) . . 294
MODIGLIANI, "Girl in Sunday Clothes" (223) 311
MONET, "Madame Monet Embroidering" (226) 309
Negro Sculpture, Bushongo-Baluba, sixteenth century, "Figure" (227) 361
PACINO DI BONAGUIDA, "Saint Bartholomew" (228) 413

PAGE

PASCIN, "Seated Figure" (229) 473
Pennsylvania Dutch Painting on Velvet, "Still-Life with Bird" (231) 344
PICASSO, "Composition" (232) 59
   "Girl with Cigarette" (233) 475
   "Harlequins" (234) 23
   "Still-Life" (235) 476
PIERO DELLA FRANCESCA, "Discovery of the True Cross" (11) . . 132
   (School), "Marriage of St. Catherine" (15) 22
PINTO, BIAGIO, "Checker Players" (406) 341
POLLAIUOLO, ANTONIO, "Hercules Crushing Antaeus" (102) . . . 403
   "Hercules Overcoming the Hydra" (103) 403
POUSSIN, NICOLAS, "Summer, Ruth and Boaz" (365) 164
PRENDERGAST, MAURICE, "Idyl" (236) 99
RAPHAEL, "Madonna: la Belle Jardinière" (369) 427
   "Transfiguration" (427) 446
REMBRANDT, "Hendrickje Stoffels" (373) 274
RENOIR, "Bathing Group" (239) 163
   "Mademoiselle Jeanne Durand-Ruel" (240) 310
   "Noirmoutier" (242) 283
ROUSSEAU, le douanier, "People in Sunday Clothes" (243). . . . 284
   "Woman in Landscape" (244) 131
RUBENS, "Holy Family" (245) 162
   "Judgment of Paris" (151) 97
RUYSDAEL, SALOMON VAN, "Halt" (5) 222
SETTANNI, LUIGI, "Russian Ballet" (246) 343
SEURAT, "Port of Honfleur" (248) 330
Smyrna Sculpture, fourth century B.C., "Grotesque Figure" (249) . 382
Southern French Master, fifteenth century, "Pietà" (428) . . . 244
Southern French Master, second half of fifteenth century, "Villeneuve
   Pietà" (384) 244
SOUTINE, "Seated Woman" (250) 383
TERBORCH, GERARD, "Concert" (385) 224
TINTORETTO, "Origin of the Milky Way" (154). 78
   "Woman of Samaria" (251) 151
TITIAN, "Assumption" (438) 447
   "Disciples at Emmaus" (391) 150
   "Entombment" (392) 77
   "Man with Glove" (394) 428
TURA, COSIMO, "Pietà" (395) 60
UCCELLO, "Rout of San Romano" (159). 119
Upper or Middle Rhine Master of c.1410, "Garden of Paradise" (109) 401
UTRILLO, "Church of St. Aignan, Chartres" (252) 384
VELÁSQUEZ, "Infanta Marguerite" (396). 275

LIST OF ILLUSTRATIONS

PAGE

VERMEER, JAN, "View of Delft" (113) 221
VERONESE, PAOLO, "Baptism of Christ" (253) 152
    "Burning of Sodom" (400) 79
Wall of Gallery, Barnes Foundation (254) . . . . . . Frontispiece
WATTEAU, "Game of Love" (160) 253
Westphalian Master, c.1400, "Healing of Lazarus" (255) 448

BOOK I

INTRODUCTION

CHAPTER I

THE PROBLEM OF APPRECIATION

THE OBJECT of this book is to endeavor to correlate in the simplest possible form the main principles that underlie the intelligent appreciation of the paintings of all periods of time. We shall seek to show, briefly, what is involved in esthetic experience in general; after that, to give an account of the principles by which painting may be judged and so intelligently enjoyed; finally, to illustrate these principles by applying them to particular painters and tendencies in painting.

The approach to the problem of appreciation of art is made difficult by the unconscious habits and preconceptions which come to us from contact with a society which is but little interested in art. When other interests, such as those of a practical, sentimental, or moral nature, directly affect the esthetic interest, they are more likely than not to lead it astray, and the result is what may be called a confusion of values. Before trying to tell what the proper excellence in a painting is, we must make clear what it undeniably is *not*.

We miss the function of a painting if we look to it either for literal reproduction of subject-matter or for information of a documentary character. Mere imitation knows nothing of what is essential or characteristic, and documentary information always has an ulterior practical purpose. The camera records physical characteristics but can show nothing of what is beneath the surface. We ask of a work of art that it reveal to us the qualities in objects and situations which are significant, which have the power to move us esthetically. The artist must open our eyes to what unaided we could not see, and in order to do so he often needs to modify the familiar appearance of things and so make something which is, in the photographic sense, a bad likeness. What we ask of a painter is that, for example, in a landscape, he should catch the spirit of the scene; in a portrait, that he should discover what is essential or characteristic of the sitter. And these are obviously matters for judgment, not for photographic reproduction or documentary cataloguing.

INTRODUCTION

By a common popular misconception, a painter is often expected to tell a story and is judged by his ability to make the story edifying or entertaining. This is not unnatural, since we are all ordinarily interested in real things because of the part they play in the story which is life. A work of art may, incidentally, tell a story, but error arises when we try to judge it by the narrative, or the moral pointed, instead of by the manner in which the artist has used his materials to produce a work of plastic art; when, in other words, a literary or moral value is mistaken for a plastic value.

Scarcely less destructive to genuine esthetic appreciation is the confusion of technical proficiency and artistic significance. Art is not only an expression of the artist's creative spirit, but also a kind of handicraft, a skill in employing a special technique. As in other handicrafts, some natural ability combined with instruction and practice may enable a person to handle a paintbrush; for one real artist there are hundreds of capable craftsmen in paint. It is not especially difficult to learn to recognize these technical devices; but it *is* difficult to recognize greatness in the effects obtained, to distinguish between professional competence and artistic genius. To look merely for professional competence in painting is academicism; it is to mistake the husk for the kernel, the shadow for the substance.

This error is really more serious than the novice's confusion of plastic art with narrative, sentiment, or photographic likeness, because the novice usually knows that he is such and is willing to learn, but the academician supposes himself to have learned already, and his mind is usually closed to the existence of anything but technique. With his eyes fixed upon the forms in which the living spirit of the past has embodied itself, he neglects the contemporary manifestations of that spirit, and often refuses to see or acknowledge them when they are pointed out to him. This is the reason why the most formidable enemy of new movements in art has always been, not the indifferent public, but the hostile academician. The public does not know that what he says applies only to technique, and not to art itself, and is correspondingly impressed. His motive need not, of course, be a conscious motive, and doubtless often is not. The mere fact of novelty, to one who has systematically addressed himself to the old and familiar things, is an irritation. It challenges precious habits, it threatens to overturn judgments with which the academician has identified himself, and which are in consequence dear to him. Pride joins hands with natural human inertia to oppose what is living in the interest of what is dead.

These errors and confusions arise because the ordinary observer has never really learned to see. He can recognize familiar objects, and the traits in them which would be of practical importance or sentimental concern in real things, but such recognition is in no proper sense perception or vision. It identifies the object only for the purpose of passing on to something else—uses, consequences, or private fancies which are no part of its intrinsic character. People often suppose that there is some secret about art, some password which must be divulged before they can discover its purpose or meaning. Absurd as such an idea is, it contains the important truth that seeing is something which must be learned, and not something which we all do as naturally as we breathe.

To make apparent in more detail the necessity for learning to see, we shall consider briefly the psychology of perception. The obvious instruments of perception are our sense-organs, by which impressions reach us from the external world. Such impressions, however, convey nothing to us unless we can interpret them, attach meaning to them, and interpretation is possible only to one who can bring the residue or record of past experience to bear on any particular situation with which he may be confronted. At any moment, the sum total of our actual sensations is a chaos: we are besieged by a medley of sights, sounds, feelings of warmth or coolness, of bodily comfort or discomfort, by far the greater part of which have no connection with one another, and which could not possibly enter into any single experience. To be conscious of anything in particular, to retain our sanity, we must disregard nearly all of them, fixing our attention upon those which fit into some intelligible scheme or picture. But the connections which bring about intelligibility, which "make sense," have all been learned from past experience; this experience, retained in memory, is called forth as occasion for it arises. It then directs our attention to the significant aspects of the existing situation, to which it gives form and meaning—which, in a word, it enables us to perceive.

We have all had the experience of being in an unfamiliar situation, and finding ourselves unable to see more than a fraction of what is going on in it. The machinery in the hold of a steamship, the babel of voices when many people are speaking in a foreign language, the actions of those with whose manners, customs, and traditions we are unfamiliar—all these things are likely to appear to us as so much confusion and blur. Our difficulty is both that we do not see and that we do not comprehend. We see and hear something, and we can at least recognize wheels and shafts in the machinery, vowel sounds and consonant sounds in the words spoken, gestures and goings to and fro in the actions of the strange people. But we perceive vaguely, and much of what is happening escapes us altogether. It is only after, and by means of, understanding, that we can perceive with any precision, or notice more than a small part of the details in the scene before us. What we do see is hazy, scanty, and without perspective. We overlook the important and significant, and the odds and ends that come to our attention are jumbled together without rhyme or reason. Our senses, meanwhile, may be as acute as those of another who misses nothing in the picture; but we have not learned to use them, and he has.

The expression "to use our senses" is an indication that seeing or hearing is an active process, not a mere registration of impressions. After we have learned the purpose and the general plan of the machinery, we know how to look for the parts and the connections of which we were at first oblivious. When we have learned the vocabulary of a foreign language and know what to listen for, the finer shades of sound begin to stand out. We have acquired by experience a background which enables us to comprehend the machinery or the foreign language.

These are only outstanding examples of a process which is going on all the time. As long as we are really alive, we continue to grow by extending the application of our funded experience, perceiving things more and more precisely and discriminatingly, and at the same time investing them with constantly enriched meanings. The process is exemplified in every activity of life, from playing tennis or driving a motor car to practicing medicine or engaging in scientific research. As the system of meanings which makes up our minds is amplified and organized, our perceptions become correspondingly richer and more comprehensive. Vision and intelligence, in other words, are co-implicative, neither is possible without the other, and all growth involves their interaction.

This general principle furnishes us with the clue to esthetic education. We perceive only what we have learned to look for, both in life and in art. The artist, whether in paint, words, or musical tones, has embodied an experience in his work, and to appreciate his painting or poem or symphony, we must reconstruct his experience, so far as we are able, in ourselves. There is no essential difference in kind between the experience of the artist and that of the observer of his work, whatever may be the difference in their respective abilities. The experience of the artist arises out of a particular background, a set of interests and habits of perception, which, like the scientist's habits of thought, are potentially sharable by other individuals. They are only sharable, however, if one is willing to make the effort involved in acquiring a comparable set of habits and background. To see as the artist sees is an accomplishment to which there is no short cut, which cannot be acquired by any magic formula or trick; it requires not only the best energies of which we are capable, but a methodical direction of those energies, based upon scientific understanding of the meaning of art and its relation to human nature. The artist illuminates the objective world for us, exactly as does the scientist, different as the terms are in which he envisages it; art is as little a plaything, a matter of caprice or uncontrolled subjectivity, as is physics or chemistry. What has made the study of science valuable and fruitful is method, and without a corresponding method of learning to see the study of art can lead only to futility. We must understand, in other words, what the distinctive aspects of reality are in which the artist is interested, how he organizes his work to reveal and organize those aspects, the means which he employs, and the kind of satisfaction which rewards his efforts when they are successful. Only in the light of such an understanding can any one build up the habits of perception and background in himself which will give him admission to the world of esthetic experience.

CHAPTER II

THE ROOTS OF ART

ART, LIKE every other human activity, has its roots in the fundamental needs of our nature, and provides one of the ways in which these needs find satisfaction. It was formerly believed that "beauty" is something which exists independently in nature, like magnetism or gravitation, and that it can be defined without reference to human wants and interest. Innumerable attempts to find such a definition have proved futile, and it is now recognized that the understanding of art must be sought in psychological principles.

Everything that human beings do is ultimately dependent upon the feelings that things and acts arouse in them. Some experiences are immediately felt as satisfactory, others as unsatisfactory, and life consists in an effort to secure the former and avoid the latter. This is a fact which requires no justification: human beings are so constituted as to have preferences, and behind preferences, in the last analysis, we cannot go. Reason or intelligence can show that one particular preference conflicts with another, and often guides us by making clear which of the two represents the more comprehensive good, but it can never prove anything a good which does not lead, directly or indirectly, to some experience valued for its own sake. We are often compelled to accept privation and pain, but only for the sake of a positive value which outweighs their unpleasantness.

To say that an experience is of positive value, that it is worth having for its own sake, is to say that in it an instinctive prompting finds fulfilment.[1] To eat when we are hungry, to turn away from what disgusts us, to be victorious when our will is pitted against that of another, are things felt to be good in their own right; they are satisfactions of instincts and are enjoyed immediately, for their own sake. Of course, the enjoyment is greater as the range of instinctive gratification is broadened. Victory means the immediate

[1] See Mary Mullen, *An Approach to Art*, pp. 13, 14, Barnes Foundation Press, Merion, Pa., 1923.

experience of triumph; it may also mean the accomplishment of remoter ends which have an instinctive appeal of their own; and the confluence of these separate satisfactions heightens our enjoyment in the experience of victory. In general, the ideal is approached as our instinctive promptings are harmoniously united in every act. Then every experience gains value from all the resources of our nature, and suffers loss from no sense of desire thwarted or damage done to any of the interests which we have at heart.

The enjoyment of art is one of the experiences which are desirable for their own sake. It is, of course, capable of acquiring other values also. It may enable us to make a living; it may improve our morals or quicken our religious faith; but if we attempt to judge a work of art directly by its contribution to these ends, we have abandoned the track. A work of art presents to the spectator an opportunity to live through an experience which by its own quality vouches for its right to existence, and whatever other value it has depends upon this value. If it lacks this, it is a counterfeit.

Art, in other words, is one of the ways in which instinct finds satisfaction. It differs from the ordinary manifestations of instinct, however, in that it does not take the form of a course of practical action. We read the poem, look at the picture, listen to the symphony, but we are not thereupon prompted to do anything further, as we are when we are moved by some actual object to fear, anger, or affection. This does not mean that the experience is passive, that we simply allow the esthetic object to do something to us while we do nothing in response—a suggestion conveyed by the definition of esthetic experience as contemplative. To hear the symphony, to see the picture, if the hearing and seeing are genuine, is the antithesis of idle reverie; it requires the energetic coöperation of all our powers, and nothing is more fatal to it than an attitude of relaxed and diffused attention. What distinguishes the response to works of art is that it takes the form of understanding, not merely intellectually but with our whole personality; of re-creating in ourselves, so far as we are able, the experience which the work of art records and embodies. This is an intensely active process, and often requires a much greater expenditure of energy than would overt action aiming at some practical end. It is, however, a different kind of activity from that ordinarily associated with instinct, and our next problem is to see wherein the difference lies.

[9]

faction which instinct finds in comprehension, in imaginative realization, is one which is intrinsic to the process of bringing out, not something added afterwards: the person who comprehends and appreciates the work of art shares the emotions which prompted the artist to create. The artist gives us satisfaction by seeing for us more clearly than we could see for ourselves, and showing us what an experience more sensitive and profound than our own has shown him.

We all take some pleasure in seeing how things look, in observing their color, their contour, their movement, whether they are moving in our direction or not. In so far as we are successful in finding what is characteristic, appealing, or significant in the world about us, we are, in a small impromptu way, ourselves artists.[2] But the man who is an artist because the interest in understanding and depicting things is a master passion with him, sees more deeply and more penetratingly than we do, and, seeing better, can also show better. His interests compel him to grasp certain significant aspects of persons and things of the real world which our blindness and preoccupation with personal and practical concerns ordinarily hide from us.

[2] See Mary Mullen, *An Approach to Art*, p. 23, Barnes Foundation Press, Merion, Pa., 1923.

CHAPTER III

EXPRESSION AND DECORATION

IN THE preceding chapter we have seen that emotion about an object or situation, when controlled by intelligence, assumes the form of interest in the nature of the object, and results in a clear and coherent perception of it. As interest thus develops, experience becomes more and more illuminating: the qualities and meanings of what is experienced are more penetratingly discriminated and more systematically organized, both with one another and with the whole background of experience which makes up the observer's world. To the extent that any individual makes it his established purpose to see his world as significantly and comprehensively as possible, his experience is esthetic, even though he may be able neither to see very deeply nor to communicate his experience to other people.

The artist differs from the ordinary person partly by his ability to make what he sees a public object, but chiefly in the range and depth of his vision itself. The first depends upon technical training and competence, but this simply as a matter of skill is far from qualifying any one for the production of authentic works of art. A work of art is a creation, and the creation is not accomplished in the act of embodying in a material object what is already in the artist's mind, but in the act of insight into the objective world by virtue of which it assumes form and order. Hence the artist is primarily the discoverer, just as the scientist is; the scientist discovers abstract symbols which may be used for purposes of calculation and prediction; the artist, the qualities of things which heighten their human significance. What these qualities are depends upon the individual artist and the medium in which he works. The comic, the pathetic, the ironic, the sublime, and the tragic are aspects of experience which can best be expressed by the writer, since they appear fully only in situations which develop in time, and a picture, though its perception takes time, obviously cannot depict a course of events. The painter is not debarred from the use of such values, since he can show manifestations of them in

[13]

the visible world—the satire of Goya or Daumier, the natural majesty of Claude le Lorrain, the religious mysticism of El Greco, the human poignancy of Rembrandt are obvious instances—but the qualities which lie most immediately in his province are those more directly apprehended by sight. Color, line, light, mass—these things, as immediately experienced, are illuminated for us by the painter. Upon them he focuses the funded experience which, richer in him than in the ordinary man, enables him to single out whatever is moving or significant, and set it in the context of relations needed to reveal its intrinsic nature. This revelation of significance is what constitutes the expression of the artist, and the fact that it *is* a revelation, not merely a game or indulgence in make-believe, appears from the dissatisfaction which we feel when the object set before us turns out to be illusory or fraudulent. Expressive form in other words, always involves the perception of something real.

This statement does not imply that art is photographic, a mere registration of fact, or that its reality can be recognized by the untrained observer. Neither in art nor in science is it true that he who runs may read. Science makes no attempt to catalogue particular things and describe them literally. For the world that anybody can see it substitutes a world that nobody can see, but which is immensely useful for purposes of control. Its tests are objective and verifiable, but they cannot be made except by those who have a highly specialized training. Recognition of the fact restrains intelligent people from forming any opinion about controversial scientific questions, but many a man who would not dream of having his own view about the cause of cancer or the structure of the atom has not the slightest hesitation in dismissing Stravinsky or Joyce or Cézanne or Matisse as unintelligible or absurd. It is evident that the meaning of truth in art requires further explanation.

It is impossible even to raise the question of reality about form in art until the artist's purpose or design is grasped. The meaning of "design" will be explained in detail in Book II, Chapter I, but its general relation to purpose is testified to by ordinary speech. A design is an intention, usually understood as including some idea of the means to be employed for its realization. No work of art can possibly be intended or designed to reveal an actual situation in its entirety, but only some selected aspect of it, and the artist's presentation need include only so much as is involved in exhibiting that aspect and its relations. In literature, for example, the most realistic novel does not and cannot attempt to tell everything about a character's life and environment; the recital would be meaningless if it were possible. It aims at extracting the essentials; but the essential itself varies with the author's intention or point of view. Fielding, Zola, and James Joyce are all in their way realists, but their methods, the phases of reality which they sought to set before the reader, were totally different, and the success or failure of any of them cannot possibly be judged by the standards applicable to either of the others. Likewise with Rembrandt, Velásquez, and Cézanne. The relation of method or technique to design, as it appears in plastic art, will be discussed in a later chapter; it suffices here to point out that the definition of artistic expression as perception or grasp of reality does not restrict such perception to any predetermined form.

The meaning of unity in art follows from what has been said about the relation of art both to interest and to the real world. The unity of an experience requires that the instinctive promptings which find satisfaction in it should be in harmony with one another, that no unreconciled conflicts of attitude should exist to keep the experiencing agent at cross purposes with himself. This is the subjective aspect of unity; objectively, it involves the coherence of the situation itself, an interpretation of it which takes account of all its relevant qualities, and brings them together in a consistent presentation. An individual in a novel or play must act "in character": all that he does must follow naturally from the point of view and set of purposes attributed to him and the circumstances in which he is placed; at the same time the novelist's general conception of his character and the part assigned him in the plot must be brought into conformity with the impression to be created by the novel as a whole. Similarly with a painting: unity requires that everything needed to produce conviction, to make the kind and degree of reality prescribed by the design, be included; nothing less, but nothing more; too little or too much color or solidity or linear accentuation, which would de-realize or overemphasize any aspect of the picture, would correspondingly impair its integration and leave it an assemblage of fragments, not an organic whole.

The correlate of unity is variety. Unity is satisfactory only when it embraces a diversity of particular details or phases; otherwise it falls into monotony. This is true of life and of all the arts. Any one can avoid conflicts and difficult situations if he narrows his interests sufficiently, if he avoids, whenever possible, the opportunities for a rich and full life; but the result is tedium, and ultimately intellectual and emotional starvation. In music, the most unalloyedly harmonious interval is the octave, which is so uninteresting, however, that it hardly seems to constitute harmony at all. In literature, characters which exemplify a single quality only, such as chastity, covetousness, courage, or cowardice, seem, just because of their consistency, to be not realities but phantoms. Coherence, in brief, means not mere sameness but sameness in difference: not the unity of grains of sand, but of parts of an organism which complement each other but are not all cast in the same mold. In painting, variety appears not only in multiplicity of detail, but also in the envisagement of every object in terms of all the plastic means. The criterion of reality, in other words, requires that a middle course be steered between uniformity and diversity, that an artist, in depicting a situation, should see it as a whole; but also that he should see it with the complexity needed to bring into play as many of the spectator's interests as are compatible with the design.

Hitherto we have considered the esthetic interests which are directed upon more or less individualized objects, the presentation of which is intended to carry conviction. A work of art, however, is not only a vehicle of imaginative insight, it is a material thing, and as such it must be itself pleasing. This sort of appeal, which may most appropriately be termed "decorative," is present in the different arts in varying degree. It is at a minimum in prose fiction; in poetry it is more important, though even in that, sound and rhythm of words depend so profoundly on the meaning that their isolation is almost impossible. In painting, however, the direct impact of colors and shapes on the senses is very important. The "decorative arts" proper depend wholly on such qualities as are immediately apprehended. In scrollwork, fabrics, rugs, embroidery, carved paneling, naturalistic motifs are either absent or so conventionalized that their interest is almost wholly independent of what they represent. The beauty of nature is itself decorative, in so far as nature is perceived, not as the dwelling-place of man and the theater in which his energies work themselves out, but as a simple spectacle which may delight the eye. Flowers, jewels, rainbows, sunsets, the sweeping curves of hill and valley, all satisfy our need to perceive vividly, abundantly, and in ways congenial to our natural powers.

In works of art, decoration has a certain amount of intrinsic importance, but if made an end in itself and not supported by reference to the real things with which all our human interests are bound up, it has no higher status than that of a rug or piece of bric-a-brac. This is an extreme case and is probably never realized in fact, even in the most abstract painting. Any indication of the third dimension, or of solidity in masses, since these involve a measure of representation, confers some expressive quality upon a picture. However, the expressive aspect may be of slight importance, and a portrait, landscape, or group of figures may be a mere pretext for exploring the possibilities of color-harmony or color-contrasts, of pattern of line or light. Matisse is an example of such decorative accentuation and so too, to some extent, are the French primitive painters, in whom spatial depth, solidity, realistic movement, and the representation of human values are sometimes subordinated to characteristics that make their appeal more definitely to the eye than to the imagination.

A number of distinguished painters suffer, when their forms are analyzed, from undue preponderance of primarily ornamental quality. In their work we find a special skill in organizing decorative elements into rich and distinctive forms which merge to some extent with the structural elements. But when we abstract the respective elements, decorative and structural, we see that the structural form is of varying degrees of thinness. Almost all of Botticelli's work comes within this category. In his famous painting, "Allegory of Spring" (90) * and also in his "Birth of Venus" (91), we find a marvelously fluid, graceful line winding in and around all the objects and making a succession of patterns which add to the charm of the line. But when we look for equivalent value in the other factors which make up the total plastic quality of the paintings, we see only thinness. In other words, the facile, extraordinary, almost flamboyant decorative forms are accompanied by so little structural plastic substance, that we look upon the paintings as primarily high-grade decorations which cannot be considered seriously as works of great art. A step further toward fusion of the two elements is found in the work of Rubens, in which, although the decoration is accentuated, there is usually a solid substructure of other plastic elements with which the decoration merges sufficiently to give a composite plastic form of distinction.

* This number and all similar documentation by numerals, throughout the book, refer to the "Catalogue Data," listed in the Appendix, p. 479.

In all painting really of the first rank, decoration and expression are *combined*, not only in the sense that the picture contains both, but so organically related that the colors and contours which give immediate pleasure to the eye also build up the expressive form. In Giorgione, El Greco, or Renoir, it is impossible to point to one area or detail of the picture as expressive, another as decorative; every part is both. Anything in life that is decorative and nothing else is merely cosmetic in function; what renounces all appeal to the sensibilities is bleak, frigid, or uncouth, an abstract demonstration, not a work of art. Esthetic unity requires the presence of both decoration and expression, though it leaves open the possibility of a relatively greater emphasis on either, provided the other is presented sufficiently to assure the reality of the whole. In Giorgione and Renoir, the scales are weighed, on the whole, in favor of decoration; in Rembrandt and Cézanne, on the side of expression; the result tends toward charm in the former, power in the latter, but in either case balance is maintained, and there is no sense of impoverishment in any respect. Penetration or power, and decorative charm are, in short, the two essential qualities in any work of art.[1]

Intermediate between expression and decoration stand what may be called transferred values. These are values which do not belong to an object in its intrinsic nature, but serve to enrich and diversify the perception of it. The exquisite surface-quality of Vermeer, Chardin, or Renoir, which may have the quality of enamel or velvet, need not actually reveal anything in what is portrayed, and still less need the elaborate transferred values of Matisse—which often lend to human flesh the texture of a tile or ceramics—contribute anything to essential realism. Such values correspond to the more fanciful types of simile and metaphor in poetry, which do not convey any really enlightening insight into what is de-

[1] The distinction between the two classes of art, designated respectively classic and baroque, seems to be due entirely to the preponderance of either the structural or the decorative elements. In sculpture, Michelangelo is, in this sense, baroque, and the best Egyptian sculpture of about 2500 B.C., is classic. In Michelangelo's famous statue of "Moses" (417) at Rome, we find a preoccupation with decoration so great that it detracts from the obviously solid and truly sculptural character of the work as a whole. In the Egyptian sculptures of the period named, especially those represented in the De Morgan Collection in the Louvre (314), there is a three-dimensional sculptural treatment of great solidity in which the decorative elements are very much in abeyance. The effect of these Egyptian statues is one of unalloyed satisfaction, of deep peace; but in Michelangelo's work the satisfaction is disturbed and often abolished by the tinge of ostentation suggested by the ornamental details.

scribed, but embroider it with images which have their own appeal, and so heighten the general effect produced upon the reader.[2]

We have hitherto considered art as a way of seeing, and its values as arising partly from the artist's account of his discoveries in the world which he shares with all of us, partly from the immediately agreeable exercise of our powers of perception. In judging a work of art, however, something more must be taken into consideration—the originality of the artist. There is a common misunderstanding of originality which identifies it with complete independence of any other artist's influence. The absurdity of such a view appears as soon as we remember that to see at all requires a background of funded experience, and that no man can build up such a background by his own unaided efforts. An individual completely isolated from the past would have as much chance of developing his own art as he would of discovering his own mathematics and natural science. We see only by utilizing the vision of others, and this vision is embodied in the traditions of art. Each of these, as will be made abundantly clear in our later discussion, represents a systematic way of envisaging the world; taken together, they record the perceptions of the most gifted observers of all generations, and form a continuous and cumulative growth which is one of the most important parts of the heritage of civilization. Tradition, however, may be used either as a storehouse of instruments for the resourceful, or as a crutch for the crippled. The moment it ceases to suggest and begins to legislate, academicism sets in. A painter is an artist, in other words, only if he is able to select from the work of his predecessors the forms which are adapted to his own designs, modifying them as his individual needs require, and recombining them in a new form which represents his own unique vision. Correspondingly, the observer or critic can only assess the originality of a painting, its artistic importance, if he himself knows the traditions and can judge what the painter has added to them. We can learn to see the art of the present, in a word, only by learning to see the art of the past.

[2] For more extended discussion of the psychology of transferred values, see Barnes and de Mazia, *The Art of Henri-Matisse*, Chapter VI, Charles Scribner's Sons, New York, 1933.

[19]

CHAPTER IV

THE ESTHETIC VALUES OF PAINTING

I. ART AND SUBJECT-MATTER

THE EXPRESSION "subject-matter" as applied to art is usually ambiguous in the extreme. Sometimes it refers to scarcely more than the title of a particular picture, which is merely a means of identification and has not the slightest esthetic significance. More often it represents the scene or object depicted, considered in isolation from the artist's treatment of it; this is equally irrelevant, but it is undoubtedly what, for the vast majority of people, determines the esteem in which a picture is held. A pretty picture is for them one which portrays a pretty object; the more beautiful the object, the greater the painting. This is a superstition which does not call for further comment, but the reaction against it may easily fall into an error which has had considerable vogue in less unenlightened circles—the denial to art of any concern whatever with subject-matter. Such a denial is plausible only so long as the term in question remains undefined.

The content of a work of plastic art includes two sets of qualities—those which evoke feelings of the same general kind as the emotions of everyday life, and which may be termed "human values," and those which are common to all perceived things (colors, lights and shadows, contours, spatial intervals) which constitute plastic values. The former are usually designated by names used for corresponding objects which have an independent existence, with which they may therefore easily be confused. A painting of the Crucifixion, for example, may be said to represent an event which occurred many centuries ago, but this is its subject rather than its subject-matter. Van Eyck, Fra Angelico, Grünewald, and Tintoretto, not to speak of innumerable other artists, all painted pictures entitled "Crucifixion," but the actual subject-matter [1] is different

---

[1] Professor Dewey prefers to use the term "substance" in the sense here given to "subject-matter." See his discussion of the point in *Art as Experience*, pp. 110–114, Minton, Balch & Co., New York, 1934.

Andrea del Castagno (77)

Design characterized by contrasts, distortions, and the use of a swirl.

Piero della Francesca, School of (15)   Analysis, page 405

This fifteenth century painting is one of the prototypes of modern
design effected by means of contrasts and distortions.

[22]

Picasso (234)

Similar to painting on opposite page in the use
of line, color, and space to effect design.

El Greco (206)

in each painting; it is the individual artist's conception of the event on Calvary, and in none of them, of course, could it possibly be said to copy what actually occurred. There is a generic sameness about the feelings called forth by all the pictures, though even that varies very widely: van Eyck's (35) and Grünewald's (55) versions have a poignancy and an effect of psychological realism which is largely lacking from Fra Angelico's (82). In any case, however, the emotions are not such as would be aroused by inanimate things, however drawn, colored, and composed: they are all called forth by an awareness of human suffering and compassion. In so far as this is the case, in so far as there is appeal to such sentiments as sorrow, pity, wonder, awe, irony, contempt, a painting may be termed an illustration, though not in any derogatory sense. Confusion of values arises only when the spectator is moved, not by what the artist shows him, but by what he does *not* show him—the historical event. The interest in that is wholly adventitious, and if allowed to play a part in determining judgment of the picture it can produce nothing but distraction.

Illustration is a legitimate artistic effect, but only when it is united with the other elements in the substance of the painting— the plastic form. We have already indicated the general meaning of form in its subjective sense, as the organization of experience which arises from the unity of personality, but form is also a quality in things as they actually exist, and this objective sense of the term raises the problem which must next be considered.

II. THE NATURE OF FORM

The word "form," like "subject-matter," has been a catchword in so many discussions that its use is at present equally ambiguous. It may, however, be given a perfectly definite meaning, both as it actually is used in common speech, and as it should be used when applied to art.

In common speech, form is that which gives to anything whatever —a table, chair, locomotive, or aeroplane, as well as a painting or symphony—its distinctive character. All objects in the world have certain attributes which we term qualities when we are referring to things, and sensations when our own experiences are in question. For example, a table is brown, smooth, hard, and cold; it is also oblong, three feet high, and its color varies according as it is in light or in shadow. But the sum total of these qualities is not what we mean when we say the word "table," for another object might have all these qualities and be not a table or anything that looks like one. We perceive it as a table only when we see those qualities *in certain relations* to each other, the relation of each one of its parts to the other parts and the relation of it as a whole to other objects. That is, to grasp it as an individual thing is to see those relations, to see the form which gives the essence of the thing, makes it what it is. Every object of which we are conscious has such a form, and until we have grasped its form we cannot be said to perceive the object. In a table, the form consists of a network of relations in which color, hardness, illumination, etc., are arranged in a certain definite spatial order. Both for ordinary consciousness and for art, impressions without form, if they exist, are meaningless.

In the form of a human being, we find a more complex series of relationships: there is a certain expanse of brow, broadness or narrowness of face, ratio between breadth of shoulders and height. It is the perception of these relationships that gives us the form of a man when stationary. For the form of a man in movement, the relation is between his position at one moment and his position at another moment: the way in which arms and legs are bent and straightened, in which the body sways with each step, etc. The form of a man speaking or singing is made of a series of relationships established by the tones of his voice: a rich voice has many overtones, it is a fuller chord than a thin voice; monotony of voice is absence of inflection, of change in pitch or volume. Each of these, a rich, thin, or monotonous voice, is a form made up of a different series of relationships. Finally, if we consider the man as a whole, as an ensemble of physical, intellectual, and moral qualities, only those things are recognized as characteristic of him which are seen in relation to the rest of what he is and does, and to the situation in which he exists and acts.

Much of the confusion and ambiguity in the use of the word form has resulted from ignoring the obvious fact that no object or situation has one form and only one form. A man may be French, a Jew, an engineer, a thief, a celibate; New York is a city, a financial center, a harbor; in each case the man's or the city's form varies according to the grouping of relations which determine each category, and no single form represents either the man or the city in concrete fulness. Which of the various aspects we select to designate the man or the city depends upon the most representative or characteristic experience we have had with them, and also, of course, upon the interest which is at the moment in control of thought or perception. In general, the depth and power of a mind or personality is measured by the variety and subtlety of the forms accessible to it, and by its power to illuminate the whole of the object, which is a complex of many forms.

Whenever we use the word form we mean that matter is organized into a distinctive entity; but the matter organized may be itself form in relation to other matter. For example: the United States is an organization of separate states, and within that organization the United States is the form and the states the matter. If we abstract any one state and consider it in relation to its component counties, the state becomes the form and the counties the matter organized into the form of a state. An exactly analogous situation is found in painting. Subsidiary to the plastic form, which is the unification of all the matter of the canvas, there exists a number of minor forms made up of color, line, space, and these latter enter into relations with each other and make more complex forms. The plastic form comprises all the forms made up of the various elements, including the pattern which organizes the decoration.

Form, in its widest sense, is the plan of organization by which the details that constitute the matter of an object are brought into relation, so that they unite to produce a single esthetic effect. This is true of a painting, a symphony, a piece of sculpture, a poem, drama, novel, or essay. In the case of each, form dominates all the subtypes of the matter which enter into the work of art. In the form which we term symphony, its contained matter—chords, melodies, movements—are brought into the particular relations which make that form a symphony. In painting, the matter—line, light, color, space—is unified into the form we term plastic unity. The more fully the work of integration is carried out, that is, the greater the formal unification of all the constituent matter, the better the painting, the symphony, or the statue.

We see, therefore, that forms may have infinite variety, that the greatest scope exists for the artist to integrate his matter into forms in which the only limits are the possibilities of his medium, his own imagination, and his own technical skill. Failure to recognize this protean character of form is responsible for the vast amount of absurd writing on art which would limit plastic form to that particular expression which the critic happens to prefer. Such an attitude is invariably the mark of incapacity and academicism. The use of a particular plan of organization, or form, depends upon purely personal characteristics, like temperament, vision, sensitivity; and a painter is an artist in so far as he is endowed with these qualities and is able to reveal them in his work. Consequently, he alone can determine the form his painting must take. In condemning an artist whose form is personal, distinctive, and original, the critic is asserting that art must conform to standards which are basically mechanized or stereotyped, a conception which would empty it of all savor of life. Imitation defines academicism, and conjoined with mere technical skill it sets the standard of whatever type of painting happens to be popular. Academicians such as John Singer Sargent and Robert Henri use Manet's technique but fail to capture its spirit of life. Childe Hassam, Redfield, Garber, and a host of others play the same rôle in relation to Claude Monet. Whistler represents a dead academic synthesis of Velásquez, Courbet, and the Japanese. Derain's form has been successively an imitation of the surface-qualities of Cézanne, van Gogh, Matisse, Picasso, Bronzino, Courbet, Corot, and Renoir.

III. FORM AND TECHNIQUE

The foregoing discussion shows that form constitutes the essence of an object, that which gives the object its distinctive individuality, makes it what it is. In painting, the forms which a painter creates reveal unerringly the organization of his mind and character. Just as the forms of things themselves are protean, many-sided, varying under different circumstances and at different periods of time, so also are varied the forms which an artist may create. The painter's individuality finds expression in what he sees to be distinctive and characteristic in the real world, and, since it is form that confers individuality, this amounts to the perception of a specific form. But the rendering of different forms requires different technical means, different styles; it is thus that "the style is the man." The point may be made clear by a few illustrations, beginning with Claude le Lorrain, the father of landscape-painting. If we consider landscape-painting as a purely objective affair, as an attempt to render with literal fidelity the appearance of meadow, stream, forest, and mountain, we shall note points in which Claude fell short of his successors, and consider him merely as a stepping-stone to later men, to Constable, Corot, Monet, or Cézanne. He will seem to be inferior to Monet in ability to show how color is affected by light and shadow, to Courbet in grasp of the naturalistic reality of individual objects, in the force and vigor he can lend to the rocks, trees, and human figures in his landscapes.

Cézanne surpassed him in his eye for the essential and living in nature, in ability to discard the irrelevant and lend solidity and substance to masses in three dimensions.

To hold these relative disadvantages against Claude is to mistake the meaning of esthetic intention and form. The artist must be judged by what he tries to do; the fact that forms of one sort are absent from his work does not detract from its value if it contains the forms which reveal what he was interested to show. Claude was interested in nature, not for any independent life it might contain in its parts, but as an embodiment, on a large scale, of human feelings. It was the landscape as a whole, "the spirit of the place," which moved him and which prescribed his individual designs; and it is precisely that design, that presentation of subtle relationships between the elements in his composition, that gives the romance, the glamour, the mystery, the grandeur, the melancholy, the majesty, which are associated with the larger groupings of natural objects. For that general effect, too much individuality in the parts of the composition would be destructive. The comparative lifelessness of detail in trees, rocks, etc., the absence of what is arresting or moving in separate figures, really contributes to the impression at which he aims. The fact that he often had his figures painted in by others is therefore not a reflection upon his art, but an indication that he could recognize what was really indispensable to his purpose and leave what was incidental to assistants.

Claude's form was thus the design by which large effects are rendered, and for this his style was admirably adapted. Manet aimed at an effect quite opposite to that of Claude. He was not trying to portray the epic quality which may attach to a wide expanse of landscape, but the distinctive, natural quality of individual things. For Claude, the particular detail was submerged in the picture as a whole, and had no importance in itself. Although he did not simplify, but painted details with considerable fulness, the attention they received was perfunctory. Manet's objects and figures are much more simplified; but the few details selected for emphasis succeed in individualizing the object much more than do Claude's more literal and diffuse representations. The effort to give what is unique in the things of ordinary life, to show their essential quality, appears in Manet's brushwork and in his rejection of the third dimension and of chiaroscuro. Manet was not interested in things as a part of a panorama, but in things as they are in themselves, with only enough relation to other things to show their characteristic function; hence his design was flat, while Claude's was set in deep space.

An analogy with literature may enforce the contrast, and show the parallel between style and subject-matter. Claude lived in the century of Milton; Manet in that of Maupassant. The seventeenth century still aimed at monumental effects, such as those of the Renaissance; it was the century of *Paradise Lost*. The nineteenth century, especially the latter half of it, had a much more restricted vision, but saw much more clearly and penetratingly what came within its range. Manet's form was a distinct thing in itself, representative of himself and of the spirit of his age. To censure him because he lacks the scope and poetry of Claude would be as unjust as to censure Maupassant because he lacks the amplitude and magnificence, the elevation of sentiment and the sweep of rhythm, which represent Milton's form and the spirit of his time.

With Cézanne we have an esthetic purpose different from either that of Claude or that of Manet, and a correspondingly distinctive technique. Cézanne shared Manet's interest in real things, but he sought to represent more clearly the dynamic relations between things. Neither painter attempted merely to be literal, both tried to render the essential. For Manet's general form, however, flat painting was more expressive, while for Cézanne's, the essential was defined in terms of solidity and spatial relationship in three dimensions. This concern, combined with the impressionistic interest in color, necessitated the use of a new form. He saw in things an organization which could be rendered by the use of color in connection with a series of distorted planes. To express this organization, he created his own technique or style, and the results prove the efficacy of the means.

Academic criticism necessarily fails to estimate justly the work of any artist, because its fixed standards are inapplicable to a world which is in a state of flux. Every technical device is correlated with a definite esthetic purpose; it is a means, not just of showing things, but of showing something in particular. Unless we have seen what the artist intends to show we cannot tell whether the means are appropriate or inappropriate. When an artist takes over the technique of one of his predecessors without sharing the vision which animated it, he takes over a mortal body but loses its immortal soul. He becomes an academic or eclectic painter, and his work suffers a loss of all vitality or individuality. This is not true of a painter who genuinely works in a tradition, because he has seen for himself what the tradition has to show him, and uses its technical means not mechanically but intelligently. Like everyone who has really grasped a principle or method, he is able to make fresh applications of it; it is a means of seeing by which his eye is opened to something not previously seen or put down. In that fresh applications are made, the originality of the painter is vindicated: Bellini, Giorgione, Titian, and Tintoretto, all worked in the Venetian tradition and each created new forms of his own which greatly enriched that tradition.

Cézanne suffers no loss of individuality because his work shows him to have learned from Michelangelo, El Greco, and Pissarro. From Michelangelo he learned the value of muscular accentuations in achieving solidity; from El Greco, he learned the value of distortions in enriching design; from Pissarro, he learned the value of color used in connection with light to make color more structural and more moving. But all of these technical means he so modified and so welded into a form which is truly his own, that a new and distinct creation emerged. Derain, in contrast, cannot with accuracy be said to have learned from Cézanne and the host of other painters whose methods are clearly seen in his work. He has appropriated their methods, but he has not seen for himself what his mentors saw, and his borrowings from them accordingly become not methods but tricks of technique. Derain is an eclectic; like the Bolognese painters of the end of the Renaissance, he has appropriated the devices of other men without creating anything new.

IV. PLASTIC AND OTHER VALUES

We have said that what an artist places before us is a series of forms, which appear to him as significant, and which were productive of the emotion which he seeks to embody. Since, as we have noted, every real object or situation contains a multitude of forms, it offers the artist an almost indefinite wealth of resources for esthetic effect. Not all of these resources, however, are available to the artist as a worker in a particular medium. Music, literature, and pictorial art, each makes its own selection from the mass of forms which are presented by the real world; and the problem of the extent to which these selections overlap, the extent to which a picture or a symphony may properly be also dramatic or narrative, is one of the most difficult in esthetics. We have already distinguished between plastic form proper and illustration; the problem which now arises is to understand how far they can be united without confusion or distraction of interest.

There is an analogous problem in music. "Absolute" music is usually considered as a higher type of music than that to which words are to be sung. Words represent ideas, and definite ideas are only casually or adventitiously associated with the emotions which music arouses. Hence, opera, song, and indeed program-music too, are condemned in contrast to sonata or symphony. On the other hand, when we compare, let us say, a symphony by Haydn with Beethoven's *Eroica* and *Fifth*, it is impossible not to be conscious of a difference of a semi-literary quality. Beethoven's own title for his *Third Symphony* is *In Memory of a Great Man*, and the symphony is heroic in essence, as Haydn's is not. Our appreciation is of the intrinsic quality of the music itself, which has the objective quality indicated by the title, and our enjoyment seems to be for that reason not the less but the more esthetic.

In contrast, let us consider Tschaikowsky's overture entitled *1812*. With it there is a definite program which narrates Napoleon's invasion of Russia and his ultimate defeat there. After a solemn passage, suggesting the sacrificial frame of mind in which a nation springs to arms for the defense of its soil, we hear the *Marseillaise*, which struggles in the orchestra with the Russian national anthem, amidst the noise of battle. The Russian hymn is at first given out in snatches, abruptly broken off; but it gradually becomes firmer, and is at last triumphantly played through, while the *Marseillaise* wavers and disappears, and chimes and trumpets unite in a pæan of victory. The pleasure afforded is largely amusement at a *tour de force*, and it is difficult not to feel that we are in the presence of what is essentially musical vaudeville. The device of representing a war by contention between the national anthems of the nations concerned, and of making music mimic a battle, seems unimaginative and childish. The total effect is sensational and offensive rather than esthetic. We feel that the association between the *Marseillaise* and France is, from the point of view of music, entirely adventitious, and similarly with the Russian hymn. The composer has attempted to stir the emotions appropriate to music by use of the symbols of nationalism. It is almost as though a painter, to suggest danger, were to show us a railway signal-board standing at the angle which directs an engineer to stop his train. The idea would not be really embodied in the painting itself, any more than a man's character is contained or implied in the name "Smith" or "Jones," or the story of Waterloo set forth in Napoleon's green coat and cocked hat.

In this fact we find a clue to the general principle of the distinc-- tion between legitimate and illegitimate use of subject-matter. In so far as the spectator or listener or reader must depend upon the resources of his own information to read the qualities of the subject-matter into the artistic representation, the effect is illegiti- mate. An artist, however, is entitled to such effects as he can really incorporate into his rendering of a subject. In the second move- ment of the *Eroica* symphony, Beethoven actually makes us feel the spirit of tragedy in the music itself, and we do not need to know the story to enjoy the music.

The same principle appears in the field of plastic art. We have subject-matter employed at the lowest level when there is no real plastic equivalent for the narrative or sentimental theme. In an ordinary magazine illustration, the familiar devices are shuffled and recombined, the old tricks are rehearsed again, but there is the same absence of any individual perception, of any distinction in execution, that we find in the words and music of popular senti- mental ballads. Even great artists sometimes resort to illustration not firmly established on a foundation of plastic form: Delacroix is entitled to great distinction as an artist if only for his contribu- tions to the brilliant and powerful use of color; but he was also highly romantic and liked to portray fervid emotions, in which forms are quite original, at least in the sense of being unusually striking. What he felt as heroism and romance, and depicted by exotic scenes and exaggerated gestures, seems to us now not sub- lime but overdramatic, if not bombastic. This fondness for Byronic stage-properties points to a defect in his observation of the things existing before his eyes. If his sense for the dramatic had sharpened his observation and enabled him to see in the real world the qual- ities he admired, both his grasp of form and the drama which he seeks to portray would have been better. Tintoretto also painted subjects of a highly dramatic nature but he gave us the plastic equivalent of the human values intrinsic to the situation, so that while in Delacroix we see flamboyance and melodrama, in Tin- toretto we find the peace that esthetic satisfaction always yields.

In Goya, Daumier, Glackens, and Pascin, we find illustration brought to such a high level that it becomes great art. All of them inform us about the situations they portray, but the means employed are truly plastic, used with individual expressiveness and extraordinary grasp of the significant. The pleasure we get from their work is of plastic origin in that the story they tell, while interesting in itself, is entirely subsidiary to the form in which the illustration is embodied. Color, line, space are arranged in forms which create, give individuality to, the comic, ironic, or satiric in the situations depicted. Their forms are significant because of the imaginative vision, originality, and power of their creators.

Velásquez and Renoir have the power of giving plastic form to values of subject-matter at a still higher level. Each had a distinctly personal vision as well as command over the resources of painting, color, drawing, composition, design, which permitted them to render the essence of the subjects which they treated. Renoir is the more poetic of the two. His painting catches the spirit of youth and springtime and vitality; he sees and draws forth the joyous and glamorous in the world. Velásquez is a realist, but his realism is penetrating to a degree that carries it far beyond mere literalism. He illuminates his subjects, not by adventitious ornament, but by a simplification and a self-effacing detachment which allows their inner nature to manifest itself through strictly plastic channels. Both men had an extraordinary eye for seeing which of the qualities of the real world lend themselves to plastic reproduction, and at the same time display the intrinsic nature of the objects into which they enter. In neither is the painting, as something over and above what is represented, merely an end in itself. The ornamental motif in evidence in Renoir is so fused with the structural elements that an enriched plastic form emerges. The picture sheds light upon what is represented, and this revelation of the world has a value which, though in the strict sense illustrative, is truly plastic or pictorial, and not at all "literary."

It is often considered that with the advent of Courbet and Manet the values of subject-matter disappeared from plastic art, since these painters, and the majority of their successors, painted anything whatever. In this they undoubtedly show a contrast with their predecessors from Giotto to Delacroix. There is a serious fallacy, however, in arguing from the fact that painting no longer confines itself to a particular sort of subject to the conclusion that it has lost interest in subject-matter altogether. We do not ordinarily care whether we have one particular coin or bank note, or another, so long as their value is equal. When Manet and his successors said that the subject did not matter, they meant merely that the qualities in which they were interested could be found in any subject whatever. Manet believed that all things are interesting for what they are in themselves, not for some pose which they can assume. He was more truly interested in subject than, for example, David, since he could find something worth recording in anything, and not only in the "noble," that is, the stiff or affected. Manet was interested in life and David in death.

It is a serious misconception to suppose that subject-matter must be limited to individual things. In a cubist picture, the thread of connection with individual topics or objects may be very slight, and what makes the picture moving is certainly not the human values of the individual thing represented. For example, it may show a violin disintegrated into many planes, all revealing partial views, seen from various angles, rendered with every degree of distortion, and recombined into a form which is plastic but not representative, and which may have a charm and an emotional force of its own. The degree of resemblance between picture and original may be so slight that, but for the title, identification would be impossible. Even when identification is made, esthetic satisfaction may be increased little if at all.

This instance proves that forms may be charged with esthetic feeling even when they represent nothing definite in the real world or when what they represent is clearly without appeal in itself. This may seem like a *reductio ad absurdum* of the view that esthetic value has anything to do with the values of subject-matter. But a hypothesis offered by Mr. Laurence Buermeyer seems to us to explain the situation satisfactorily. His theory is as follows.

All emotions are at least in part generalized: they are called forth not merely by particular things or situations, but by virtue of universal qualities which these things contain. This is true of the ordinary emotions and also of the esthetic emotions. When we cannot find in a picture representation of any particular object, what it represents may be the qualities which all particular objects share, such as color, extensity, solidity, movement, rhythm, etc. All particular things have these qualities; hence what serves, so to speak, as a paradigm of the visible essence of all things may hold in solution the emotions which individual things provoke in a more highly specialized form. It may give us a realizing sense of space, of externality, of colorfulness, of mobility, and along with these a distillation of the feelings which spacious, colorful, moving objects provide. Mr. Buermeyer adds plausibility by suggesting analogous cases of relatively vague apprehension or feeling. When we hear such words as "and," "but," "although," "therefore," we have usually little or nothing in the way of mental imagery, and yet there is no lack of meaning. We grasp something, even in the absence of any mental imagery: consciousness is not the less real because it is generalized. Again, music awakens very definite emotions, even in the absence of any perceptible objective reference. One air may make us sad, another joyous; neither may call up any definite reference whatever, and the cause of the difference may defy analysis; but the effect is incontestable. In other words, feelings travel far afield from the objects that first excited them, and it is therefore a mistake to suppose that a feeling has no objective reference because its object has no clear resemblance to the object that served as its original stimulus.

If Mr. Buermeyer's hypothesis be true, cubistic pictures of the kind mentioned only represent a stage beyond that of impressionism. The impressionists were interested in any or every object, because every object had its own characteristic form or quality which might be given pictorial representation. The cubists are interested not in the qualities which distinguish, let us say, an apple as an apple, or a woman as a woman, but in the qualities which are common to both as parts of the visible universe. Indeed, between the impressionists and the cubists there stands a painter, Cézanne, who seems to represent a transitional type. His figures do not seem obviously "natural" and "lifelike," as do Manet's; they are sometimes distorted out of any close resemblance to the objective things which they represent; and yet they seem to have even a more intense reality than Manet's. This reality is not that of literal representation and it does not depend exclusively upon such things as depth and apparent tangibility; it is more generalized but not therefore less objective.

What we have been contending for is the fact that reference to the real world does not disappear from art as forms cease to be those of actually existing things, any more than objectivity departs from science when it ceases to talk in terms of earth, air, fire, and water, and substitutes for these the less easily recognizable "hydrogen," "oxygen," "nitrogen," and "carbon."

Critics differ so widely in their estimate of the esthetic value of any particular form or set of forms that what to one seems merely literary or photographic, seems to another a profound and searching grasp of essentials. The principal reason for difference in judgments of all kinds lies in the fact that no two men have the same fund of experience, and consequently no two men are precisely on a par in their ability to follow the lead given by a painter. Above a certain level, appreciation is always in part the creative appreciation of one who is acutely sensitive to forms or who has a large mass of funded experience. In such cases the individual is rarely able to gauge the precise extent to which his enjoyment comes from his own resources and is not intrinsic to the work of art.

For instance, Gauguin's Tahitian pictures, which are his most distinctive achievements, may have an appeal by virtue of their subject-matter. Their exotic, even lurid, quality may seem either a genuinely esthetic value, like Constable's power of catching the spirit of an English countryside, or merely meretricious, a device for stimulating a palate weary of the more sober scenes of an older civilization. Putting to one side the question of Gauguin's properly plastic virtues, we may say that the question is one of individual taste and interest. There are people who constantly desire experiences as different as possible from those with which they are familiar, who are chiefly concerned to add to the sum of their sensations. Such experiences are vicarious adventures, a living of a more exciting life than their own humdrum world provides. There are, in contrast, people who prefer to discriminate between those experiences they already have had and thus to classify, order, and penetrate deeply into a relatively small segment of life. Both interests are legitimate; extensive experience has a value as well as intensive; but primary devotion to either makes the other appear inferior. Constable will seem comparatively tame to the man of one temperament; Gauguin, crude to a man of the other. The bent of mind which makes Constable's work seem fertile in suggestion leaves its possessor unresponsive to alien scenes and incapable of being stimulated by them to imaginative excursions of his own; and the same is true, with rôles reversed, of the man of opposite bent. In general, if we are shown something which awakens no echoes in ourselves it may seem merely literal or photographic or dry or superficial: the only clue that is meaningful to us is one which our interests will prompt us to follow up. By the same token, science may seem dry and trivial or mechanical to those who have no desire to understand the world intellectually; and poetry seem tedious, futile, or trifling to those who care nothing for imaginative understanding. Each is right in his own sphere, and wrong only in supposing that his sphere leaves room for no other.

In contrasting Gauguin with Constable, we have been referring to the attitude of the human being of average culture rather than to the highly equipped specialist primarily concerned with the esthetic significance of plastic elements. The plastic form in Gauguin's work is obviously thin and feeble compared with that in Constable. When Gauguin's work stimulates a spectator to the point of esthetic fulness, we have clearly a case of temperamental preference for subject-matter usurping the function of an external stimulus of a purely plastic nature. That is a legitimate esthetic experience, but it amounts to a kind of interpretative criticism which an individual's own personality reads into the painting. It means merely that a plastic form need not be in itself very strong to set in vibration the chords of sympathy which, once under way, increase in volume and power and carry the individual into a world of esthetic experience which is to a large extent of his own making rather than that of the painter. In the case of Constable, the plastic form is powerful enough in itself to move a trained observer to greater esthetic heights than the plastic form in Gauguin. He need have no preference for the subject-matter and still have the capacity of interpretative criticism that comes from native sensibility and a rich fund of experience. A disinterested judge would be able to say, and on good psychological grounds, that there is a tinge of sentimentalism in the Gauguin enthusiast.

V. FORM AND MATTER

We have hitherto spoken of art-values only in relation to form, and have made only casual mention of the material or matter which is organized into forms. We have seen that the distinction between form and matter is only relative; that we cannot think of form and matter as two independent variables, making their separate contributions to the total esthetic effect of the work of art. Matter apart from form is never to be found, since what is matter in relation to more generalized form, is form with relation to other matter: a state, which is matter in its relation to the United States, is form in its relation to the counties in that state. It is now necessary to show in detail how the two values are not really two, but one; that is, the apparently separate values of matter are really included in the values of form.

Let us consider the distinction between the two as it appears on a first glance. If we contrast a painting with a drawing, or with a photograph of the painting, the painting seems to differ from both the drawing and the photograph in that it adds to the skeleton of form, the enriching material of color. Since any good painting is better than a photograph of it can possibly be, the value of the painting seems to be that of the form, as given in the bare outline, plus that of the material. In a similar way, when a symphony is transcribed for the piano, the loss in effect seems to be due to the subtraction of the orchestral color lent by the varying timbre of the different instruments. Again, when a prose synopsis of the ideas in a poem falls short in emotional quality of the poem itself, we are likely to suppose that what makes the difference is the loss of such sensuous effects as rhythm and rhyme. A moment's reflection will show that all such suppositions are erroneous and that they arise from the improper limitation put upon "form" of which we have already spoken. In the case of the poem, the ideas when prosaically expressed cease to be really the same ideas because every word has a wealth of associations, derived from its use in many contexts, and all these associations enter into the content of the poetic idea when it is expressed by their aid. When it is stripped of associations and reduced to what can be given by abstract symbols, all its relations are disturbed and it ceases to be the same idea, the same "form." The form is the living body, and the symbol is the bare skeleton. To translate

> When to the sessions of sweet silent thought
> I summon up remembrance of things past

into "When I indulge in unuttered reminiscence" is not to give a new material setting to an already existing form; it is to lose a great part of the form itself.

The same is true in music. The piano transcription of a symphony loses the qualities of orchestral color and other relations which give the symphony its unique form, that is, make it what it is. A part of the form goes when the matter is changed. The sounds characteristic of the piano require a form of their own, one essentially different from that suitable to the orchestra. Otherwise, the best piano music would be that which most nearly reproduces the orchestral effect, and this is not the case. Chopin's works for the piano are better than Liszt's, and for the reason that Chopin's effects are properly pianistic, while Liszt's are conceived for the orchestra. It is the mark of an inferior symphonist that his works lose little if so transcribed, for it shows that his orchestral forms were defective to begin with. In really good music, even the shift from one key to another makes a difference. Once more, form and matter are not two separable things, but only distinguishable aspects, like the length and the direction of a line. The form that is merely added to matter is mechanical; the matter that is merely added to form is redundance and ostentation.

We find the same principle to hold in painting. The color which is added to the lines of a drawing or the tones of a photograph does not simply add a sensuous value to a form already given. It enters into the form itself, and the better the painting the truer this is. There are, of course, paintings in which the form is really not painted but drafted, with color added as an ornament; such paintings, as for example those of David, lose comparatively little when photographed; but the fact constitutes a reflection upon the original quality of the work. To overlook the functional value of color and treat it as simple decoration is to misconceive the purpose of painting and to lose sight of its specific medium. It is to make painting an inferior substitute for sculpture, or else mere illustration.

The reason why it is possible to photograph a painting at all is that different colors have different light-values, so that in a photograph they appear as varying shades of gray. In a painting, however, there are light- and shadow-effects, degrees of illumination, which are directly represented, as in chiaroscuro. In a photograph, these also are presented by grays, and the two correspondences overlap and obscure one another: a light gray may represent either a yellow or red, or a brightly lighted blue or green. In other words, two entirely different sets of relationships are fused, and the specific quality of each is lost. This means that a part of the form simply disappears, for the color is a part of the form and not an extraneous addition to it.

The loss of form with loss of color is to be found in reproductions of work so little colorful as that of Daumier. Daumier worked with somber tones, qualified by light and shadow; but the effect of the light on the tones is extremely important. Drawing of this character gives the effect of mass, of both inertia and movement, the qualities which give Daumier's work its power. When the double effects of light-contrasts and color-contrasts are reduced to a common denominator of gray, the massiveness of his forms is largely dissipated. With any painter who depends upon elaborate or novel color-effects, with Titian, Rubens, Delacroix, Renoir, Cézanne, or Matisse, the impoverishment of form in the reproductions is enormously increased. This principle explains the futility of the universal practice in colleges, universities, and popular lectures of using photographs, even colored ones, to give an adequate idea of the paintings themselves.

In Renoir, drawing is accomplished largely by the use of color. Relations are indicated not, as with Ingres, by sharply defined lines of contact between surfaces on which the color is evenly laid, but by gradual transitions through intermediate tints, variously illuminated. The specific color-values are all-important for such indication of form, and without them the form is thin and tenuous. In Cézanne, the rôle of color is different, but no less important. He draws volumes not so much by varying degrees of illumination, as by patches of color and by heavy well-defined line; and since the light-values of the different colors are often indistinguishable, a photograph of a Cézanne is likely to miss almost entirely the impression of massive reality conveyed by the original. With Matisse, color is of prime interest because of the very unusual chromatic combinations employed: contrast is an important factor in the form, and the distortion of outline which may appear to be his distinguishing feature is really in large measure a means of making the most effective possible use of color-contrast and color-harmony. In a photograph, in which color cannot be reproduced, these distortions appear arbitrary, that is to say, formless.

We have stated the general principle that form and matter are two sides of one reality, not two realities. Consequently when a painter makes of a particular type of form an end in itself, it is likely to degenerate into a formula, almost a mannerism, because the form of a great painter includes his own vision and temperament, and these cannot be duplicated. An instance of such degeneration is to be found in the preoccupation of some of the Florentine painters, notably Leonardo, with sculptural form, that is, with the representation of massiveness. The general design of Leonardo's paintings was usually subordinated to the purpose of making figures appear as full-rounded as possible. The result is one obvious type of "form," which has been regarded by many critics of painting as esthetic form *par excellence*, but which may, and often has, become almost a matter of semi-mechanical ritual. The overemphasis on massiveness in Leonardo's figures detracts from the esthetic value; monotony replaces unity and variety. In many of the lesser Florentines, Luini, for example, the "form" of Leonardo, so understood, becomes no more than a piece of technical display, a trick.

It is then a symptom of esthetic poverty and one of the many varieties of academicism, to which the stock distortions in the academic imitators of Cézanne furnish a more recent analogue.

The fact that any single type of organization if exaggerated becomes mechanical, may be further illustrated by Rembrandt. With him, chiaroscuro is in very great measure the agent of design and modeling, and often with great success. He too, however, occasionally fell into the error of making something which is valuable as a means, an end in itself, and when he did so the results are as disastrous as such results invariably are. In his famous "Old Woman Cutting her Nails"(277), the effect of light is so exaggerated that we have what is essentially melodrama. It is striking but cheap, the sort of thing that suggests academicism animated by ingenuity rather than imagination animated by genius. There is "form," no doubt, but it approaches perilously close to the forms that are manufactured with a lathe, and these are discoverable in great profusion in the work of Rembrandt's imitators.

VI. QUALITY IN PAINTING

In every work of art there is something which fixes its degree of goodness or badness, and which eludes description in words. The work may have the indispensables of variety and unity, and its forms may be clean-cut and readily placed in established categories. A poem may be unexceptionable in thought and rhythmic structure; a symphony may show a good use of melody, counterpoint, and harmony; a painting may reveal skill in the use of line, color, modeling, balance, rhythm, all fused into a good design; yet the poem, the symphony, or the painting may still fall short of greatness. In other words, there is in every work of great art a pervasive and subtle quality which defies analysis and for the recognition of which no rules are adequate. The term that seems best to hint at this indescribable something is the word "quality," used in the eulogistic sense.

Attempts to describe quality, in the sense here employed, usually result in little that is convincing. But that quality does exist and that its existence is recognized, is shown by the use of the terms "first-rate," "second-rate," "tenth-rate," applied to various degrees of goodness in nearly everything in life. Above the level of superiority that can be demonstrated objectively and upon technical grounds, for example, by the traits that make a five-dollar cravat differ from a half-dollar one, or a painting by Picasso

[42]

superior to one by Redfield—above these levels we come into a nebulous atmosphere. In criticism of the finer kind required to discriminate between "Assumption" (438) by Titian and "Madonna: la Belle Jardinière" (369) by Raphael, no words can adequately tell the whole story. Ultimately it is the native sensitivity and the funded mass of experience, providing an infinite number of forms in subtle relationships, that shed illumination to the person thus equipped. Even though the quality is indefinable in words, it is not recondite and it can be at least adumbrated sufficiently to enable one to follow the clues given. In *The Egoist* by George Meredith, this adumbration is successfully achieved through the musings of Dr. Middleton as he sips his after-dinner glass of old port. Nothing he says about the wine itself would enable a reader who lacked Dr. Middleton's temperament and experience to participate in his pleasure. But by a skilful use of words and phrases relating chiefly to life in general, a whole series of associations are suggested that penetrate to the intrinsic esthetic meaning of things and enable a sensitive reader to reconstruct from his own resources an experience that conveys to him, in subtle essence, the quality of the wine.

Such is the problem of a writer who would attempt to convey to others a clear idea of the distinctive content that endows a painting by Giotto, Giorgione, Titian, Renoir, or Cézanne with that quality which belongs to the very greatest artists. There are objective facts, color, line, space, which experience enables the spectator to perceive as distinctive forms productive of esthetic satisfaction. But the forms themselves will have little significance except as decorative patterns or as indications of represented subject-matter, unless the spectator has within himself the spark of life which makes those forms living realities capable of setting in vibration feelings akin to those which the artist had when he painted the picture.

This ultimate dependence of esthetic appreciation upon something which must be felt, and cannot simply be abstractly formulated, is the final proof of the affinity between art and instinct. Every instinct confers upon its possessor a specific sensitiveness. It makes him aware of distinctions which for another may not exist, and in making him aware of them it causes him to be moved to emotion by them. The word "sensitive" ordinarily covers the meanings of both distinction and emotion. Amorousness finds attractions invisible to the cold in temperament, resentfulness discovers causes for anger to which the man of milder disposition is blind, the compassionate are moved to pity by what may leave others indifferent or even amused. In a similar way, the sense of beauty distinguishes between grades of "quality," and finds the distinction important, when those who lack it are oblivious of any difference, and consider it of no consequence if it is pointed out to them. In the final analysis it is a matter of interest, and interests, as we have seen, are themselves determined by our instincts. The distinction between quality and its absence can be illustrated but not analyzed to its ultimate constituents. We must keep in mind that it is not a separate type or department of value but a difference between degrees of merit in the values already described, that is, in drawing, color, composition, plastic unity. Quality in painting is merely another name for the successful use of the plastic means to express the artist's individual vision in terms that are objectively demonstrable to a person possessed of the trained perceptions, and the store of accumulated meanings which constitute experience and culture. The degree of quality fixes the artist's rank.

CHAPTER V

ART AND MYSTICISM

WE HAVE seen that esthetic value is something which is moving, which must be experienced, which cannot be finally demonstrated, or completely communicated to other people of different endowment. In other words, the esthetic experience is of a mystical character.[1]

Mysticism is a sense of union with something not ourselves. It is felt to be intensely real even though any one lacking the mystic's sensibility cannot be compelled to share it. In its simplest form, it is found in the understanding that we have of those whom we know and sympathize with, and it is lacking in our feelings toward those who are strangers to us. Mysticism divines a kindred animation, a will, a consciousness in what appears to the non-mystic as alien or indifferent. In it, the barriers which ordinarily shut in our independent existence appear to dissolve, the self seems to expand, and our life to become confluent with another and a wider life in which we find our true self. It is a participation in an experience in which our own individuality is absorbed and carried along like a drop of water in a stream.

The sense of union with our environment depends directly upon the degree with which such an environment encourages and reënforces our wishes. We can do nothing without some degree of coöperation on the part of things about us: we need air to breathe, food to eat, light to see with, and in general the means for satisfying our instincts, affection, anger, self-assertion. Ordinarily, however, the world compels us to circumvent obstacles, offer inducements, persuade indifference; in consequence, the sense of an alien world is rarely banished. Even the most cheerful people have, at times, the feeling of being alone, of being shut up in themselves. Those great agents of isolation—frustration and grief—are the most powerful deterrents to the mystical outgoing of ourselves in the world. But there are times even in ordinary experience when every-

[1] See Laurence Buermeyer, *The Aesthetic Experience*, pp. 142–155, Barnes Foundation Press, Merion, Pa., 1929.

[45]

thing seems as by a miracle to forward the causes in which we are interested. At such times, the painful contraction of the frontiers of the self is at least in part abolished. When everything conspires to give us what we want, everything appears to be a part of ourselves and the sense of isolation falls away. We are conscious of an immediate expansion of our individuality, and this expansion, when vividly and profoundly felt, is the same thing as mysticism. To come home from abroad, to exchange an environment of strange customs for the ease of movement and comprehension which the familiar always offers us, is likely to be an experience tinged with mysticism. In the experience of falling in love, when the thoughts, the feelings, the desires seem to find an immediate response in another individual, the self dissolves into a larger and richer existence. In all human experiences, in so far as there is truly harmony, the self is expanded, and the mystical emotion has play.

We can now understand why art and mysticism should tend to come together and coalesce. The world of art is a world which has been made by human beings for the direct satisfaction of their wishes. It is the real world stripped of what is meaningless and alien and remolded nearer to the heart's desire. Whatever man does of his own free will and for pleasure, is art in some degree; natural objects, however, discourage as often as they encourage free activity, and many of our creations, the objects made for our own use, liberate only a small part of ourselves. The material things of life and the contrivances by which material ends are achieved thus remain impotent to evoke our profounder and more personal emotions. Deeper harmonies can be set up only by objects embodying feeling and imagination, as well as inventiveness. It is these deeper harmonies, frustrated by our life in a world so indifferent to our feelings, that art sets in vibration. Through the expressive form, embodied in art, the spiritual interests which we have in the world are immediately stimulated and satisfied and the imperfect expressiveness or responsiveness of material objects is supplemented and heightened. In consequence, the world of art is felt to be endowed with the independent and yet responsive life which we always attribute to what answers to our feelings. Even the decorative quality of pictures increases their mystical effect in that it enables us to perceive readily, fully, and agreeably, and thus encourages a harmony between ourselves and what is before us. In this, it contributes to the mystical effect.

[46]

We have mysticism at its height when the harmony between the self and the world is taken as the key to all experience, when everything is felt to be full of life, and at heart one with ourselves. Then the indifference or lifelessness of most of the world is felt to be no more than illusion, and the mystic feels that he sees beneath appearances to the reality underlying them. The artists who are mystics in this sense are the mystics *par excellence*, and we find them in such painters as El Greco, Claude, and Cézanne. In El Greco, we have the Christian's mysticism, a world dominated by supernatural forces. He reveals the pervasive life that the Christian mystic finds in all human experience, and uses nature as a symbol to show the individual's fears, struggles, aspirations, defeats, and triumphs, all vitalized with the artist's intensity. In Claude, we are nearer naturalism, but nature is still humanized. Claude painted landscapes, but they are romantic landscapes interfused with something close to human life. In Cézanne, nature ceases to be the mere vehicle it was in Claude and becomes interesting intrinsically. Its vitality is its own. Cézanne takes us out of ourselves more completely than Claude, who takes us out of ourselves only to show us ourselves again in a different form.

Mystical effects, like others in art, may be counterfeited. In such a painter as Böcklin, we find an exaggerated mysticism, a mysticism which is literary rather than plastic. Its effect depends not upon plastic form, but on specious technical devices and in consequence its symbolism seems cheap and melodramatic. In the work of the American painter, Arthur B. Davies, there is the same miscarriage of intention, and a lack of command over plastic means results in literary effects that amount to mere sentimentalism. Painters of his type are feeble purveyors of the mysterious and transcendental, who lack the properly plastic force which would make of their poetry a substantial reality.

CHAPTER VI

SUMMARY

IN THE preceding chapters, an attempt has been made to show that human nature, from which art springs, also determines its forms and sets its standards. In the following chapters, we shall consider systematically the means at the painter's disposal and the success or failure of particular painters in their employment of these means. As a preliminary, we may summarize a few of the cardinal points of the foregoing discussion in order to emphasize what qualities in plastic art are needed if it is to play its proper rôle in giving satisfaction to human desires.

The relation of art to instinct is shown in the immediately satisfying character of art; to see adequately is an intrinsically satisfying experience, and plastic art is the means by which the experience becomes accessible to us. The artist saves us from the plight of having eyes and seeing not: to have an eye systematically open to what is visually appealing is possible only if we have learned the artist's lesson. Thus does art educate our interest in perceiving the world.

The world which we perceive has in it many things, color, shapes, and lines, that may exert a natural charm. The colors of a sunset, the lines of a range of mountains, a ship, an automobile, even a piece of furniture, may have an esthetic quality, and this simple quality is probably the germ of the esthetic interest in its full development. It is the analogue of what we have called "decoration," the immediate agreeableness of certain sensations and arrangements of sensations. In a work of art, however, this "*a priori* beauty," as Bosanquet calls it, is supplemented by an expressive *form*. An object is more than a pattern of lines and colors; it is an individual thing, and its form, as we have seen, is what gives it individuality and significance. Its significance may reside in its appeal to our more specific instincts, or it may be due to the realization of mass and space, of the qualities common to all material objects. In either case, the particular colored and patterned object takes on a more universal appeal, and moves us not only by what it is, but by what it suggests and embodies. Obviously, the greatest satisfaction is possible from an object which combines these decorative and expressive interests and in which what is expressed is not only the universal qualities of the natural world, but human values also. To create an effective pattern of line and color is something; if line and color are made instrumental to massiveness, to distance, to movement, that is an important addition; if the dynamic masses in deep space are so composed and interpreted as to render the spirit of place in land-scape, as in Claude or Constable, of religious elevation, as in Giotto, of drama and power, as in Tintoretto, of poignant human-ity, as in Rembrandt, the total result attains or approaches the highest summits of artistic achievement.

Each of the arts has its individual medium, and the forms and human values which it can realize depend upon the medium em-ployed. Every art inevitably loses some of the values of the real world, because stone, paint, sound, or words can each represent or indicate only a portion of our concrete experience. The artist who tries to incorporate into his art the effects appropriate to other arts, injures the esthetic effect of his work. The painter must render his human values in plastic terms; he must make an object or situation move us by its line, color, and indicated spatial re-lations. Literature and music have duration in time; consequently, relations to what has happened or is going to happen are a legiti-mate source of esthetic effect. But the content of a painting is all simultaneously present, and it cannot properly be eked out by past or future; hence the futility of narrative, or of what pass for "moral" appeals (as in Millet) in plastic art. It is impossible to put in words the criterion of plastic embodiment, to give a formula for distinguishing between what is and what is not properly in-tegrated in the visible form of a picture. But a cultivated sensibility will discriminate between the pictorial realization of the values of actual experience, such as we have them in Titian or Giotto, and a recourse to literature such as that of which Delacroix was fre-quently guilty.

The achievement possible to any artist depends upon the com-mand he has over his medium, though there is no precise corre-spondence between this command and his final rank as an artist. Manet was one of the supreme painters, from the point of view of technical mastery, but he was by no means an artist of the rank of Giotto or Giorgione. What is meant by mastery of medium may be clearly seen if we compare Manet's work with that of a very inferior man, Meissonier, who was a very competent craftsman but not an artist. He could give a very accurate detailed rendering of any material object or scene; but his work is totally devoid of any personal feeling or vision and is intolerably diffuse and feeble simply as painting. Nothing in it suggests that he saw things in the terms that paint could render: the distinction between essential and irrelevant had no meaning for him. Manet's skill in the use of paint eliminated what is plastically adventitious, and he had a feeling for what in the object represented would go into the medium of paint. It is this ability to feel the object depicted in terms of the medium employed which is the *sine qua non* of any kind of artistic achievement.

We are all familiar with the corresponding gift in literature. A man may command a good vocabulary and write grammatically; but if his phrase is never terse or pregnant, if he cannot tell when to elaborate and when to pack many ideas into a few words, if he has no sense for the metaphors underlying words, the shades of meaning and feeling that cannot be put into a dictionary, he has no more style than a set of equations or a table of logarithms. In other words he is incapable of making words do what they can, and is, therefore, not an artist. Similarly, a competent painter of illustrations may be incapable of making paint do what *it* can do. He is then nothing but an animated color-camera.

BOOK II

THE ELEMENTS OF PAINTING

THE RAW MATERIALS OF PAINTING

WHEN we look at the world, we ordinarily suppose that our eyes reveal much more to us than they do. Merely as a matter of visual sensation, we see nothing but a flat surface, made up of a patchwork of colors. These patches represent solid objects, situated at varying distances from us, but it is not the eye that informs us of the fact. We learn of solidity from touch, of space from the motions which are needed to transport us through it. Gradually, as we take hold of the things we see, we learn what visual appearances are associated with smoothness, roughness, hardness, softness, and the like. As we walk about in our surroundings we learn that an object looks larger when we are near it than when we are far from it; that its outlines become blurred with distance and its colors less vivid. Objects vary also as light grows brighter or dimmer, and as its angle of incidence varies. Thanks to experiences of this sort, our visual sensations acquire meaning, and we say that we *see* distance, tactual quality, and light and shadow. In strict accuracy, however, all that we ever see is colors spread out on a plane at right angles to our line of vision; everything else is inference. By the time we have reached years of reflection, the process of learning to see has ordinarily been so completely forgotten, the inferences have become so entirely habitual and unconscious, that it is impossible, without special training, to distinguish the signs actually before us from the meaning read into them.

Such training is indispensable to the painter, whose medium directly affects the spectator through the eye only. Considered as a physical object, a painting is also nothing but a flat surface, on which colors are spread. To make these spots and areas of color represent solid volumes in space, the painter must retrace the process of learning which we have all forgotten and recover what is sometimes called the "innocence of the eye." Only thus can he learn the alphabet of his language, and combine its letters into intelligible signs with which to communicate what he sees to other individuals. Drawing, modeling, and the use of perspective are the specific functions which the spots of color may be made to play.

In many accounts of the technique of painting, it is assumed that this process of finding visual equivalents for all the qualities and aspects of the perceived world constitutes the education of the artist. There could be no greater mistake. It does constitute the training of the craftsman; but to identify the two is to fall into the confusion between art and imitation to which we have already referred. The ability to reproduce in paint the experience of vision is merely to have at one's command the raw material of art, and may leave its possessor in no more exalted status than that of the camera. It is analogous to familiarity with the grammar and vocabulary of a language, which makes speech possible but does not in the least guarantee that anything said will be worth listening to. The history of art has often been written on the assumption that art began with fumbling and ineffectual attempts to mirror the world which anybody can see merely by looking at it, and progressed as the copy approached the original more and more closely. We have already seen that art means selection, design, the revelation of the significant, and it would be superfluous to labor the point further. Important as the ability may be, when occasion calls for it, to render solidity, deep space, textural quality of surface, or any other pictorial effect, any such effect may be superfluous or distracting in a particular design. The craftsman becomes an artist only when he employs the raw materials of painting for the creation of plastic form, and the conception of plastic form is therefore fundamental to all understanding of plastic art.

CHAPTER I

PLASTIC FORM

A PAINTING is a work of art in so far as it embodies the artist's
perception of what he finds moving and significant in the objective
world. As the expression of a coherent personality, it must have
order or form; and as the outcome of an insight which penetrates
to essentials and reorganizes surface-appearances, it must be
plastic. The word "plastic" is applied to anything that can be
bent or worked or changed into a form other than that which it
originally had, and for the painter the merely factual appearances
of things are plastic: they can be emphasized, distorted, and re-
arranged as his personal vision and design require. The means
by which this transformation is effected are color, line, light, and
space. A painting, as we have seen, is primarily concerned with
things in their visible aspects, but it may include such illustrative
values as are communicable without the intervention of any
agency other than the specific plastic means. Plastic form is the
synthesis or fusion of these specific elements. To be significant,
the form must embody the essence, the reality, of the situation
as it is capable of being rendered in purely plastic terms. A
painter's worth is determined precisely by his ability to make the
fusion of plastic means forceful, individual, characteristic of his
own personality.

Plastic unity is form achieved by the harmonious merging of
the plastic elements into an ensemble which produces in us a
genuinely satisfying esthetic experience. Plastic form is significant,
in the ultimate and highest sense, only when it is a creation: an
expression of an individual human experience in forceful plastic
terms.

The most obvious plastic element is color. It has an esthetic
value quite independent of its function of representing the actual
color of real objects. Indeed, the esthetic significance of color is
the most difficult of all to judge and is the source of much confusion on the part of novices and even of advanced critics. The
novice is subject to many pitfalls in this respect—the mere sen-

[55]

suous appeal of varying degrees of brilliance, individual preference for particular colors, unconscious comparison with well-known objects of definite color-content—none of these standards has any esthetic significance. The intrinsic importance of color, and its relation to drawing and composition, will be discussed in the chapters which follow.

Another of the basic plastic factors is drawing—and here again reigns a confusion similar to that noted in connection with color. The novice looks for the type of drawing which is a replica of the way colored surfaces of real objects intersect to form line and contour. He forgets that the artist's work is not to copy literally the lines and contours of objects, but so to select, draw out, accentuate, and modify its essential aspects, by a fusion of all the plastic means, that there emerges a *creation*, constituting his individual version of the object. Success is a matter for esthetic judgment and not for simple comparison with the original object.

In the flat surface of a painting, color and line make up all the objects depicted. If there were no attempt to indicate the fulness of spatial depth, if objects were placed as flat representations on a single plane, color and line would be the only plastic elements possible. But such a painting would have no esthetic significance unless there was an arrangement of the colored and drawn masses into some sort of relation with each other; and this arrangement is termed composition. Even in the pattern of a carpet or wall paper, composition, in this sense of relations, is present. To have an esthetic appeal, the distribution of the elements in a pattern must have such a sequence of line and mass, a relation to each other, that their arrangement, order, balance are satisfactory to our sensibilities. Thus, mere pattern is the beginning of esthetic expression in so far as it shows that the creator has chosen one particular arrangement in preference to others physically possible, but without as much esthetic significance. In other words, color and line have been *composed* and the result is a design, a union of the two to give a single esthetic effect. Design is present when the color, the line, the composition, instead of being independently conceived, mutually affect one another and form a new unit. To alter any of these elements would disturb existing relationships and would destroy that particular unity. A design is completely satisfying esthetically when that particular arrangement of masses, that particular coloring, those particular shapes and sizes of ob-

Greek Pottery (208)

Distortions of naturalistic appearances similar to those above appear
constantly in the best contemporary painting.

El Greco (207)

Design achieved largely by means of distortions and
contrasts.

Picasso (232)

Modern version of El Greco's design.

Cosimo Tura (395)

Analysis, page 411

jects, harmonize better with each other than would another set of relationships between the same elements. And this principle of unity may be said to be the ideal according to which all paintings may be judged. The design of a picture consists of the general plot or handling of the various details, and it is the factor which should be uppermost in the mind of the person who wishes to discriminate the plastically essential from the irrelevant. Design in plastic art is analogous to the thesis of an argument, the plot of a novel, the general structure of a symphony, the "point" of an anecdote: that is, the feature or detail which assigns to each of the other elements its rôle, its bearing, its significance.

A word of caution is necessitated by the present widespread confusion of pattern with design and with plastic form. Pattern, as defined on page 56 and in passages on cubism, is always discernible in a good painting, but plastic form is present only in a relatively degraded stage in the "abstract" painting represented by cubism. Pattern is merely the skeleton upon which plastic units embodying the universal human values of experience are engrafted. Critics of the so-called advanced school prove by their writings that all that they see in paintings is mere pattern, although they endow it with the oracular mystification of such terms as "plastic design" or "significant form." The needed clarification of the meaning of form is furnished by Professor Dewey in the following statement: "Unless the meaning of the term [significant form] is so isolated as to be wholly occult, it denotes a selection, for sake of emphasis, purity, subtlety, of those forms which give consummatory significance to everyday subject-matters of experience. 'Forms' are not the peculiar property or creation of the esthetic and artistic; they are characters in virtue of which anything meets the requirements of an enjoyable perception. 'Art' does not create the forms; it is their selection and organization in such ways as to enhance, prolong and purify the perceptual experience. . . . Tendency to composition in terms of the formal characters marks much contemporary art, in poetry, painting, music, even sculpture and architecture. At their worst, these products are 'scientific' rather than artistic; technical exercises, sterile and of a new kind of pedantry. At their best, they assist in ushering in new modes of art and by education of the organs of perception in new modes of consummatory objects, they enlarge and enrich the world of human vision. But they do this, not by discarding altogether connection with the real world, but by a

[61]

highly funded and generalized representation of the formal sources of ordinary emotional experience." [1]

In any design, whether or not involving distortion, there are two important principles which deserve mention. These are rhythm and contrast. It is rhythm that first strikes our attention and produces the pleasure that holds us longest. No plastic element in a painting stands by itself, but is repeated, varied, counterbalanced by similar elements in other parts of the picture. It is this repetition, variation, and counterbalance that constitutes rhythm. Each of the plastic elements may form rhythms with like elements—line with line, color with color, mass with mass— and each of these rhythms may enter into relation with the rhythms formed by other elements. The simplest form of rhythm is that in which the bending of a line is matched by similar modification in another line. This may be a simple repetition, or it may take the form of a meeting, intersection, and balance of lines in which duplication plays a small part, as in Poussin's "Arcadian Shepherds" (360). Color may be likewise repeated, varied, balanced, in such a way that the rich, pervasive powerful rhythm gives to the painting its chief characteristic, as in Renoir's "Bathing Group" (239) or in Giorgione's "Concert in the Open Air" (330). These rhythms, supplemented by rhythms of line, light, and mass, permeate every part of the picture, contribute to the composition, and form an ensemble which constitutes design in its highest estate. Such fusion of rhythms, at its best, has an effect upon our sensibilities comparable to the harmonious merging of chords and melodies in a rich symphony in music.

As with rhythm, contrast may be of various sorts. Matisse's work is an example of very successful color-contrast. Chiaroscuro, as Rembrandt used it, derives its powerful dramatic effect from the contrast of light and dark. In many Dutch landscape-paintings, a placid episode is contrasted with dramatic trees and sky. A vivid contrast between foreground and background is to be found in Fra Filippo Lippi's "Virgin Adoring the Child" (98): the Virgin and Child are disproportionately larger than the figures and masses behind them, and much lighter in color. In this case, the fact that the background has the effect of a screen greatly heightens the general contrast. The power of Giotto's Assisi compositions (18) is largely due to his success in unifying the two sides

[1] John Dewey, *Experience and Nature*, pp. 391–393, Open Court Publishing Co., Chicago, Ill., 1925. Professor Dewey's text has been slightly condensed.

of his pictures even when the contrast between them is so striking that they seem radically disparate.

Contrast also may be between different sorts of technique: broad areas of color may appear in one part of the picture, divided colors in another. This sometimes occurs in van Gogh, who also diversified his effects through contrasting direction and size of the brush strokes. The principle of all esthetic contrast is that of combining variety with unity, but it advances beyond the general principle in emphasizing the fact that variety is effective in proportion as the difference between the elements involved is unmistakable and dramatic.

To the experienced observer of paintings, it is the design that is revealed at first glance, and determines whether or not the painting is worthy of further attention. Judgment of a painting consists in nothing more than the determination of the artist's degree of success in integrating the plastic means to create a form which is powerful and expressive of his personality. Defects in plastic form are revealed by ineffective use of line, color poor in quality or inharmonious in relations, inadequate feeling for space, stereotyped, formulated, or perfunctory use of means, overemphasis of one or more of the plastic elements. In short, plastic form is lacking when the halting, inadequate, unskilled use of the means fails to effect the unity indispensable in a successful work of art. Either the artist has nothing to say or he lacks the command of means to convey an idea in plastic terms.

Painting which makes no attempt to portray spatial depth, that is, the third dimension, represents plastic form at its simplest. It may embody fluid graceful line, harmonious color, flat masses and surface-space, all so composed that the relations establish plastic form of a high order, even though quite simple. It is true that scarcely any painting is absolutely flat, even that of the Byzantines or Persians: there is usually some indication that the different parts of the painting are not literally on one plane, as are the figures in a rug. The objects almost invariably appear to be at varying distances from the spectator's eye, though this effect may be achieved in ways other than the utilization of perspective or deep space. In many Persian miniatures, for example, different scenes are depicted upon the same plane, but they are placed one above the other; thus a substitute for perspective is achieved. While the design in flat painting may be satisfying, such plastic forms remain comparatively meager and correspondingly deficient in reality.

In general, if there were no depth, there could be no solidity, no rendering of planes one behind the other, as they exist in the world as we know it. It is obvious that to render the depth and solidity of objects, the illusion of deep space must be created by plastic means. In flat painting, in which objects can have only two dimensions, they can have no depth, cast no shadows, cannot bulge or recede, and cannot be felt to be solid. Color remains superficial, sequence of line is chiefly mere pattern, light can play no rôle except to modify the quality of color, and composition is reduced to arrangement of objects above and below, to right and to left. But when deep space is conceived, color, line, composition, and pattern are endowed with new possibilities of individual and interrelated treatment, which increase greatly the painter's power to create new and more complex plastic forms which possess a multitude of relations impossible in merely flat painting.

[margin note: makes this weakens to lesser value, inte]

Plastic form and reality go hand in hand—that is, an attenuation of means results in a form which leaves out of account much of the actual quality of things which in art, as in the real world, moves us so deeply. When a painter uses any of the plastic means inadequately, the fulness, the richness of his work suffers to the extent of his lapse, for it is a characteristic of good art that it gives a reality more convincing, more penetrating, more satisfying than actual objects or situations themselves give.

[margin note: questionable]

While it is true that painting which portrays spatial depth is, in general, richer in plastic values than painting which approaches flatness, it is *not* true that mere depth or three-dimensionality of objects is the factor which determines the relative worth of such paintings. It is possible to get an effect of depth by tricks of perspective or modeling, in which event the third dimension becomes mere virtuosity and the result is that instead of reality we get a specious unreality, more unreal than a frank two-dimensional pattern. Spatial depth and massiveness of objects have esthetic value only when they are achieved by plastic means harmoniously coördinated with the other plastic elements; that is, when they function as elements in a unified design. Therefore, it is obviously absurd to judge the relative merits of two painters by the success with which they render the illusion of a mass extending into deep space. A figure by Renoir, for example, has not as a rule the massiveness of a figure by Cézanne; such a figure would not enter harmoniously into his lighter, more delicate general design; Cézanne's design, in contrast, conveys the effect of austerity and power, and anything but a massive figure would be a disturbing factor. In short, spatial depth and three-dimensionality of objects are not to be judged by any absolute standard but only by their contribution to a unified, meaningful plastic form.

The merits of relatively flat painting and of three-dimensional painting which realizes solidity and spatial depth can be compared only when we observe how the artist has used color and light. One often sees paintings, in which color is merely laid on the surface like a cosmetic; it has the quality of tinsel, of something added after the object has been constructed. Instead of increased reality we get an effect of falsity, of unreality, and the painting lacks organic unity. Color is usually not a property merely of the surface of objects as we perceive them in the real world. The gray of a stone seems to spring from its depth, to go down into the body of the stone; the color is perceived as part of the structure of the stone, so that the grayness and the solidity are felt as a single individual reality. In painting, the failure to include color in form reduces the degree of conviction, and makes the total effect relatively cheap, tawdry, unreal.

What about fauvism? Not just local color?

Not less important than color, in attaining a convincing three-dimensional character, is the use of light and shadow. In painting that is two-dimensional, light functions through modification of hue or tint so that the shade of a color is partly determined by the light that falls upon it. In three-dimensional representation, massiveness of an object is achieved by having the brightest light fall upon the point nearest to the source of illumination, from which point there is a continuous gradation to deepest shadow. In other words, solidity is rendered by color and light correlated, and that correlation constitutes the modeling of forms. It is obvious that this correlation makes possible another esthetic effect: such use of color and light that they may each form independent and separate rhythmic patterns, which in turn form rhythms with the other plastic elements. For example, in Bellini's "Allegory of Purgatory" (89), the pattern made up of the light and shadow placed in various parts of the canvas, is one of the principal components of the plastic form: it is relatively independent of the function of the light and shadow in giving indications of position and contour. Similarly, in Titian's "Man with Glove" (394), the striking pattern formed by the light, focused on the face, shirt-front, hands, and glove, renders the solidity of these various units, and also does much to organize the picture.

In the left margin, handwritten: *to give life to activate*

In general terms, the artist has used this particular plastic means to portray the essence, the reality, of the subject and also to enrich and vivify as well as unify the design.

The plastic element which determines the character of three-dimensional painting is deep space, and this is achieved by the use of perspective. It need not be literal perspective as we perceive it in the real world: it must be used plastically, that is, changed or adapted by the artist to particular needs. Perspective conjoined with the modeling makes possible what is termed "space-composition." This is something over and above the third dimension achieved by the utilization of line, color, light, and perspective to make an object appear solid. Space-composition is such an arrangement of things in the depth of space that the intervals, back and front as well as up and down and to right and left, are felt to have a pleasing relation to each other and to the objects which they separate. Space-composition moves us esthetically when each object is so placed in its particular position that we perceive the space around the object in a definite relation to the space around each of the other objects, and that all these spaces are unified, that is, composed. If there were no objects, space could not be felt as an order of definite intervals; hence space-composition involves both the objects *and* the intervals of space. It is the sequence of objects and spaces so ordered that they form a pattern, which we perceive as a thing in itself. Space-composition is successful when it is unified with the plastic form as a whole; in other words, when the painter has been so successful in suggesting planes receding, advancing, and interacting with each other, that the whole series of spatial intervals between objects, as well as the objects themselves, interests or charms us. Space-composition contributes enormously to the reality of the total effect, since in our commerce with the real world we not only see objects but move among them. We live in a world of space and we see objects in relation to remoter objects: a tree with a wall beyond it, a house against a background of hill or forest. Our mind is filled with these forms. When an artist enriches them with his deeper perceptions and feelings, and molds them into designs richer than our unaided powers could construct, we share his larger vision and deeper emotions.

We have seen that plastic form is satisfactory when all its elements and aspects are organically integrated. As one progresses in the study of plastic art, a great variety of falls from plastic unity reveal themselves. A painter, unable to enter fully into his subject, to see it in its concrete fulness and with an eye to all its relations, or one with an insufficient command over all the plastic means, is incapable of achieving a unified painting. He may single out for emphasis some one feature and slight the others, treating them sketchily, perfunctorily, or conventionally. When this happens, we have what is termed formula painting or academicism, and while the execution may be very skilful, the skill is mere virtuosity: the painter, no matter how adroit, is not genuinely an artist. Line, or light, or modeling, or perspective, or the relations with surrounding objects that enter into space-composition—any one of these may be accentuated to the point of submerging the other aspects of the object or situation. When this occurs there can be no proper integration of the plastic means, and the result is comparative unreality.

As we have already seen, the unreal is the uninteresting and we cannot accept as real what we feel does not represent an object or situation *in its concrete fulness*. This principle, so true in real life, is equally true in all the forms of art. For example, in poetry, Swinburne's spontaneity, variety, and subtlety of rhythm produce an exceedingly brilliant effect. But the flow and surge of his verse is soon seen to conceal an inner emptiness; mere rhythm is made to serve for the imaginative grasp of the subject that should vary both the ideas and their expression by all the poetic means. This constant repetition of rhythm without other poetic content becomes mere virtuosity. Verbal magic destitute of meaning constitutes unreality. In music, Berlioz and Liszt have a great command of orchestration, but their themes are almost invariably commonplace and conventional, their ideas are thin, and the orchestral dressing fails to conceal the essential triviality. Here again one factor is given an exaggerated rôle to cover up a lack of real substance, and the effect is one of showiness or melodrama, of unreality.

The conception of plastic form, as integration of all the plastic means, will be used in this book as the standard and criterion of value in painting, and hence all the analyses and judgments that follow will be an illustration of its meaning. To clarify what is meant by integration of plastic means we may anticipate the later discussion and consider Raphael as a striking example of inadequate plastic form. Raphael has often been looked upon as one of the greatest of all painters, and he was undoubtedly a master of his medium. He had a great command over line, his ability to use light to indicate contour and to make a pattern was of a high order, and in space-composition his gifts were unsurpassed. But these accomplishments were largely borrowed, his line and light from Leonardo, his space-composition from Perugino. His color is superficial and undistinguished in quality; it is thin, dull, sometimes garish, and it seems rather an afterthought in the design. His composition is almost invariably conventional; it has not the freshness and the inevitable fitness that we see, for example, in Giotto, so that for all the spaciousness and airiness of his pictures we never get the impression of a really original and powerful imagination at work. His borrowings are made in some measure his own; but they are not sufficiently changed to indicate that they are really a creation of a strong personality and a distinct mind. His subject-matter lacks originality and it has the sweetness and softness to be expected in a conventional and sentimental mind. In other words, he had no vigorous personality to serve as the crucible in which the qualities of things should be fused and welded into a new form. The result is that his particular means remained disjoined from his conceptions as a whole, and his light, line, and space-composition stand out as isolated devices, as exploits of virtuosity. He did achieve a form of his own, and his great technical skill enabled him to attain results extraordinary in their own way, but the efforts are often specious and the effects tawdry.

For examples of the use of plastic means so disintegrated as to be mere tricks or mechanical stunts, we may examine the picture by Guido Reni entitled "Deianeira and Nessus" (377). We find almost nothing expressive of the painter's individual grasp of the subject, and correspondingly there is no real synthesis of the plastic means employed. The pattern and composition are effective, but these are taken directly from Raphael and executed less competently. The impression of movement is rendered skilfully, but it is so much overdone that it suggests histrionics rather than art. The color is without charm or originality, and is simply laid upon the surface. It is so little integrated in the plastic form that another set of colors might be substituted with no damage to the total effect of the picture. What we have is a mere assemblage of devices without inner coherence and contributing to an effect that is conventional, strained, and exceedingly tawdry.

Recognition of the balance or integration of plastic means which constitutes plastic form comes only from experience in looking at many kinds of painting. There can be no rules by which to fix the degree to which variety and brilliance of color, elaboration of grouping, rhythm of line, or any other plastic effect, must be realized. Colorists like Titian and Renoir cannot be accused of overaccentuation of color: they realized other aspects of the world in plastic terms equally strong, so that it is clear that they did not conceive *exclusively* in terms of color. In the work of both of these painters we see significant line, movement, composition, effective spacing, both on the surface and in the third dimension. Color serves not as the only source of effect, but as an organizing principle. Renoir's drawing, for example, is done in terms of color, and though the incisive line characteristic of Raphael or Leonardo is absent, the effects to which line contributes—movement, fluidity, and rhythm—are rendered with great success. Although the kind and degree of three-dimensional solidity which we find in Michelangelo or Cézanne is absent from Renoir's figures, these figures do not seem vaporous or unreal. They have substance, mass, actuality, though not in the same manner and degree as do the figures in the work of painters whose primary purpose was different.

The way in which emphasis upon one of the plastic means may be united with subsidiary but sufficient realization of the others is further illustrated in Rembrandt. He employed chiaroscuro, that is, a bright area surrounded by darkness: light melting into heavy shadow serves as the technical method in most of his pictures. He avoids overemphasis of his special means by making chiaroscuro function as color more powerfully than any colors of Leonardo or Raphael. In "Old Man" (104) and "Hendrickje Stoffels" (373), minute variations in the golden-brown light give a richer, more glowing and actually more varied effect than all the colors of the spectrum used by a lesser artist. When, as in "Unmerciful Servant" (168), he introduces bright color, the effect is one of marvelous depth, richness, and fire. This same combination of economy of means and great effectiveness is to be found also in his line and distribution of masses. In space-composition the use of chiaroscuro narrowly circumscribes the space at the painter's disposal, yet in "Unmerciful Servant" the effect of roominess achieved is comparable to that of Perugino or Poussin.

In general terms we may say that in painting, as in all other forms of art, whatever quality is selected as setting the dominant note must be ballasted and made real by being shown in a context of other qualities, and when this is not done the effect becomes conventional, cheap, tawdry, unconvincing, and unreal.

The "reality" which we consider to be the essence of art-value in painting may be illustrated by reference to the subject-matter portrayed by the French painters, David and Delacroix. In David, there is constant recourse to stage-settings, poses, themes, reminiscent of classic antiquity. In Delacroix's exotic, Byronic themes, there is a similar indication that the world in which we actually live is beneath the artist's serious attention. In both cases we are conscious of an artificial or theatrical quality, and this conviction that the painters are playing a game or acting a part is not affected by the fact that the histrionics were doubtless free from deliberate insincerity. What they portray of poignancy, pathos, tragedy, significance, existed in the world about them as well as in remote times and distant places. If they did not find them near at hand, we are justified in concluding that they did not know what they are, and that their portrayal of them is essentially a caricature, a set of figments out of daydreams.

This condemnation of "classicism" and "romanticism" is not based upon literary considerations, but upon plastic ones: antiquarianism or sentimentalism betrays itself in limited and unoriginal command of plastic means. The painter does not draw inspiration for his art solely out of his own personal experience but depends upon other painters for the methods by which his pictorial effects are produced. David's "classic" calm, or rather coldness, is due to a line which he took from Raphael and Mantegna and which they had taken from ancient sculpture. It is not something which he actually saw as a part of a personal and coherent view of reality, but a studio-device to which the qualities of color, mass, and space were added as an afterthought. These qualities do not really fuse with the line to produce an impression of reality, but remain adventitious, just as the "noble" or "distinguished" figures and situations painted remain strangers and phantoms in the world in which we actually live.

The same is true of Delacroix. The stormy emotion, the exaggerated gesture, and violent drama are almost as spectrally unreal as David's "nobility," and they point to the same inability to *see* the actual world about him. Delacroix does not seem so artificial either in subject-matter or in plastic quality as David, because romanticism was for him less a pose than classicism was for his predecessor, and because he did more to modify and reorganize what he took from others. His color represents an advance over Rubens' in that he showed a degree of originality in the methods he took from him. Consequently, he seems more real, and so more interesting and a greater artist, than David.

We realize how essentially fantastic David and Delacroix were when we compare them with later painters. The concern with actually existing scenes, persons, and situations made of Courbet and his successors the legitimate successors of Velásquez and Goya, in making us see the objective qualities of things, divested of the subjectivism that constituted the romanticists' exhibited world of self. To sympathy with Courbet's insight we owe the important painters of 1870—Manet, Monet, Degas, Sisley, Pissarro, Renoir, Cézanne—and their imaginative telling of the story of life in a real world. Of that group, Renoir and Cézanne deal most objectively with the whole range of experience as men find it verified in themselves, free from the trifling, the insignificant, the preoccupation with theory, method, virtuosity, or personal vanity. If one looks beneath the dissimilarity of techniques, Renoir and Cézanne are seen as close kin in dealing with the fundamental, universal attributes of people and things. Both treated the familiar, everyday events that make up our lives. We see, feel, touch the particular quality that gives an object its individual identity. Each of the painters created a world richer, fuller, more meaningful than that revealed to our own unaided perceptions. Each mirrors, so vividly, a world we know by having lived in it, that we get a sense of going through an actual experience. Both are great artists because they make art and life one by convincing us of the truth and reality of what they see and feel and express.

CHAPTER II

PLASTIC FORM AND SUBJECT–MATTER

WE HAVE seen that the value of a painting resides in its plastic form, not in its subject-matter; but that does not mean that the appeal of the painting, as a concrete reality, is not due in part to what is shown in it. Subject-matter and plastic form are not in any absolute sense separable. It is true that relevant judgment or criticism of a picture involves the ability to abstract from the appeal of the subject-matter, and consider only the plastic means in their adequacy and quality as constituents of plastic form. In that sense, a picture of a massacre and one of a wedding may be of exactly the same type as works of art. We may abstract from each the form which is made up of the plastic elements— line, color, space, light—and determine the quality of that plastic form as an organic, unified fusion of those elements. Until one has formed by study and long experience the habit of doing so, the intrinsic appeal or repulsion of subject-matter itself will constitute the chief interest found in pictures. Many painters who are unable to master the means of plastic expression, seek to awaken emotion by portraying objects or situations which have an appeal in themselves, independent of any artistic conception or rendering of them. This attraction, dramatic, sentimental, religious, or erotic, though it is all-important in determining popular preference, is plastically and esthetically irrelevant. A popular vote for the best painting at academy exhibitions always results in the selection of a picture representing a mother and child, or a nude, or a pretty landscape, even though the one chosen has no qualities that entitle it to be called a work of art. This sin is not of modern origin but dates from the beginning of painting, and many pictures in the Louvre, the Uffizi, and all other large galleries owe their reputation and their preservation almost solely to the character of the subject-matter.

It is no easy task for a novice to banish from his mind the independent interest of the subject-matter and to fix his attention upon the manner in which color, line, space, and light are employed and interrelated; it involves the breaking up of a set of old, firmly riveted habits and the beginning of new ones. But, as in other activities where genuine interest drives, once the new habits of seeing are established, they operate almost automatically, and the tendency to be distracted by irrelevancies ceases to be a stumbling-block to perception. For example, of the hundreds of paintings upon detailed analysis of which this book is based, scarcely a score are known by the author in terms of their subject-matter, whether that be, in its general nature, religious, sentimental, dramatic.

Difficulty is ordinarily encountered in appraising justly a painter who habitually accentuates human values, religious, sentimental, dramatic, in terms not purely plastic. Raphael sins grievously in this respect as do Fra Angelico, Mantegna, Luini, Murillo, Turner, Delacroix, and Millet; and for that reason they are all second- or third-rate artists. Even more important painters, such as Rubens, are not always immune. The error, indeed, is the same as that we have already discussed, in that it is usually from the excessive use of some plastic device that the overexpressiveness of subject-matter results—although the two are not fully identical. Ingres's effects are melodramatic in the plastic sense— they are dramatically linear—but not in the expressive or emotional sense, as are so often, say, Delacroix's. The criterion for both of these forms of melodrama, the plastic and the expressive, will appear as we consider command over plastic means. When mastery of means is assured, when there is a definite balance of one means with another, there is a legitimate esthetic effect: the appeal of the subject-matter is integrated with the plastic form, and whatever the subject-matter there is no sentimentality or melodrama. In other words, the values contributed by the subject portrayed are not specious or extraneous and any degree of emotional appeal is properly esthetic. A painting may be dramatic, religious, or concerned with sex to an indefinite degree without being specious, cheap, pornographic, or tawdry. The principle is precisely the same in the other arts. Only the hopelessly prudish could find vulgarity in *Madame Bovary* or *Anna Karenina*, even though their subject-matter, marital infidelity, is the same as that of neighborhood gossip, the newspaper, or the divorce court. It is the manner of conceiving a subject, the ability to do it justice in terms of the artist's materials, that determines whether the effect shall be esthetically satisfying or unsatisfying. Paintings which are illustrations and nothing more, constantly tend to be

[73]

either literally photographic or completely conventional in conception, and thus to be without any esthetic substance of their own. Here again the criterion is that of reality: any quality or effect taken in isolation is uninteresting because unreal.

Success or failure in integration of the values of subject-matter with plastic qualities can only be made clear by concrete illustration. In Titian's "Entombment" (392), the subject is solemn, sad, pathetic; but the solemnity and pathos are restrained and dignified. So much for the obvious, represented subject-matter. When viewed plastically the picture presents a group of figures unified into a firmly-knit, self-enframing, oval composition, similar to, but more complex than that in Giotto's "Lamentation over Christ" (287). The drawing is highly expressive of movement and gesture but does not indicate exaggerated grief or despair, such as we find in treatments of the same subject by many lesser men. The color though glowing does not flaunt itself, but is of a subdued richness which pervades the whole canvas and contributes to compositional unity. The robes in the bending figures to the right and left are brighter in color and serve as a sort of secondary frame, enclosing the members of the group, and setting them off from the background. The color, in other words, functions as an organizing principle. Finally, the use of light, powerfully enhanced by color, brings out the figure of the dead Christ, and is so distributed over the whole canvas as to form a pattern in itself, reënforce and harmonize the color-values, contribute to the composition, and heighten the sense of mystery and awe characteristic of the event depicted. In this painting it is both the intrinsic interest of the event and the perfect coördination of all the means, color, light, line, space, which make up the total esthetic effect and establish the painting as one of the great achievements of plastic art. One need not, however, be a Christian, or indeed have any special interest in the event itself, to obtain from the painting the rich human values, the nobility, intrinsic to sympathy, solemnity, tragedy. These values are rendered plastically, by means of color, light, line, mass, space, all unified into a rich, rhythmic design.

In the Titian just discussed, the subject-matter itself is characterized by restraint, but quite the opposite qualities may be realized esthetically provided there is fusion of the plastic means. In paintings by El Greco and Tintoretto, the subject-matter is often violent, tumultuous, or ecstatic in character, but it is so rendered in plastic terms that we get a sense of satisfaction and peace. In many paintings by Delacroix, in contrast, the turmoil in the subject-matter infects the plastic treatment, coördination is impaired, and the picture becomes theatrical. In Guido Reni the balance between subject-matter and plastic means is usually completely destroyed, and what is put before us is almost devoid of art-value. Even in the works of the greatest artists perfect fusion of plastic means is by no means always attained. For example, in Titian's "Christ Crowned with Thorns" (390), there is a tendency to overemphasis of light, to sharply drawn line more nearly like Raphael's, and the melodramatic element begins to creep in at the expense of plastic form. In Paolo Veronese's "Burning of Sodom" (400), the plastic design is perfectly realized by a fluid rhythm of line, color, mass, and space, all gracefully flowing in the same direction and giving a plastic form fused completely with an intense and dramatic subject-matter; in his "Jupiter Destroying the Vices" (401), on the other hand, motion and drama almost completely lack plastic equivalents.

The religious theme is realized best in plastic terms by Giotto and El Greco, with an effect of great dignity and peace in Giotto, and of mysticism and ecstasy in El Greco. With lesser men the religious theme becomes perfunctory, trivial, or specious. Fra Angelico represents a certain stage of this descent, and although his pictures have a certain charm, mainly decorative, they owe their popularity chiefly to religious and sentimental narrative. In Murillo, the decay of the Spanish religious tradition is much further advanced than that of the Italian in Fra Angelico; the mysticism of El Greco has become an insipid sentimentalism, with resort to exaggerated lighting and a sweetness which suggests the consummation of Luini's and Andrea del Sarto's exploitation of Leonardo's worst features; or literal representation—for example, sadness in a face depicted by a few lines bent in certain directions— is palmed off as expression. In Millet we have humanitarian religion, unsupported by the necessary plastic means, with the inevitable sentimentalism. In Correggio there is disbalance between the values of subject-matter and values truly plastic: his women tend toward sweetness, in the manner of Leonardo and Raphael, and he too makes an excessive use of light. In his "Jupiter and Antiope" (307), though the color is pleasing, the distribution of masses effective, and the general pattern of a high order, there is a tendency toward superficiality in the color, together with a lack of variety, of richness; light is overemphasized; the flow of line stands out in relative isolation; the drawing is flabby; and there is also a suspicion of triteness in the composition. There is more light, and more sweetness, than a perfectly balanced plastic form permits.

Many of Renoir's pictures show the charm of feminity in a lyric or idyllic setting which in the eyes of a superficial observer is likely to verge upon mere prettiness. But Renoir's mastery of his medium enabled him so fully to realize his conceptions and to surround charm with a wealth of plastic qualities, that the distinctive poetic charm is achieved by legitimate means. In the presence of a fine Renoir we feel that he was deeply sensitive to obvious, but very real, sources of delight in the world, but that he saw them so objectively, so thoroughly interwoven with the other qualities of real things, that his version of them is free from any touch of sentimentality. His interest in subject-matter thus takes form in terms that are plastic in high degree.

Delicacy, grace, even fragility can be found in many of the greatest paintings, as in Velásquez' "Infanta Marguerite" (396); in these pictures the artist's grasp of plastic essentials is so sure that the quality of the subject-matter lends a heightened charm.

The development of painting in modern times took place in large measure contemporaneously with the revival of classic culture which we know as the Renaissance. Attention at that period was fixed upon the sculpture of ancient Greece and Rome, and classic traditions and themes inevitably appeared in the painting of the time. This classic influence was of great value so long as it was thoroughly assimilated, merged with the spirit of the age, and rendered in plastic terms individual to the artist. Such merging is always a matter of degree; in the work of Giorgione, for example, the heritage from the Greeks was completely incorporated in the artist's own spirit. In Michelangelo and Mantegna, on the other hand, the themes often seem to be lifted bodily from Roman sculpture, and there is the inevitable failure so to embody these themes in a setting of line, color, space, as to make them really live. The integration is accomplished perfectly in Claude's use of a Virgilian glamour and romantic mystery: there is no hint of falseness, of a sluggish imagination taking refuge in mimicry. He was able to make the ancient spirit live again under another sky, and to give an adequate and very personal plastic form to a world conceived both classically and romantically.

Titian (392)

Cézanne (178)

The design in the above two paintings is very similar in structure and expressive content: the interrelationships of plastic elements result in a form which submerges the associated values of different categories of subject-matter in a distinctive esthetic experience, basically similar with the two pictures, yet qualified by the individuality of each artist.

[77]

Tintoretto (154)

In this painting and the one on the opposite page, dramatic subject-
matter and plastic form are successfully merged.

Paolo Veronese (400)   Analysis, page 431

Bellini (89)

Analysis, page 418

In contrast we find in the French painter David the classicism which is a mere formula, a rattling of dry bones. In Ingres the classic tradition is also clearly seen. It inspired him, as it did Raphael, to a vivid sense of the effects possible by emphasis on clear-cut and pervasive linear quality, and his use of these effects was vigorous and personal. But David's classicism was destitute of any personal insight or vision, and his conventionality is reflected also in his stereotyped rendering of every aspect of subject-matter. His frigid correctness is superior to the self-conscious antiquarianism of the British pre-Raphaelites only in that he knew more about his métier and could make a more skilful use of his brush.

We have seen that plastic deficiencies that are not due to simple technical incompetence, almost always take the form of over-accentuation in one or another of its various types. The reason for this is that a painter who has nothing of his own to show, but who possesses a certain amount of technical skill, can only imitate what some one else has shown. Usually, he borrows the more striking features, the mannerisms, makes a formula out of the original; the result is overemphasis of what is borrowed and relative neglect of everything else. When a painter has great technical skill, he may do this so successfully as to deceive the inexperienced observer; hence, if we are to understand and judge any painter justly, it is necessary to know at least something of the history of painting. The salient features of this will be sketched briefly in subsequent chapters; but first a more adequate account of the plastic means will be given.

CHAPTER III

COLOR

As we have seen, color is the fundamental plastic means, and the other elements, line, light, and space may be regarded as modifications or aspects or results of it. Color has an effect which depends upon its intrinsic quality, independent of all relation to the other constituents of the picture. We all know, and the fact may be experimentally verified, that some colors produce quiet and restful effects, others are flamboyant and exciting to the sensibilities, so that the specific sensations of color with which a picture presents us have much to do with its appeal, both immediate and permanent. In Raphael, for example, the color, simply as sensuous material, is rarely good and when abstracted from the other plastic elements, it is usually like the colors in a cheap rug or fabric—either dull or overbrilliant. In Giorgione, Cézanne, or Renoir, on the contrary, immediate sensuous charm of color pervades and heightens all the more complicated effects. The result is not unlike that which simple physical charm gives to personality, in making moral and intellectual qualities more vivid and appealing, more intensely *felt*, as well as judged favorably or approved.

Variety or richness, and harmony, add greatly to "quality" in color, both in the picture as a whole and in the separate parts, elements, or units. In Giorgione, Titian, Rubens, Renoir, Cézanne, there seems to be no limit to the multiplicity of hues and tints introduced into the simplest object, an orange, a cup, a hand, a lock of hair; yet these color-chords are invariably units in themselves. The effect of unity in diversity is repeated again and again, with successively more comprehensive units, until we come to the picture as a whole, which seems a symphony of color, in which the direct sensuous appeal is enormously heightened by the sense of the relations between the colors employed, with each color setting off and being itself set off by all the others.

In order to appreciate the esthetic significance of color in the great modern painters, we must be acquainted with its use by the

[82]

Venetians, above all by Giorgione, Titian, and Tintoretto. These painters employed colors which are intrinsically pleasing, and are diversified and harmonized to yield magnificent effects. Renoir advanced beyond the Venetian tradition by utilizing the contributions made by Rubens, the eighteenth century French painters, Delacroix, and by the impressionists, so that in the richly decorative aspects of his surfaces he is without a peer. On the other hand, the extreme richness, the voluptuousness of his color, detracts in some measure from his strength: there is in Cézanne a greater effect of power.

In contrast, Leonardo shows a relative barrenness of color. In both the London and the Paris version of his "Virgin of the Rocks" (141; 345), the color not only lacks obvious appeal, but in its variation throughout the picture there is a lack of inventiveness, of a sense of the possibilities of variation and harmony. It is mainly tone; when the tone is lighter in shade it seems to have an effect merely of shininess, when darker, of muddiness. Color itself, and color-relations, detract much from the value of his plastic form.

It must be remembered that sensuous charm or richness in color is not the same thing as brightness. Colors which are bright without being rich or deep give an effect of garishness or gaudiness, and the general effect is of superficiality. In Lorenzo Monaco and Baldung Grien among the early painters, and in Kisling, a modern artist, bright color gives no sense of glow or splendor, while in Daumier and Rembrandt, though the colors are very subdued, the effect is anything but drab or dingy.

Variety of color does not mean variety in the sense of employment of all the colors in the spectrum. Rembrandt's subtly modified dark tones suggest a great variety of color, and Piero della Francesca used chiefly a silvery blue so varied in shade, so tinged with light and shadow, that his repertoire of color seems extremely rich and the economy of his means appears only upon analysis. If Delacroix's colors were taken out of his canvases and arranged side by side, his vastly greater actual variety would be revealed, but a good Piero hung beside a Delacroix would show that Piero was the greater colorist.

We have hitherto used the word "richness" in a way that might be construed to mean "variety," as when we say that there is great richness of color in Renoir, and comparatively little in Perugino. But there is another sense of the word for which

[83]

we may find a synonym, by a figure of speech, in "juiciness," as something opposed to "dryness." This is present nearly always in the greatest masters of color, in Titian, Constable, Delacroix, and Renoir. Its opposite, dryness, is not, however, a term of unqualified reproach. Poussin is a great artist and an important colorist, yet the color in his pictures is almost invariably dry. The distinction is thus not always one between good and bad, since there are esthetic effects to which dry color is a positive reënforcement; a painter may use very juicy color, like Monticelli, without thereby becoming an artist of the first rank. Again, if Puvis de Chavannes had emulated Renoir in the use of juicy color, his own distinctive form would have suffered rather than gained. The most important difference in color-quality appears when we consider the relation of color to light, composition, modeling, etc. Color combines with light to form what may be called atmosphere, and this may be a most important element in esthetic effect, as in the Venetians, in Rembrandt, and in the impressionists. Furthermore, light has a direct influence upon color, enriching it by an internal luminosity, and the incapacity to take advantage of this influence is a serious defect in plastic form. In the world of real things, color changes in quality under different degrees of illumination, and the ability to utilize the alteration so effected is an important part of the painter's command over his materials. When light is not properly used in connection with color, plastic reality suffers because of the absence of the modification and enrichment that light works upon color. Instead of bringing out and revealing new harmonies within color, the light seems to efface color and act merely as a substitute for it. In Leonardo and Raphael, too much light overemphasizes the contrast between light and shadow, and, in addition, the light fails to make the color function vigorously. The contrast between light and shadow is even more striking in Rembrandt, but his handling of color-indications is so skilful that the chiaroscuro is utilized as an enhancement of color and not as camouflage for lack of it.

The use of light in connection with color as atmosphere is to be seen conspicuously in the Venetians, in the painters of the Barbizon school, and in the impressionists. It appears earlier in the work of the fourteenth century Florentine, Masaccio. In the real world, atmosphere blurs the outlines of objects at a distance from the eye. This naturalistic effect is in Masaccio's painting enlarged in esthetic value by an addition of color to the simple haze of nature. Except among the primitives, almost all painters reproduce the blurred outlines of distant objects, but the effect of atmosphere as a luminous color in which all things float is not universal in painting. Sometimes, as in Whistler, it is an obvious imitation of mist; sometimes it is a source of melodramatic pseudo-romance, as in Turner; but when employed with discrimination, as in Claude and the Venetians, it is a powerful reënforcement having its own esthetic effect. It is usually golden in Claude, in the Venetians it is golden with an admixture of brown, and in Corot it is silvery. As a translucent atmosphere, a circumambient glow, it supplements or blends with the local colors, augments decorative quality, aids in knitting the composition together, and thus functions as an important element in the plastic form.

The rôle of color in drawing and composition is as important as its joint function with light in creating atmosphere, but it may be more conveniently discussed in the chapters dealing with those topics. There remains one other important distinction in the use of color to be discussed at this point. Color may or may not seem to be a part of the actual structure or mass of an object. As we have seen, the usual manner of rendering solidity is to show a graduated increase in light or shadow. Such modeling was developed to a very high degree of perfection in Leonardo and Michelangelo, and since their time it has been the usual method of giving the impression of solidity. But modeling has a richer plastic value when the artist is able to make color an integral part of the solid structure. The Venetians were the first to realize this structural use of color and it became an important plastic resource in subsequent great painters, notably, Constable, Delacroix, Velásquez, El Greco, Renoir, and Cézanne. In Giorgione, Titian, and Tintoretto, a solid body does not appear as something which has substance in itself independent of color. The substance seems to be built up out of color, that is, the color seems to go down into the solid substance and permeate it. In every detail in Titian's "Man with Glove" (394), for example, color seems to be the actual material out of which the form is wrought. In contrast, Leonardo's effects of solidity are largely independent of color: there is not a great deal of color at best, and what there is is usually superficial. In Ingres's paintings, we usually get the impression that the form was completely fashioned or modeled before any thought of color entered the painter's mind; the result is a lack of the solidity which accrues when color is used structurally. The color is often quite pleasing, but it tends to be a mere decorative adjunct, without organic plastic function.

Another kind of pervasive color-effect is best illustrated in Giotto. His color is not structural in the Venetian sense, though it is an integral part of the general form of the picture. The atmosphere is usually as clear as crystal, and the colors stand out like jewels, in contrast to the Venetian glow in which there is a suggestion of translucency amounting at times to a haze. In spite of this crystalline transparency of Giotto, the pervasive color, into which reddish, yellowish, and bluish tints merge, is extremely marked, and adds much to the elevated and mysterious effect. The religious character imparted may be expressed if we say that in Giotto the world is *transfigured*, and that the limpid, sparkling color-glow is the main agent in the transfiguration. In Rembrandt, though the actual color is very different, we find the same mystical effect, the same sense of reality without any approach to photographic representation, and here too the effect is due to the same extreme sensitiveness to color-values and ability to render them by subtle yet unmistakable means. Indeed, the mysticism which art at its best conveys seems to attach itself in a peculiar degree to the masterful handling of color, and points to the fact that color is *the* source, *par excellence*, of the highest "quality" in painting.

Another form of color-effect is that in Piero della Francesca. In him we have neither the solid structural use of color, nor the juiciness which is so often a sign of great ability in color-handling. His color is unmistakably dry. His total effect, of an all-embracing coolness, requires exactly the colors which he uses. The basis of this effect is blue; but it is a blue so infinitely diversified by light that it becomes a whole series of blues with only the most subtle distinctions between them. They are so juxtaposed and blended with other harmonious colors, cool greens, grays, reds, as to provide a complete set of new and distinctive color-forms. This dominant note of coolness is Piero's characteristic form, and is perfectly blended with the drawing, composition, expression, etc., to create a distinctive note of the highest esthetic excellence.

Fra Angelico used a pleasing bright blue but with less sense of harmony with other colors. Instead of the pervasive charm of Piero or the brilliance and power of Giotto, we have a staccato effect as one color follows another across the canvas, and this, though it constitutes a color-form of a kind, is not esthetically very moving. The color-relations are too reminiscent of those of other painters, and this deficiency is made more serious by the fact that they are usually superficial.

The foregoing illustrations embody effects perceptible when we isolate color from all other plastic elements and consider it as a thing in itself. But there are types of definite color-designs other than the glows or suffusions of which we have been speaking. The use of color to make a design is well illustrated in Soutine, a contemporary painter. Soutine's characteristic form is that of intense movement, of passion, and his choice and combination of colors is peculiarly adjusted to this effect. His hot, juicy, vivid, and varied color is the antithesis of Piero's, yet both men achieve color-design of a high order. In Tintoretto's "Paradise" (387) and in Renoir's "Bathing Group" (239), the rhythmic flow of color is an essential part of the general effect of fluid, graceful, swirling movement, and forms a rich color-design which plays its own part.

A somewhat similar effect is to be found in Poussin, whose color is rather dry, and though it cannot be called superficial, is not deeply structural in its function. But its flow and rhythm extend to every part of the canvas and make up a design well in harmony with Poussin's general form of delicacy and "choiceness." The color-design reënforces his linear and compositional rhythms, and appears as a distinguishable but perfectly merged element in his plastic form.

Leonardo rarely makes color function successfully in the design; in "Mona Lisa" (343) he approaches the goal, but in his "Bacchus" (341) the color adds but little to the design. Indeed, one of the chief reasons for denying to Leonardo a place among the greatest artists is his inability to merge light with color, as they are merged whenever either appears at its best, as in Giotto, Giorgione, Titian, Tintoretto, Dürer, van Eyck, Rembrandt, Cézanne, and Renoir.

In Perugino, although the color is not deeply felt or organically used and lacks juiciness and richness, it is occasionally, as in his "Combat of Love and Chastity" (358), in keeping with the design, which is, on the whole, light and delicate, tasteful rather than moving. In Raphael, there is almost no real color-sense. If we abstract the other elements and look for a color-design, we usually find nothing of great esthetic significance. Everything else, light, line, placing of masses, modeling, pattern, is practically complete without color. Usually his color is taken from other

painters and used with little or no individuality though occasionally, as in "Virgin with Blue Diadem" (371) and "Woman with
Veil" (80), it does contribute to the ensemble effect. In his famous
"Madonna: *la Belle Jardinière*" (369), one must be able to ignore
the color to enjoy the fine linear effects and feeling for space. The
color is garish and drab, in spite of the bright red of the dress.
The good modeling with light loses its force because of the
absence of color, which is called for to make the figure live. The
effect is doughy and pasty, as of a statue in soft plaster. Raphael's
inferiority as a colorist appears again in the contrast between his
"Count Baldassare Castiglione" (367), in which there is lack of
harmony in color relations, and Titian's "Man with Glove"
(394). In both pictures the color is present mainly as tone, but in
the Raphael it is superficial, dry, monotonous, and it has little or
no value as a design; in the Titian, subtle but rich color-chords are
present and enhance the ensemble.

In "Ascent to Calvary" (351), by Simone Martini, the bright
colors make a pattern lending vivacity to a picture which is essentially illustration, rather than a complete plastic form. Their
brightness does not make them really moving; nevertheless their
ensemble effect fits in well with the general form of the picture.
In Mantegna, the lack of quality in color-relations and their
failure to form a unity are sometimes positive drawbacks. That
this is not due to the specific colors used is apparent from the fact
that the dark greens which appear in the Louvre pictures by him
(349; 350) are used by many other painters, and with no effect of
dulness or muddiness. In "Agony in the Garden" (143), he appears
to better advantage, for there color does function successfully in
unifying the design and enriching plastic form.

In the use of color, academicism is very common. Raphael is an
instance of this at a comparatively high level of skill; in his imitators, Guido Reni and Giulio Romano, the imitation of Raphael
is doubly academic and is not merely indifferent but offensive.
The Venetian glow becomes an academic device in the lesser
painters of the school, Palma Vecchio and Sebastiano del Piombo:
an overaccentuation, a melodrama, with imitative character
testified to by overemphasis, in practically every detail. In the
Barbizon painter, Rousseau, Claude's color is academicized, with
resulting artificiality and feebleness; the same is true of van Dyck,
in relation to Rubens. The Poussin tradition becomes academic,
cheap, and tawdry in Le Sueur, whose color is hopelessly gaudy and

trivial. His plagiarism is obvious and is unredeemed by any plastic force or reality.

The foregoing discussion, brief and incomplete as it is, shows how superficial is the view of nearly all the critics that color is a relatively unimportant element in painting. This view is definitely stated by Roger Fry; it is stated and then retracted by Berenson, but the judgments on pictures to which he gives expression in his books on the Italian painters, show how little he really appreciates the rôle played by color in plastic art. In esthetic criticism of lower order, such as Mather's, there is no evidence of any intelligent conception of the function of color in painting. The importance of Giotto as a colorist, for example, is entirely overlooked, and so is the function of color throughout the whole Florentine school, which is said to be preoccupied with "tactile values," that is modeling—really a very secondary matter. Again, in the Venetians, though the rôle of color is emphasized, its significance is never explained even in general principles, and the organic and structural functions of color are totally ignored. These critics fail to see that by far the most important aspect of color is not its sensuous quality but the part which its relations play in organizing a picture. That color-relations are all-important in plastic form, that composition at its best is effected by means of color, is one of the most weighty facts in esthetics, and it is one to which the great majority of writers on plastic art seem to be totally oblivious.

CHAPTER IV

DRAWING

DRAWING is often understood as a function of the line which defines contour and marks off adjacent objects from one another. The only conception of drawing, however, which does justice to the plastic function here in question is that which includes in its meaning the whole process of *drawing out* whatever aspects are significant for the painter's design. We have already seen that all art is selective, concerned only with certain phases of its subject-matter, and that even these phases are never literally reproduced. They are emphasized or even distorted in various degree, and set in a new context by which their esthetic significance is enhanced. This selection and interpretation is the essence of the expressive act; in it all the artist's powers are called into play and put on trial; it is what really constitutes drawing. In terms of plastic art, drawing is a fusion of all the plastic means, an interrelation of line with light, color, and space, the esthetic value of which is proportionate to the degree of union achieved. In drawing of the very first order, line is not a sharp demarcation between adjacent areas of color, but is color itself, either as an actual narrow colored band, as often in Cézanne and Matisse, or as an area into which the color overflows from the objects on either side. The latter form of drawing, which originated with the Venetians, attained in Renoir its supreme degree of perfection. Even when there is no overflow of color, as in such early painters as Giotto, van Eyck, and Dürer, clean-cut line may be so well harmonized with the other plastic means that perfect integration is achieved. Unreality appears only when line stands in isolation, when there is no organic relation between contours and what they enclose.

The relation of line to drawing is, however, very close. We speak of a summary or digest of essential features in anything as an "outline"; to portray is to "delineate"; and the features which make any one what he is are his "lineaments." A pen-and-ink drawing may be an excellent illustration, in the esthetically expressive as well as the illustrative sense. Hence the use of line is the natural point of departure for a discussion of drawing, provided the fact is kept in mind that line is *plastically* significant only in so far as it is related to the other elements in the form as a whole.

Painting developed out of mosaics. In them, the definition of contour was of necessity absolutely distinct and this distinctness remained for a long time characteristic of painting. In Cimabue, the line of demarcation between one object and another is very clear-cut, so that the surface of the canvas is divided into what might be called color-tight compartments, and the line between them seems to belong to neither compartment. Line so used produces a rigid fixity in the movement and expression of all the figures so that the impression of actual movement is lacking. Also, there is comparatively little integration of the lines of separate objects in a linear design in the picture as a whole. After Cimabue, line became more integrated with light, with color, and with composition, so that these elements are recognizable only upon abstraction and analysis. At the start, the pictures seem like line-drawings to which color, light, etc., were applied after the design was essentially complete; subsequently, the drawing was conceived in terms of all the plastic elements, with the result of a great increase in unity, reality, and moving force. In Giotto, line is no longer literal or isolated but a simple, terse, and forceful factor the significance of which can be fully grasped only with the aid of the imagination. The line is still clear-cut, but the color and light on each side are merged with it to give an ensemble effect of more convincing reality than is possible from line alone; in other words, the line gets its force from the relations it assumes, and thus becomes plastic. In the drawing of individual objects, and of the picture as a whole, the sequence of line and mass is fluid, rhythmic, and harmonized to make up the total design.

In Masaccio, we have the first important step toward naturalistic effects in drawing, in the employment of blurred outline. In Andrea del Castagno, the sharpness of line is diminished through the use of a swirl, and this necessitates further simplification and abandonment of mere literalism, with the result that the expressiveness of the line, and its use in abstract design, is further heightened. In Fra Filippo Lippi, line is less expressive and powerful than in Masaccio and Andrea del Castagno, but there is an increase of grace and decorative quality, which adds a fresh enrichment to design. In Uccello, the line is stiffer, less fluid, and more varied in direction; by reason of these qualities it has a quite peculiar effect in achieving individual patterns. Line is still very sharp in both these men, and has little or no effect of movement, even when the subject-matter is ostensibly dynamic.

In Piero della Francesca, line is more reënforced by color, and the general design is much more elaborate, varied, and powerful esthetically. He gets many of the effects of drawing by means of color, without abandoning the clearly separate character of the two elements. The absence of movement or drama in his drawing is required by his generally quiet and detached style.

In Botticelli line gives the effect of active movement, but it is so isolated, elaborated, and overworked that plastic unity is largely lost. The line forms an intricate series of arabesques, so feebly supported by the other plastic means that the drawing is not really an element in structural form, but is rather decoration. The result is an effect of facile virtuosity which is superficially attractive but has little moving force. The line forms a pattern but is rarely an integral part of the design, and is used without consideration of the appropriateness to subject-matter: in his religious pictures, for example, it produces a tendency to an incongruous swirl.

Leonardo's sharp line also stands out clearly, but, since it is merged with the modeling and plays a more integral part in the design, it is much less of an overaccentuation than Botticelli's. In "Mona Lisa" (343), for example, the lines in the sleeves and in the background really give an impression of solidity and depth, as compared with the merely decorative quality of the more elaborate linear pattern in Botticelli's "Birth of Venus" (91). Leonardo's line was taken over by Raphael and made more incisive, more dramatic, more rhythmically varied, and on the whole a more interesting feature of the design. In both men, it often tended toward literal expression and oversweetness, and this is not entirely counterbalanced in Leonardo by the three-dimensionality of his masses, or in Raphael by the impression of vigorous movement. Raphael's line is prodigal rather than terse, and consequently lacks the high degree of expressive power which comes with economy of means. His line is very sharp, is quite independent of color, and the light, by which it is complemented, heightens the sense of overdramatization.

In Michelangelo, line and color are distinct but are so well related that the drawing has a quality of great strength. His drawing was a modification of that of Signorelli and Cosimo Tura, but he merged it in a special way in the form as a whole, and used it to give more melodramatic expression to subject-matter.

The drawing of the Venetians was an advance over that of their predecessors in that they made a systematic use of color and of blurred contour. Because of their structural color and atmospheric glow, the definition of areas by sharp lines was neither necessary nor desirable for the general design. The earlier Venetians, Bellini and Carpaccio, retained the use of sharp line and merged it well with color and light, though not sufficiently to attain the convincing reality found in Giorgione and Titian. In Giorgione the contours are comparatively little blurred but they do not stand out and cause the attention to be centered on themselves. Titian often uses a broad line of contour which is sometimes relatively isolated from the form and, while it adds to decoration, very frequently weakens expression. Sometimes Titian's line is so loose that the objects seem to melt into surrounding space, and this represents the expressive function of drawing achieved with the minimum of means. Here line, color, and light are fully synthesized, and drawing reaches the highest estate as yet attained.

In Tintoretto, linear contour is often accentuated as a narrow band of color, but the line, light, and color are all completely merged in the form of a swirl which is the most effective means of representing powerful movement and drama, and may also be adapted to other purposes. When the swirl is toned down and used to depict the hard, clear quality of textures, the organic use of the color prevents the clear demarcations from seeming like isolated lines, and the effect is one of greater solidity and reality. In Paolo Veronese, the line is also sometimes accentuated as a band of color as in Titian and Tintoretto, but on the whole contour is sharper than in the other important Venetians. In his "Burning of Sodom" (400), line pervades the whole picture, flows from object to object, and gives the effect of motion in a particular direction by its general disposition through the canvas. This pervasively unifying line is characteristic of all the best Venetian painters.

Poussin's line is more Florentine than Venetian. It is extremely graceful, elegant, delicate, charming, but it has not the power of that of the best of the Venetians and is less firmly supported by structural color. It is less incisive than Raphael's or Leonardo's; but both of these modifications are well adapted to Poussin's designs, and they function very effectively in both decorative and expressive rôles.

[93]

In Rubens, contour is sharper than in Titian but less sharp than in Raphael. His swirl necessarily gives the effect of broken line, so that within the confines of a surface there is less of the broad, unbroken area of color which throws hard contours into sharp relief. His line is repeated rhythmically over and over, and contributes strongly to the effect of animation and movement, but is less convincing and powerful than Tintoretto's, in which color is more deeply fused with all the other plastic elements.

Rembrandt's drawing is accomplished with extreme subtlety and economy of means. The merging of light, line, and color is so perfect that minute analysis is required to differentiate between them; in addition, the effects are more restrained and so more powerful esthetically, than those of Rubens. There is perfect differentiation of masses, and yet the actual marks on the canvas by which this is done are scarcely perceptible. His subtle line is infinitely more expressive than Botticelli's or Raphael's in conveying feeling and characteristic movement or gesture with the utmost sensitiveness. There is a similar subtlety in Velásquez but of a lesser degree. El Greco's line is so distorted and so varied in direction, length, and proportions as to give an impression of emotional frenzy carried to the highest intensity. But the effect is not melodramatic—the activity of the line is perfectly matched by similar activity in the light, color, and all other plastic factors.

Upon close inspection, Claude's drawing of individual units seems inferior to that of the greatest painters in that his line lacks terseness, individuality, expressiveness. But if we examine the drawing of the picture as a whole, we find linear effects formed by the sequence of masses instead of by the definition of one mass against another, and that larger line is fluid, varied, rhythmic, and distinctive. Claude's design required the rendering of the lineaments of a total scene, which he was able to do better by slighting the drawing of the details of individual objects. In Boucher the line is quite hard and partakes of Botticelli's qualities of grace and sensuous charm, with much decorative and little real expressive power. Its sharpness imparts a delicate cameo-quality. Watteau and Fragonard show softer contours, with a general tendency to diffuseness; the imperfect fusion of line with color results in rather weak drawing. In Chardin the contour is sharper, but the drawing is so sensitive, expressive, and tempered with light and color, that it seems subdued and makes a strong but unobtrusive element in the plastic form.

[94]

David's drawing, skilful but hard and cold, is fundamentally academic; Ingres's is far more varied, rhythmic, and sensitive, and is more original. The classic feeling of coldness is present and the line is very tight; but there is a sense in which it is more effective than in any other painter. Although Ingres's pictures may almost be said to be made out of line, the line does much more than define the meeting-place of two distinct objects. It renders the basic feeling of the surfaces depicted without much aid from color and light, so that the line is the groundwork of the painting. In a measure, it does for Ingres what chiaroscuro does for Rembrandt, that is, gives an equivalent for the other plastic means. Of course, line cannot give the full equivalent; but it does function organically, and so is far less of an overaccentuation than it is in Botticelli, in whom it is little more than a pattern. Ingres's use of line is really art and not mere virtuosity, but it is not the greatest art, partly because this particular means is inadequate to bear the full weight of plastic form, partly because Ingres lacked the freshness and depth of insight of the really great masters: he did not have a great deal to say.

Daumier was another master of drawing, though of quite a different sort. His line is often broad at the contour, as in Titian and Tintoretto, but is more broken in continuity. It is highly vigorous, concentrated, expressive, and it coöperates with light and modeling to give an effect of great weight and solidity combined with activity. In some paintings his drawing is comparable in power and expressiveness with that of Rembrandt, and is executed by a coalition of line, light, and color.

Delacroix's drawing is relatively negligible from the standpoint of original plastic expressiveness. In line, light, and color it derives from Rubens, and is too often perverted to noisy purposes that are obviously narrative and psychological. This psychological motif was rendered with much more effect by Degas, who added the flexibility, variety, and skill of Ingres, and made a form in which the psychological expressiveness of line is given an adequate plastic embodiment. In Degas' paintings, as distinguished from his work in pastel, there is a tendency to rely too much on line without sufficient support from the other plastic means, so that in spite of the genuineness of his effects his paintings do not reach the highest level of achievement.

Courbet's line is comparatively hard, but his total drawing is firm and has distinction and power in conveying his particular realistic effects. In Manet, line is merged well with the other plastic elements and his drawing successfully avoids imitation and achieves a very distinctive design. In Claude Monet, line is often almost dissolved in an excess of light and color, and the result is a loss of vigor, expressiveness, and strength of design. There is not the firm structure beneath the veil of color and light that there is in Renoir and Cézanne.

In these later men, the contributions of all previous painters are in large measure summed up and revised to make new forms. In Renoir, drawing is derived fundamentally from the Venetians, but it is extended in range of expressiveness by an infinitely better fusion of line and light with color, and by his own modification of the brushwork of the impressionists. Color flows over contour more freely in Renoir than in any previous painter; line, as an independent entity, practically disappears in his latest work, without in the least compromising the masses outlined against one another. Objects are thus enriched by the wealth of color-relations which enter into them, and at the same time the broader, more fluid drawing eliminates non-essentials and reveals inherent quality as the Venetian drawing, even at its best, never does. In Cézanne, the tradition of Michelangelo, Tintoretto, and El Greco, who employed distortions to get strength, is passed through the channels of impressionism, and emerges with a new note of significance and reality, heightened by planes intersecting in perspective. In a still later painter, Glackens, we have a general style similar to Renoir's, modified by the psychological expressiveness of Daumier and Degas, but even more simplified and especially illustrative of posture, gesture, and movement.

Drawing, in brief, is good art when it is free from confusing elements, like isolated literal contour or overdecorative quality; when it is so condensed, so simplified that it carries in itself sufficient revelation of objective fact to enable us to grasp the essence, significance, conviction of objective reality in the things portrayed. In short, drawing consists not in the literal reproduction of linear contours or shapes; it is a mark of the artist's ability to resolve the lines of demarcation into separate parts, select certain parts for emphasis, and recombine them into a new ensemble that is a form in itself, not merely a duplication of the shape of an object. Line gets power by what it does to what is contained between the lines; that is, as with all other forms, its essential characteristic resides in the relations it assumes and creates. A line in isolation is rarely to

Rubens (151) Analysis, page 433

This painting and the ones on the three following pages show how similar subject-matter has been treated in the interest of design by old and modern painters.

Giorgione (330)

Analysis, page 422

Prendergast (236)

Matisse (220)

be considered in a painting; it gets form from its relation to other lines; its value in the hierarchy of art is determined by its significant use in connection with the other elements—color, light, space, mass, shadow—which make up drawing.

A man's drawing is as distinctive of himself, of his personality —his candor, reality, freedom from affectation—as is his face, his writing, or his psychological make-up as revealed by analysis.

CHAPTER V

COMPOSITION

As DRAWING constitutes the way in which significant aspects of things are selected, drawn out, and molded in accordance with the painter's design, so composition is the whole process of ordering, organizing, and unifying the plastic elements in the form of a picture. Conventionally, the term "composition" has been applied to the distribution of masses, but this is an unjustifiable limitation of its meaning. The compositional units of a picture may, but need not, be masses; they may also be areas of color, islands of light, linear arabesques, or any means whatever by which balance and unity are secured. The Venetian glow, Rembrandt's chiaroscuro, Renoir's color-suffusion, and Matisse's pattern of color-compartments, all serve to unite every part of a picture in a rhythmic, organic unity. In modern painting especially, in which the use of relatively abstract design is very extensive, all the parts of the picture are more nearly on an equal footing compositionally than in the primitive and Renaissance pictures, the organization of which is usually focused about individual volumes or groups of volumes. In tracing the development of composition, therefore, we shall begin with the distribution of masses, which may most conveniently be designated "mass-composition," and observe the way in which, as time goes on, composition becomes more fluid and more organically related to the use of color. Composition by means of color represents the supreme form of plastic integration.

There are a number of general types of mass-composition which are constantly encountered and which require examination. The simplest form is that of a central mass with balancing figures to right and left by which bilateral symmetry is attained; this form is usually that of a pyramid, and achieves the sense of stability and rhythm in an obvious form. It is illustrated in most of Raphael's Madonnas, but with him it is so stereotyped as to indicate a poverty of imagination. However, this form, although in itself trite, may be combined with other qualities, color, light, line, of such personal and distinctive character, as in the Castelfranco Giorgione (50), that it is redeemed from banality. Greater personal expressiveness is achieved in the distribution of masses when instead of a complete bilateral symmetry we have volumes different in kind but similar in function, which surprise and yet fulfil the normal desire for balance. In Titian's "Disciples at Emmaus" (391), the number of figures on the left of the central figure is greater than on the right, but there is in addition on the right a window opening out on a landscape, which adds to the interest of the design; thus unity is not disturbed and variety is increased.

In the foregoing, it is their relation to a central mass that ties together the separate masses. The central figure is usually in these cases the one of greatest interest, so that there is an obvious parallel between plastic and narrative or human values of the several units. But the object that ties up the parts of a picture may be in itself trivial from the illustrative point of view as, for example, the Cupid in Titian's "Jupiter and Antiope" (393), or the tree in Cosimo Rosselli's "Pharaoh's Destruction in the Red Sea" (423). A radically different type of composition is achieved when the central mass is not the main focus of interest as in Giorgione's "Concert in the Open Air" (330), or is discarded, as in some of the Assisi Giottos. In these pictures the elements are kept from falling apart by subtle relationships, by which the artist's feeling for grouping is expressed. This "feeling for grouping" means a feeling for harmonious relationships, and in plastic art it may vary independently of the other factors: in Raphael, for example, it is much better than his color.

In a good painting all the factors are integrated, and disposition of masses is one of these factors. Paintings of the highest value are composed with color, so that the two factors, composition and color, are blended. In Piero della Francesca and Giotto, firm integration makes their pictures highly personal and individual. In Giorgione's "Concert in the Open Air," the color-rhythms bind the picture together, along with the sequence of line and mass. In Titian's "Entombment" (392), the color, rich, varied, and deep, permeates the entire canvas and ties the units together. The color in the cloaks of the bending figures, at the right and left of the central group, functions as a frame to enclose and unify it. In Tintoretto's "Paradise" (387), the rhythmic succession of color unites with the rhythm of line to give the effect of swirling movement which is the keynote of the picture's design. Here, as always, the greater the fusion of means the more living, convincing, real, individual, is the effect, and the farther removed from mechanism or academicism.

Another adjunct to composition is the distribution of light. Here, as with color, the light represented in various parts of the canvas often forms a pattern in itself. A figure or object functions quite differently according to its place in the pattern of light, which is a distinguishable but inseparable part of the plastic form. The pattern of light in Titian's "Man with Glove" (394) is vital to the composition. In other words, the manner in which a picture is composed is an essential part of the total design, and must be judged as subsidiary to it; and this is the reason for the futility of all academic rules for judging composition in isolation.

The lines which define the contours of objects have an important function in composition. In Courbet's "Painter's Studio" (308) and in Poussin's "Blindmen of Jericho" (361), the figures are held together not only by their placing with reference to a central point, but by linear effects carried over from one mass to another. The whole composition flows, it is never static. When abstracted the line is seen to form a pattern in itself which is made up of a series of subsidiary patterns all merged with one another. This interweaving of line in combination with a central figure is very important in all closely-knit compositions. In Leonardo's "Virgin, St. Anne, and the Infant Jesus" (346), or Raphael's "Holy Family, of François I" (368), the figures, both as wholes and with reference to their parts, are focal points in a network of lines in three dimensions. The way in which linear patterns contrast with each other, reënforce each other, may be infinitely varied according to the feeling of the painter for space-effects. In Uccello's "Rout of San Romano" (159), linear effects constitute the chief compositional factor in the plastic form, which is clearly separable from and independent of the subject-matter. This again illustrates the necessity of judging all plastic elements in relation to design. Judged by academic standards, the Uccello would be uncomposed, but with the design in mind the relation of the parts to one another at once becomes apparent. In its abstractness, Uccello's form resembles that of the cubists, and cannot be judged by any criterion of representative accuracy.

Individual figures or masses do not always operate singly as compositional units: they may be perceived as part of a whole group which functions as a unit, as in powerful compositions on a large scale. In that case there is a subsidiary composition within the group, just as in a symphony we find several movements each one a composition in itself. In Francesco di Giorgio's "Rape of Europa" (321), for example, the entire group of trees and foliage plays the part of a single mass, within which the individual trees, branches, and leaves make up a subordinate composition. Similarly in Rembrandt's "Unmerciful Servant" (168), the three figures at the right are a single mass balancing the single figure at the left; within that mass the individual elements are clearly distinguished and make up an interesting composition in themselves. This subordinate composition will in a great painting fit into and enhance the general design; in an inferior painting it may be good in itself, but it may fail to integrate with the total design. In Botticelli's "Incidents in the Life of Moses" (418), there are two separate pictures which do not unify into a single composition; in Cosimo Rosselli's "Pharaoh's Destruction in the Red Sea" (423), a similar double theme does unify. In Titian's "Assumption" (438), this integration of different groups is present in a very high degree, the rhythms of line and mass being reënforced by light, color, and space, all binding the picture together in a harmonious unity, with human values and plastic values perfectly merged. A similar compositional problem in Raphael's "Transfiguration" (427) is treated by superficial and specious means.

Transition to space-composition may be made if we consider relation of figures and masses to background. In work of the greatest esthetic power many features of composition depend upon representation of the third dimension. Even in painting which tends to be flat, such as Matisse's or Manet's, not everything depicted is shown as on the same plane, and though spatial depth is not emphasized, it is by no means eliminated. The relation of a single head, as in a portrait, to what is back of it, should be considered a part of the composition of the picture. This relation is partly determined by color, partly by compositional means in the narrower sense. The pattern of lines in a portrait may be carried into the background, or there may be superficially no relation, as in the Pisanello "Princess of the Este Family" (359). Here the background of foliage and flowers may seem plastically unrelated to the girl's head; really, however, the relation is an organic one established by duplication of rhythmic patterns. In Fra Filippo

Lippi's "Virgin Adoring the Child" (98), the relation between the central figures and the background is exceedingly important, though the objects in the background are felt like the pattern on a screen. On the other hand the background may be extremely simple, as in Rembrandt's "Hendrickje Stoffels" (373), or Titian's "Man with Glove" (394), in both of which, by means that are very subtle, the figure is distinguished, set out from what is back of it. The effect of infinite depth achieved in both these pictures is an extraordinary triumph of space-composition. In Rubens' "Baron Henri de Vicq" (380), though the placing of the head against the background is effective, the means employed, that is, sharply contrasting colors, are obvious and more facile, and the lesser economy of means reduces the esthetic value in comparison with the Titian and Rembrandt.

Space-composition is achieved largely through use of perspective and is at its best when color is the chief constructive factor in it. But skilful perspective is not the same thing as effective space-composition. The difference is that in effective space-composition not only is the illusion of depth rendered, but the intervals, the relations of distance, are intrinsically pleasing and represent personal feeling instead of literal imitation. The mere representation of distance has no closer relation to art than the work of the surveyor or civil engineer. Objects well composed in space are not huddled or crowded: each object is in its own space, each has elbow-room, no matter how small the space may be. The ordering of these relationships constitutes the space-composition of the picture as a whole and is an important source of esthetic pleasure.

In architecture and sculpture, where space is actually present, there is the same distinction between a vital, personal arrangement of spaces which gives the *feeling* of depth or extensity, and the inability really to conceive the object in three-dimensional terms. Primitive Negro art shows this power of conception in three dimensions, while in much of Greek sculpture it is comparatively lacking.

In composition in three dimensions, all the effects of two-dimensional composition are amplified. Thrust and counter-thrust, balance, rhythm, the effects of light and shadow, are heightened in variety and power. The sense of real space, harmoniously subdivided, appears in Claude, in Poussin, in Perugino, in Raphael, in all the great Venetians. In regard to space alone

Raphael is a really important artist. He and Perugino were doubt-less influenced to achieve it by the clear air and mountainous country of Central Italy, in which striking relations of masses in obvious deep space are almost forced upon the attention.

In practically all of Poussin's pictures we find not only a clear indication of distance everywhere, but great appeal in the intervals themselves. The masses are related backward and forward as well as on the surface of the canvas, and these relationships form an integral part of the general plastic design. This design in space is reënforced by color, both in its appealing sensuous quality and in the relations of the colors to each other, and by line and light and shadow; all these elements combine to give a distinctively clear, light, airy, and charming design. In Giorgione's "Concert in the Open Air" (330), the relation of all parts of the landscape to the blue and golden distance contributes greatly to the impression of mystery, romance, and glamour. Claude's effects are more romantic, more majestic, and they would be impossible but for the unlimited spaciousness of his pictures, which gives reality to the vast patterns of light. In addition, the ways in which the intervals are proportioned and related to one another are also immediately pleasing in themselves. A final example of space-composition is Giotto's: his perspective, from the academic standpoint, is very faulty, but he had the utmost genius for placing objects, in deep space, in relations which are varied, powerful, absolutely unstereo-typed, but always appropriate and in harmony with the general design.

Space-composition, like the other plastic functions, reaches its greatest height when color takes the most active part in it. Cé-zanne's dynamic organization of volumes in deep space is a partial illustration of this compositional rôle of color, since color is the material and organizing force in all his painting; but an even better example is to be found in Renoir's work, especially that done after 1900. Color extends over contours so freely that spatial intervals are felt primarily as color-relations, and in many of his paintings a suffusion of color floods every part of the picture, uniting each compositional element with all the others in an indissoluble entity.

Space-composition shares with the other plastic factors the pos-sibility of becoming academic, usually through overaccentuation. An example of this is found in Perugino's fresco, "Christ Giving the Keys to Peter" (422), in which the grouping of the figures and the linear patterns on the pavement cheapen the effect by their extreme obviousness. In Turner's "Dido Building Carthage" (158), there is the same overdramatization of space, but in this case the theft from Claude is so obvious that the picture is plagiaristic rather than academic.

BOOK III

THE TRADITIONS OF PAINTING

CHAPTER I

THE DAWN OF MODERN PAINTING

In order to show the general nature of the traditions which have played an important part in the development of painting, and how they are utilized and modified by individuals, it is necessary to consider briefly the historical aspects. Old traditions constantly emerge in even the most recent painting, as, for example, Tintoretto in Soutine, the Persian miniatures in Matisse. One can judge of the individuality and importance of a painter only by referring to the sources of his effects, and by observing how these effects are combined with those from other sources. If the artist is a real creator these effects pass through the crucible of his own personality and emerge as new forms. If they are seen to be destitute of organic relationships, the painter is a mere imitator or academician, or an eclectic such as Derain.

Painting, which evolved from mosaics, had reached the highly developed form seen in the Pompeian frescoes, painted prior to the first century (407). In these, line, light, modeling, and perspective are used to depict solid figures and deep distance in well-organized three-dimensional space-composition. Byzantine mosaics and panel paintings are substantially in a single plane, that is, flat, and really amount to little more than colored patterns with an illustrative appeal. Although many of these are positive creations of definite art-value, their subject-matter is usually stereotyped or unreal, with little or no sign of personal expression. Convention was the rule and individual expression the exception. The esthetic effects spring from color and line composed harmoniously into what is really decoration. The slight reliance upon light, modeling, and perspective, and the use of a rigid line resulted in figures stiff and not individualized, and in highly formal compositions with very simple rhythms.

The Ravenna mosaics, executed in the fifth century (411), depart from this flat decorative pattern by introduction of perspective, illumination, modeling, and their application to more naturalistic subject-matter, so that they are more expressive. Increasing expressiveness through command of a greater number of plastic means, and increased personal feeling in the painter, will be traced in the history of the traditions.

Cimabue (c.1240 – c.1301) is more representative of the Byzantine mosaic tradition than of the form attained in the Pompeian frescoes. His compositions are in the main flat although his figures are modeled in well-defined three-dimensional forms. In his "Virgin Enthroned" at Assisi (16), and "Virgin Enthroned" in the Uffizi (92), there is the same Byzantine composition—a central figure and exact bilateral symmetry achieved by an equal number of figures on each side, with linear patterns and shapes in each balancing those in the corresponding figure on the opposite side. The contours are very sharp, that is, the drawing is chiefly linear, and the color is obviously laid on, with neither the Venetian structural use nor the merging shown in Giotto. The color lacks brilliance but there is effective color-harmony, partly due to the above-noted bilateral symmetry. In general the figures are static, without animation, and the expression of the faces is uniformly doleful and almost bovine, without individual variation. There is slight indication of perspective and the planes are few and close together. The stereotyped expression, the sharp line, and the superficial color, with lack of realism in the figures and objects, give the whole a painted rather than a real effect. The composition is well balanced but it too remains inert. The design is largely one of color-compartments only slightly varied by the rather monotonous contrasts of light and dark. There is skill in the employment of the traditional formulas, and the religious character of the subject-matter, in keeping with the spirit of the time and free from sentimentality, yields an austere, effective form which must be judged, in view of the state of plastic art at the time, as of considerable esthetic importance. A dignified rhythm pervades both the figures and the component parts of the figures and objects. The Byzantine form is beginning to take on the qualities of life, but it is still quite stylistic and comparatively unreal and other-worldly.

Giotto (1266–1337), one of the most important painters of all time, whether he be judged by what he contributed technically or by the esthetic power of his creations, made the next step in the development, and it was an enormous one. The transition from

Cimabue is illustrated strikingly in the Uffizi, by Cimabue's "Virgin Enthroned" (92) and Giotto's "Madonna Enthroned" (95), in which the composition is essentially the same.

In the Giotto, the Byzantine tradition is shown in the formalized pattern and the bilateral symmetry of composition. Its esthetic value is increased by the intensification, amplification, and enrichment of color, which is of much finer sensuous quality and less obviously laid on. The color-harmony is pervasive and is an important agent in unifying the picture. The light not only heightens color, but forms with shadows a subsidiary pattern, as in the deepening of the folds of the gowns. The sensitiveness, expressiveness, and rhythmic quality of Giotto's line is greater, the tactile values are increased, and in spite of the static character of the picture it is much more convincingly real than the Cimabue. The decorative quality and rhythms are increased by the duplication of naturalistic textural effects, which also make possible special notes of color-harmony. There is also a new contribution in the expression of the faces, in which the set dolefulness of Cimabue is replaced by a tendency toward beatification. The use of perspective, though still relatively slight, is increasing; there is more space as such, though in the space-composition the gold halos remain as an adventitious aid. Although the spirit of the times is still in evidence, there is a decided step away from the stylistic Byzantine form, and toward naturalistic painting.

Giotto's special qualities are best shown in the frescoes at Assisi (18) and at Padua (284), and these are of such epic character that they are analyzed with considerable detail in the Appendix. The style in the set at Assisi is quite different from that in the series at Padua, but the essential Giotto form is present in both.

It will suffice here to state only those characteristics which have a bearing upon the relation between plastic means and the human values resulting from their effective use in rendering subject-matter. Giotto is always direct and simple both in what he does with the plastic means and in the story he tells—they dovetail, go hand in hand, balance. We feel the rightness of everything. His originality is astounding, it seems never to be exhausted. This is seen at Assisi in the unusual methods of composition and at Padua in the variety of effects attained by means in themselves essentially unvaried. The result is an overpowering wealth of relationships of forms. He abstracts the essence of real things and presents them by legitimate plastic means—a fine example of the rendering of human values in painting without regard for details of subject-matter. In Giotto, we may ignore the story, yet when we look for the story it is there, and told simply and directly. It is dramatic in the best sense of the word, that is, it is vivid, moving. He renders deep universal human values by means of line, mass, planes, color of high quality, and marvelous use of light as illumination and pattern. As a draughtsman he had few equals: his drawing is tersely expressive of an infinite variety of unmistakable meanings. Not, as in Botticelli, so decorative that we see chiefly the line; nor as in Ingres, emphasizing pattern or arabesque; nor psychologically saturated as in Degas—Giotto's line is *all* these and all in solution. His color is as moving esthetically as it is in the Venetians and it moves us by the way it works in and around line, mass, space, to weave them into things distinct in themselves —a series of rhythmic designs that fuse into a plastic form of overwhelming esthetic power. What Giotto means to us depends upon what we bring to his paintings in background and temperament. The stories he depicts are irrelevant. By sheer mastery of plastic means, he compels us to enter that union with the world which is the basis of religion, whether pagan or Christian.

Those critics who laud the Padua frescoes at the expense of those at Assisi, mistake the technical shadow for the esthetic substance. The Assisi frescoes represent a gifted, personal, and daring use of means of his own invention. In those at Padua his composition is more conventional, and his highly individual effects, such as the pervasive color-light atmosphere, and the daring use of architectural units as main masses, are less in evidence. It is true that the Padua works contain a greater number of units made by the relations between the objects employed, but this fact is comparatively irrelevant when compared with the succession of massive esthetic onslaughts by the Assisi frescoes: the observer is at first overwhelmed and then astounded and delighted. The Padua frescoes charm by suavity of effects, rich, varied, and gentle, but they lack the monumental power of those at Assisi.

CHAPTER II

THE FLORENTINE TRADITION

GIOTTO marks the beginning of the Florentine tradition. Its debt to him is enormous, for practically all the Renaissance methods find their origin in his work. His use of perspective opened up a world of values possible only by the ingenious utilization of deep space; his modeling added lifelike three-dimensional qualities to figures and endowed them with conviction; he replaced the overdecorative static Byzantine linear pattern of light in folds of draperies by a few simple folds preponderantly vertical, modeled by color and light related to line, and grouped on each side of a central broadly rounded one-piece area; his atmosphere and color gave an increased naturalistic quality to objects and situations which hitherto had been at the best merely symbolic. These factors—perspective, space-composition, modeling, atmosphere, and a new use of color—were each made the subject of special experimentation by later artists and yielded the brilliant results which we find in the high Renaissance. These artists, each of whom added something definitely constructive toward the ultimate results, were Masaccio, Leonardo, Uccello, Andrea del Castagno, Michelangelo, and Piero della Francesca. Although the last-named was not a Florentine, he, like other great men from all parts of Italy, had absorbed the developments that came from Florence and made them a part of a tradition which became universal. We can best appreciate the fundamental greatness of that tradition if we note briefly the individual contributions of the various important Florentines, and the important heritage which they bequeathed to modern and contemporary painting.

Masaccio (1401–1428) led the way toward the naturalism of later painters: his figures look more like actual people, less otherworldly than Giotto's. His line is less clean-cut than Giotto's, so that contours are blurred rather than sharp, and his drawing gives the feeling of natural movement. It is realistic in the best sense, that is, imaginatively realistic, unburdened by literal representa-

[115]

tion, and is the origin of that of later great draughtsmen, such as Rembrandt, Goya, Daumier, Glackens, Pascin. It expresses the essence of drama tersely, in good plastic terms, and with no alloy of speciousness. That is true of Giotto also, but the means employed are different; in Masaccio the effects tend more toward the naturalism which increases as we recede from medieval painting. Linear perspective is used with an emphasis that tends toward the literal representation of distance; it is more literal than in Giotto, but Masaccio combined it with color in such a way that there is an effect not only of aërial perspective but of an atmospheric haze pervading the whole painting. Thus, deep space, with its great possibilities of new effects and new values, assumes increased importance.

Masaccio's color-scheme departs from Giotto's in that the delicate pinks and blues are infused by deeper tones of red, brown, orange, green. The composite effect is that of great though subtle color-power: many tones of red, blue, tan, and green pervade the browns and deep slate hues and give to the rich, glowing, and powerful ensemble a vague and appealing peachblow tone. It is Masaccio's mastery of color which makes his space-composition so wonderfully subtle and effective and gives to his drawing its unique grace, charm, and emotional drama. His "Adam and Eve Expelled from Paradise" (83), for example, is drawn with exquisite fluid grace, mainly by accentuated patterns of light and dark pervaded through and through with rich, subtle color. It is doubtful if any painter ever rendered more convincingly the feeling of actual movement than is revealed in these two figures: their very stride is seen, felt, emotionally experienced.

Masaccio's suffusion of color makes his atmospheric veil more evident than the Venetian glow. It suggests Rembrandt, and though it is a union of color and light without definite chiaroscuro, there is in both Rembrandt and Masaccio a glamour, a mystery, and a feeling of austere dignity. Occasionally, as in the small figure at the left in "Saint Peter Healing the Sick" (85), Masaccio resorts to chiaroscuro as positive as that of Rembrandt and with results quite as satisfactory. It is possible that Rembrandt had noted Masaccio's methods and was influenced by them. The atmospheric veil perceptible in Masaccio is apparently the precursor of the colored atmosphere which is so often found in later painters, notably the Venetians, and which the impressionists made one of the principal factors in their method. Objects located in the

Byzantine Mosaic (412)

Masaccio (87)

Analysis, page 396

Uccello (159)

Showing sacrifice of naturalistic rendering in the interest of design.

Giotto (20)   Analysis, page 391

middle distance, and still more those in the background, are blurred in comparison with the relative clarity of those in the foreground. This rendering of the effects of distance again recalls the work of the impressionists, and again illustrates Masaccio's tendency toward naturalism.

His advance toward modern painting is shown by the greater use he made of colorful light both in modeling and in the formation of a definite pattern. The solidity of figures achieved by this modeling indicates a departure from Giotto, and his accentuation of light is greater; both of these are steps toward more naturalistic painting. In short, Masaccio represents a positive advance over Giotto in the use of all the plastic means—line, color, light, perspective, space—toward a new plastic form of individuality and power.

In painting up to the time of Uccello (1397–1475), subject-matter had played an important rôle, but, as we have seen, a painter's importance is to be judged by his ability to fuse subject-matter with the plastic means. It has been emphasized repeatedly that esthetic experience is purest when we disregard all associated ideas suggested by the subject-matter and confine our attention to the plastic form in which the story is embodied. Uccello proves the truth of that statement, for if we condemn him because of the quaint, the naïve, or the grotesque, represented in his subject-matter, we miss entirely the artistic significance of his work. His obviously accentuated perspective has misled critics into patronizing him as an inferior artist obsessed by perspective; the fact is that Uccello is one of the great creators of the early Renaissance. His unique plastic form is not a by-product of his preoccupation with perspective but a clearly felt purpose achieved by the intelligent and skilful use of all the plastic means, including perspective. His use of perspective is never such that he attempts to apply it to all the objects depicted. Instead, he deliberately selected certain objects and to only certain phases of them applied rigidly the laws of perspective. We see that same general principle used by Cézanne, Matisse, and Picasso in dealing not only with perspective, but with other plastic means, when literal representation of objects or situations is far from their intentions. An artist is great in proportion as he has the ability to select and modify phases or characteristics of actual things and so to rearrange them as to create a new form, a thing in itself, radically different from its original in nature. This was what Matisse meant when he said to a critic, who had remarked that he never saw a woman like the one Matisse had painted, "But it is not a woman—it is a painting." So with Uccello, his subject-matter is not like anything we have ever seen in the real world. In his "Rout of San Romano" (159), the horses have the appearance of rocking-horses cavorting with exaggerated movements, and all the figures have a rigidity quite non-human. The lack of realism is heightened by a tendency of the background to recede not naturally but suddenly toward the top of the picture, in a manner resembling that employed centuries later by Pissarro, Manet, Degas, Cézanne, Renoir, who increased the power of their design by abolishing the current, more or less literal, representation of distance. In short, Uccello used perspective deliberately to establish a new and more moving relation of things to each other; in other words, to achieve a design, a plastic form, of his own creation. His success in that respect entitles him to a very high place among painters even of the great era in which he lived. If we disregard the story in his battle-scenes in which nobody is fighting, and look at the lines of the stiff figures, spears, and staffs, and at the placing of the objects in deep space, we find an interplay between colored angular planes and rounded contours of unrealistic objects, which establishes a series of relationships of such rich esthetic reward that our attention is not distracted by the narrative. The exaggerated, unrealistic dramatic movement is merely a novel and highly successful means of forming a design the elements of which, line, color, space, and mass, function plastically. Uccello's form is primarily that of bizarreness, and like all esthetic forms it is to be judged as a thing in itself, purely by its effect esthetically. Critics who treat Uccello as simply an experimenter in perspective paving the way for later artists who used perspective more realistically, show an utter confusion of the history of technique with relevant plastic criticism.

Another Florentine whose importance has been inadequately recognized is **Andrea del Castagno** (c.1410–1457). His distinction is due not so much to skilful use of the plastic means of his predecessors, as to his ability to endow these means with a new note of power and strength in design. One of his chief technical devices is a swirling unit of well-integrated line, light, and color which later men, Rubens, El Greco, Fragonard, Renoir, Pascin, and others, employed as an element in their individual techniques. In the

Cenacolo di S. Appollonia at Florence which is reserved for his work, a whole series of frescoes proclaim his distinction and strength. There also is a fresco, "Saint Eustachius" (79), said to be by one of his unknown followers, which is very rich in the successful use of the plastic means in the style of the master. His "Pietà" (78) produces an impression of moving esthetic power akin to that of Michelangelo, but it is executed with much simpler means and without obvious muscular accentuations. It has reality, power, and charm, which spring from a wonderful series of relationships between masses and spaces; these are interlaced by the dignified, balanced, simplified use of line, light, and color. In contrast to this simplicity, "Last Supper" (77) gives the same effect of strength and power through the medium of an infinite series of forms of much greater complexity. It would be difficult to find, aside from El Greco's work, a painting composed of greater variety of intricate patterns formed by the harmonious relation of line, light, color, and space. There is a complex and moving pattern in each of the figures, in all parts of the bodies, hands, heads, etc., in the table and all its parts, in the wall, in the textiles, bench, and floor. The separate patterns of light, line, space, color, flow with rhythmic throbs and fuse into each other and into the total plastic design. Deep and rather dark colors pervade this astounding richness of forms and enhance the effect of abstract dignity, solemnity, austerity, and power.

Fra Filippo Lippi (c. 1406–1469) is not generally considered to be among the monumental figures of early Florentine painting, but he has a form which is uniquely his own, which, in certain respects, allies him to modern and contemporary painting. He has neither the rich imaginative power of Giotto, the strength of Andrea del Castagno, nor the expressiveness of Masaccio. When compared with the work of these or even lesser men, Lippi's conceptions are usually stereotyped and lacking in personal distinction. Yet his effects are at times charming, quite individual, and significant from the standpoint of modern design. His ability to place a figure or a group of figures against an elaborate background and obtain a particular effect, is almost unique among the early painters. The qualities of the foreground and of the background are at first sight radically disparate, yet the two are linked into an organic whole by means so subtle that only one experienced in observing modern painting can recognize the essential unity of the picture. The point is illustrated by his "Virgin Adoring the Child" (98). The good-sized figures of the Virgin and Child are painted in bright and delicate color, which strongly reënforces their fluid, highly expressive, rhythmic line. The background, in which distance is represented by elevation toward the top of the canvas, is filled with a very large number of extremely clean-cut objects, drawn in minute realistic detail, too large for their apparent distance from the plane of the picture, and with outlines unblurred by anything suggesting atmospheric haze. The innumerable planes in the background are packed close together, so that their effect as a whole is that of a screen, vividly contrasting with the figures in the foreground, which are surrounded by free open space. This contrast is heightened by the generally dull, somber color in the background, which has only occasional scattered notes of brightness. Superficially the two parts of the picture are incongruous and unrelated, but when they are considered plastically, without regard to naturalistic accuracy, the unifying relationship becomes apparent. Both are rhythms: the figures a set of rhythms of color, line, and light; the background a highly complex rhythmic organization of intertwining colored planes; and the two sets of rhythms, embracing all the plastic elements, move in perfect accord with each other. Additional links between all parts of the picture are forged by the painter's fine feeling for the relations between exotic, non-naturalistic color. In all these respects, Fra Filippo Lippi makes a highly distinctive advance upon his predecessors, and anticipates not only the impressionists but also, and even more closely, Rousseau, *le douanier*, Matisse and other contemporary painters.

In contrast to the foregoing Florentines, whose skilful use of plastic means entitles them to be classed as creators, the work of another Florentine, **Fra Angelico** (1387–1455), whom the public, as well as many critics, consider a great master, is really of very inferior plastic value. He was an eclectic who represented a regression from the men who lived up to high standards, from whom he took the plastic ideas which he never succeeded in merging into a powerful and distinctive form. Even at his best he leans heavily upon Giotto and creates little if anything of his own. His line is that of his master Lorenzo Monaco, from whom he borrowed also much of his pattern and considerable of his color. It is true that Fra Angelico's color often has a pleasing sensuous quality, but he rarely succeeded in making it function organically in a painting.

Color remained a series of staccato ejaculations, which often re-enforce linear representation and sometimes make pleasing patterns; but the latter remain things apart which serve no purpose in promoting or effecting plastic unity. In the rare instances in which his composition is satisfactory from the standpoint of ordered arrangement of masses, there is little or no evidence of originality. His use of perspective is either perfunctory or an over-accentuation of Uccello's, and the effect is unconvincing esthetically. The spacing is fairly good but the figures function compositionally only as elements in groups; individually they have little bearing upon the general design. His modeling by light and shadow, though skilful is specious rather than convincing, and there is little distinction in the pattern formed by light. His plastic shortcomings are made more evident by the nature of his subject-matter, the appeal of which is narrative or sentimental. Fra Angelico is a good example of how technical skill can be combined with lack of the ability to use it to produce a distinctive plastic form. His popularity is due to the illustration of themes of deep religious feeling, and not to his power to convey them in good plastic terms. His drama is literary, not plastic, and is, therefore, unreal. His abundance of detail is merely representative and inventorial, and is treated largely by means of line which approaches literal depiction of fear, humility, piety, abnegation, suffering. All this substitution of literary values for plastic equivalents is unconvincing; we feel it as affectation, sentimentality, unreality. The emotion portrayed is out of all proportion to the plastic content of the form, so that while skilful as illustration, it is superficial as art of the pretensions it assumes. In general, the most favorable verdict possible of the vast majority of his paintings is that they offer a pattern of harmonious colors which serves as a setting for a sentimental story told in terms that are literary rather than plastic.

Piero della Francesca (c.1416–1492), while of Umbrian birth, may be regarded as Florentine, because he develops largely from Giotto and is free from the eclecticism that characterizes the Umbrians in general.

Piero is of interest primarily for his effective designs, both in his pictures as wholes, and in their parts. His subject-matter has comparatively little of the intense religious elevation of Giotto, or of the dramatic force of Andrea del Castagno. His attitude toward religion is one of cool detachment, and the effect is one of composure and dignity. These results he obtains by the skilled use of plastic means, of which the most important and characteristic is color. The basis of his color-scheme is a cool blue, which pervades everything, and is so effectively, though subtly, varied with light and related to other colors, that its variety seems infinite. This blue is probably the single note that is uniquely, inimitably his own, and it produces powerful varied esthetic effects both by itself and by its relations to other elements of his design. The quality of the blue is tremendously moving; wherever he puts it, it animates the picture; it is not a mere sensuous note, but a positive form. He uses it frequently in association with a series of whites that have the quality of rich old ivory, to render surfaces of marvelous charm. In comparison with this blue, his other colors, such as red and brown, approach the conventional; but into objects whose color, for example, green or purple, has a general feeling-tone akin to that of blue, he infuses a unique vitality that functions actively in reënforcing other dynamic plastic relations. This blue is so infinitely varied by light, and particularly used in relation to space, that it is really many kinds of blue, yet upon analysis the general feeling-tone identifies it as basically the same blue, infinitely varied.

This achievement of an exceedingly rich color-effect by means of the greatest simplicity—the way in which a single color is made to function sometimes as a mass, sometimes as the element that gives space its distinctive character, and sometimes as the means of unifying compositional elements—shows Piero's rank as an artist. His blues accomplish something comparable with Rembrandt's achievement in chiaroscuro. The color is not juicy as with Rubens; not, as with Giotto, jewel-like, varied and yet blended into a suffusion so subtle as to escape any one but a connoisseur. But it is extraordinarily adapted to his design, and establishes a distinctive form, in which it functions through harmonies and contrasts, and also aids in modeling, composition, and movement. It is not of the airy eighteenth century French quality, but while it carries weight it is not heavy; it is just fine, convincing, quietly powerful.

His composition, like Giotto's, is on a large scale, and shows great power of unifying the design in spite of disregard of conventional rules. His masses are often distributed in unorthodox fashion, but are always effectively welded into a single composition. Like the greatest masters, he accomplishes this welding by the aid of all the plastic means through the medium of color. Often a spot of light functions as a mass, as in "Exaltation of the Cross" (12), in which it is combined with blue in a pattern of clouds. His space-composition is not so striking as that of Perugino and Raphael; but every plane is clear-cut and distinguished from every other plane, and no matter what the complexity of the work the number of planes is never increased to the point of confusion. Even in battle-scenes, while there is a complex, striking pattern, a clean-cut organization is maintained. As an esthetic effect, Piero's space-composition is in many ways better than either Perugino's or Raphael's because it does not stand out as accentuation, but is merged with the plastic means; it is more varied, and color adds quite a particular charm to the spatial intervals. Piero's command over light as an element of design is especially noticeable; he uses it both to make a pattern in itself and to aid in modeling. All the objects in his pictures swim in a lovely quiet light, enriched and varied with color. His lighting of figures is never obtrusive; even when the light-pattern is accentuated, it so effectively heightens the quality of color that the impression conveyed is not of overemphasis but of more powerful reality. He models with light and color so subtly that it is often difficult to see how the three-dimensional character is attained. The faces often seem to be cast in one piece in which light and shadow and color are scarcely distinguishable; but of their solid, three-dimensional character, there can be no doubt.

Piero's drawing is such that it gives the effect of rigidity to figures, which is not felt as a drawback but as a charm, and indeed a strong contributing factor to the general graceful naïveté. His ensembles are of great distinction; the keynote is coolness, detachment, power. Subject-matter is rendered in its essence by means properly plastic. One must be familiar with Piero's work to appreciate Cézanne, Renoir, Picasso, and Prendergast.

With Botticelli, Leonardo, Raphael, Mantegna, and Michelangelo, the influence of antique Greek and Roman sculpture becomes the dominant one in Renaissance painting. The flowing line of Greek sculpture was so much the vogue that nearly all the painters of the late Renaissance used it as the basis of their individual expression. It was Botticelli's chief source in achieving imposing decorations. Leonardo used it, accompanied by the rather cloying sweetness characteristic of late Greek sculpture, and went even further toward the sculptural effects of the ancient Greeks in his preoccupation with modeling. In Michelangelo the conception is almost more sculptural than pictorial.

Botticelli's (1444–1510) work may be classed mainly as decorative illustration, rarely as full plastic expression. His line is extremely rhythmic, but it lacks the reënforcement by the other plastic elements necessary in painting of real importance. His color, which is almost uniformly either dull or garish, offers only the superficial pleasingness of feeble color-combinations. It has neither structural value nor organic functional power, and his compositions are usually conventional. In his "Incidents in the Life of Moses" (418), the composition falls apart; in his "Birth of Venus" (91), the composition aims at simplicity but achieves incongruity by overdecoration of the few component structural elements. By the skilled use of light, of space, and graceful fluid line, he sometimes attains to considerable esthetic value, but it is much more a pattern than a synthesis made up of varied plastic units. As an artist he is mediocre because his means are limited. He was a master of line, but he had no fine discrimination in using it; for example, in his big religious pictures, his swirling line gives a feeling of virtuosity instead of the richer values accessible through a command over all the plastic means. His line builds a series of arabesques of much charm in their rhythmic movements; but that is mere decoration, an accentuation of a detail which stands out in isolation instead of being merged with the other plastic elements into a unified design. A comparison of Francesco di Giorgio's "Rape of Europa" (321) with Botticelli's "Allegory of Spring" (90) reveals the difference between rhythmic line reënforcing other elements, and the same line exaggerated to the point of obscuring them. As with Leonardo and Raphael, much of the popular appeal of Botticelli rests upon illustration rather than upon plastic value.

Leonardo (1452–1519) is one of the great outstanding figures in the history of art, but his popularity is due chiefly to factors that have little to do with art itself. He was a scientist more than an artist, and while his researches produced results that have had an enormous influence on painting since his time, these results promoted academicism quite as much as real creation. Most of what is bad in Raphael is due to the influence of Leonardo, and Leonardo's positive contributions were soon academicized by his followers

Andrea del Castagno, School of (79)

Showing the swirl used by subsequent painters, including Tintoretto,
El Greco, Rubens, Fragonard, Delacroix, Renoir, and Pascin.

Fra Filippo Lippi (98)

Rousseau, *le douanier* (244)

Modern version of Florentine form.

Piero della Francesca (II)

Analysis, page 398

into a formula which has served as a counterfeit of art for several centuries. Leonardo himself derived from the Greeks and from Verrocchio, but what he absorbed was reworked by his own powerful mind into a new and definite form. His positive contribution was a manipulation of line and light into a modeling of figures whose three-dimensional qualities are outstanding. In this, however, the central idea came from the Venetian, Giovanni Bellini. Leonardo rarely seems to be able to control his medium: in his Uffizi "Annunciation" (97), for example, the surface has the quality of ordinary fence-painting. Although his color is sometimes appealing, as it is to a certain extent in "Mona Lisa" (343), it is usually indifferent, so that the shadows are dull and the paint almost muddy. This defect is apparent even in his sketch "Adoration of the Magi" (96), one of his best works. His line, though vigorous, is constantly overaccentuated, as in "Saint John the Baptist" (344), and so is his light. It is the overaccentuation of light that produces the melodramatic tinge so constantly present in his work, and which is to be seen in both the London and the Paris versions of "Virgin of the Rocks" (141; 345). He was rarely able to make light function economically and subtly and as a real equivalent for color, as did Rembrandt. When he uses light and color together, the light seems to be laid on and does little or nothing to animate, enrich, and heighten the color-effects, as it does in Rembrandt, Giorgione, and the other great colorists. To give expressiveness, he abstracted line and light from their legitimate place in the ensemble of plastic means and debased them in the portrayal of the adventitious, literary, narrative, or sentimental aspects of subject-matter. There are rarely to be found in his work plastic equivalents for the human values of subject-matter, as we find them in Giotto, Titian, Tintoretto, or Rembrandt. We find instead preoccupation with solidity of figures, indifferent color, rather tight line, a tendency to overlighting, all of which throw into relief subject-matter in which excessive sweetness of expression is the almost constant feature. His real status as an artist is revealed best by a comparison of his sketch "Adoration of the Magi" (96), with almost any of his finished paintings. The sketch reveals his fine sense of composition and his great command over space, light, and line. Though merely a skeleton it is so rich in elements harmoniously combined into a strong plastic unity that it has greater esthetic value than the majority of his finished paintings. In it we see what Leonardo could do in planning a composition, and we are able to judge how much he lost by his frequent failure to use color effectively and by his overemphasis of light in modeling and in the general design. Walter Pater's essay *Leonardo da Vinci*, in his book *The Renaissance*, unwittingly reveals how well an artist can be represented in his true essence by brilliant writing that never comes within sight of the essential qualities of his subject.

Michelangelo (1475–1564) succeeds in giving a sense of power mainly by modeling with light and shadow, and accentuation of muscular contours in the figures. The sources of his inspiration were Greek sculpture, and also the paintings of Pollaiuolo, Verrocchio, Signorelli, and Cosimo Tura; but these influences are incorporated in a form which is Michelangelo's own creation. His light and shadow are welded into a three-dimensional solidity which is the main factor in his rhythmic and effective designs, both in individual figures and in the composition as a whole. Subsidiary to this are the muscular accentuations, which make a pattern that unifies with the main design and contributes to its strength. These means are so varied in the series of frescoes in the Sistine Chapel (419) that there is no suggestion of monotony. Michelangelo's color is, on the whole, conventional and without distinction but in his best work it serves as an efficient adjunct to the mass-composition.

His line is extremely vigorous and terse, and is so broken up and related to other lines that it has a positive decorative quality which enhances the total esthetic effect. At times there is lack of perfect fusion and the resulting overdecorative effect detracts from the strength of the plastic unit. Like Raphael, Michelangelo is a great illustrator, but in the dramatic themes of his frescoes, we are often conscious, as with Raphael, of a disbalanced melodrama. His "Last Judgment" (420) is a powerful design of three-dimensional forms, moving in rhythmically ordered space, but the dramatic movement has the stridency seen often in Rubens and usually in Delacroix. The intensity, the exaltation, the terror, in this fresco are rendered so speciously that the expression remains one of overdramatized emotions, achieved mainly by patterns of light, line, and shadow. It is impossible not to feel in Michelangelo that there is a deliberate striving for effects not strictly within the limits of painting, effects which partake of the nature of illustration. It is certainly true that his imagination was sculptural, and the range of his means in painting was quite restricted when compared with that of other great painters. One detects in his frescoes the claims of the sculptor and of the literary poet in conflict with the proper function of the painter. At any rate, his paintings do not realize the scope of effects possible in painting as do those of Giotto, Giorgione, Rembrandt, Velásquez, or Renoir.

Raphael (1483–1520) had wide knowledge of what other painters had contributed to art, an extraordinary facility and ability to use paint, a fine sense for the grouping of masses, an unsurpassed feeling for space-composition, and he was in active contact with a rich and vital civilization. But his work, judged by what it contains of plastic value, provides the perfect example of a first-rate virtuoso who was far from being a first-rate artist. His superlative skill and knowledge enabled him to obtain striking effects, but he was in reality an eclectic, even though his works have a characteristic Raphael quality. The origin of what he has to say is always discoverable, and his borrowings are not fully modified into a creation of his own. The more he is studied, the less original he seems and the more his dapperness, grace, charm, and skill are seen to be superficial. His frescoes in the Vatican (425) are mainly academic tricks: sharply contrasted directions and accentuated perspective are calculated to strike the eye, and give vivid illustrative instead of plastic values.

His command of plastic means was very unequal. His good sense of arrangement and his fine feeling for the ordered sequence of objects on the same plane and in deep space are left without adequate support. His color is almost uniformly thin, dry, and lifeless, even when bright; it is nearly always without structural quality, and without unifying effect on the composition. His lack of feeling for color makes his light seem unreal, because when light falls upon color it not only fails to animate it but heightens the effect of its thinness, dryness, and superficiality. This defect was Leonardo's also, and Raphael took it over. His drawing is done almost entirely by a line derived from Greek sculpture and from Verrocchio's and Botticelli's attenuated versions of the classic spirit. Though his line is incisive, graceful, and varied, it is isolated from color, so that it detracts from reality: it is preoccupied with the literal representation of contour, movement, direction, and perspective. This linear overemphasis, inability to use color, and unbalanced use of light, all contribute to the lack of conviction in his figures and masses generally.

[135]

Raphael's mass-compositions, while skilfully executed, essentially follow Leonardo's formula; they lack real vigor, are usually of the conventional bilaterally balanced type, and are unaided by color. From Leonardo also he borrowed the method of using light and the sentimental sweetness, but he was unable to attain to the skill of Leonardo's modeling. His greatest accomplishment, effective space-composition, came directly from Perugino. It stands out as an accentuation, especially when an attempt is made to merge it into an organic design in which the badly used other plastic elements must enter. In consequence of all these deficiencies the composition which at first glance seems so effective, never sustains analysis: one finds virtuosity and eclecticism instead of plastic unity.

Raphael was a great illustrator, but his illustration instead of supplementing plastic form constantly supplants it. The passage of time has dimmed the interest of his subject-matter for the person of non-antiquarian culture. It displays an excess of unappealing drama, as in "Saint Michael Crushing Satan" (370) and in "Descent from the Cross" (416), or an inane sweetness and sentimentality, as in nearly all of his Madonnas. The subject-matter brings clearly into relief the spuriousness of his effects and his general lack of personal force. As an illustrator he is inferior to the best of his contemporaries, to Goya, Daumier, or Degas of the last century, and to Picasso, Glackens, or Pascin of our own age, all of whom give the essentials of a situation plastically and with conviction. Like Leonardo, Raphael relied upon the relatively trivial, adventitious, and literary. As a result of all these unorganized and indiscriminately selected elements, his work seems artificial, formalized, devoid of spontaneity, an effect which is increased by the fact that even his best organized pictures are better painted in some parts than in others. In short, we rarely find in Raphael a powerful, original conception, uniformly and adequately rendered in plastic terms. He will always be the ideal of those who seek in art the easily accessible, the agreeable, and superficial; that is, the antithesis of profundity and real personality. His appeal is to facile sentimentalism which has little to do with art but which offers a fertile field for critics who delight in flights of irrelevant rhetoric.

SUMMARY OF THE FLORENTINE FORM

Florentine painting starts from Giotto. In Giotto's design the essential points are an intensely expressive, terse line, novel and powerful composition, and a uniquely effective use of color. The result is a series of relationships, extremely rich in plastic content. The feeling for effective compositional organization is present in all the great artists working in the Florentine tradition, Masaccio, Andrea del Castagno, Uccello, Piero della Francesca, Pollaiuolo, Leonardo, Michelangelo, and Raphael. It is to be seen in a less powerful form in Fra Filippo Lippi; in Botticelli, it has become attenuated to essentially a linear decorative pattern; in Fra Angelico it has fallen away to little more than a set of pleasant color-relations; in Ghirlandaio, it has gone almost completely to pieces. In the most important members of the school the **mass-composition** is almost invariably good but in Botticelli, Leonardo, and Raphael it tends to academicism. In Masaccio and Piero della Francesca it is almost as original and powerful as in Giotto, and in them as in him it is reënforced by light and color, as it is also in Michelangelo.

Color is at its best in Giotto, who alone among the Florentines used it as effectively as the Venetians, though in a totally different manner. In Piero della Francesca, feeling for color compares well with that of any other painter, but his work is less variedly rich than that of Giorgione and Titian. In Masaccio, the color is very rich and it acquires a new function by its combination with light to produce an aërial perspective and an atmospheric effect which contribute to an intense realism. Michelangelo's color is secondary to patterns of light and dark, and is without distinction. The Florentine use of color, and the Florentine form in general, may be described as relatively austere in comparison with the Venetian. Even when the color is at its best, as in Giotto, it has not the depth and juiciness of the Venetian: it is more ethereal, jewel-like, or cool than luscious and warm. There is no Florentine who has the sensuous splendor of Tintoretto or Titian, or whose color gives the abstract feeling of power which those great colorists achieved. The Florentines dealt much more with religious **subject-matter** than the Venetians, so that their concerns were more remote from human affairs. This remained true even when the dominant religious motif was modified by the classical. In the incorporation in plastic art of human values, especially of the more natural, spontaneous kind, they were therefore inferior to the Venetians, as we shall see in our discussion of the Venetians in a subsequent chapter.

Drawing was developed by the Florentines to a high degree of perfection, although the comparatively limited function of color as a reënforcement of line makes their draughtsmanship less effective than that of later painters. In Giotto the presence of pervasive color minimized this deficiency. In Masaccio and Piero della Francesca color reënforces line, and Michelangelo's drawing is at times well merged with his color; but in Botticelli, Leonardo, and Raphael, color and line remain quite distinct. Andrea del Castagno's line is terse, vigorous, and made more powerful by the use of a swirl akin to that developed later by Tintoretto and Rubens.

Modeling is achieved mainly by light and shadow, with little recourse to structural color; it has a high degree of conviction in Giotto and Masaccio; in Leonardo and Raphael the light is usually exaggerated and dissociated from color, and in Michelangelo the emphasis upon volume is more sculpturesque than pictorial.

The general effect of the Florentine form is that of delicacy, while that of later men, like Titian, Tintoretto, and Rembrandt, is robustness. This delicacy tends to weakness in Raphael, to mere decoration in Botticelli, to sentimentality in Leonardo, to a miniature-effect in Fra Filippo Lippi, and it is a part of Piero della Francesca's coolness; but in every case it distinguishes them from the more full-blooded Venetians. In space-composition, the airiness of Giotto, of Piero della Francesca, and of Raphael has a delicacy that is comparatively absent in Claude or Cézanne. This same delicacy appears in the Florentine use of **light,** even when it is weakened by overaccentuation, as in Leonardo and Raphael. Combined with color to make atmosphere, as in Masaccio, light takes on a robustness approaching that of Titian.

In short, the Florentine form at its best is constituted by a strong sense of design, executed in delicate, harmonious, but not structurally used color, with expressive line, convincing modeling, effective lighting, and rhythmic, spacious composition. Some individual painters added characteristic contributions of their own to this form, others allowed it to become unbalanced, weakened, and cheapened.

The obviously numerous and important characteristics of the Florentine form show the one-sidedness of Berenson's estimate of their principal achievement in painting. He asserts that this is their realization of "tactile values," that is, that the effects are similar to those perceived by touching three-dimensional objects. It is true that this does appear in Giotto and Piero della Fran-

cesca, but along with many effects of far greater esthetic significance. It is to be found further developed in Masaccio, but so are
aërial perspective, atmosphere, and other elements of realism which
influenced profoundly the whole subsequent history of painting.
It is most apparent in Leonardo, but even in him it is secondary
in esthetic significance to his general sense of composition. When
tactile values do appear as the sole or outstanding quality of his
pictures, the fact constitutes a defect and not a virtue. Berenson's
estimate of that one element as the chief contribution of the
Florentines indicates that he overlooks the importance of delicate,
pervasive color, of rhythmic movement of plastic units, of light
in many rôles other than as an element in modeling, and of design
in the largest sense. And to overlook these elements is to miss the
esthetic significance of painting.

It remains to relate the Florentine contribution to art to that
of subsequent painters. Giotto's work has in it the germ of most
of what gives modern art its value. Other members of the Florentine school made individual advances which anticipated practices
which continued down to the present day. The Florentine general
effect of delicacy combined with power and conviction is largely reflected in Poussin, and through him it greatly influenced the whole
course of French painting. The step taken by Masaccio toward
naturalism was enormously influential in the process of bringing art
from preoccupation with another world to interest in the world as
it actually is; more particularly, his development of drawing foreshadowed the Venetians, and also Rembrandt, Goya, Daumier,
Renoir, and other important artists. He worked line, color, and
space into the perceptible atmosphere and realistic aërial perspective from which developed the luminous, colorful atmosphere of
Claude, the Barbizon painters, and the impressionists. With the
same elements he created the haze and the chiaroscuro which
in Rembrandt developed into the means of realizing a profound
mysticism.

Uccello's development of design and especially pattern finds a
parallel in many modern and contemporary artists, including Cézanne, Matisse, Prendergast, Seurat, and Picasso. His treatment
of the background as a contrasting screen rather than as realistic
representation, which is also to be seen in Fra Filippo Lippi, anticipates the impressionists, and van Gogh, Gauguin, and Matisse.
Piero della Francesca's color and to a considerable extent his line,
light, modeling, and general design, were used by Picasso and

other moderns in the development of plastic form through pervasive color-effect. Andrea del Castagno's swirl is an anticipation of that of Tintoretto, Rubens, and Delacroix; his draughtsmanship forecasts that of Goya, Daumier, Renoir, Glackens, and Pascin; and in his color, line, and space, there are also suggestions of forms characteristic of Rembrandt and El Greco.

The Greek influence noted in the painters of the high Renaissance continues in Poussin and to a certain extent in Claude, and it is the chief stock in trade of the neo-classicism of the early nineteenth century. The fluid line of Ingres recalls the incisiveness of Raphael's line and the decorative quality of Botticelli's, both of them clearly Greek in origin.

The influence of Leonardo and Raphael upon subsequent painting is seen particularly in modeling and in composition. This influence on the whole has been deplorable, since academicians and purveyors of literature and sentiment have at all times drawn sustenance from it. Michelangelo's anatomical accentuations reappear in varying degrees in painting since his time, notably in El Greco, Rubens, Cézanne, and Pascin. All painting since the Renaissance has been so much influenced by the Florentine tradition, that it cannot be properly understood or judged by any one unfamiliar with the work of that school. The converse of that statement is also true, namely, that the meaning of the Florentine tradition is only fully revealed by the development that has followed from it, and that Giotto, Masaccio, Piero della Francesca, and the artists of the high Renaissance are not fully comprehensible by those unable to understand and appreciate the most modern movements in painting.

CHAPTER III

THE SIENESE TRADITION

THE SIENESE form as a whole is more decorative than it is plastically expressive of profound human values. Compared to Giotto or even Cimabue, works like those of Simone Martini, of Memmi, and of the Lorenzettis, sink to a lower level of art because, despite their highly decorative character, they are more narrative and sentimental than truly plastic. The foundation of their form is the Byzantine tradition which they made more graceful and endowed with delicacy and an intime feeling, but they lack the depth of expression, the great variety of forms, the high plastic quality, seen in Giotto and his great followers. Occasionally, however, as in Ambrogio Lorenzetti's panels in the Vatican, "Legend of St. Stephen" (426), color attains to a distinction comparable to that of the great Florentines, not only in variety and pleasing sensuous quality but in the formation of compartmental patterns with their own high esthetic value.

The outstanding characteristics of Sienese painting are: a prevalence of green in the substructure of flesh; an accentuatedly angular treatment of rocks in landscape; an exaggeration of the white of the eyes and an elongated downward slant of the lids toward the temples, whereby an expression of sharpness is conveyed by the eyes; sinuous rhythms in draperies; a distinctive use of light, color, and line in the rendering of folds in garments, and in a type of drawing which we have termed "Sienese droop."

The "droop" consists of a flow of light and color joined integrally with line and rendering a distinctive down-flowing movement of contour and mass in figures. It differs from the Florentine method which tends to depict movement by sequence of line: the Sienese droop represents a fuller plastic drawing, because of its fusion of line with light and color. The droop is anticipated to a certain extent in early French and German miniatures and woodcuts; and in the form developed by the Sienese it was used creatively in several types of German and French primitives.[1] The

[1] See Barnes and de Mazia, *The French Primitives and Their Forms*, pp. 81 and 318, Barnes Foundation Press, Merion, Pa., 1931.

[141]

Sienese treatment of folds in draperies is based only partly upon the Florentine development of the Byzantine method; it retains more of the Byzantine patterned effects, the rigidity of which is converted into fluid rhythms and movement by sinuous lines and scroll-like edges, and by an accentuated fluidity in the relations between broad bands of light on the crest of folds and bands of color which parallel the highlighted area on each side.

In **Duccio di Buoninsegna** (1260–1339), the usual Sienese stress upon psychological states, especially sweet sentimentality, is attenuated by a form which claims greater attention because of its essentially plastic quality. The set doleful expressions, the static character of his figures are well embodied in patterned forms made up of color, line, and light-and-shadow. The practice of the Byzantine color-compartments is continued but with less accentuation, and the color is modulated with light and gives a feeling of reality, though slight, to fabrics. The color is usually rich with a tendency to juiciness, but occasionally it has the dryness of about that of Cosimo Tura's "Pietà" (395). Duccio was evidently the originator of the Lorenzo Monaco - Fra Angelico color-scheme: his colors partake of the general lightness of Lorenzo Monaco's and Fra Angelico's, but are less bright, less glaring, less staccato, and better related. The charm of his color-ensembles is due to his feeling for relations between unusual colors, as for instance, a pink robe with broad areas of light and a deep green, similarly lighted. Color-distortions are particularly noticeable in the painting of flesh: green or blackish-gray faces are vividly patterned by contrasting pink or red highlights on the cheeks, nose, and lips. This method of flesh-painting gives a sort of diffuse character to Duccio's drawing of faces, which thus differs from the usual type of Florentine drawing. His contour, in general, varies from a heavy line of contrasting color to a sharply linear effect. There is a tendency to a broken line in the definition of cloaks and shoulders, and to swaying curves in draperies, with internal linear patterns of folds organized in geometrical shapes. Three-dimensionality of objects is usually well realized by modeling with light and shade, and perspective is adequately rendered in effective space-composition. In many of his pictures Duccio continues to use the Byzantine ancona, that is, the division of the composition into several individually framed compartments. The tendency in his large paintings is toward the traditional bilaterally balanced composition; in his small pictures, he is less conventional and often strikes bizarre notes of great originality His plan of organization and execution adds a naïve delicacy, charm, and greater naturalism to the Byzantine form.

Ugolino da Siena (c.1280 – c.1340) resembles Duccio in general form. His figures are more active, there is a greater feeling of movement throughout his compositions, and the facial expressions are less doleful. His color is somewhat brighter, with a greater use of ivory, but in general his pictures, though well organized in terms of color, lack the depth, power, and plastic simplicity of Duccio's best work.

CHAPTER IV

THE VENETIAN TRADITION

THE CHARACTERISTIC Venetian tradition appeared much later than the Florentine, and never really represented the austere Christianity of the Middle Ages. The influence of the Renaissance operated strongly, but the classic feeling is more thoroughly assimilated and incorporated in a new and characteristic form. In the best period there was a successful union of traditions, subject-matter was brought closer to the earth, and hence there is a greater naturalness in the Venetian form at its best than ever appeared among the Florentines.

The first of the Venetians to merit serious attention is **Giovanni Bellini** (c.1428–1516). He inherited the academic tradition of the fourteenth century but reworked it into a richer form which contains the germs of the work of the greatest Venetians, Giorgione, Titian, and Tintoretto. The most important of Bellini's contributions was in the realm of color: he made color seem to enter into the solid substance of objects, and he also used it as a means to create a circumambient atmosphere by which the effect of color in unifying composition was greatly increased in power. It seems probable that Bellini got the latter idea from Masaccio; but he converted it from an atmospheric haze into a pervasive swimming color-glow which surrounds and sets off the particular objects and contributes a further element of both unity and variety to the picture. Both the structural use of color and the glow were less in evidence in Bellini than in his successors. The glow does not yet suffuse the whole picture, but is confined to certain areas, and is often more silvery than golden, though the reddish-brown quality is beginning to appear. This limitation of the glow to certain areas, together with the partial use of structural color, is seen in his large altarpiece "Madonna and Saints" (437).

Bellini's use of light was epoch-making in two respects. First, his modeling by light and shadow was taken over both by his great successors at Venice and by Leonardo, from whom it descended to Raphael. Bellini's modeling is more convincing than that of these Florentines because he achieves solidity without the overaccentuation that became virtuosity in Leonardo. Bellini's second great achievement by the use of light was the construction of a complex but unified pattern which Giorgione, Titian, and Tintoretto used later with marvelous results. His mass-composition often remains on the whole within the academic formula, though his compositional design is enriched by new combinations of color, as in "Madonna of the Little Trees" (430), and by graceful, fluid line, and patterns within patterns to such an extent that the effect is decidedly novel. The importance of all of these achievements becomes apparent from the indebtedness of the later Venetians to Bellini. For example, the poetic treatment of landscape, and its combination with figures to the enhancement of both, which we find in Giorgione, are anticipated in Bellini's "Allegory of Purgatory" (89), in which there is also the germ of Tintoretto's mingling of light and color in the rendering of texture. Bellini's use of color to build up the structure of objects anticipates Titian, although in Titian sharpness of line gives place to a more convincing blurring of contour. In Bellini's work there is the dignity, avoidance of sentimentalized expression, and the uniform control of the plastic means, characteristic of the Venetian school at its best, therein contrasting with the opposite traits of Leonardo and Raphael. He was a very great painter, who is overshadowed by his successors only because they made even more impressive use of his means.

In the work of **Carpaccio** (c.1455–1525) we see Bellini's feeling for design elaborated into more complex compositions, and also the tendency of the colorful atmosphere to become more crystalline and, at times, more silvery. His space-volume compositions depart from the conventional central mass and bilateral symmetry, and his three-dimensional objects take on a rhythmic order in deep space, so that his compositions are perceived as processions of rhythmic units. He is among the greatest masters of space-composition: his very expressive handling of space was perhaps his most distinctive contribution to the Venetian tradition. In all parts of his pictures, there are intricate organizations—of light, line, color, space, three-dimensional volumes—which merge into the strong central design. He enriched the tradition also by great skill in the employment of architectural detail to enhance expres-

[145]

sion, and by quite a sensitive rendering of the spirit of place. His "Dream of St. Ursula" (431) brings home to us, by the similarity of general subject-matter to Vermeer's, how far superior Carpaccio was to Vermeer both in originality of conception and in technical skill.

Giorgione (1477–1510) merged all the good in the traditions of his time into a new and distinctive form, in which are visible more of the values of painting than in the work of any other artist up to that time, if one realizes the importance of color. The foundation of his form is color; it is of the utmost richness in itself, and it functions as a unifying agent in the design through the medium of the Venetian glow. In addition, the color is presented in an infinitely varied series of units, in themselves harmonious rhythms that move in and about all parts of the canvas, weaving themselves into a general design that has an emotional power equal to that of the richest symphony. In Giorgione color is of great sensuous charm and decorative quality, blends with the light, welds together the composition, and contributes to the power and expressiveness of the drawing. He has an equally great control over the use of light. It affords a general illumination which we feel to be perfectly natural, the antithesis of Leonardo's and Raphael's artificial lighting; it also aids in modeling and in unifying composition, and it forms minor patterns which enter harmoniously into the total design. The line is always expressive, rhythmic, and fluid. It helps to build structure and to decorate it, and is not isolated from either the structure or the decoration. The composition, at its best, is entirely liberated from academic shackles, is wonderfully varied, perfectly realized in three dimensions, with beautiful spacing; the masses are convincingly solid, and are knit together by sequence of line, light, and color. All this is accomplished without suggestion of overemphasis of any element: even the ubiquitous color is never out of place and never stands out by reason of excessive brightness. This supreme merging of all effects endows every part of the canvas with intrinsic interest as well as with integral and esthetically significant relations to every other part. In "Sleeping Venus" (73) and "Concert in the Open Air" (330), there is not a spot that is either uninteresting in itself or a mere transition to some other spot of greater interest: the eye cannot rest anywhere without finding the fullest satisfaction.

These plastic qualities are the legitimate foundation for an expression that is probably the most poetic in all painting. The note is primarily lyric, idyllic, Arcadian; it is free from weakness and softness, and becomes stronger the more it is considered. The elevation of Giotto, the grace of Masaccio, the strength of Andrea del Castagno, the drama of Tintoretto, the mystery of Rembrandt, are all present in solution. The intense but deep and restrained human feeling, the glamour and mystery of nature, the peace and the mysticism of all-embracing natural religion, produce a total effect which is, in the best sense, sublime. Giorgione's unique endowment as an artist is shown in the Castelfranco "Madonna with St. Francis and St. Liberal" (50), which was painted at an early age and under influences comparatively academic. Into a composition which, by itself, would be formal and stereotyped, he injected a wealth of plastic and human values which make one forget the triteness of the compositional arrangement.

The early work of **Titian** (c.1477–1576) has most of Giorgione's qualities, though in a weaker form; for instance, his "Christ and the Magdalen" (156) presents the Venetian glow, the manner of using light, the richly diversified composition, the lyric quality of Giorgione; but these characteristics are slighter, less convincing, less poetic. Subsequently, Titian's work became less arcadian and more dramatic, until it covered nearly the whole range of expression. It gained in splendor and positiveness of color, elaborateness of design, gravity, depth, and majesty. It offers plastic embodiment to the most lofty themes, and although it never reaches quite the height of Giorgione at his best, it is infinitely more extensive in scope. The Giorgionesque quality never entirely disappears but gradually merges into a new form which makes Titian's later work very different in total effect.

Titian's painting of flesh is more varied in the different figures than is Giorgione's, and its surface is usually dappled or mottled by a subtle pattern of unaccentuated semi-shadows which melt smoothly into intervening, loosely defined areas of light. This dappled surface became a feature of the flesh-painting of Tintoretto and Paolo Veronese, each of whom introduced variations in appearance by technical devices of his own.

Titian's drawing differs from Giorgione's in the use of a broad line of contour; Giorgione's contour is usually formed by a deepening of the shadows, rarely by a definite band of color. Often

Titian's linear contour is isolated, not merged with the form, and the drawing is less expressive. His drawing is seen at its best in "Man with Glove" (394); in this picture drawing is a fusion of line, light, and color. The figure melts into the background, without any sharp contrasts of line, of color, or of lighting, and yet it is perfectly distinct. It stands away from what is back of it, but the means by which that separation is effected are exceedingly subtle. There is general economy of means, of the highest type: the design is extremely simple, and yet every element in it is utilized to the utmost. The background seems to recede to infinity, but by the use of what means it is impossible to say. There is very little bright color: the subdued tones seem to glow, and the harmonious color used structurally blends with light and gives subtle color-chords and an effect of solid reality.

The same dignity and effectiveness in embodying the values of what is presented appear also in "Disciples at Emmaus" (391) and "Entombment" (392). The effect of solemnity, of quiet, deep drama, places these paintings among the greatest in existence. Similar rendering of religious feeling unobtrusively, convincingly, profoundly, is repeated on a larger scale in "Assumption" (438), in which the design is more complex than any attempted by Giorgione. It has great wealth of secondary designs and positive symphonic or epic effect.

The standards characteristic of Titian's best work are not always maintained; in fact, in any large exhibition of his work—for instance, that held in Venice in 1935—the academic and banal nearly always outnumber the creative and excellent. In his "Christ Crowned with Thorns" (390), there is an overuse of light, comparable to that of Leonardo and Raphael, and the effect is chiefly melodramatic. In "Saint John the Baptist" (434), a similar yielding to Leonardo's preoccupation with light and line has a deleterious effect upon the strength of the expression. But Titian's best work represents an extremely important contribution to painting: his influence upon later artists was perhaps unsurpassed. Titian's forms are so important and so rich, and they are achieved by such a varied and skilled use of technical means, that no brief general summary could do justice to either the forms or the technique. It is only by detailed study of particular paintings, such as has been attempted in our analysis of his "Assumption" (438), that one can obtain an adequate idea of his extraordinary versatility and power.[1]

[1] See p. 429.

Giorgione (200)

Titian (391)

Analysis, page 424

Tintoretto (251)

Fine example of convincing drama embodied in well-balanced plastic form.

Paolo Veronese (253)

Tintoretto's (1518–1594) form is fundamentally that of movement and drama. The chief technical means is a modification of line tending toward distortion and its incorporation into a plastic unit which is a swirl of light, color, and line. This appears both in the minor details of treatment, and in the composition as a whole; for example, in "Artist's Portrait" (386), the swirl is to be seen in the lines of the face, in the cheeks, and in the beard. In "Paradise" (387), the whole composition is a succession of these swirling units, communicating a powerful, moving quality to the canvas. The effect of his swirl is animation and vigor: his work is less tranquil than Titian's and seldom has the idyllic calm of Giorgione's.

Tintoretto's color is rich and deep in itself, it functions organically in the composition, is very well used structurally and it gets an added power by its application in his characteristic swirling movement. In his rendering of textiles the color has usually an internal illumination which radiates light and imparts translucency; at other times, as in the background of "Susanna at the Bath" (388), the texture is more clear-cut, metallic, lustrous, than it is in Titian. The translucent effect was further developed by El Greco, and the metallic by Paolo Veronese.

In Tintoretto's organization of volumes, the more important masses are frequently placed at the extreme left or right of the canvas, as in "Susanna at the Bath" (388). When there is a central mass, as in "Paradise" (387), it is less a means for setting the composition as a whole at rest than a focus of motion. The movement is quite different from and more solidly real than that of Raphael, which tends to be isolated by his incisive line and sharp contour. In Tintoretto, movement is infused into the whole structure of the object by drawing in which color, light, and line are merged. Tintoretto showed his greatness by this ability to realize movement in good plastic terms and so to control it that he could adapt it to a great variety of subjects, from dignified portraiture to the seething turmoil portrayed in his "Paradise" (387). He adopted Titian's frequent use of a broad, often isolated, line of color defining parts of the contour of objects, a procedure used later by Daumier, Cézanne, and Matisse. One of his most important contributions was in the use of areas of accentuated light placed in contrast with broad areas of rich, deep color. By that method he achieved a particular quality of vitality and richness in the painting of the long folds of gowns. An even more striking use of this means is seen in the painting of skies. There, he used a broad area of dark color in alternation with ribbonlike streaks of light in varying degrees of width. Both the color and the light are applied in a swirling fashion, with an effect that is intensely dramatic. El Greco made this device the foundation of a technique which has influenced many of the important subsequent painters.

Tintoretto's work shows how a great man can enrich an already great tradition. To the Venetian tradition he added characteristic personal variations in light, color, line, composition, rhythmic form. He reorganized Titian's contributions to his own ends. The swirl, and a new integration of light and color, show his ability to make the necessary modification of familiar technical means to render new dramatic effects. Even the tinting of the traditional glow is changed appropriately. He is inferior to Titian and Giorgione in that his means are more obvious and less simple, his color is not uniformly so rich, and the conviction of reality in his pictures is sometimes not so strong. How important Tintoretto's contribution was is realized when we recall that El Greco derived chiefly from Tintoretto and that much of what is best in modern painting comes from El Greco.

Paolo Veronese's (1528–1588) virtues are in the main those of his predecessors, though not quite on the same supreme level. He is less lyric than Giorgione, less imaginative than Titian, less powerfully dramatic than Tintoretto. A sweeping movement, which affects his drawing of units as well as the compositional organization, is his own modification of Tintoretto's swirl. His special ability lay in portraying the spirit of festival and pageantry, and this he did successfully in enormous canvases of great decorative richness.

Paolo's flesh-painting is usually lighter in color than the other Venetians' and he uses more pink, as a rule concentrated in small areas on cheeks, knees, thighs, from which it radiates and gradually merges with the general silver- or lavender-gray tone of the surrounding flesh. This treatment, which imparts a general rosy cast to the complexion, was adopted and extended by Rubens and Boucher. Another of Paolo's innovations was the modification of Tintoretto's metallic luster into something more crisp, cool, and clear-cut. It is this quality that makes his textures appear brilliant, enameled, and jewel-like, instead of soft and mysterious, as in Titian and Giorgione. He has great ability to render the spirit of

place and the feeling of all the material objects in their own surroundings. His command over space recalls Carpaccio's compositions, but Paolo's emphasis upon the contrasting directions in
which the masses are placed, contributes a feeling of more lively
activity: a great number of his compositions open up in a large
V-shaped expanse of space, and the individual masses are practically all set at angles to each other, thus creating a complex
series of contrasting oblique rhythms which come to rest by their
own interrelationships as well as by the counterbalancing power of
the horizontal and vertical units. He modifies the Venetian glow
to a more grayish-silver tone, with more coolness but with less
glamour and mystery. Color remains structural, though it is less
glowing. Light is very well used in all its functions, to form patterns, accentuate movement, and render tactile values; its pattern
in skies, in relation to areas of shadows, gives a distinctive character to Paolo's treatment of clouds: the dramatic contrasts
achieve a compact succession of parallel, irregularly shaped,
elongated planes. He rarely reaches the artistic heights of Titian
or Tintoretto, but at his best he is able to attain fine plastic realization of his chosen subject-matter.

SUMMARY OF THE VENETIAN FORM

The chief characteristic of the Venetian form is the use of color,
first structurally, and then in combination with light, in the form
of a pervasive, circumambient atmosphere or glow. The uniform
richness of color as a sensuous element and its use to establish the
relations constituting plastic form, were the supreme achievements
of the Renaissance in painting. The Venetians conceived and
successfully realized lighting, drawing, space, composition, movement, rhythm, all in terms of color; for that reason Venetian painting represents, as a whole, the high-water mark of pictorial art.

Compared with the Florentines, there is first of all the greater
naturalness and spontaneity of feeling, which is due to an interest
much more directly turned to the actual world. A firmer integration of color with line, light, and space renders the drawing fuller
and more expressive by heightening the imaginative value of the
theme and by forming infinitely varied contrasts and harmonies.
The Venetian figures are more completely realized in terms of the
fullest experience, and there is consequently more human feeling
in them. These figures fit more naturally into the landscape, and
the landscape itself is more complete, rich, and convincing because

it is much more nature as we know it. In other words, there is an absence of that austerity which we see in the Florentines.

Because of the greater activity of color the decorative element is very much more in evidence in the Venetians than in the Florentines. Even in the best of the Florentine colorists, such as Piero della Francesca and Masaccio, the effect of the color is largely decorative rather than expressive, so that it does not so fully engage our sensibilities as it does in a good Venetian picture. Much of this sensuous richness is due to the Venetian glow which, over and above its function in holding the design together and adding to the glamour or mystery or poetry of the subject, has a direct appeal to the senses. We may say, in short, that Venetian painting not only is more fully expressive than the Florentine, but adds also the very great value of enhanced decoration. Finally, as we shall see later, the Venetian tradition had a much wider and more profound influence on the subsequent development of painting.

CHAPTER V

RUBENS AND POUSSIN

AFTER the height of the Renaissance, the center of gravity in painting shifted from Italy, Germany, and Flanders to Holland, France, and Spain. After Paolo Veronese, Venetian painting degenerated through the stage of repetition as represented by Sebastiano del Piombo and Palma Vecchio, into the crude overdramatizations of Tiepolo. Correggio used the light of Raphael and Leonardo in connection with a richer color than theirs and achieved a form not wholly borrowed. The Carraccis and other late Italian painters were purely eclectics, had nothing of their own to say, and became mere academicians. A number of gifted painters like Guardi, Canaletto, Bellotto, and Pietro Longhi came later and worked in the tradition, but they contributed comparatively little of importance.

The development of the tradition of Venice lay henceforth outside Venice itself. In Spain, El Greco developed Tintoretto's color and his distortions into a new expressive form; Velásquez derived his color from the school as a whole. Poussin merged the Florentine and Venetian traditions into a new, delicate, French form, and through him the whole characteristic French style since then was extensively influenced. Claude transformed the glow into his appealing atmospheric effects, and thereby brought the tradition into bearing upon all modern landscape-painting. But the chief agent in carrying over the Renaissance effects to modern painting was Rubens, whose influence was a determining factor in the forms of Watteau, Lancret, Boucher, Fragonard, Pater, Delacroix, the impressionists, and Renoir, as well as contemporary artists such as Pascin and Soutine. From Rubens developed also, through van Dyck, the school of English portraiture.

Rubens (Flemish, 1577–1640) grafted upon the Flemish tradition the contributions of the Italian Renaissance, especially of the Venetians. From the Flemings he took the tendency to realistic treatment of textures and of details in general, the rather superficial and arid color, and the general quality of weight. All these

[157]

were modified in his work by the Venetian influence, especially that of Paolo Veronese. His color is fundamentally derived from the Venetians but is so transformed by his own gifts that a new and characteristic color-form evolves. The color seldom attains to the structural quality of Titian's, and in the loosening of line by flow of color over contour he never equaled the great Venetians. The pinkish or reddish suffusion of color is his own quite personal version of the Venetian glow. His drawing and modeling were inspired by the Florentines but were so modified by the Venetian and his own color and technique that the influences are merged creatively. His line resembles somewhat that of Raphael, but is so much broken up into short curves that it is more varied in movement as well as in decorative quality, and has a quite particular animation. In many of his paintings the classic influence is clearly apparent, but that too is modified away from the academic feeling of Raphael. The muscular accentuations which Signorelli, Cosimo, Tura, and Michelangelo used in modeling were taken over, modified, and adapted by Rubens, but their effect is rather soft in comparison with the majestic result which the same means afford in the prototypes.

Rubens' fusion of the various influences above noted yielded the most characteristic of his plastic means: a swirl of broken light, line, and color, which is the peculiar instrument of his individual effects of animation, movement, and drama. This swirl differs from that of Andrea del Castagno; it is brighter in color, but it is used with so much abandon that it is less moving esthetically. It is more nearly allied to the swirl of Tintoretto and Paolo Veronese, but is less powerful than Tintoretto's, and on a smaller scale than Veronese's. In Rubens the swirl is found in all the units of the picture and imparts a strikingly rhythmic character, a feeling of indefinitely repeated movement to all parts of the canvas. Hence the general effect of drama not only in the action of the figures, but also as a contributory note in backgrounds and draperies. Even his modeling of flesh is affected by the pervasive swirl-motif: bands of contrasting color parallel within the volume the curves of the contour. The combination of vigorous movement with bright color and hot light, gives a striking, sometimes a melodramatic effect. Rarely is there that perfect equilibrium which results when all the elements alike contribute to the ensemble. While his effects are original they have neither the fulness of expression nor the richness of decoration of Giorgione, among the Renaissance painters, and Renoir among the moderns.

Rubens' form has both advantages and disadvantages. Naturally, it is best in the depiction of scenes of violent action and turmoil. It tends inevitably to the overdramatic, grandiose, and flamboyant, and also to softness and mere prettiness. Many of Rubens' own pictures have all of these defects, and in his imitators they become the chief characteristics. Attributes intrinsic to the design made it tend toward the specious and academic unless its use was controlled by a fine, discriminating intelligence, restraint, and a sense of depth and dignity. Softness and prettiness are paramount in van Dyck, and through him degenerated into the stock traits of Reynolds, Gainsborough, and the other English portrait-painters. It is also apparent in Fragonard and Watteau of the eighteenth century French school, and becomes greatly exaggerated in their imitators. In Jordaens the attenuation of Rubens' plastic form becomes specious melodrama, while in Delacroix's very uneven work are to be found both a successful use of Rubens' form and its degeneration into obvious histrionics. Rubens cannot be ranked with the greatest painters, with Giotto, Giorgione, Titian, and Rembrandt, because of lack of economy of means, simplicity, and restraint, and also because of a certain flabbiness of fiber. His spirit is grandiose rather than noble or elevated, noisy rather than perfectly convincing, and his means are obvious rather than subtle. His work rarely indicates that he had a grasp of the deepest human values, and compared to any of the supreme painters he is lacking in the sense of mysticism. Nevertheless, the contributions which he made to art were enormously influential upon later important men. Through him the Renaissance traditions descended to modern art and he also added to them powerful and original features of his own creation. His influence has been greater than that of Rembrandt and Velásquez, probably because their work, being more individual, subtle, and unapproachable, lent itself less to use by other men. Rubens, more than any one else, determined the development of later Italian, Spanish, and English painting. He was the chief inspiration of the eighteenth century French school represented by Watteau, Boucher, Lancret, Pater, and Fragonard. Through Constable and Delacroix he played a large part in fixing the form of impressionism, and the debt owed him by Renoir and Cézanne is obvious. From the point of view of the history of painting he is, therefore, a very important figure.

[159]

Poussin (French, 1594–1665) may be compared to Giorgione in that he took what was good in the traditions of painting and fused it masterfully with his own personality in a definite, highly individual creation. He had great command over the plastic means and he used them to construct an infinite variety of distinctive forms of a graceful, delicate, poetic charm. In him, is found the whole of the Italian Renaissance in solution, and so individualized that his own personal quality is felt to dominate the Italian. There is a lightness and grace in his drawing and color, an airiness in his space, a suavity in his patterns of light and in his illumination generally, a novel rhythm in the distribution of masses in his compositions, which make a new form, French in spirit and equally Poussin's own.

His work represents the reaction of a highly sensitive and rarely gifted Frenchman to the qualities in Italian painting that gave the Renaissance its greatness. Poussin is one of the few great colorists: he had a fine feeling for the sensuous nuances of different colors and a rare power to make color function in harmoniously composing his canvases. The color-areas harmonize both with adjacent areas and with those in remoter parts of the canvas. This color plays as important a part as line, space, or mass in unifying the components of groups of figures, and in organizing the various groups in a unified whole: it flows from one group to another and between the figures and objects within each group. His color must be appraised as a thing in itself and not in the terms of the great Italians. He never achieves the solidity with color that makes Titian's figures and objects so firmly real, nor do his canvases swim with the rich glow of the great Venetians. All such use of color would be foreign to the suave, graceful delicacy which is inherent in Poussin and which constitutes his own form. His color is delicately structural, and there is a glamour of overtones which makes a gentle, pervasive glow. His color undulates with the line and is integrated with the line and light in a highly expressive drawing, of the choicest delicacy.

Poussin's figures have such a precision, a grace, and ease of posture, and are so infinitely varied in position, height, spacing, that they always have an arresting charm. In "Blindmen of Jericho" (361), the composition offers no end of rhythms up and down, in and around the central masses, the separate groups, the collected group. Few if any of the Renaissance masters exceed his capacity for compositional use of linear rhythms, as shown in this picture.

Botticelli (90)

Analysis, page 405

Rubens (245)

Renoir (239) Analysis, page 466 Fragonard (316)

The Renoir represents a modern version of the Venetian tradition as it evolved through Rubens and the French eighteenth century painters.

Poussin (365)

He converted Raphael's decorative and illustrative line into something more substantially expressive by merging it with the other plastic elements.

The many porcelain- or enamel-like surfaces in Poussin arise from a refining and delicatizing of the clear-cut, metallic color-quality found in Tintoretto and Paolo Veronese. His subsidiary designs of light or of the folds in garments, also suggest the Venetians, and occasionally his anatomical distortions follow those of Michelangelo, but always with due modification in the direction of the characteristic Poussin form. Light often plays a very distinctive part in his compositions: focused upon objects or areas in various parts of the picture—frequently in far distance, upper center, and lower foreground—its pattern actively contributes to the rhythmic character of the organization. His volumes are usually set in more clean-cut planes than are the masses in Venetian compositions; correspondingly, in his adaptation of Venetian painting of draperies, planes are also more in evidence in the patterns made by the lighted and shaded color-areas of the folds.

He advanced upon his predecessors by recasting their traditions into a new form, but his work represented no great step in the direction of modern painting. He was rather the last of the Renaissance than a constructive factor in post-Renaissance painting. The classic spirit in the Renaissance appealed to him strongly and it is reflected with his characteristic delicacy in the drawing of figures and compositional use of architectural features. In this respect he recalls the work of Mantegna, but the cold, rigid, stone-like quality of Mantegna's figures has melted into delicate and fluid grace of form and posture. In spite of Poussin's great gifts of space-composition, and his utilization of it in the treatment of outdoor scenes, his landscapes are conceived in the Renaissance tradition as settings for his themes rather than as things interesting in their own right. In "Funeral of Phocion" (363), the details of the landscape function compositionally like figures. This general classic and Renaissance feeling makes Poussin seem less modern than his contemporaries, Rembrandt, Claude, and Velásquez, or even Rubens. Poussin must be considered as a fine flower of the Renaissance, to the traditions of which he added a quality of choiceness made up of charm, suavity, and delicacy reënforced by strength.

CHAPTER VI

THE IMPORTANT SPANISH PAINTERS

El Greco (c.1541–1614) was a pupil of Tintoretto. We have seen that a particular feature in Tintoretto's form is a fusion of line, light, and color in a swirl which produces very dramatic effects; the line is undulatory, so that it tends toward distortions of the shapes of objects; the light is accentuated in ribbonlike streaks; the color is deeply structural, organizes the compositional units, and has a pleasing sensuous quality. These particular plastic elements were taken over by El Greco and made the foundation of a new and distinctive form that shows a powerful use of the imagination in obtaining rich and varied decorative designs. In his early work these elements were used in almost their original forms, so that at that period his paintings seem to be almost literal reproductions of Tintoretto's except in subject-matter. But very soon El Greco's line grows finer and more animated, the metallic and translucent qualities of Tintoretto's color become more vivid and lustrous, and the ribbonlike bands of light become broader and enter into more dramatic contrasts with adjacent color. As his particular form develops, these lines, color, and light are worked into the most amazingly intricate patterns in all parts of the canvas, and these subsidiary designs enter into an extremely complex design, a rhythmic surge of tremendous esthetic power.

El Greco's great command over line, light, color, space, and design released him more completely from the limitations of realistic subject-matter, and enabled him to build a series of unique abstract forms of such power to compel attention that the spectator has little concern with the subject presented. All the plastic elements are distorted deliberately in the interests of design: line becomes nervous, serpentine, and writhing; color, iridescent, phosphorescent, ghostly, and vaporous; light, flickering, eerie, and almost ghastly. But these qualities of line, color, and light overflow one into another and make El Greco's distinctive form of writhing movement, flamelike in its pervasive power and intensity.

An examination of his work incites admiration for the imagina-

tive scope that conceived so great a variety of plastic forms embodying human values in diverse subject-matter. At times, the
plastic elements appear to be reeling in disequilibrium as the
emotions of excitement and anxiety dominate the scene. At other
times, the perfect balance of the plastic means through which the
subject-matter is expressed, yields the effect of deep peace. A
wide range of human feelings get adequate plastic embodiment
through marvelous combinations of a really very limited number
of plastic means. The linear elements are so animated, so nervous,
and so often repeated in a particular unit, that they seem to form
almost a tangle. The simple and stark colors—red, green, yellow,
blue—take on a series of relationships through variation by light
and become a shimmering mass of variegated tones which in-
sinuate themselves into the serpentine line to form units that
cover the whole gamut of color-contrasts and color-harmonies.
We see a green flow into and tinge a red, blue, or yellow of an adjacent object and give it a lurid, vaporous, unearthly effect. In
another part of the canvas, a crimson red transforms itself through
gradations and admixtures of light to become, further on, sometimes a lavender, sometimes a flame tinged with an ultramarine
highlight. An indigo blue is bathed with light and emerges a
steely gray, a deep ocher is varied to a lemon yellow. Shadows
take on these many variations of red, yellow, green, or blue and
enter as a part of the serpentine unit of merged line, light, and
color. Everything is distorted into a pattern, even the shadows,
and particularly the contrasts of bright colors, vivified and dramatized by broad streaks of light, and set against a comparatively
dark background. We see a design in every plastic unit, every part
of the canvas, and in the canvas as a whole. Each unit shimmers,
glows, and flows into a pattern with other units—it is movement
itself, but with an eerie, lurid quality that makes the drama other-
worldly. No other painter has ever achieved the deep, supernatural
mysticism of El Greco's religious subjects. The same effect is felt
to some degree even in his realistic portraits. In our materialistic
age his subjects have comparatively little appeal; but his design,
his plastic forms, are as moving to-day to the sensitive spectator
as his subject-matter was to the Christian mystic of the seventeenth
century. His distorted figures—with the narrow oval faces, crooked
noses, squinting eyes, strange brows, ears set at extraordinary
angles, elongated fingers, twisted arms, swollen legs—are things in
themselves and are their own esthetic justification. To seek in

them representative naturalistic values is to overlook both their intention and the total significance of art. The distortions are necessary to the design and prove that out of objects resolved into their elements an artist can produce something that moves us more than anything we find in nature.

It is only since about 1880 that El Greco has emerged from his obscure position to recognition as one of the greatest artists. Before that date critics shared the popular confusion of the values of representation with the values of art. With the advent of the great men of 1870—Courbet, Manet, Degas, Renoir, Cézanne—critical observers began to see that plastic form is something in itself of infinitely more esthetic value than literal subject-matter. An intelligent study of modern and contemporary painting will reveal that its values depend to a large extent upon a plastic content substantially akin to that which makes El Greco's work art of the first magnitude.

Velásquez' (1599–1660) work is so individual and his means are so subtle that it is not easy to classify him in the great traditions of painting. The influences of his predecessors are present but they are in solution and converted into distinct entities that bear few surface indications of their origins. The chief influence was that of the Venetians: Titian's and Tintoretto's color and Carpaccio's sense of design and feeling for space took on new meanings in Velásquez' work. From the Flemish he took the green-and-brown color-scheme, enriched it, and applied it to new ends. Compared to the Dutch his browns and blacks in textiles are more lustrous, and his realistic effects in portraiture are more subtle.

His colors are the Venetians' but they are cooler and they rarely have the depth, richness, and surface-charm of their prototypes: a feeling of paint is nearly always perceptible in Velásquez' surfaces. Nevertheless, his colors balance and enter into harmonious relations with each other and with the other plastic elements in designs of color-contrasts individual to Velásquez. Color is conjoined with a light of a quite peculiar clearness and sharpness, which also has its own functions as illumination and as pattern. At times, light and color make a silvery atmosphere that bathes the whole painting with a rich fluid charm. His line is firm, flows gently into forms of sharper contour than in Titian, builds linear patterns resembling Carpaccio's, and contributes to an effect of poised movement equaled by few other painters. His modeling is rarely in evidence

as such, and is used with skill and subtlety to achieve varying degrees of three-dimensional solidity, that harmonize with the particular character of the design. Rarely did any other painter put
as much subtlety into space-composition or adapt it more fittingly
to a great variety of purposes. With all this superb command of
plastic means goes a quality of impersonality, a detachment, a
freedom from accentuated emotion. Velásquez sees an external
object with an eye to its essential character; consequently, there is
great simplification, elimination of everything not intrinsic to the
thing presented. He differs from Rembrandt in being less imaginative, concerned more with what can be actually seen with the eye,
and less with the life in the object that can be divined by sympa-
thetic insight.

This impersonality of spirit is attended by a concealment of his
technical execution: by his mastery of the use of paint, all the
plastic elements are so completely merged that to detect the separate operation of any of them is seldom possible. In Titian, even
when color is most successfully integrated, there is the sense that
color stands out, that is, that color is the stuff out of which the
picture is made. In Velásquez, *nothing* stands out; color, light,
space, composition, rhythm of line and mass—all these factors are
vital constituents of the form, but no one of them alone is what the
picture is essentially made of: it consists of them all, in the measure
and proportion required by the design. Each element plays its
assigned rôle and never overplays it. Velásquez' design is richly
varied by well-balanced and unified subsidiary motifs; it is subtle,
convincing, entirely personal, and is an embodiment of delicacy,
charm, power, dignity, reality, mystery, peace.

Many great painters have found in Velásquez the source of developments that have been epoch-making. Goya adopted his form
as a whole and recreated it with much individuality. In nearly
all of Chardin's work is Velásquez' feeling for spatial relations
and for the essential reality of objects. He had a profound influence upon Corot; and Courbet's painting of figures, his color-
scheme of cool grays, greens, and blues, and his feeling of outdoors
in landscape, derive from Velásquez more than from any other
source. Manet learned from Velásquez the value of simplification
and much of his way of using firm brush strokes. In both Courbet
and Manet we see the selective and generalizing power that enabled
Velásquez to detach the essential elements of objects and present
them in their pictorial significance stripped of redundancy. Im-

pressionism owes much to Velásquez through the adaptations of Manet's technique, and of Courbet's color and naturalism, and through these men he exerted indirectly an important influence upon Renoir and Cézanne.

Goya (1746–1828) is highly important both in portraiture and in that form of illustration which, because of its adequate plastic embodiment, is really art. As a portrait-painter he is inferior to such men as van Eyck, Dürer, or Titian; but in illustration it is a question whether he has ever been surpassed. His derivation is chiefly from Velásquez in painting, and from Bosch and Brueghel in black-and-white illustration. His form, though stamped with the mark of his own virile personality, is less strong than Velásquez'. As an illustrator he resembles Bosch not only in plastic gifts but in penetrating and often ironical insight into character. In some of his best figure-pieces Goya owes also much to Chardin, but never reaches Chardin's heights in richness of plastic units, subtlety of relationships, depth of color, richness and charm of surface, or fulness of expression.

Goya's own characteristics are a great facility in the use of paint, a fine sense for the compositional relation of objects to each other, and an ability to render movement and character by extraordinarily expressive drawing. His psychological characterization is extremely effective, though in a measure it suffers from the painter's personal comments: there is a tendency to exaggeration of the qualities which made the subject attractive or repellent to Goya himself.

His powerful line and his relative deficiency in sensuous quality of color often emphasize the comparatively linear quality of his work, although the line is better merged with light and color than it is in Ingres. His line is not so sharp as Ingres's, it is shorter, and in defining contour it is wavy rather than continuously incisive. This short broken line gives fluidity, movement, and animation instead of Ingres's static rigidity. Frequently a line of light softens the contour and helps the transition of space from figure to background. Except for the type of painting characterized by dramatic light-and-dark effects anticipating Daumier,[1] Goya's work is usually airy, delicate, light, floating, as well as simple and convincing. His color is luminous and skilfully blended with light, but, as in Velásquez, the surfaces are rarely free from the feeling of

[1] E.g., Goya's "Witches' Sabbath" (172).

paint. The individual colors are harmoniously related to each other in color-forms which make up designs of considerable plastic significance. Often there is but little structural quality and as a result his pictures suffer in general solidity and strength. For this color-weakness there is considerable compensation in the excellent mass-composition, in which forceful line and placing of objects at irregular, but subtly varied, spatial intervals, combine to give to the whole painting a stirring sparkle, animation, and expressiveness. In this, color plays its part but chiefly because of its arrangement in pleasing patterns. The most successful use of color is in modeling flesh and textiles, in which, tempered by light and unobtrusive shadow, color in conjunction with line, makes interesting patterns and also renders a sense of solidity. His skilful painting of gauzy, diaphanous stuffs yields rich decorative effects and a general feeling of lightness and delicacy. Light is used with great skill, and without overemphasis; it provides general illumination and forms appealing patterns both in figures and in backgrounds. This effect of light depends largely on Goya's superlative technical skill, as do also his subtle effects of space. Space-composition accounts for no small part of his delicacy and grace: it is always esthetically moving; it appears at its best in the relationship of figures to background which is often accomplished with an economy of means so perfect as to defy detection of technical methods.

In spite of his plastic gifts, Goya's illustration and psychological characterization often outrun his plastic organization, and the result is a lack of balance. Contributory to this is the fact that his color is not of the highest quality; moreover, his lack of impersonality interfered with portrayal of the qualities which lend to persons and things universal significance. This plastic inequality and deficiency in emotional detachment combine to place his work, in spite of its many excellences, in a rank lower than the highest. What Manet and the other impressionists owe to Goya is obvious, but he has also been an influence for bad in inspiring the flood of feeble academic pictures by Gilbert Stuart, Sully, and the Peales which disfigure so many walls in American museums.

CHAPTER VII

THE GERMAN TRADITION

THERE were several centers of primitive German painting, the most important of which are Bohemia, Franconia, and Bavaria, in the south; the Rhine region, including Cologne, in the west; Westphalia in the north-west; and Hamburg and Hannover in the north. All of these primitives stem from Byzantine and early Italian traditions, and each type shows certain general characteristics that differentiate the German tradition as a whole from the French and the Flemish.

Each of the above-noted German centers developed a distinctive style, due to geographical, historical, local, and individual influences or conditions. In the south, particularly in Bohemia, the form is a direct outcome of the Florentine and Sienese traditions; in Cologne and along the Rhine, the Italian influence was interfused with French and Flemish; in Westphalia, Franconia, Bavaria, Hamburg, and the Hanseatic country, the paintings were chiefly regional interpretations of Bohemian transcriptions of the Italian traditions. Of all these early German types, the Bohemian and Cologne schools contributed most to the formative stage of the tradition.

GENERAL CHARACTERISTICS OF GERMAN PRIMITIVES

The Byzantine and Italian features are embedded in a form that evokes a quite characteristic feeling of both heaviness and delicacy combined. The delicacy relates to surface-details of miniature-like elements borrowed from the French or Flemish, or of color-and-light relationships retained from the Italians; and since the handling is crude rather than subtle, the delicacy tempers but does not fundamentally alter the inherent heaviness or coarseness of the German form.

The heritage from the Byzantines consists of the two-dimensional patterns; the gold or uniformly colored background which is, at times, studded at regular intervals with a decorative motif; the application of color in sharply defined compartments; the general symmetrical disposition of masses which, however, is enriched by a greater abundance of linear rhythms and a more varied use of light and color. Accentuated, detached, or superposed highlights in modeling are additional Byzantine derivations. Planes are placed one behind another rather than in the flat Byzantine manner and hence give the effect of spatial recession and its accompanying complexity of color-relationships.

The color in general is mainly derived from the Italians and is arranged in compartments which blend well with the light-patterns. Sometimes the color retains the dull somberness of the Umbrians and of certain types of Byzantine panels, but as the tradition develops the color-scheme often assumes a brightness close to that of the early Florentines and Sienese, even the garishness of such men as Lorenzo Monaco and Fra Angelico. At other times, the color has a certain depth as well as good sensuous quality and fine relationships. The drawing of textiles by juxtaposed parallel areas of color and light, which is a Sienese derivation, renders a measure of solidity and of textural quality, but the patterns thus formed, as well as those on brocades, gold background, or other gold ornaments, are usually coarse and crude in comparison with corresponding features in the Italians. A characteristic German feature is the use of parallel striæ indented upon the gold surface, often running in a single oblique direction, independently of the enveloping roundness of a garment or the curve or movement of individual folds or objects. Occasionally, too, the indented striations are replaced by hatchings of thin black lines.

Drawing, in general, remains sharply linear as in the Byzantines and Italians, but the Germans usually add a certain rigidity to the flowing willowy figures of the Sienese, a rigidity which bestows a character of charming gauche naïveté upon the early German tradition as a whole. This rigidity produces at times an effect closely akin to that of Uccello's linear rhythms and distorted perspective. In contrast to the Italians, the Germans lack the feeling of austerity, of grandeur, or majesty: their art reflects a more homely interpretation of religious subject-matter.

THE BOHEMIAN SCHOOL

The Bohemian versions of Italian features and methods gave direction to the German tradition as a whole and to the particular forms it assumed in various parts of the country. The Bohemian characteristics appear in the two most important and typical pictures of the region, the "Votive Picture of the Archbishop Očko v. Vlašim" (408) and "Wittingau Altarpiece" (410).

The principal influence upon the Bohemian school in general is that of the Sienese version of Byzantine traits, with practically all Sienese earmarks in evidence.[1] Tommaso da Modena and other Italians, whose forms are essentially Sienese, worked in Prague in the second half of the fourteenth century, and Bohemian painters visited Italy; these two facts explain the Sienese influence. The Bohemians added a more ponderous color, a type of drawing that accentuates distortion, a more naïve and cruder type of expression, and quite individual decorative effects. All of these features became basic in the entire German tradition. The Bohemians modified the Sienese type of drawing and modeling by using a preponderance of light over color, particularly in the treatment of draperies. The areas of light often include the entire rounded volume of a fold, so that in effect the drawing is by means of colored light rather than by either illuminated color or color-and-light pattern. A frequent use of brownish glazes or transparent washes over part of flat gold motifs in brocades, achieves an effect of modeling and depth in folds, across which the brocade pattern lies flatly without any foreshortening.

Another characteristic of Bohemian painting is that the individual masses, figures particularly, bulk so large in proportion to the space enclosed by the entire picture, that, in contrast to the Sienese, Bohemian compositions are often sequences of emphasized individual masses rather than of grouped units commensurate with the expanse of space employed. Still another departure from the Sienese is a more dramatic effect of color-contrasts, due partly to the Bohemian use of accentuated lighted areas in conjunction with a use of somber browns. This drama of contrasts, and the above-noted disproportion between masses and space, are obviously responsible for a great part of the heaviness which the Bohemians engrafted upon the Sienese form.

The chief importance of the early Bohemian school is its influence upon the entire subsequent German tradition: the "Wittingau Altarpiece" (410), for instance, is the obvious source of Master Francke's drawing, color, presentation of subject-matter, and, particularly, compositional organization; the general Bohemian

[1] Sienese droop, flowing rhythm of draperies, fluid area of light on crest of folds, scroll-like edges of folds, green cast to complexion, slant of eyes and elongation of eyes toward temples, irregularly crenellated rocks.

use of color and light in drawing was adopted by the Lower Saxony Master of the Laurenziuskirche Altarpiece who worked in Cologne, and it was continued by the Cologne masters in general. Other Bohemian features which became fixed in the German tradition as a whole are: the grotesque type of drawing characterized by distorted proportions of the human figure, such as large heads and squatty bodies; decorative patterns of wounds; stylized rufflelike clouds; and the general undercurrent of crudeness, coarseness, or even raucousness in color-relationships. About the middle of the fifteenth century, the Bohemians acquired a certain delicacy in the treatment of details, and developed a method of painting chubby faces with pursed lips. Both of these later characteristics persist in the fifteenth century German tradition as a whole, and were emphasized by the Cologne and Rhine region painters. From the fifteenth century on, Bohemian painting is weakened by admixture of various Flemish and other German elements, and becomes stereotyped and academic in interpretation and execution.

PAINTING IN THE RHINE REGION

Early Rhenish painting is divisible into three stages, represented by: (1) The early German modification of the Byzantine form as, for instance, in the "Ingeburge Psalter" (52), and the Rhenish panels "Scenes from the Life of Christ" (378). (2) The concentration of influences and tendencies which materialized into the distinctive Cologne school of the fourteenth and fifteenth centuries. (3) The paintings, variously classified as of the Middle-Rhine or of the Upper-Rhine region, which, while close to the Cologne form, offer local characteristics and, at times, considerable individuality—for instance, "Madonna and Child, with Female Saints" (41) and "Garden of Paradise" (109).

PAINTING PREVIOUS TO THE COLOGNE SCHOOL

The first of these stages, that preceding the Cologne school, is indicative of German tendencies rather than establishing a definite German form. This work is really of Franco-German origin, born of the reciprocal influences between French and German primitive forms.[2] Its general tendency is German because the contributions of the Rhine painters, although influencing French artists, were

[2] For analytic study of this type see Barnes and de Mazia, *The French Primitives and Their Forms*, pp. 140–146, Barnes Foundation Press, Merion, Pa., 1931.

absorbed more completely by the Germans. The miniatures in the manuscript known as the "Ingeburge Psalter" (52), belong to this borderland type. These miniatures reveal a step toward typical German features in the exotic character and glare of their color-scheme, the brilliance of burnished gold, the dead uniformity in surface and texture of flesh, the modeling of draperies by a central band of light on folds, which are edged with color-band contours, and the representation of hair by an active pattern of curvilinear strands. Another example of German characteristics in their formative stage is furnished by the Rhenish panels "Scenes from the Life of Christ" (378). The identifying traits here are: the weight and solidity of color; the light-and-color pattern on folds, not so sharply linear or angular as in the Byzantines and the "Ingeburge Psalter" (52), is of a type midway between the angular fluidity of folds in the "Ingeburge Psalter" and the freely flowing movement typical of the later Germans; the sequence of color and light in modeling combine into units that have a degree of three-dimensional solidity approaching that in the Bohemian and Cologne schools' adaptation of the similar Byzantine pattern; modeling in general tends toward rounded volumes rather than flat planes; the Sienese-droop type of contour-drawing involves volumes as well as outline; the technical execution in the drawing of hair is practically identical to that in other German primitives of the same period.[3] In these Rhenish panels, as in the German primitives specified in the footnote, faces, hair, beards, and white textiles are drawn with brownish lines over flatly colored areas. Other points of kinship exist also in the treatment of iconographic detail and in the general presentation of subject-matter. Minor differences are found in the modeling of the flesh: three-dimensional quality is obtained in the Rhenish panels by spots of white highlights on nose, nostrils, chin, cheeks, ears, and knuckles, and in the other German primitives referred to, by broad red smudges on cheeks, lower jaw, and neck.

THE COLOGNE SCHOOL

The Cologne school represents the most active and perhaps the most important phase of early German painting. Its early mem-

[3] E.g., the Cologne "Crucifixion, and Four Scenes from the Life of Christ" (58); the Cologne "Annunciation" (59) and "Presentation" (60); and the Frankfurt "Altenburg Altarpiece" (108).

bers, chiefly anonymous, were co-heirs with other northern schools of German painting to the Bohemian version of the Byzantine and Italian traditions, and to the influences of the early German woodcuts, the primitive Rhine-region painters, and the French miniaturists, particularly Honoré.

The importance of the Cologne school in a study of the German tradition as a whole can scarcely be overestimated. The antecedent influences of the Byzantine, Italian, Bohemian, and French traditions became, in the Cologne school, crystallized in a distinctive, characteristic form. It not only produced pictures and masters of outstanding individuality and creative power, but it profoundly influenced practically all of the important later German painters. The work of Strigel, Grünewald, and Dürer, for instance, though enriched by Flemish and other German influences, follows essentially the form developed by the Cologne painters. From the same source came much of the inspiration of important painters of the Netherlands: the drawing of Bosch and of Pieter Brueghel, for instance, is clearly founded upon essentials perceptible in the work of the Cologne Master of "Mount Calvary," of Stefan Lochner, and of the Cologne Master of "Life of Mary." The Cologne school was also one of the formative elements in the development of one phase of the French primitives—the Franco-German form.[4]

GENERAL CHARACTERISTICS OF THE COLOGNE FORM

The Cologne painters in general show more imagination in the creative use of antecedent traditions than did the Bohemians, and greater versatility in the treatment of composition, in the handling of color, light, and space, and in drawing and modeling. In composition they followed the Byzantine-Italian prototypes in the use of bilateral symmetry, gold background, gold halos, ancona type of altarpiece, and compact sets of planes; but their composition is more varied, less conventional than the Bohemian, and their distribution of masses and of plastic units is further away from the prototypes. Their organization of units produces, in general, a great feeling of liveliness, due partly to the multiplicity of units of subject-matter actively participating in the episode depicted, and partly also to units treated emphatically as decoration. Bilateral

[4] See Barnes and de Mazia, *The French Primitives and Their Forms*, pp. 140-166, Barnes Foundation Press, Merion, Pa., 1931.

disposition of masses is relieved of static quality and monotony by the activity of rhythms and contrasts in subsidiary components, by the quality of the color, and by the vividness of the drawing.

The color has lost the almost constant dulness of the Bohemians', and acquired some of the brightness of the Italian color-scheme, particularly the Lorenzo Monaco - Fra Angelico type. It has the Italian brightness, compartmental arrangement, and effect of staccato rhythms; but it differs from the Italians in basic essentials: the tones are heavier, harsher, and more opaque; the contrast-relations tend toward the abrupt rather than the subtle; the general color-key is often dominated by a high-pitched yellow gold; the pattern of light is more pronounced than in the Italians, and the relationship between color and light is more active.

Light is so used as to yield quite characteristic effects. It is accentuated in small and large areas, more or less circumscribed by contrasting adjoining color with which it forms vivid patterns and contrasts; it enhances decoration by helping to form color-chords, and by its own vivifying pattern; it contributes to dramatic expression and to the character of the composition by lively highlighted spots, streaks, and areas; it participates in expressive, decorative, and compositional movement by the flow of light and color in the drawing and modeling of figures and draperies.

Drawing is a product of the creative use of several antecedent factors. The linear definition of areas and volumes, often by a narrow dark-colored or inklike independent line, probably derives from early German woodcuts. The linear swirl in the drawing of hair, beards, and draperies attests a source in the early Rhenish painters and miniaturists—for instance, the illustrator of the "Ingeburge Psalter" (52)—and in the French form of Honoré. The linear drawing is bent to many characteristic distortions which render both active movement and psychological states —fear, joy, suffering—with a high degree of vividness, distinction, and plastic reality. Its chief characteristic is an intermingling of curvilinear gracefulness with rigid angularity which imparts to the distorted, often grotesque, proportions of figures an appealing awkwardness, and a charming naïveté to the depiction of either reposeful states or alert and vivacious attitudes. The drawing of faces and features, which is forecast in the Bohemians, reaches its fullest degree of integration in the work of Stefan Lochner. The faces are comparatively large, oval, delicately curved, with broad high forehead and pointed rounded chin. Eyes, nose, and mouth, drawn with short fluid curves and often in detail, occupy a rather small area of the face and thus accentuate the characteristic expanse of forehead and cheeks. Eyes are heavy-lidded, take on a circular rather than an elongated shape, and have the dark of the iris emphasized rather than the white of the eyeball. Proportionately large heads on short bodies often give a characteristic squatty appearance to figures. Hands, frequently elongated, are not only very expressive but also active as decorative units. The fluidity of the Sienese droop, so prevalent in the Bohemians, is retained but it is transformed in appearance and effect, in part by its relationships to the differently proportioned figures, in part by its content of color and light. The Cologne painters' more sensitive feeling for relationships between colors and between color and light, gives greater individuality to the patterns of folds than exists in the Bohemians. Decoration in general is more deeply embedded in the form than is usually the case in other German primitives, with the exception of Master Francke.

Modeling of flesh and draperies, which stems from the Florentine-Sienese-Bohemian form, develops into two distinctive Cologne types. One of these, close to the Bohemian, consists of a juxtaposition of parallel color-bands, related to broad color-contour, and enclosing a lighted band in the center of the volume. In the other type, more frequent in late than in early work, the gradation of color in the flesh is very subtle, involving no abrupt changes in light and shadow, with the exception of accentuated, usually small, spots or streaks of highlights. The result is a smooth, slowly curved surface of volume, the one-piece effect of which is hardly disturbed by the depth of the eyes, the chubby nose and chin, and the pursed full lips.

Space is clean-cut with no perceptible atmosphere, although an effect of glow results from the reverberation of bright color-units and the glitter of gold. The foreground and middle distance are punctuated by numerous compactly grouped volumes and planes, while the distant background is usually a uniformly colored area, which is either patterned or plain, and often of gold. In the best work, the color-relations between the figures or objects placed against the uniformly colored setting, convey a feeling of ambiency and receding space.

Landscape as a setting for figures is treated as a decorative framework in a manner characteristic of the school. The landscape recedes into distance through a series of variously lighted green areas which form a horizon by their abrupt contact with either the background of single color or gold, or the blue of the distant hills or sky. There is practically no use of the Italian blue in aërial perspective and no intermediary tones or gradations between foreground and background. Hills and mounds are rendered in broadly painted, comparatively flat areas of cool green, slightly modeled on the upper contour by a darker green or brownish tone. Thus generalized the landscape becomes a series of large geometrically shaped rhythmic areas, which interlock with a sort of zigzag movement. This carries the eye into the distance and at the same time affords a simple patterned setting for the detailed figures and objects in the foreground.

After the middle of the fifteenth century, Flemish traits greatly modify the Cologne tradition but seldom entirely submerge its distinctive character. Under the influence of the late Antwerp school the Cologne form deteriorated into utter banality.

The "Altarpiece—Life of Jesus—from the Cologne Laurenziuskirche" [5] (70), painted by an unknown master of Lower Saxony (active c.1360 – c.1380), shows a kinship with much earlier painting in that region—for instance, the "Antependium from the Cloister of Wennigsen a. Deister" (124)—which already had added a slight German flavor to the essentially Byzantine foundation of its form. In the Laurenziuskirche panels the Bohemian and Italian traits are synthesized in a new entity with increased expressive and decorative content. The color is superior to the Italian in sensuous appeal, in its diversification by light into rich and variegated color-chords, and in its greater weight and solidity. The drawing, with its apparent gaucheries and odd distortions, not only gives to its Bohemian derivations fuller expressive and decorative values, but is a consistent feature of a more original, more comprehensive, and better organized design. States of mind are rendered vividly and convincingly without the monotony of the early Bohemians nor the almost uniform dolefulness of the early Italian and Flemish painters. The deep religious subject-matter, the human values of sorrow, pity, and reverence, picturesquely reënforced by rich color and naïve drawing, are embodied in a plastic form of such reality that the

[5] In the Lutheran Church at Netze, the "Altarpiece" (268) bears so many characteristics in common with these Cologne panels that it may safely be assumed to have been painted by the same man.

Lochner (69)   Analysis, page 438

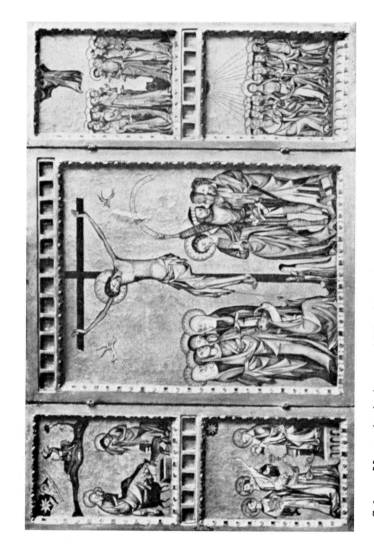

Cologne Master, beginning or middle of the
fourteenth century (58)

Analysis, page 437

Master Francke (120)

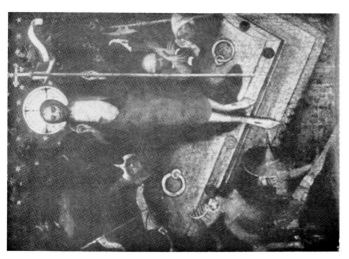

Bohemian Master, end of
fourteenth century (409)

Holbein (336)

Huber (213).

depicted tragedy is suffused with a sense of profound esthetic satisfaction.

Stefan Lochner (c.1400 – c.1451) came from the Bodensee region, but worked in Cologne in the trend of the local tradition, to which he gave a new distinctive form by refining several of its features. The type of faces already described as characteristic of the Cologne school reaches its most complete phase in his work. His type of drawing and his use of Italian color are forecast in "Madonna with Pea-Blossom" (65) and "Saint Veronica" (258), both of the Cologne school of the beginning of the fifteenth century and probably by the same so-called Cologne Master of "Saint Veronica." Lochner had greater technical skill and command of his medium than any previous member of the Cologne school, and the finish of his work contrasts strikingly with the naïveté, the apparent crudity of, for instance, the "Altarpiece—Life of Jesus—from the Cologne Laurenziuskirche" (70), though the painter of the latter was a more important creative artist. Lochner drew on the early Flemish form in general, and upon the Florentine-Sienese-Bohemian for the type, expression, and general drawing of faces and figures, the tendency toward pyramidal mass-composition, and the use of a gold background. He sometimes modified the relation of foreground to gold background by curving the junction line between the two, thus producing an appearance of concave space. The early Italian influence is perceptible in the disposition of objects in space, in the utilization of architectural features, and in the color. To every plastic aspect borrowed, Lochner gives a new and individual form. His range of colors is very extensive; it includes delicate, Fra Angelico-like tones to which is added a structural function comparable to Bellini's, and hence an added depth; some of the hues are bright, others somber, but both alike are pleasing, and of a richness rarely equaled by the early Germans.

Stefan Lochner's treatment of landscape by minutely detailed rendering of grass, flowers, and other objects, is the vehicle for a kind of drawing which harmonizes with the charm and delicacy of his general design. Lochner's line-drawing is comparable to the best of the Florentine and Sienese. Sharp outlines, sometimes broadened by colored shadow, are reënforced by a delicate light-and-shade modeling, occasional contour of reflected light, and color-chords richly illuminated; and many choice and subtle dis-

[185]

tortions offer striking patterns and vivid depiction of states of mind. The grotesqueness, active movement, and caricature-effects in his "Last Judgment" (67) are probably the source of similar effects in Bosch, Brueghel, and Cranach. Dürer also doubt-lessly owes much to him. As usual with the Germans, Lochner adds weight to the Florentine tradition, and consequently a con-viction and power lacking in most of the early Italians.

The dominating influence of van Eyck, van der Weyden, and Bouts upon the Cologne school after the middle of the fifteenth century is illustrated by a series of eight pictures, the "Lyversberg Passion" (64), supposedly an early work by the **Cologne Master of "Life of Mary"** (active 1460–1480). The Flemish influence is obvious in the expression of faces, in the treatment of folds and draperies, and in the arrangement of figures, landscape, and other details. The German painter's contribution consists of brighter color, more numerous geometrically shaped patterns of color, line, and light, and brilliant gold backgrounds. The colors, more garish than those of the contemporary Italians, are well related, and are applied partly in uniform areas, partly in areas varied by light and color-chords. Modeling is done chiefly by light and shadow, and the textural quality of flesh tends toward wooden-ness. Gold brocades are indented in coarse parallel striations as if mechanically done by an instrument. With few exceptions, the arrangement of masses is asymmetrical, with one side usually composed of a large number of compactly placed figures, the other side comparatively empty; but even when the space is most densely packed it is never overcrowded, and the succession of intervals is full of charm. This dramatic and highly effective space-composition is further enhanced by the light which floods the interspaces, and by the varied and striking linear pattern.

In the other, presumably later, works by the Cologne Master of "Life of Mary"—for instance, "Crucifixion" (61) and "Scenes from the Life of Mary" (257)—the Flemish influences continue but the handling is less conventional, the color richer and better related, and the general quality more refined. In many of the pic-tures by the Cologne Master of "Life of Mary," the familiar German background of gold is retained, but space and a sense of natural landscape are rendered creatively, and with a delicacy further developed in the German tradition by the Cologne Master of "Holy Kinship" (*Meister der Heiligen Sippe*), Strigel, and Dürer.

[186]

The later German artists owe much to the Cologne Master of "Life of Mary": for example, Grünewald adopts his mass-composition and depiction of active movement; Schongauer's Colmar panels, "Christ's Passion" (57), are scarcely more than conventional repetitions of the treatment of subject-matter in "Lyversberg Passion" (64); Dürer's painting of hair and gowns is an enriched transcription of that in "Scenes from the Life of Mary" (257); the germ of Strigel's color, movement, and general expression in his "Conrad Rehlingen and his Children" (264), is seen in two pictures by the Cologne Master of "Life of Mary": "Saint Barbara with Donor and Seven Daughters" (62) and "Saint Katherine with Donor and Eight Sons" (63).

Barthel (or Bartholomäus) Bruyn, the Elder (1493–c.1555) is extraordinarily skilful, and his use of the Flemish, Italian, and German traditions is competent, but he adds nothing very personal to them.

RHINE–REGION PAINTING CONTEMPORARY TO COLOGNE SCHOOL

This type, variously classified as Middle-Rhine, or Upper-Rhine tradition, is illustrated by three pictures of distinction, "Garden of Paradise" (109) of c.1410, "Madonna and Child, with Female Saints" (41) of c.1420, and "Mary with Female Saints" (72) of c.1420–1430. They differ from the Cologne type mainly in that their color-pattern is greatly increased in decorative character, chiefly by the miniaturelike rendering of details in fabrics, foliage, and jewels, executed with great technical skill. The ensembles recall, by their appealing color, drawing of figures, and meticulous rendering of detail, the work of van Eyck, Memling, the early French and Flemish miniaturists, the French diptych panel, "Madonna in Garden" (75), and the contemporary Cologne form represented by Lochner. In common with German painting in general, color has a weighty feeling whereby the lightness and daintiness borrowed from the other traditions are reinterpreted in a characteristic German manner.

Other traits common to this group of Rhine-region pictures are: volumes so grouped in compact receding planes that their placing emphasizes the lateral extension of the group from side to side of the picture; the chubbiness of faces often exaggerated, and all the faces in a single picture usually executed alike in their drawing, distortions, modeling, color, and facial expression.

PAINTING IN WESTPHALIA

In the thirteenth and fourteenth centuries, painting in Westphalia follows the general German adaptations of Byzantine features. Its distinguishing traits are a relatively more marked archaism, accentuation of angular patterns and, at times, masklike faces with peculiar distortion of features, such as extraordinary slant to the eyes and accentuatedly curved eyelids.

Konrad von Soest (active c.1404) is the outstanding figure in the Westphalian tradition. His work as represented in Bad Wildungen[6] and Münster[7] is perhaps more Italian in color, compositional arrangement, and general lightness than that of the other early Germans.[8] Von Soest's fine feeling for plastic organization is shown by his ingeniously varied distribution of line, masses, and color-patterns, in a design marked by the activity of planes, appealing units of space-composition, and effective rhythmic contrasts. He is also a great colorist. In his "Altarpiece of Crucifixion" (26), bright, fresh, cheerful, and delicate pinks, blues, and ivories, are interspersed with dark colors, especially a blackish green. The result is a strange somber dignity merged with brightness, which imparts to the ensemble a combined effect of the color-schemes of Fra Angelico and of Uccello. The color-scheme and gold setting recall similar decorative effects in Persian miniatures, in Fouquet's miniatures, in "Legend of St. Ursula" (48) by the Bruges Master of "Legend of St. Ursula," and in Memling's "Scenes from the Legend of St. Ursula" (49). The colors convey no real textural feeling: flesh is like alabaster or wood, and the faces resemble masks; objects have but slight three-dimensional solidity and very little tendency to a light-and-shadow modeling. Draperies lack the familiar early German accentuated pattern of light and are rendered by broad color-areas which function less

[6] "Altarpiece of Crucifixion" (26).

[7] "Crowning of the Virgin" (266) and "Outpouring of the Holy Spirit" (267).

[8] In this Italian derivation as well as in several characteristics of his drawing, pattern of hands, color, and compositional organization of the subject-matter, Konrad von Soest is allied to the painter of the "Marienkirche Altarpiece, from Göttingen" (126), and his work resembles also, but to much less extent, the Hannover "Golden Panels, from Lüneburg" (125).

as light than as units in the total color-pattern. The subtle patterns made by highlighted spots and streaks of paint do not disrupt the one-piece type of modeling reminiscent of Piero della Francesca. The fluid and graceful drawing portrays vivid, animated, and intent facial expressions. Distortions resemble the general Westphalian type only in the slight slant of the eyes and occasional masklike faces. His distortions are quite individual in character: pointed chin; accentuation of the white lower part of the conjunctiva; elongation of feet and hands; fingers slender, elongated, and bent backward; the little finger and thumb separated from the compact central mass of the three other fingers. This peculiar treatment of the hands creates a number of interesting and varied patterns in harmony with the dainty linear grace of numerous other decorative motifs, such as patterns made by crisply profiled heads, highlights on flesh, arabesque silhouette of dogs, demons, etc., curvilinear scrolls, ruffled stylized clouds, and linearly highlighted drawing of angels placed against a dark setting.

Von Soest's departure from the conventional German treatment of draperies and brocades also contributes to the individuality of both his total form and its decorative character. Draperies proper are painted in broad areas of generally light color, and the gold pattern in brocades is rendered in broad smooth areas, only occasionally marked by commalike indentations and not patterned by the familiar German striation of indented parallel lines.

Von Soest's work embodies a fine and very personal integration of plastic and human values and is outstanding among early German primitives.

Master of Liesborn (active c.1465) derives basically from Lochner but with the Italian influences so much in the ascendency that his form is a curious combination of Florentine and Cologne school features. His characteristic, charming, delicate coloring has the general lightness and freshness of Fra Angelico's at its best and is engrafted upon the heavier general German form. His versions of the gentle and graceful characteristics of Lochner, at times, lead to a soft effeminate sentimentality and to a mechanical type of drawing and painting, particularly apparent in the rendering of flesh. Faces in a single picture seldom vary either in color or drawing, and they seem flat and often masklike, with little feeling of solidity. The rather uniform pink or grayish-pink of their surface is delicately mottled by slight color-chords which merge into the smoothly modeled unit of flesh, realistic in texture and appearance. In three-quarter views of faces, the absence of foreshortening of the more distant cheek, and the use of a black outline along its contour, make that part of the face seem to come forward and thus accentuate the masklike appearance. His best work shows a fine feeling for design but the majority of his paintings are either mediocre or academic.

PAINTING IN HAMBURG REGION

This section of Germany developed no single typical form. Its outstanding figures, Master Bertram and Master Francke, were both influenced by the Bohemians, but each was distinct from the other in their adaptations of German and Italian traits.

Master Bertram (active c.1379) was mechanical and formalistic in drawing, color, modeling, and in the pose and facial expression of figures. Attitudes are ungainly, drawing is clumsy, the feeling of naïveté in his work seems affected, color has a fence-paint quality, and the range of its effects is very limited. The flesh of wooden, unreal texture, is rendered in a reddish-coppery hue, mechanistically used and scarcely varied by light or by shadow. Similarity in facial expressions is increased by an unvaried distortion of mouths which consists of the accentuation of the center of each lip. Draperies and other objects, even though patterned with folds or with streaks of light, likewise appear artificial and are devoid of color-charm, and his use of the Bohemian shadows in glazes over gold brocades is mechanical. Figures, animals, trees, and other objects appear as rounded wooden masses set in planes, but with such lack of distinction in space-relationships that they function chiefly as representative objects and symbols. Master Bertram's form as a whole may be summed up as story-telling representation of a low order.

Master Francke (active c.1424), judged by his work in the Hamburg Museum,[9] is one of the most important and individual

[9] "Adoration of the Kings" (114); "Bearing of the Cross" (115); "Birth of Christ" (116); "Christ, Man of Sorrows" (117); "Entombment" (118); "Flagellation of Christ" (119); "Flight of St. Thomas of Canterbury" (120); "Martyrdom of St. Thomas of Canterbury" (121); "Resurrection" (122); "Women of the Crucifixion" (123).

of the early German painters. His form embodies a creative use of traits found in the early Italians and Bohemians: from Uccello he takes the color-scheme of ivory and brownish green, the accentuated linear patterns, the pose of figures, and the skilful and picturesque treatment of space. His debt to the Sienese appears in the use of green shadows in the painting of flesh; and to the Bohemians he owes the general foundation of his drawing and the method of treating draperies and brocades. The striking red background studded with stars of gold, and the tendency to a definite compositional arrangement of units in planes, recall the Bohemian "Wittingau Altarpiece" (410). He far surpasses the Bohemian artist in technical skill, as well as in the variety and subtlety of effects in both decoration and expression. His color is richer, more solid, and better lighted, and his space-composition is infinitely superior. His extensive use of compact planes that often interpenetrate, creates a rhythmic series of distortions, movements, color-patterns, all finely coördinated in the total design. The color-units and color-relations, particularly in the painting of flesh, recall effects familiar in French and Spanish primitives. His color is sometimes glaring but is usually of good sensuous quality enriched by a deep glow and numerous color-chords. Indeed, Master Francke is one of the greatest and most individual colorists in the German tradition.

VARIOUS OTHER INDIVIDUAL VERSIONS OF THE GERMAN TRADITION

Konrad Witz (c.1398–1447) was born in Switzerland but worked in the German tradition. The essential feeling of the fourteenth and fifteenth century Italians, especially of the Florentines, appears in his clear atmosphere, the bright colors in his figures, and his linear drawing, each feature transformed and made weightier by union with German traits. His "Christ on the Cross" (46) is Italian in color-scheme and Flemish (van Eyck) in its mass-composition, miniature-quality, enamel-like surface, the dark green in the landscape-setting, and in the drawing and modeling of figures.

Witz' space-composition is of a high order. Masses often appear like sculptured or carved wooden blocks, set at very clean-cut intervals from each other. His color is often raucous, its surface tinselly, and its application like that of fence-paint, but on the whole he relates colors successfully and brings the plastic units together in well-integrated designs.

Martin Schongauer (1445-1491) is, in nearly all of his work, an academician who used the Cologne and Flemish forms to paint pictures which are not leavened by high quality of any sort. He did achieve, however, in his "Madonna in the Garden of Roses" (54), one picture of high excellence: a richly decorative plastic expression of deep human values is executed in solid, well-illuminated color that glows almost like Titian's. The form, however, is too close to Memling's to pass as an important creation. His chief claim to plastic distinction is skilful manipulation of line to produce effective linear rhythms. His color is usually dry and rather superficial, and its defective relationships to light and shadow make it seem comparatively muddy. Technical ability of a high order enabled him to produce a number of small, charming, delicate, clean-cut, well-lighted pictures, but in spite of their appeal they lack any fundamental originality. His narratives are more literal than plastic, and the Italian and Flemish subjects and manner of handling become in his work conventional and much less effective.

Bernhard Strigel (1461-1528), in his best work,[10] makes very individual creative use of some of the strongest features of the Cologne-school tradition. Upon the Cologne Master of "Life of Mary," he drew for his general color-scheme, spatial organization, vigorous drawing, and general feeling of landscape; he adopted Lochner's treatment of draperies and general expressiveness, and he utilized the characteristic compositional arrangement of the tradition. Strigel's color is at times very rich, and is finely related in greatly varied rhythmic ensembles. The union of light and color is so complete that in brilliantly illuminated areas, the color is felt as strongly as the light, while darker areas suffer no loss in richness or luminosity. His technical execution is skilful and ingeniously varied; for instance, the modeling of flesh sometimes has a one-piece effect not unlike Piero della Francesca's and Domenico Veneziano's; at other times a brownish reddish-yellow attains to greater weight and textural realism than in Dürer's and Holbein's use of a similar color. Line is usually sharp, and unites

[10] E.g., "Saint Norbert as Protector" (43); "Sibylle von Freyberg" (265); "Kaiser Maximilian I" (443).

with light and color in graceful, flowing, rhythmic curvilinear patterns akin to, but heavier than, Dürer's. A particularly effective form of space-composition is achieved by a succession of receding planes of different size and color; in portraits this effect of successive planes is often heightened by a small window on the side of the picture opposite that occupied by the figure, which is placed against planes of drapery, wall, or screen. This striking and individual note was later much employed by Tintoretto. At his best, Strigel renders character solidly and convincingly, without virtuosity or mechanical tricks, in original and well-integrated compositions. Much of his work is, however, banal and academic portraiture.

Mathias Grünewald (active c.1485 – c.1530) created a very personal form by his masterly use of space and color in a fusion of Italian, Flemish, and German characteristics. Depth is sometimes rendered in the manner of Uccello, sometimes extended to infinity, and the units of space-composition are usually enlivened and enriched by unusual and appealing patterns of color, line, and light. His drawing is sharply linear, the contours forming extraordinary linear patterns which, at times, convey a feeling of quivering movement in a manner anticipating El Greco's. These linear patterns are usually fused with color and vivid and unusual light-patterns in an esthetically moving organic whole, which carries the profound emotional state portrayed.

Grünewald's color is essentially that of the German version of the early Florentine color, and occasionally, as in his greatest painting "Crucifixion" (55), deep and rich color-chords enliven many parts of the picture. His masterful use of space and the vivid, often eerie, lighting, lend great power to the bizarre color-effects. Color-ensembles vary from an adaptation of the Uccello-Flemish dark greens and browns to a delicate color-scheme like Fra Filippo Lippi's, and to the bright, bizarre, and even garish color often seen in the Cologne Master of "Holy Kinship." Grünewald's work is uneven and much of it is rather academic, but as embodiments of personal vision and the creative utilization of preceding traditions his outstanding achievements, for example "Crucifixion" (55) and "Entombment" (56) from the Isenheim Altarpiece, bear comparison with the greatest pictures of all time.

The post-primitive phase of the German tradition rose to its supreme height in **Albrecht Dürer** (1471–1528). His point of departure was the form developed by the Cologne school at its best, under the influence of the early Florentines and van Eyck, but it was the native German elements rather than the Flemish and Italian accretions that most influenced him. In delicacy and expressiveness of line, in the filiform painting of hair, in the rendering of textiles, and in mass-composition, Dürer owes much to Lochner and something to the Cologne Master of "Life of Mary," but his color is richer and more essentially expressive. The narrow inklike line of the early German painters occasionally also reappears in Dürer. Whatever he took from any source was usually recreated in a unique and personal manner.

Dürer's forms are greatly varied. His early work, exemplified by a number of portraits of himself and of his father, has a comparatively subdued color-scheme, which seen from a distance gives the impression of uniformity; but the color is so interspersed with light and related to shadow and space that differences slight in themselves produce an effect of rich variety. His color, moreover, is wonderfully subtle, flowing, and harmoniously organized. With a grayish-blue, grayish-green, or other subdued color, Dürer accomplished what Rembrandt and Daumier did with golden browns; that is, an effulgence radiates from within the color, and the color so dominates line, light, and space that the effect is one of extreme color-power. No less appealing are the extraordinarily fine and active rhythms of space and light, and the delicate interior linear patterns, reminiscent sometimes of van Eyck, and made up of hair, wrinkles, and facial features in general.

Dürer's line is usually clean-cut, light, fluid, graceful, and curvilinear in tendency. Its expressiveness is due to its integration with the other plastic elements, a fact which becomes strikingly apparent when his Louvre drawing "Erasmus" (312) is compared with Holbein's drawing "Head of Man" (337) in the same gallery: Holbein relies exclusively upon line, to which shadows have been added; Dürer's line, light, and shadow are fused in a single plastic unit, infinitely more expressive of character.

In Dürer's pictures of the period after 1500, the color-scheme becomes bright, as in "Girl's Portrait" (30), "Adoration of the Magi" (94), "Apostles John and Peter" (259), "Apostles Paul and Mark" (260), and even daringly brilliant, as in the Berlin "Madonna" (34), in which the conventional colors of the early Italians are related in a harmonious ensemble, more German than Italian, and arranged in striking patterns of color-areas and lines.

This picture seems to represent an experiment of Dürer, an adventure outside his usual form, in which he succeeds in getting rid of the raucous tinsel-quality of bright colors in a manner similar to Matisse's. In its background, for example, two areas of very bright and vividly contrasting color are brought into relation by a narrow band of ivory, which thus has the same plastic function as many of Matisse's broad colored contours. Some of Dürer's portraits, for example "Head of Woman" (31), recall Bellini in their broad and relatively loose drawing.

The flesh-painting in Dürer's later portraits lacks the eerie, lurid quality of his earlier work. The ivory-white complexion of the Louvre "Self-Portrait" (313), for example, is abandoned in favor of a variously toned reddish-yellowish hue, comparatively monochromatic like Holbein's, but differentiated from that and from every other German portrait-painter's by a pinkish tinge. This color enters into harmonious relations with the light, delicate colors of the rest of the picture and forms an ensemble quite characteristic of Dürer. In spite of detailed representation, Dürer's portraits carry conviction by their profound grasp of character and their fully realized plastic embodiment of dignity, strength, gentleness, serenity, and poetry.

Dürer's large compositions [11] are far inferior in all plastic essentials to his portraits and small-scale pictures, and are interesting chiefly for their fine space-composition, and because they show his interpretation of the antecedent Cologne form as it came through Lochner.

In his work as a whole, he creates out of the German tradition a new form from which the characteristic heaviness is eliminated and all the force retained, a form which has a fluidity, grace, charm, and power completely distinctive of himself.

The influence of Dürer on German portraiture is exemplified by the work of **Martin Schaffner** (c.1480 – c.1541), **Wolf Huber** (c.1485–1553), and **Peter Gertner** (active 1521–1540), each of whom made Dürer's creations the basis of personal expressions. In Schaffner the outstanding plastic quality is a subtle use of space both in the composition of groups or single figures and in the sense of infinity in the background. Faces are modeled either with a one-piece effect reminiscent of Domenico Veneziano or

[11] E.g., "Adoration of the Trinity by All the Saints" (440) and "Ten Thousand Martyrs of Nicodemia" (441).

with a cameolike surface, varied by linear patterns, which is characteristic of van Eyck, Mantegna, and Dürer.

Gertner took over Dürer's delicately colored patterned stuffs and general type of flesh-painting, and related figures and brightly colored backgrounds in harmonious, boldly patterned color-ensembles.

Huber adopted Dürer's filiform painting of hair, and general manner of drawing, but his figures, dressed in dark, flowered stuffs, are usually set against a background of landscape dominated by a bright, charming, and well-illuminated blue, somewhat reminiscent of Bellini's.

The work of **Lucas Cranach, the Elder** (1472–1553) falls into two general types—portraits, and groups of figures moving actively in landscape-settings. In the latter the drawing and flesh-painting follow models found in Lochner, Dürer, Leonardo, Metsys, Mabuse, and the late Antwerp school; his surfaces are occasionally rich, but in the main the paintings are comparatively heavy and mechanically executed. To the Flemish tradition he adds weight and an appealing pattern of sensitive line derived from Dürer but which in Cranach has much the same virtues and defects as Botticelli's. As a rule his portraits also lack originality, insight, or essential plastic strength, even though many of them have considerable decorative value, due more to the varied and striking color-contrasts between figure and background than to the color and linear patterns in the figures themselves.

Hans Baldung (Grien) (c.1475–1545) follows the Cologne school in color and space-composition. To the bright colors of the Cologne painters he adds a glaring raucous quality; his colors enter into linear compartmental arrangements productive of weird, speciously attained, dramatic effects. In his "Vanity" (439), he discards strident color, overemphasizes patterns, and attains to genuine artistic achievement by a convincing color-ensemble and very effective space-composition. This accomplishment is rare in Baldung, for in most of his work the discordant colors have the tinsel-quality of such inferior Italians as Dosso Dossi, Andrea Solario, or Carlo Sasaccio. His use of paint is mechanical, and the gross discrepancy between the quality of execution in different parts of the same picture often entails serious plastic disintegration. He resembles Holbein in literalism, and depends much upon rhythmic pattern in features and garments, obviously an imitation of Dürer's. Despite skilful execution, his work is, in general, destitute of force, dignity, or essential expressiveness.

The work of **Hans Holbein, the Younger** (1497–1543) ranks with that of Dürer, Titian, and Rembrandt in popular esteem and financial value. Although born in Basel, his stock was German and his form is based upon that tradition after it had assimilated the contributions of preceding schools. His short life was full of rich experiences that came from wide travel in northern Europe, England, and Italy, and from meeting many of the outstanding characters of the time, many of whose portraits he painted. The foreign influences on his work are correspondingly numerous, and include those of van Eyck, the Flemings in general, the Florentines, and the Venetians. His use of the traditions shows no evidence of deliberate imitation and is sufficiently personal to merit some distinction but not to justify his reputation as a great artist. Frequently his pictures are mere hash-ups of the contributions of preceding painters.

Holbein is essentially a portrait-painter whose means are more photographic than plastic. His extraordinary skill enabled him to reproduce meticulously the literal detail of ornaments and fabrics in the manner of, but vastly inferior to, that of Domenico Veneziano and other Italians. Compared, in this respect, to the sixteenth century French painters, Corneille de Lyon and the Clouets, his coarseness and heaviness are flagrant.

Holbein's color has about the same structural character as that of the best of his German predecessors but his rendering of textural quality is unconvincing: flesh has usually the uniformity of putty, or a wooden character, destitute of the vital quality of flesh; the reddish-brown tone of the complexion is repeated mechanically, with no adaptation to the specific character of individual faces or hands.[12]

Throughout the picture his fusion of reddish-brown color with light is in essentials a version of the Venetian glow, with much the same compositional function, but its effect is feebler, it is monotonously employed, and it partakes of the aridity and bleakness of the individual colors which enter into it. The monotony of his surfaces is often relieved by linear patterns in faces, figures, and incidental objects, which testify to the fact that Holbein is a

[12] E.g., "Anne of Cleves" (335); "Erasmus" (336).

greater draughtsman than painter. The apparent richness in "Ambassadors" (138) is due to superficial illumination rather than to any depth or glow from within. When Holbein uses bright colors, as in "Anne of Cleves" (335), the result is a patterned rather than a colorful picture.

The plastic element that Holbein uses with most success is space. Often a multitude of units in all parts of the canvas are finely placed in space and interrelated in a complex design, which is enriched by sharp line and effective contrast of light and shadow. Yet fine as are the individual units and their relations to one another in groups, the groups lack any such organizing force of color as is to be found, for example, in Carpaccio, and they fall short of integration in the total form.

Holbein's two portraits of "Erasmus" (27 and 336) are satisfying realizations of character in good plastic terms. Apart from these, his pictures chiefly represent the virtuosity of an able craftsman. His figures, compared to Dürer's, lack grace, fluidity, vitality; they seem merely posed. As an artist, his chief claim to distinction is that he rarely fails to relate color, line, light, and space to each other; the relationships, however, remain superficial, for the individual means are too easily distinguished, and do not unite in an organic expressive form. Photographic representation skilfully executed probably explains Holbein's popular appeal.

CHAPTER VIII

THE FLEMISH TRADITION [1]

THE FLEMISH tradition, prior to Rubens, has a distinctive color-scheme, founded on a greenish brown, and different from that of any school of Italian painting. Tempered with light to make a rhythmic form, this color-scheme gives an effect quite unlike that of the Italian grays, blues, pinks, and golds; it has an intrinsic vigor and solidity, and the lighting prevents the tendency to heaviness from becoming objectionable. Even when the color is bright, it is arid compared with Italian color. The general effect of the form is dignified and quiet, and conveys a feeling of ambient atmosphere. The painting of stuffs and landscapes is done with fulness of perspective and of detail and with considerable skill, but in the best men of the school the detail is rarely so emphasized as to distract the attention: accentuation is dissolved in the uni-fied form of the whole painting. Compared with the Italians, the Flemings seem heavy, and this holds true even in the case of such Italians as Carpaccio, who also employed detailed textural repre-sentations, but who retained the unmistakable Italian delicacy. The Flemings, however, are not wholly at a disadvantage because of the heaviness, since it gives added solidity, weight, and dignity. Sometimes, the tendency to miniature-painting, which appears well marked even in so great a painter as van Eyck, becomes the characteristic form of virtuosity and academicism of the school. There is also a disposition to make use of religious subjects of a sentimental type.

Flemish textiles are as a rule less decorative and more naturalis-istic than those of the early Italians; that is, their units portray the actual fabric rather than serve as color-areas in a patterned composition. Although thickly painted, especially in the shaded areas which often are raised on the edges, their surface is relatively smooth and glossy. A stress on the local color of the material rather than on patterns of light and shadow or on modulations of color, together with a detailed depiction of representative elements, is

[1] See also discussion on Rubens, p. 157.

chiefly responsible for the heavy and realistic character of the Flemish draperies. The Flemings obtain the gold appearance of brocades by means of a brownish-tan layer of paint which is either hatched or dotted with thick yellow highlights that are varied in direction, size, and degree of accentuation. The colored intervals between the brocaded motifs are often raised above the surface of the lighter parts, as is also the outline of dark color around the golden-yellow pattern. Flemish folds, with their balance of decorative and expressive values, represent a synthesis of the rigid linear patterns of the Byzantines with the modeling by light, line, and color of the Italians. The resulting, highly patterned drapery is a series of predominantly triangular motifs each unit of which adequately represents texture, solidity, weight, and movement.

In its effect upon subsequent painting the Flemish tradition is as vital as any other: for example, upon the work of van Eyck and his followers are founded many of the chief characteristics of the German and French traditions as represented by such important men as Dürer and Fouquet; while the Flemish color-scheme and general weightiness incorporated in the work of Rubens exercised its effect upon much of the best post-Renaissance painting.

Jan van Eyck (c.1385–1441) is the most important of the northern artists and stands further away from Italian influences than any other of the Flemings. He is the originator of the distinctive Flemish form with its characteristic color-scheme, clear-cut drawing, and the miniaturelike painting of detail in features, objects, stuffs, and landscape. He handles all the plastic means adequately and with equal skill, variety, and originality. Line, light, color, and space, each makes appealing patterns of its own; and these patterns enter into harmonious relations with each other to effect compositions of great distinction and power. While his pictures seem almost photographic, they are unified plastic ensembles. His portraits represent supreme examples of an artist's legitimate use of the plastic means to convey the reality of human character with dignity, strength, and power. His "Man's Portrait" (135), in the London National Gallery, can justly be put on a level with a fine Rembrandt: it seems to have been breathed upon the canvas; it represents the supreme degree of technical skill in the perfect example of art concealing art. His vigor and subtlety are illustrated by a triumph of color-power attained by means of colors that are of almost surface-thinness, yet carry an effect of structural

Flemish Master, active c. 1480 (190)

van Eyck (35)

Flemish Master, fifteenth century (189)

Lucas van Leyden (216)

quality. The landscape-background in his "Crucifixion" (35), for example, is as solid, real, powerfully moving, and fine as Venetian landscape at its best, and is realized without the obvious structural color. The relatively thin surface-colors are so related to one another and so enriched by light, that they emerge with a new meaning as a series of color-forms which, at a distance, have the character of miniature-painting plus the solidity of the Venetians. The figures and the cross are flooded with light, the colors in the gowns are glowing, and this light-element placed upon a relatively dark background produces an effect of quiet drama, appropriate to the pathos and tragedy of the scene. No "Crucifixion" in the Italian school has greater conviction, more appeal, or plastic rightness than van Eyck's. Absolutely Flemish in the use of all the plastic means, he owes little if anything to any of the great Italians except what every artist, since the thirteenth century, owes to Giotto. But the debt of numerous subsequent painters to van Eyck is enormous and testifies to his importance in the traditions. His influence is clearly traceable throughout the whole Flemish school and extends to the French fifteenth and sixteenth century painters, especially Fouquet and the Clouets, as well as to the Cologne Masters and the later Germans, including Dürer and Holbein. Indeed, much of what is best in Dürer comes from van Eyck; for example, the manner in which line and color in the flesh are related to wrinkles and features to make patterns which, while highly expressive of character, also constitute surfaces that are no less interesting in themselves than as representation. Dürer's merging of colors in the background of portraits is very similar in quality to van Eyck's, and these two masters have also a similar ability to weld into a moving ensemble the individual patterns made up of color, line, light, shadow, and space.

Van Eyck's originality and his contribution of a new, characteristically Flemish, form are comparable to Giotto's revolutionary transformation of the preceding Byzantine form, to Bellini's enrichment of the Italian tradition, and to Dürer's and Cézanne's creative innovations. He not only stands at the head of the Flemish movement which he originated, but his forms constitute the source of some of the most significant features of important succeeding traditions.

Petrus Christus (c.1410 – c.1473), starting with the tradition of van Eyck, adds to it a polished surface such as is often seen in the best of the Florentines. There is a glow and sheen in the painting of particular objects or textiles which sometimes degenerates into the quality of tinsel; but at its best it anticipates the exquisite polished surface in van der Heyden, Berckheyde, and Vermeer. Most of Petrus Christus' work is in portraiture. He models with light and color blended to make rich color-chords, and free from drabness or muddiness even in the shadows. There is an enrichment of patterns by light, shadow, and color, which makes his faces more interesting than those of any other Flemish painter except van Eyck. Petrus Christus' "Marco Barbarigo" (130), for example, compared with van Eyck's "Man's Portrait" (135), both in the London National Gallery, falls short of the color-power and the convincing characterization in the van Eyck. Petrus Christus manifests a fine sense of color-relations, by which colors very close in tone are so differentiated by linear contour that background and figure form a contrast. His linear patterns are taken from van Eyck, but his color is on the whole less solid. At his best, he sometimes attains to the composed, dignified, characterful, facial expressions of van Eyck, but with less depth of color and with a little more heaviness, more akin to Strigel's. Compared with the sixteenth century French painters, such as the Clouets and Corneille de Lyon, Petrus Christus is more solid, weighty, varied, and characterful, but his form as a whole shows too little departure from van Eyck's to establish him as a creative artist of the first rank. His paintings other than portraits show him to be a great master of space and of general composition. Space-composition, for example, in "Deposition from the Cross" (270), varies from a subtle arrangement of the objects and intervals in the foreground to an appealing relation between widely separated objects in the background.

The work of **Roger van der Weyden** (c.1400–1464) shows more tendency toward pose and psychological literalism than the painting of such men as van Eyck, Bouts, or Lucas van Leyden. His form is more delicate than solid, he makes light dominant throughout the painting, and, in spite of the delicate charm, the net result is rather slight. His tendency to miniature-painting in landscape— walls, trees, and other objects—recalls somewhat van Eyck, but the form is much thinner. His enamel-like color-surfaces, while pleasing, have comparatively little of the rich porcelain-quality characteristic of the surfaces found in the good Dutch artists. The color-areas are by no means bleak or devoid of attraction, but their richness is somewhat diminished because of the rather mechanical and overaccentuated use of light. Light is his general means of unifying his pictures, while in Bouts, for instance, the color more fully serves that function. Van der Weyden's integration of light, line, and color is more successful in grass, flowers, and trees, and secures a greater degree of conviction than in faces, in which the effect is comparatively superficial. He depends too much on light and shadow for his modeling and shows too little ingenuity and variety in the linear patterns. His color, while delicate and well supported by light, functions chiefly as a decorative pattern for religious story-telling. A few notes, at times, recall the solid colors used later by Vermeer, with the difference that in van der Weyden the rich, solid color appears only in parts of the painting, while in Vermeer's best work there is equal solidity throughout and equally effective merging with light or shadow. Facial expressions, even when intent, usually lack the color-relations needed to give plastic support to their photographic representation. It is the relative neglect of color and overemphasis upon light that exclude van der Weyden from the higher artistic ranks. On the whole, his pictures are rather academic; they are precise, detailed, photographic, slight, and more posed than convincing.

The chief contributions of **Dirk Bouts** (c.1400–1475) to the Flemish tradition consist in his unconventional patterns and in his new relations of light and color. His kinship to van Eyck is seen in vivid psychological characterization, which, because of coördinated use of the plastic means, does not descend to mere illustration.

The linear aspect of his work is generally pronounced. Line defines contour sharply, much in the manner of the early Florentines, and is organized into striking and appealing patterns reminiscent of Uccello, of the Cologne Master of "Life of Mary," and of Bosch and Brueghel. His drawing sometimes has a tendency toward the expressiveness of Bosch, but falls short of caricature; it renders with full plastic conviction the intentness of people actively doing things without pose or affectation. His strongly realized backgrounds and bright figures in foregrounds make integral wholes, as van der Weyden's do not, with a corresponding gain in plastic power.

Bouts' color follows the general Flemish tradition, as exemplified by van Eyck and Memling. It is heavier than that of the Italians, is of comparatively little structural value, but it is by no means a mere filling-in between contours. His color is juicy for a Fleming and contrasts advantageously with the general dryness of Gerard David's. It is richer and deeper than Roger van der Weyden's and less conventionally arranged. The colors are usually well coördinated with light, so that illumination of color results in plastic units of great charm and conviction. His light is less a general illumination than van der Weyden's, and there is a relative isolation of the light-pattern from that of the other elements, even when space-, light-, and color-patterns merge well into an ensemble; consequently, the light-patterns are very striking. His color, while rich and illuminated, has relatively little internal glow. Bouts' "Entombment" (128) shows that he can achieve with light colors what he does so well with dark ones; it is very much in the spirit, color-scheme, and general treatment of Piero della Francesca.

His flesh-painting is done in the manner of van Eyck. He models by similar means of light and shadow fused with color varying from an ivory tone, through various shades, into a yellowish red. A comparison of the pictures of Bouts and Memling in the London National Gallery reveals that Bouts' painting of flesh is more varied and interesting, less mechanical, less wooden than that of Memling. His painting of details in figured stuffs has the accurate, meticulous character of the school of van Eyck.

The surfaces in Bouts are enamel-like, and his color gives the effect of stuffs in a manner somewhat similar to Vermeer's in "Girl with Turban" (112)—a manner midway between Ingres's and Tintoretto's. In the use of space he often follows Uccello: the horizon is lifted to the top of the picture and the spatial intervals are organized in unconventional and well-realized units, reënforced by patterns made up of all the plastic means, especially line and light. His fine patterns of light and shadow, and his ability to make light function as a general illumination and as a means of organizing a picture, are carried over into his portraits. These become triumphs of integrated means, though they are not of the quality of van Eyck's or Dürer's.

Hans Memling's (c.1430–1494) derivation from van Eyck is obvious in drawing, in psychological characterization, in the static quality of his figures, and in the miniature-painting in landscape-settings. His detailed painting of stuffs, such as rugs and draperies, is quite miniaturelike in effect but his landscapes, though detailed, are broader than Roger van der Weyden's. The attention to detail in trees, leaves, and other similar objects is counterbalanced by a frequent use of a broad, relatively uniform, flat, blue band at the horizon, simplifications in facial features such as lashless eyelids, and a tendency toward broad spots of color in background figures. This contrast effects a general design quite different from van Eyck's. In Memling's portraits, the facial expressions, somber and set, maintain the same tendency to rigidity, the composed dignity, and the intentness to be noted in van Eyck. Figures, however, are less solid, and often wooden in comparison with those of van Eyck or Petrus Christus, and they show less variation in the hues of the flesh. His "Woman's Portrait" (354) in the Louvre is an exception: it offers a wealth of wonderful patterns of line and light used in relation to rich ivory and slate gray-blue colors; the effect is both delicate and convincing. His portrait "Duke of Cleves" (144), in the London National Gallery, is also a striking picture: its color is rich, and in the one-piece modeling of the face it achieves a higher degree of textural realism, with less mechanical use of paint than is usual with him.

Memling's method of painting flesh and textiles is generally so unvaried that the effect is rather mechanical and lifeless, although monotony is somewhat relieved by interesting shadows and patterns. His contours are sharply linear and well related to color, and the color-scheme is the conventional brown-green hue with very little of the Italian blue. His comparatively indifferent use of light in general illumination makes his work as a whole somber, and his color, insufficiently vivified and diversified, often seems monotonous. Compared to van Eyck, his color lacks glow and structural quality, and is drier, less varied, and not so rich, even when brighter. In his "Seven Joys of Mary" (262), there is an attempt to vary the usual Flemish color-ensemble by an injection of the Fra Angelico range of pinks, yellows, and blues: the effect is decidedly heavier than in the Italians and more closely akin to that in Lochner; indeed Memling's work often has numerous points of affinity with Lochner's in drawing, color, and general form. He is far inferior to van Eyck as an expressive artist and as a technician, and he is less original in his variation of traditions than Bouts or van der Weyden.

Hugo van der Goes (active c. 1435–1482), one of the most important Flemish artists, works in the van Eyck - van der Weyden manner, to which he adds individuality by the frequent use of a line of reflected light to define contour. This feature was taken over by many French painters of the fifteenth century, notably those belonging to the school of the so-called Master of Moulins. His color is brighter than Memling's and is heavy compared with the Italian. The Germans—Cranach in his drawing of figures, and even Dürer—also owe much to van der Goes.

Hieronymus Bosch (c.1460–1516) is famous chiefly as an illustrator, particularly as a caricaturist. His drawing is a modification of that of the Cologne school, especially of Lochner's adaptation of the early Italian line, to which Bosch added the element of caricature. The majority of his work portrays grotesque or ironical scenes of everyday life in which the comical phases are emphasized. He also painted a number of religious pictures of great dignity, and in these the drawing is as expressive as that in the scenes noted above. In other words, he was able to adapt his ability of portraying character to both the sublime and the ridiculous. So fascinating are Bosch's powers as an illustrator that his importance as a colorist is likely to be overlooked. But the truth is that the illustrative force of his work is fundamentally due to a powerful plastic form of which color is one of the chief elements. The framework of this color-construction is a background of contrasting colors arranged in an unusual and striking pattern, a sort of screen, against which are set a great variety of units made up of line, color, space, and light. These individual units also furnish striking notes of color-contrast. His drama is thus plastically legitimate: contrast, rhythm, thrust and counterthrust, appear in a succession of convincing plastic units.

Bosch's extraordinarily expressive and varied drawing is due to much more than line, terse and expressive as that is: a fusion of line, light, and color renders the essence of an object or a situation. His highly expressive figures, in a word, gain added meaning in that they are forceful color-units, located in well-ordered space, and arranged upon a vividly patterned background. That is his design, his plot, his theme. From his success in fitting these smaller units into the general scheme of color-patterns with all-pervasive rhythms, Bosch derives his importance as an artist. Studied from this point of view, his work reveals decorative qualities almost as absorbing as the turmoil and drama which his figures so vividly enact.

Bosch is a great master of space: his rhythmic colored units are set at intervals of great variety, while distance is rendered some-times almost literally, and at other times by elevation toward the top of the canvas—a distortion which enhances the interest of the pattern. His color is, in general, Flemish, with echoes of the early Germans in a quasi-structural effect to which is added a consider-able degree of surface-charm. His light, while generally not accen-tuated, illuminates color by interspersion; it also forms light-patterns recognizable in the general framework which can be analyzed into their ultimate small units almost as readily as can his pervasive color-patterns.

The work of **Gerard David** (c.1460–1523) is usually dry and cool, compared with that of Bouts or Memling. There is little charm, quality, or variety in his application of paint, and excessive monotony in figures testifies to his lack of imagination. Although occasionally as in "Crucifixion" (272), representative and plastic forms are combined successfully, David's work is in the main a technical version of the classic Flemish tradition. In general, his chief virtue is an attractive arrangement of predominantly linear patterns.

Quentin Metsys (c.1460–1530) is chiefly interesting as showing the decadence of the Flemish tradition through an infusion of flashy academic Italian traits. He was extremely skilful as a painter, but his bright color and accentuated light result chiefly in melodrama, and his form is essentially eclectic. He thus paved the way for the degeneration of the Flemish form into the low estate represented by the Antwerp school.

Joachim Patinir (c.1480–1524) has his name given to many pictures which are obviously not the work of the same man. Among those which approach a similar general form, some achieve very dramatic effects by contrasts of somber color and areas of light. Though these effects are striking they are more specious and less truly plastic than those found in van Leyden. While these pic-tures are mainly patterns with only a fair degree of color-organiza-tion, they have sometimes, as in the Vienna "Baptism of Christ" (442), considerable abstract esthetic power.

Adriaen Isenbrant (c.1485–1551) shows a close kinship at times to Memling and at other times to Gerard David. He often excels

Memling in expressive power and variety of technique, and his color is richer, deeper, and better used compositionally than David's. His color-scheme is usually darker than Memling's, but admirably organized patterns of light save his pictures from somberness. The line is usually broken in continuity and contours are rather blurred; these are merged with well-illuminated color to secure a loose, floating, graceful quality not unlike that of the Venetians. In his "Nativity" (273), a glow akin to Titian's pervades part of the picture. This rather hazy atmosphere, combined with nicely placed and very charming light-patterns, distinguishes Isenbrant from most of the Flemings. His mass-composition is effective, though there is little emphasis upon space. Modeling is done with so much interfusion of color that the accentuated light in the highly illuminated areas, and also the shadows, seem deeply colorful; this is true even when the color is a pale ivory.

Lucas van Leyden (1494–1533), though born in Holland and generally classified among the Dutch painters, follows chiefly the Flemish methods which he merges with the German and Italian traditions. He owes something to Dürer in the derivation of his very expressive line and to Bosch in certain characteristics of his drawing of faces and figures. His work does not in general bear the Flemish stamp, but he has evidently adapted, added to, and modified the Flemish form and achieved a distinctive personal creation. He towers far above Flemings such as Gerard David and Roger van der Weyden in his more effective and original utilization of the traditions and the plastic means, especially light. He is a supreme master of light, both in its use as an instrument for creating patterns and in its skilful adaptation to different themes. Combined with color light becomes, as it does in Salomon van Ruysdael's landscapes, the principal means of unifying his compositions. It is also accentuated in a quite special manner, akin to Leonardo's, to yield an effect of drama, but its better plastic integration makes the drama much more convincing than Leonardo's. In the relation of light to dark areas there is also anticipation of Tintoretto and El Greco.

Van Leyden's color interspersed with light yields a rich colorglow, whereby charm and conviction are added to the rather heavy effect characteristic of the Flemings. His imaginative use of color is revealed in variations that extend from harmonies of somber tones to well-merged blues and reds which are light and delicate and yet solid. Flesh has a rather lurid quality, reminiscent of some of the early Florentines, but the addition of color to light-and-shadow modeling achieves a richer and more individual character than in the Florentines. Color-relations, reënforced by light, lend a convincing reality to stuffs, the decorative value of which is also enhanced by striking and unusual rhythms and patterns. His outlines, sharply linear, are often broken into sections and become expressive movements suggestive of Dürer. Sometimes these movements are short swirls which impart a Rubens-like feeling of vivacity. His best and most characteristic pictures are highly patterned compositions in which the division of the surface into planes is the dominating trait, almost as obviously as it is in cubistic designs. His supremely skilful use of light makes this distribution of planes very effective and yields results similar to those seen in the work of the modern American artist, Demuth.

Van Leyden's backgrounds are more broadly painted than is usual with the Flemings. They are not literally rendered but distorted to make a sort of screen, which serves as a setting for the story in the foreground. In portraiture, he follows van Eyck and his school in an almost photographic reproduction of detail. His "Man's Portrait" (142) resembles, in its light-pattern, Antonello da Messina's "Condottiere" (355), but the Italian painting is the more mechanical and artificial, and the less plastic of the two. His most important picture, "Adoration of the Magi" (216), reveals an artistic status not inferior to that of van Eyck at his best.

Pieter Brueghel, the Elder (1525–1569), is more German than Flemish in his relation to the traditions. By the use of brighter color and more actively moving figures he adds vivacity to the usually rather static Flemish form. His color, though not actually structural, usually has the adequately constructive quality of the Cologne Masters. He ranks among the great colorists for much the same reason that Bosch does: his general framework is a striking pattern of contrasting colors maintained throughout the picture by a well-integrated series of rhythmic plastic units functioning as subsidiary color-patterns. In his general pattern, the broad areas of rather uniform color serve also as patterns of light, and the illumination of color places him among the great masters of light. Areas of a rather brownish tan are often juxtaposed with greenish areas, and upon the background so formed are scattered trees, houses, animals, and other masses, which constitute the secondary units in the composition. Brueghel's patterns are pronouncedly linear. Line is very expressive and is obviously derived from Bosch and the early Cologne painters, especially Lochner and the Cologne Master of "Life of Mary." Its great variety appears when it is contrasted, in similar compositions, with the monotony of Cranach's. It is nearly always sharp, dividing color-areas into clear-cut sections, which make up the very interesting patterns already described. These rhythmic patterns of line and mass anticipate contemporary tendencies in design.

The many figures, composed of color, line, and light, which seem at first sight to be scattered at random all over the picture are in fact the units in a varied and effective space-composition, which achieves the effect of charming landscape extending through vast distances. The designs have plastic unity of a high order in that the foreground, the seat of varied and active movement, is contrasted and yet merged with a background of landscape which serves as an expressive and decorative foil to the activity of the figures.

Brueghel renders the spirit of place sometimes with the lightness and delicacy of pastel as, for example, in "Harvesters" (269), at other times, with as much vigorousness as in Vermeer's "Little Street" (9). Like Bosch, he is a great illustrator whose figures are plastic units, in which essentials are rendered without over-accentuation of any sort. The actively moving figures are elements in a well-integrated general design and hence truly expressive. The stories told, though sometimes biblical in theme, are saturated with the local spirit of homely peasant-life, often with a rustic humor verging upon the grotesque. The intense psychological realism is so well executed plastically that illustration never clashes with pictorial organization.

Antonio Moro (c.1519 – c.1578) adds to the Flemish tradition a deep, rich, and solid color, that gives to his best work some of the general quality of the great Venetians.

CHAPTER IX

THE DUTCH TRADITION

THE INFLUENCE of the seventeenth century Dutch painters upon the art of other countries has been enormous. The Dutch landscape-form is, apart from Rembrandt's portrait-painting, the most important in this respect, because it is obviously the most original and most expressive of the Dutch spirit. Genre-painting, as it appears in the best pictures of Vermeer and Pieter de Hooch, has also determined the character of the work of many subsequent painters, but unfortunately it has inspired imitation more often than artistic creation. A much greater influence for good was that of Dutch still-life; this type of painting, indeed, was more important because of its effect upon such artists as Chardin, than because of any achievements of its own. Hals has also had a considerable influence, chiefly technical. His great skill with the brush pointed the way to some of Goya's and Manet's best effects; but in lesser men it operated chiefly to inspire displays of virtuosity, barren of genuine esthetic significance.

Jan van Goyen (1596–1656), more important than his Dutch forbears, Gerritsz and van der Velde, ranks as an artist with his contemporary Claude le Lorrain. Both van Goyen and Claude felt the intrinsic interest of landscape, and each contributed a new landscape-form, personal, profound, and distinctive, which was the inspiration of many subsequent painters. While Claude painted the majesty, grandeur, and mysticism of nature in epic terms, van Goyen reported episodes of the Dutch countryside and seacoast, overflowing with a charming intime poetry. This quality of intimacy became dominant throughout the Dutch school and appeared even more clearly in the genre-painters. In this, as well as in his technical use of the plastic means, van Goyen was a forerunner of Constable and the Barbizon painters.

The basis of van Goyen's design, like that of all his followers, is a dramatic contrast of light and dark areas in the composition. His pictures are bathed in light and organized by light: light used not only as a pattern but as a reënforcement of all the other plastic means. Against a general light-and-dark pattern in the background and overhead, are set the rhythmic series of his compositional masses, and this contrast provides the essence of his very moving drama. The suffusion of these masses with light gives life to them and enhances the general drama of the design by a pervasive reënforcement of line, color, and space.

Van Goyen's color is deep, rich, varied, yet delicate and charming. Its general tone is that of ivory, subtly varied with nuances of yellow, gray, and green; in conviction and power it surpasses anything Hobbema accomplishes with heavier and brighter colors. Quiet, yet rich, color-chords pervade the contrasting light and dark areas and masses in the composition, and endow them with depth and conviction. These color-chords are rhythmically placed in spatial relations of infinite variety, which add a further delicacy and reality to the general form. Out of color also are constructed the material objects in the picture, boats, houses, trees, etc., and with such economy and supreme command of means that it seems to be the color that renders the essential quality of the material. The Ruysdaels followed him in their treatment of material objects, using brighter colors, but they never equaled him in strength and conviction.

In composition in three dimensions, though van Goyen is less successful than Salomon van Ruysdael in emphasizing the intervals between masses and achieving the effect of general spaciousness, his command of space is commensurate with the character of the scene depicted. His compact compositions are never crowded or jumbled, and in extensive organizations there is an airiness combined with an effective placing of masses, which adds to the charm of nature.

Van Goyen was in the best sense a great draughtsman: his drawing renders characteristic individuality by a fusion of light, color, and line. Objects are convincing because color enters into their essential structure. In his work the essence of Dutch landscape and of the Dutch tradition in painting—the dramatic contrast of light and shadow—are rendered both by light and by color, and his integration of all the plastic means is more successful than that of any of his rivals. He was the first to discover and portray by plastic means the poetry and charm of nature as nature appears in Holland.

Salomon van Ruysdael (c.1600–1670) obviously owes much to van Goyen in general composition, in the use of color and light, and in the treatment of skies, but the debt does not compromise his own individuality, expressed in a powerful and characteristic form. His subject-matter is usually not, as often with van Goyen, harbor scenes: he turns to the countryside—fields interspersed with groups of trees and houses.

His plastic superiority to Hobbema is shown by a comparison of his "Halt" (5) with Hobbema's "Water Mill" (3). Ruysdael's powerful design is realized through the medium of a marvelous use of light. The accentuated light, colored with a rich ivory, flows through the spatial intervals, vivifies the color in the objects, and makes a charming pattern in clouds, housetops, wall, and stream. This finely organized unit is dramatically contrasted with a dark unit, into which enter the houses, trees, cows, and figures in the foreground. This pattern with its luminous color makes the Hobbema, in contrast, seem drab: in the latter the light fails to lend glow to the color or to give plastic organization to the picture, so that the light-dark drama remains isolated and specious, while in the Ruysdael the light, working throughout the picture, reënforces and unifies all the other plastic elements.

Ruysdael's color is neither very solid nor profound, but, brightened and diversified by light, it forms everywhere a rich variety of harmonies and contrasts. These yield a charm of surface, though the charm remains superficial when compared with the profundity and weight attainable by the use of structural color. This is not to say that Ruysdael's objects lack the degree of solidity requisite for his purpose: his subject-matter, Dutch landscape, is better adapted to treatment by accentuation of light and space than by emphasis upon structural color. Color and solidity of objects are thus appropriately made secondary to space-composition, and, in this, color plays its rôle by appearing as a diffuse illumination, thus adding conviction and interest to spatial intervals. Indeed, one of his chief accomplishments is his ability to fuse light and color in a homogeneous entity which includes the whole picture. In this he anticipates in a measure the impressionists, though his foreground, middleground, and background remain clearly distinguishable.

Ruysdael's stature as a great artist was heightened by his rare gift for putting quality into paint: in his delicate porcelainlike surfaces the colors seem to flow into each other as they do in mother-of-pearl—an effect seen at its best in Vermeer's "Little Street" (9), and in van der Heyden and Berckheyde. This superb technical skill enabled Ruysdael to attain successfully results which, examined in isolation, may seem like mere *tours de force*, but which, in reality, are supreme artistic achievements. For example, in "Halt" (5), above analyzed, the accentuation of light comes perilously close to speciousness, but its use as a reënforcing and synthesizing agent for all the other plastic means brings the picture within the field of great art. Ruysdael combined a fine intelligence with an extraordinarily skilful technique.

Adriaen Brouwer (c.1605–1638) is usually classified as Flemish but his form is typically Dutch. He cheapens the tradition by an excess of illustrative features and by overaccentuation of light-and-dark contrasts. Feeling for landscape is supplanted by preoccupation with compositional relations on a small scale: houses and trees give the effect of chairs and tables, and his landscapes are really magnified interiors. This is apparent in his "Halt" (28), in which the surfaces of rock, grass, ground are not only brittle but cottony. The majority of Brouwer's work consists of interior scenes—usually groups of persons in active movement—which are for the most part high-grade illustrations.

One of the sources of Corot's inspiration is traceable to **Paul Potter** (1625–1654), whose landscapes, episodic in character, are bathed in an atmosphere of charm, delicacy, and placidity. Potter is akin to Claude le Lorrain in that his interest is less in the detail of figures, masses, objects, than in the general spirit of place. His space-composition is very charming and his use of light effective. The poetry of his landscapes is chiefly due to lyric power of color, sensitively related to light and atmosphere. His color is slight and lacking in depth, but there is strength and eloquence in his color-relations and color-suffusions. In general feeling, Potter is light in comparison to Claude—just as Corot is light in comparison to Courbet.

Jacob van Ruisdael (c.1628–1682) added practically nothing of his own to the landscape-form of his predecessors. His color is somewhat brighter than Salomon van Ruysdael's, but his inability to merge it with light and to put quality into paint deprives his pictures of color-power and makes them comparatively thin and mechanical. His use of the familiar contrasting light and dark areas is specious: his light remains a relatively isolated series of spots, which never really fuse with color to reënforce it. The effect is rather stereotyped and superficial: his cascades and streams, for example, often seem metallic, with none of the actual feeling of water. In his hands Dutch landscape has become attenuated to a conventional form, which seldom reveals either individual vision or ability to paraphrase with distinction. The Barbizon school probably owes something to his manner of rendering forest-scenes, but on the whole his pictures are painty, papery, feeble, and unconvincing.

Meindert Hobbema (1638–1709) follows the traditional Dutch landscape-form. His composition consists of a rather uniform distribution of volumes around a house, which has almost invariably a red roof—the red being used in connection with large masses of accentuated light that heighten the contrast of light and dark. The effect is specious when compared with the union of light, color, and line in van Goyen. The limitations of Hobbema's form in comparison with those of van Goyen and Salomon van Ruysdael have already been discussed. A further appraisal of Hobbema's caliber may be made by a comparison of two very similar compositions, his "Water Mill" (3) and Jacob van Ruisdael's "Landscape with Water Mill" (4). The Hobbema is much stronger in every way: in fact, the Ruisdael looks like a weak imitation of it. Hobbema's greater technical command over his means is obvious, though in general his themes and the manner of their treatment are too similar to those of other painters to indicate much imagination. In this picture his color is of better quality, more solid than Jacob van Ruisdael's, and more finely organized and related to the other plastic means.

In general, Hobbema's color-scheme is a dark green with spots of lighter green on the leaves, relieved and enriched by red roofs, and varied by the grayish-green structure of such objects as wharves, houses, and logs. These various color-components are distributed in minor notes throughout, so that a sort of rhythmic pattern of color enlivens the picture. While his color is in some areas enriched by light, the light is more often merely laid upon it, so that there is no adequate luminosity of color. This trick of spot-lighting, especially perceptible in the trunks of trees and on the edges of wharves, roofs, and similar details, makes the color seem superficial rather than essentially expressive. The color-ensembles are well coördinated, no one color is used at the expense of any other, but in none of them is there the richness which comes from the successful structural use of color fused with light. It is the heaviness of color, rather than structural quality, which gives a weighty solidity to the masses. His skies are always of the conventional Dutch type: light clouds interspersed with dark ones form the foundation of his dramatic effects, but the lack of balance in the plastic means makes the drama mechanical. Occasionally, he rises to great heights, but even in his best pictures he falls short of Salomon van Ruysdael's ability to coördinate light and color: Hobbema's shadows are less colorful and less convincing than his lighted areas. On the whole his compositions have too little originality and are too uneven in their plastic quality to be considered important works of art.

Frans Hals (c.1580–1666) displays the characteristic Dutch fondness for drama and for textural effects, both in the surface of his canvases as a whole and in the rendering of particular objects. He had incomparable technical skill, apparent especially in his use of the brush: he simplified detail often to the point of executing it with a single brush stroke. Unfortunately, this obvious technique is usually employed in a spirit of display, with no rendering of essential character as Velásquez or Manet attained by the same means. The brush strokes also add to the general drama of the picture, but speciously, and the melodramatic quality is often increased by the fact that all sorts of other devices—theatrically posed figure, exaggerated gesture and facial expression, obvious contrast between figure and background—constitute the basis of the drama. His color is dry, either drab or overbright, and superficial, he lacks fundamental originality and grasp of deep human values, and in spite of his good disposition of masses his virtuosity rarely achieves real esthetic significance.

Rembrandt (1606–1669) ranks with the greatest of artists in originality, plastic power, and in the universality of the emotions his work calls forth. His form is wholly characteristic, has never been successfully imitated, and is achieved by less obvious use of the plastic means than that of any other artist of the first rank. His means are chiefly light and shadow, used in the combination known as chiaroscuro, by which he is able to depict a whole gamut of powerful emotions deeply tinged with mysticism. His line and color are limited in variety, but through their merging with chiaroscuro they give a richness and depth of color, and effects of strong linear patterns infinitely more varied and moving than

Vermeer (113)

Analysis, page 452

Terborch (385)

those which many artists of high rank obtain from intricate line and bright color.

Rembrandt's chiaroscuro is anticipated in some of the work of Masaccio and Andrea del Castagno, in whom, however, it is only incidental. In Caravaggio it was used more nearly as a mere technical instrument. With Rembrandt it becomes a method systematically employed and used with such consummate skill that it appears not as a technical stunt or trick but as the only natural and inevitable means of showing what he had to show. Through it color assumes quite a new quality and greatly increased power. The actual colors are very limited in range, usually somber and rarely very bright, but in conjunction with chiaroscuro they assume a great variety of color-forms of immense expressive power. Dark colors, usually brown, go from darkness, through varying degrees of light, to rich, glowing gold and back again to darkness in a pleasing graceful flow reënforced by lines, spots of light, and masses, all merging into a moving, harmonious design.

With line and space his chiaroscuro also works miracles. Drawing mainly by linear effects, as we see it in Botticelli, Leonardo, or Raphael, does not exist in Rembrandt: the outline is so related to the chiaroscuro as to achieve a distinctness of contour by means so subtle that it is impossible to say how the work is done. A dark figure against a background hardly less dark, becomes a mass which stands out with fine three-dimensional solidity from a background that recedes to infinity. With means of equal subtlety, he renders the different feelings of hair, flesh, fur, and other textures, and when these are juxtaposed the edge of demarcation is perfectly clear, though there is no line to speak of, and the difference in the tones employed almost escapes detection. The intervals between masses are so distinct, and the atmosphere so positive, that each figure moves in its own world of space, but one that relates itself with other spaces and forms rhythms full of simplicity and charm.

No other painter has so combined economy of means with richness and convincing reality. His wonderfully effective design is obtained by the rhythmic ordering of lines, masses, and spaces, and by harmonies of color blended with light and shadow. He has not the obvious decorative surface-quality of Paolo Veronese or Rubens, but his expressive forms are so interrelated that decoration is fused with expression in a perfect unity.

Rembrandt's technique makes the physical appearances of

things illuminate in a supreme degree their intrinsic quality, their significance from within. He seems to feel the life by which anything is animated and to make it visible. There is somewhat the same quality in Giorgione, but it concerns an Elysian life and is therefore more remote. Both are poetic, but Rembrandt's is the less obvious poetry, the mystic poetry of the things nearest us, which ordinarily escapes us. It represents the consummation of what Bosanquet calls "the home-coming of art," the discovery of profound meaning in the here and now. Rembrandt is a realist, but his is the real as interpreted and not merely, as in the case of Velásquez, observed. In the portrait of "Hendrickje Stoffels" (373), the rendering of the quality of things is far from literal, but it gives us the essence of the things as felt. In this sense, Rembrandt is the most mystical and religious of painters: with everything adventitious, remote, or perfunctory left out, the mystical essence of religion is extracted and made one with the essence of human values. In him imaginative interpretation of the actual world reaches its greatest height, with perfect plastic realization, and with complete avoidance of anything not capable of being rendered in plastic terms.

Rembrandt's ability to attain this fulness of expression is very unequal, and probably the majority of his paintings are defective in this respect. In "Unmerciful Servant" (168), "Hendrickje Stoffels" (373), and "Old Man" (104), we see him technically at his best. In "Old Woman Cutting her Nails" (277), chiaroscuro is overaccentuated, with the specious and tawdry results that are nearly always found in the work of his imitators. His influence upon subsequent painting has been great, but only a few painters have been able to utilize his contributions to new and personal ends. The most successful in this respect was Daumier, although other men, like Hobbema, Bonington, and Monticelli, have used a modification of his principles with some degree of success. It became a stock trick with the Dutch genre-painters and sank to the status of a threadbare banality.

Dutch painting after Rembrandt is chiefly concerned with landscape and genre. Rembrandt had comparatively little direct influence on the painting of landscape, but his chiaroscuro lent itself well to the treatment of interiors and of the life lived in them, and the spirit of his work was not unlike that of simple scenes and everyday affairs. Hence, genre-painting was influenced by him, though none of the genre-painters could possibly be called his successor, for none had his poetry, his magic. The general effect of genre-painting is intimacy, an obviously though not profoundly appealing human quality; this, combined with very great technical skill, and a minute attention to the treatment of textures, fabrics, and still-life, constitutes the characteristic Dutch form. In the best of this group, Vermeer and Pieter de Hooch, the skill is more than virtuosity because of perfect adaptation of means to ends. With few exceptions, however, the Dutch fell short of the highest rank: their form suffers from the relatively trivial nature of its preoccupations.

Jan Vermeer (1632–1675), retaining the traditional Dutch contrast-motif, applies it to new themes which he develops into an individual and distinctive Vermeer form. To the Dutch tradition he adds an increased colorfulness and a tendency to generalization of detail. He is Dutch also in the generally small-scale character of his effects, but he goes beyond his predecessors in rendering the intime, and he approaches the crystalline, quasi-miniature effect achieved by van der Heyden and Berckheyde.

His work is very uneven. In his best pictures, "Little Street" (9) and "View of Delft" (113), he reaches the highest ranges of art, chiefly through his consummate use of color. This has, first of all, a strong sensuous appeal, due to the unique quality of the color itself, especially of the characteristic blues. Its richness and sensuous charm are heightened by the great variety of relations of immediate color-harmony. Color is mottled and fused with light that diversifies the tones and lends a glow to the whole canvas, which thus appears as an ensemble of vivid, perfectly unified color-chords. The realistic textures and fabrics are mere details in the general symphony of color.

In the best of Vermeer, color has, as in no other Dutch painter except Rembrandt, full structural significance, and drawing is a perfect merging of light, color, and line. Contours vary from an accentuated broad line to complete absence of line. The masses thus constructed are bound together by rich, rhythmic linear patterns, color-relations, and pervasive light in compositions which are felt as colored rhythmic sequences of volumes in deep space.

It is an enormous step down from Vermeer's above-mentioned pictures to such others as "Cook" (6), "Girl Reading Letter" (7), "Letter" (8), or "Girl with a Pearl Necklace" (45). Plastically,

[227]

these consist of little more than an obvious, isolated pattern of light, which shines upon color and cheapens it: color is not illuminated from within, and there is no organic color-ensemble. The result is a photographic reproduction of subject-matter with the adventitious appeal of young womanhood. "Diana at the Bath" (111) is an almost literal repetition of the Leonardo-Raphael tradition with overaccentuation of light and superficial and speciously bright color. In these pictures the plastic means are not integrated in an organic whole. In contrast, his "Little Street" (9) and "View of Delft" (113) are representative of some of the highest achievements in painting: they are very individual expressions of the intimate appeal of everyday things of life, of the spirit of place, of Holland, and of the Dutch tradition itself.

Pieter de Hooch (1629–c.1683), like Vermeer, was very uneven in his work. At his best, as in "Court of a Dutch House" (139), he organizes his canvases with light and a color-glow which catches the quality of real sunshine; the light, though accentuated, is not overaccentuated, and his color in general is inferior in quality and depth to Vermeer's. Relative absence of structural color and frequent excess of light often diminish the general effect of color-power, and reduce his work to mere illustration. Even at best, the emphasis put upon literal representation of subject-matter is considerable, but then his adequate command of means lends conviction to the narrative; much more often the illustration is set in a striking pattern of light with superficial and unorganized color. The bright color, sunlight, and clear-cut line amount to no more than an exercise of virtuosity, although there is always a residue of charm.

With **Gerrit A. Berckheyde** (1638–1698) and **Jan van der Heyden** (1637–1712) a distinctive variation of the Dutch landscape-form appears. It preserves the light-dark motif, the episodic character, the spirit of place, and a certain placidity, but it differs from what has gone before in its subject-matter, which becomes urban and approaches that of interiors and genre-painting in general. Both men had an extraordinarily fine feeling for the grouping of masses and the relation of these groups to one another in compact, serrated, well-organized arrangements of three-dimensional units. The result is a very appealing form of space-composition, enhanced by the rich color of the objects and their greatly varied spatial intervals. These two painters applied the miniaturelike effect of

[228]

Pieter de Hooch and Vermeer to landscape and obtained much the same precious, porcelainlike charm of smooth, glossy surfaces. Because of an increased range of reds, blues, ivories, and yellows their pictures are more richly colorful than most Dutch landscapes. Red and ivory are used very much in the manner of Vermeer, but with less solidity in the objects. Although van der Heyden's color is somewhat more structural than Berckheyde's, the latter has a greater gift for color-illumination. No matter what the depth of shadow or darkness in tone, Berckheyde's ability to put effulgence in a pervasive color-ensemble is marvelous.

Berckheyde, like van Goyen, makes accentuated light the focus about which the other plastic means are organized and given added effectiveness. The light-pattern is so merged with a suffusion of illuminated color that the whole canvas has the effect of a bouquet. His surfaces are even richer in color-chords and more charming than van der Heyden's; in this respect "Flower Market" (2) is comparable to Chardin at his best, though the color, not so deep or solid, carries less conviction. This defect is to a large extent compensated for by the quite particular power of the rich color-ensembles found in both his work and van der Heyden's, a power that gives to their work an individual flavor which adds something to the best of the Dutch tradition.

Dutch still-life and genre-painting greatly influenced Chardin, and through him it affected Courbet, Manet, Cézanne, and numerous important contemporaries, including Matisse. Of the purely genre-painters, Brouwer was one of the most powerful; the level is sometimes high in **Dou** (1613–1675), **Terborch** (1617–1681), and **Metsu** (1630–1667); it declines through **van Ostade** (1610–1685) and **Steen** (1626–1679) to the poor academicism of that time, which persists in much of the popular painting of to-day. It becomes narrative or mere virtuosity without plastic unity.

CHAPTER X

THE FRENCH PRIMITIVES [1]

THE FRENCH primitive paintings are not numerous, and they all fall within a comparatively limited extent of time—a little more than a century. After 1500 the tradition had lost its primitive character and had either crystallized in the type represented by the Clouet school or degenerated into banal academic imitation of the Italians, as in Cousin, Perrier, and the like. Nearly all the early French paintings are anonymous, and little is known about the circumstances of their production: existing classifications are practically all arbitrary and plastically meaningless. It is necessary, therefore, to decide the origin and relations of the early French tradition from the pictures themselves, and to distinguish the different types with reference to earlier traditions to which they show intrinsic kinship.

French fresco-painting shows much less influence than Italian upon the panel-painting which succeeded it. It was never really indigenous to France, though its fundamentally Byzantine and Italian character assumed a French cast which presents a number of general qualities and incidental features analogous to those of the more authentic French expressions of plastic art. A far more important influence was exerted by the French miniaturists and illustrators of illuminated manuscripts, who developed forms of compelling individuality and force. This influence extended into Italy, Flanders, and Germany, especially into Italy, where it contributed to the richness of Italian panel-painting; it largely laid the foundations of the French plastic form, fixed the general character of delicacy and subtlety, and profoundly affected the characteristic use made of all the plastic means. The form thus established was adopted, with the necessary modifications, by artists in stained glass and tapestry, and their use of it was of such high excellence that panel-painting itself was enriched in return by the new plastic devices and themes. Thus nourished and strengthened

[1] This chapter is a brief summary of the research entitled *The French Primitives and Their Forms* by Barnes and de Mazia, Barnes Foundation Press, Merion, Pa., 1931.

by the interplay of these forces, the French tradition acquired a vitality which enabled it to resist submergence by the more powerful art-streams of Flanders and Italy when these invaded France. The foreign streams did indeed leave their marks, which are often more obvious than the delicate French strain; but the basic French form, instead of being obliterated by the invaders, assimilated them and maintained its own intrinsic character. When the French form is resolved into its plastic components, the fact becomes clear that what lends distinctive significance to the whole is the set of elements native to the French soil.

The foreign traditions which appear in early French painting had already been extensively intermingled before the French made any drafts upon them, and their separate influences cannot therefore be precisely distinguished. The Italian tradition, as already noted, was particularly influenced by the French miniaturists, many of whom worked in Italy, and consequently when it entered France it fused readily and naturally with the indigenous tradition to yield results of the lightness, delicacy, and colorful harmony exemplified in the Louvre "Entombment" (324). The Flemish tradition, when it made its way into the north of France, had already assimilated from the Italian a pervasive influence which affected, as a rule, not any single plastic element but rather the form in its entirety. The different types of French painting cannot, therefore, be rigidly separated; they represent tendencies, not compartments; but a definite classification can be made in accordance with the predominance, in each type, of a particular tradition or combination of traditions.

TYPES OF FRENCH PRIMITIVE PAINTING

There are five important and clearly distinguishable types of French painting. The first may be described as the French Italo-miniature tradition, referred to in the last paragraph; in this the close relationship to the miniatures is very apparent, as well as to the Italians. In space-composition, linear effects, and employment of decorative motifs, these pictures follow the miniaturists, but their color-schemes and subtle color-organization as well as their integration of color with line and space, are Italian in derivation. In the Louvre "Entombment" (324) and the Louvre "Pietà of Our Lord" (325), the Italo-miniature type is pure, but in the Berlin "Crowning of Mary" (37), and the Bargello diptychs,

"Madonna in Garden—Calvary" (75 and 74) and "Adoration—Crucifixion" (76), there is an additional German influence, chiefly in the presence of a relative heaviness.

In the second class of pictures, here designated as that of the Franco-German borderland form, the German influences are more extensive—sufficiently so to diminish materially the French character of the form. The heaviness, both in general style and in execution, is clearly in evidence, and there are other features distinctly German—for example, drawing by means of light and color in juxtaposed areas, a particular application of highlights in modeling—but the grace and decorative charm are indubitably French. A typical example is the Louvre polyptych, "Altarpiece of the Virgin" (326). In another picture of this group, "Holy Trinity" (137), the affiliations with a Germanic form are much closer, indeed so close that the picture is classified, albeit erroneously, as German in the London National Gallery. There is the same heaviness, a color-scheme closely approaching Lochner's, and much similarity in the painting of particular details; but the use of planes, the type of modeling, and the employment of ivory tones in relation to the German elements in the color-scheme, dilute the German stock with a French strain.

The third type—the Franco-Flemish—shows a fusion of French with Flemish characteristics. It has two subclasses, in one of which [2] the Flemish influence is comparatively pure (subject to the reservations above noted, that the Flemish school had already been permeated by Italian traits); in the other there is a direct Italian influence.[3] In pictures in which comparatively pure Flemish influences are predominant, there is expressive line, and a considerable degree of realism in space and modeling, which conveys more nearly the effect of real depth and solidity. What transforms these qualities into something distinctively French is their brighter and more glowing color, their grace, and their subtlety. The Italian influence in the second subclass appears chiefly in the color, which is brighter than in the other subclass, organized in ensembles with very different relations; but what is taken from the Italian is not directly copied, it is assimilated and refashioned into a perfectly distinct French form.

[2] E.g., "Legend of St. Bertin" (40); "Birth of the Virgin" (192); "Mary Going to the Temple" (193); "Saint Roch" (196).
[3] E.g., "Salome" (1); "Circumcision" (194); the so-called Master of Moulins's "Magdalen and Donor" (352).

The elements constitutive of the fourth—the Italo-French—type are fully present in their pure form only in one picture, the "Altarpiece of St. Etienne" (110) from Gréolières, but that picture is so striking, original, and distinctive that it must be regarded as establishing, in itself, a completely individual type. This type includes, in some measure, the Bonson "Altarpiece of St. John" (47) and the Louvre "Scenes from the Life of St. Andrew" (327); but the resemblance is only partial in the case of the Bonson picture, and is very tenuous indeed in "Scenes from the Life of St. Andrew." The former of these two pictures has a considerable Italian element with only a slight French complexion, and the latter is less French than Sienese. In its pure form, the type has a derivation exclusively Italian, though there are no predecessors, either Italian or French, to which the characteristics in the Gréolières altarpiece may be directly traced. In its general delicacy and the fineness of its color-relations, it is thoroughly French and could not possibly be attributed to any other tradition.

The fifth type has as its most important representatives the Cimiez (53), Louvre (Villeneuve) (384), and Sospel (428) Pietàs. Each of these is primarily a synthesis, of which the most important ingredients are Flemish and Italian, but which includes also certain German and Spanish features. Both Flemish and Italian elements are present in the composition; there is some degree of bilateral symmetry, but the transverse body of Christ provides a note of variation in the balanced right-and-left placing of the other figures. The characteristic French flattening of objects appears, though the objects are more than mere surfaces of color. Heavy execution and ridged surface of paint, somber color, and dramatic contrast of light and dark, present in varying degree, ally these pictures also somewhat to the Spaniards. The thirteenth century Spanish migration into parts of southern France probably accounts for the presence of these particular traits. Although the pictures lack French delicacy and grace, the ivory tone, the dryness of color, and familiar textural and surface qualities bring them certainly within the French tradition.

In addition to these more important classes there are a number of other types of pictures which show French traits, but they are unimportant both intrinsically and as examples of the French tradition. Such are those by the followers of Bréa, by the so-called school of Amiens, and the pictures with affiliations predominantly Spanish; most of these tend toward eclecticism.

French portraiture includes works of very different degrees of merit, but they have not a sufficient number of plastic features in common to distinguish them as an important individual type. Almost without exception they are definitely of the Franco-Flemish class.

GENERAL CHARACTER OF THE FRENCH PRIMITIVE FORM

All five types of the French primitive paintings have in common a set of fundamental characteristics which establish their distinctive French form. They all display a pervasive gentleness and delicacy, and a simplicity which embraces drawing, composition, and the use of each of the plastic elements. Their compositional organization has its source largely in the form and technique of early stained glass and is in broad areas of color. The resulting color-pattern is differentiated by specific relations between color, line, and space from the corresponding patterns in the Italian, German, and Spanish primitives, all of which are more closely related to the Byzantines. An additional point of distinction is that in the French the color-areas are composed in compact planes, with reduced spatial depth, a form of organization which embraces background as well as foreground; in Italian backgrounds, in contrast, the masses are set in comparatively realistic deep space. Such emphasis upon compact planes, with reduced perspective, is characteristic of the entire French tradition, from its inception to its latest exemplification in such men as Picasso and Matisse, and is most in evidence when the tradition is most typically French.

The general French primitive form is fundamentally decorative, a fact which largely determines all its plastic aspects. The expressive form is sufficiently convincing to assure plastic reality, but there is little or none of the realism of such other early men as Masaccio or, in a very different manner, of van Eyck. The reduction in the depth of space, together with the accentuation of planes, is a manifestation of this decorative tendency, in which the deficiency in depth is counterbalanced by patterns of interspaces created by the varied and compact organization of planes. In the Gréolières "Altarpiece of St. Etienne" (110), for example, the position of the planes of color, placed close together before and behind each other as well as to the right and left, results in an unusually appealing treatment of space, with no atmosphere or glow of color; and the same general type of spatial organization prevails in most of the other important paintings of the tradition.

EMPLOYMENT AND TRANSFORMATION OF ANTECEDENT DECORATIVE FEATURES

A considerable number of the devices taken over by the French primitive painters from earlier schools of art and given a new character and function, have a primarily decorative significance. Typical of these is the ornamental gold background. Derived from the Byzantine mosaics and preserved for a while by all the early traditions, it gives place in the Italians as early as Giotto's time to the representation or at least suggestion of infinite space, and is practically abandoned after Fra Angelico. In the French frescoes an area of flat color appears instead of gold; in many of the miniatures the gold retains in large measure the effect of a screen, and in the panel-painters it still has much of that character. Among the Flemings, naturalistic settings were introduced early and soon became the rule; the Germans, like the French, used decorative gold backgrounds but the effect was more nearly that of a unit in an ensemble of bright and glaring colors; the actual color and the color-relations lacked the subtlety and delicacy of the French, and the inscribed ornamental pattern was coarser and more mechanical. The French pattern on the gold setting is usually drawn with a technique of minute indented dots placed close together and organized in rosettes, stylized foliage, and flowing curves. Both the technique and the color-ensemble related to the gold had their origin in the miniaturists.

Another type of decorative patterning in the French primitives developed from early classic and Oriental sources. The all-over checkered background, a distinctive feature of the French miniatures and stained glass, is in all probability an outgrowth of geometrical patterns which originated in Egyptian textiles, Greek vases, African carvings, and Moorish decorations. The actual diapered backgrounds of the stained glass and miniatures almost completely disappeared in the panel-paintings, but their generalized effect persisted in the geometric arrangement of many color-areas, especially in floors. Checkered floors, often giving the effect of tiled patterns, occur in a number of early traditions, but the French are less realistic than the Flemish or Italian, and simpler and more subtle than the German or Spanish.

A third feature of the decorative pattern in which previous traditional practices are employed is the enframing border, painted or stippled around the background, which continued a universal practice in early Greek, Egyptian, and Byzantine art. Like other decorative features, this persisted much longer among the French than among the Italians. It had an even more extensive use in miniatures and stained glass; in panel-paintings, the borders have less internal patterning, less contrast with the rest of the background, and their effect is therefore less purely decorative, more definitely compositional.

The margins of many of the early miniatures and manuscripts were ornamented with finely detailed foliage and small animal figures. These were sometimes organized in planes, and fragmentary depiction of a natural setting was added to the usual screen-setting. In a few of the illuminated manuscripts there are recognizable landscapes, though they are still primarily decorative. In the early frescoes, such as those in the Chambre de la Garde-Robe at Avignon (25), the setting of episodes in a leafy, swirling, highly decorative background was a similar anticipation of later landscape, with a general type of decorative organization analogous to those in the thirteenth and fourteenth century miniatures but with a richer and more intricate interplay of plastic relationships. Still another version of the early landscape-form appeared in the French tapestries of the fifteenth century, for example in "Concert in the Open Air" (328), in which the execution of the background is more detailed than in the Avignon frescoes (25), and also in the series of tapestries entitled "Lady and Unicorn" (404) and "Scenes of Seigniorial Life" (405).

In all these miniatures, frescoes, and tapestries, the background of landscape is highly decorative, a stage-setting against which the figures are placed, not an integral part of nature to which the figures are really felt to belong. The authentic quality of natural landscape first occurs in the illuminated manuscript "Book of Hours of the Duc de Berry" (51), of about 1416, illustrated by Pol de Limbourg and his two brothers, especially in the calendar scenes, the general characteristics of which reappear in so many important French paintings that they may be regarded as establishing a typical French tradition of landscape-painting. There is an abundance of detail in Pol de Limbourg's landscapes: every feature is drawn with microscopic fineness, and contour; local color, and position in space are clearly set forth; but the design controls every aspect so completely that the effect is not that of an inventory but of a plastic whole. In this there is a resemblance to van Eyck, but the French pictures are more simplified and much less realistic as to exactitude of detail. In French panel-painting the delicacy and lightness of the miniatures is preserved, but there is more generalization and what is borrowed from other traditions is tempered with characteristic decorative quality. Of these other traditions, it is the Flemish which on the whole is nearest the French in treatment of landscape, doubtless largely because it too had undergone the influence of the miniaturists; but the French tradition, in spite of the intermingling of the two strains, remains simpler, lighter, less realistic, more delicate and decorative than the Flemish.

COLOR

The decorative character of the early French form determines also its color, in panel-painting no less than in stained glass, frescoes, and miniatures. Its characteristic effects are those of pervasive delicacy, subtlety of relationships of a very high order, and a coolness and dryness reminiscent of the early Italians. Its decorative function is maintained in spite of the frequently crude application of paint, which results in the dull, dry, coarse surface generally associated with house and fence painting. Except here and there in a few late fifteenth century paintings, French color has little or no structural function nor is it combined with light and shadow in chiaroscuro.

The influence of the miniaturists upon Italian painting, already noted, had before the beginning of the fifteenth century left its mark on the delicate, decorative color of the Italian primitives. Hence it was natural that the French painters should draw extensively on both the Florentine and Sienese for their color-gamut, and that their color-ensembles should so largely reflect the feeling of the miniatures themselves. The keynote to the general French color-scheme is an ivory tone which appears in all parts of the canvas, and which was probably derived from the effect, in the miniatures, of transparent color-washes applied to ivory parchment. A similar ivory occurs in the Italians, but is there of a different surface-texture: that of the Italians generally resembles cardboard, but in the French it varies from a dry, chalky, porcelain, alabaster, or stucco quality to the warm textural feeling of

[237]

actual old ivory. Its plastic function, established by its relation to other colors and to light, line, and space, is also quite distinctive in the French. Often in the painting of flesh the ivory is shaded with light brownish tones and overcast with a delicate, soft, creamy, lavender-rose tinge, so that from a distance the individual tones coalesce in a composite hue which may conveniently be termed "peach-blow." This may be observed in its most typical form in the Gréolières "Altarpiece of St. Etienne" (110), and its source identified in the early miniatures, in the flesh-painting, for example, of "Roman Breviary" (24).

Upon the foundation of ivory are built up the color-ensembles characteristic of the various types of French primitive painting. That of the Louvre "Entombment" (324), which best represents the French Italo-miniature type, is everywhere of extreme delicacy, with many nuances and subtle relationships, and the influence of the miniatures appears in the technique and use of gold. There is sufficient flow of color between adjacent areas to soften the pattern and produce a general effect of color-pervasion, and this is heightened by color-chords which result from subtle infiltration of light throughout the picture. A gentle surface-glow of color adds to the pervasive delicacy and charm.

In the Italo-French type, exemplified in the Gréolières "Altarpiece of St. Etienne" (110), color is more powerful, color-contrast is relatively accentuated, and the pattern is more sharply compartmental. As in the "Entombment" (324), color is of Italian origin, but the Gréolières picture is more closely allied to the frescoes than to the panel-paintings of the Italians, and among the Italians it most resembles Piero della Francesca. Both pictures are delicate and subtle, but they are very definitely distinguished from each other by the complete absence of all miniature-quality from the altarpiece.

The color of the three characteristic French Pietàs—from Cimiez (53), the Louvre (384), and Sospel (428)—differs from that of both the foregoing pictures: it has no miniature-quality, no lightness, delicacy, or brightness, but is opaque, heavy like the Spanish, and somber like the Umbrian, and is dominated by dramatic contrasts of large light and dark areas. It is French, however, in its dryness of surface and in the subtlety of tonal relations within the general dark ensembles.

There is no characteristic form of color-design in pictures of the Franco-German borderland type, but in those belonging to the Franco-Flemish category the Italian influence remains stronger than that which comes direct from Flemish sources. It plays its part in the transformation of Flemish color less by specific modification of individual tones or relationships than as a pervasive tendency which operates upon the general character of the color-ensemble, and is often the chief instrument by which the French painters conferred their individual quality upon what they borrowed from the Flemish.

DRAWING

Drawing in the French primitives is predominantly, though by no means exclusively, linear. This is a natural consequence of their compartmental organization as patterns of color-areas, and of their origin in the miniatures, in stained glass, and in other primitive traditions, all of which go back to the Byzantine. Their contours are generally sharp, but they are more varied, expressive, and organically integrated with the form as a whole than those of the Byzantines; they not only constitute decorative patterns but draw out the general graceful rigidity which characterizes the French primitive form in all its variations.

This rigidity is obviously a survival from Byzantine painting, but its original angularity and stiffness are converted in the French by finer execution and by subtlety of color-relations and modeling, as well as by more fluid and delicate line, into a peculiar graceful naïveté, gauche in character, but largely dependent for its distinctive effect upon this very gaucherie. Contours remain sharply linear or angular, but the figures seem less artificially posed than the Byzantine, and are plastically more expressive.

Other characteristic distortions are adapted by the French from the traditions of their time. Elongated figures, which are also prevalent among the Byzantines, were taken over by the Italians and the Flemish, and from them by the French; in the Italians they tend to be flowing, in the Flemish stiff or rigid; the French frequently combine the two characteristics, further modifying both by their own characteristic simplifications and bringing the general effect into harmony with their general naïve gaucherie.

The use of elongated figures is chiefly in evidence in pictures of the Franco-Flemish type; in those related more closely to the Italians a different type of drawing appears, also a departure from literalism, but less obviously distorted: the distinctive down-flowing movement of contour and mass, which we have designated the "Sienese droop"—occasionally anticipated in French miniatures, German woodcuts, and French frescoes—is adopted in several types of French drawing, and when imaginatively transformed and thoroughly integrated in the French form it yields an increased delicacy and heightened expressiveness. When its linear aspect is isolated, however, or the conventional Sienese pattern is followed, the effect is mechanical or lifeless. It is seen at its best in the Louvre "Entombment" (324) and "Pietà of Our Lord" (325), in each of which the downward movement in the Madonna's figure is united with subtle modeling and delicate color, and the whole effect is gentle, convincing, and charming; in "Altar-Cloth of Narbonne" (323), in contrast, too exclusive emphasis on line and resemblance to the Italian prototype result in academicism and plastic unreality. Whatever the degree of integration of the Sienese droop, its linear movement is pronounced and it carries out the general theme of rhythmic line which is of great importance in French drawing.

In the Franco-German type of French primitives, appears a number of distortions borrowed from the Germans, most of which tend toward a vivid depiction of psychological states, or toward the grotesque. In the originals, the Cologne school, for example, the psychological and narrative interest is very strong, even when the plastic organization is of a high order; in the French, as might be expected, realism is less, and decorative quality more, in evidence; but the squattiness of the figures, which sometimes reaches deformity, the vivid facial expressions, the use of streaks of light and sharp line in the drawing, and frequently the actual rendering of faces, hands, hair, and other parts of the body, testify to the German influence. The German sense of life and movement is preserved, but the execution is finer, less heavy in the French, and color is more subtle both in its intrinsic quality and its relations to the other plastic elements.

Line plays an extremely active part in determining the design in all phases of the French primitive form, but its importance is perhaps best illustrated by the extent to which it is employed in the drawing of faces. Eyes, nose, lips, and chin are often represented by greatly simplified linear definitions, with decorative effects absent from either Flemish or Italian faces; this resulted, in all probability, from the influence of the miniatures, in which the limited repertoire of means made line inevitably the chief instrument of drawing. Faces are sometimes primarily silhou-

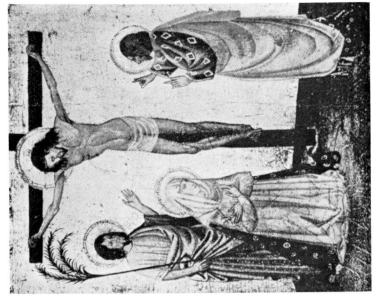

French Master, fourteenth
century (191)

French Master, active
c. 1400 (195)

French Master, fifteenth century (110)   Analysis, page 458

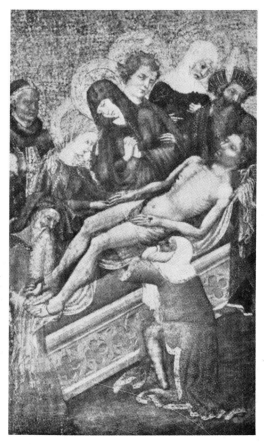

French Master, end of   Analysis,
  fourteenth or beginning   page 456
  of fifteenth century (324)

Southern French Master, second half of
fifteenth century (384)

Southern French Master, fifteenth century (428)

[244]

ettes; rhythms of linear pattern frequently serve as the means of compositional unification between faces, figures, and background; occasionally a heavy line plays the part of shadow, at other times a pink line forms part of the contour of facial features. Line is used extensively in the Germans also to define facial expression and to make patterns, but that of the French is lighter, more clear-cut, plastically richer, and more varied and individual.

THE PAINTING OF FLESH AND DRAPERIES

The painting of flesh has its native French roots in the ivory tone already discussed, which was derived from the miniaturists. Modeling is in general chiefly Florentine, with gradations of light and shadow conferring a measure of solidity upon color-areas, but in some pictures the light and shadow are more patterned, in the manner of the Flemish. The delicate terre-verte which sometimes modifies the color used in modeling is an echo of the Sienese, and through them, of the marked green shadows of the Byzantines. In many of the Franco-German borderland pictures, streaks of light are adapted from the German version of this Byzantine trait, and from the Byzantines are derived the ridges of paint which diversify and pattern the surface of the flesh, and in this way contribute to modeling. These derivations vary in importance in the different types of French painting, but the distinctive French form is maintained in each. All alike are far from realistic: solidity is never carried to the point of interfering with the organization in planes, and the texture is never that of actual flesh: it conveys instead, the feeling of chalk, wood, stucco, alabaster, or porcelain, in harmony with the general exigencies of decorative treatment and the particular design in which it occurs.

A similar synthesis of traditions occurs in the painting of draperies, which is given its specifically French form chiefly by the quality of color and the drawing of folds. The naturalistic Flemish treatment of textural quality had comparatively little direct influence on the French, and when closely imitated resulted only in academicism, but when combined with more decorative Florentine elements and authentic French color, as in the Aix "Salome" (1) and the Berlin "Legend of St. Bertin" (40), it provided the basis for a considerable degree of expressive conviction, achieved without detriment to the characteristic French form. In the latter picture, by a very successful union of color and light the actual effect of a diaphanous material placed in deep space is secured, with a convincing essential realism which heightens the decorative charm. Similarly the traditional Italian bright color, contrast of light and shadow, and sharp flowing line, while mechanically employed in some French pictures, is organically incorporated in the form of the Louvre "Entombment" (324) to produce draperies of the utmost individuality and charm. Subtly related, flowing color and light in delicate nuances, with sharpness of line tempered by the absence of any abrupt color-contrast, lend a subdued richness, an appealing softness, and a light, almost floating quality to the fabrics.

In the French treatment of folds in draperies, the outstanding characteristic is the relative suppression of space, the primarily decorative use of the folds, with sacrifice of realism and often also of plastic strength. This tendency toward reduction of folds to comparatively flat surface-pattern prevails in the whole early French tradition, from the heavy solid Pietàs (53; 384; 428), to the light and delicate "Altarpiece of St. Etienne" (110). In the best representatives of the tradition the plastic deficiency is compensated for by the sensuous appeal of the color, the effective relations between color-areas, or the quality of the surface.

In the folds, as in the other details of the French form, the general Byzantine influence reappears, with the usual addition of grace to rigidity, but the more direct influences are Florentine, Sienese, German, and Flemish. Folds reflecting the Florentine influence are comparatively few in number, preponderantly vertical, unobtrusive, long and graceful, and slightly modeled by light and shadow. The Florentine character is not usually much changed, but the rhythms become more fluid, subtle, and delicate, and the use of light is also more subtle. The fluid rhythms and pronounced pattern of Sienese folds occur in a number of French pictures, but the folds are more numerous and the pattern stands out more clearly because of the more precise shape of areas of light and shadow. Frequently also the slow curves of the Sienese drapery give place to a more definite arabesque-movement. In Franco-German borderland pictures appears, in varying degree, a fluid softness in the folds, resulting from gradations of light and shadow within a single color, derived from the Bohemian and Cologne painters, and earlier anticipated in the French tradition itself in the work of the miniaturist Jean Pucelle. From the Flemish are adapted numerous triangular motifs in the arrangement of folds, but texture is less realistic, the geometrical pattern is as a rule less sharply defined, and even when it is most accentuated it remains superficial and contributes almost nothing to depth.

SUMMARY

The French primitive form was rooted in that of the miniaturists, to which are united elements derived from the Byzantines, Florentines, Sienese, Flemish, Germans, and Spaniards. Reënforced by kindred forms in fresco-painting, stained glass, and tapestry, it maintained its vitality in the presence of all foreign traditions, and at its best it assimilated from the alien forms the elements needed for its own growth, giving them its own distinctive character and manner of organization. For their primarily decorative design, the French primitive painters adopted a style of drawing and composition, and a use of space, line, and color which emphasized such aspects of the world as grace, delicacy, subtlety, gentleness, and charm. This limitation of interest explains and, in a qualified sense, justifies the absence from their work of structural color, deep space, realistic depiction of texture and movement, dramatic action, and complex large-scale effects. Their number included no one of the range or power or importance of van Eyck or Giotto; but in establishing a form of consummate delicacy, grace, and charm, firmly founded on plastic essentials, they gave to French art a pictorial expression which has since been added to, broadened, and deepened, but has never undergone a break in the fundamental continuity of its development.

THE CLOUETS, CORNEILLE DE LYON, AND THE LE NAINS

The **Clouet school** developed through the influence of two painters from the Netherlands—**Jean Clouet** (1485–1540) and **Corneille de Lyon** (c.1505 – c.1575)—who settled in France in the sixteenth century. Their work is little more than a delicatized version of the van Eyck - Petrus Christus type of portraiture. **François Clouet** (c.1510–1572), the son of Jean, carried on the tradition. The style of the numerous portraits ascribed to the Clouets or to Corneille de Lyon is very formalistic and so readily imitable that it became the stock-in-trade of the majority of portrait-painters of the period in France. It may be said, therefore, that most of the pictures attributed to the Clouets or Corneille de Lyon are the work of painters of greatly varying degree of sensibility and technical skill. Indeed, even pictures supposedly authenticated as the work of Jean Clouet,[4] Francois Clouet,[5] or Corneille de Lyon differ radically in their form and manner of execution. It is impossible to establish distinctive marks of difference between the work attributed to Jean Clouet and that given to his son François. The pictures of each of these painters vary in the type of drawing, in the quality of surface, texture, and tone of flesh, and in degree of technical proficiency. At times the drawing is sharply linear and at other times contours are loose. The flesh is sometimes of natural color with pink tints on the cheeks, sometimes red in general tone and almost Venetian in solidity, and at other times the flesh is whitish ivory with a semi-transparent surface of delicate, eggshell-like brittleness. Many of these Clouet type of pictures rank high as portraiture, because the fine, delicate, almost literal rendering of features and stuffs is fused in the design, with essential expressiveness given adequate plastic embodiment. The command over the medium of paint is usually very good but the close similarity of compositions indicates a lack of imagination in the use of color and in the construction of patterns.

The form of Corneille de Lyon's type of pictures is in general delicate and miniaturelike, with figures usually sharply linear, daintily and crisply drawn, and set against a background of contrasting color often of a green not unlike the verdigris of the early French miniatures. The flesh, with its translucent delicate blue-green shadows and its smooth polished surface, has the texture, tone, and general feeling of delicately modeled tinted ivory.

Antoine le Nain (1588–1648) and his brothers, **Louis** (1593–1648) and **Mathieu** (1607–1677), although they were born in France and worked in Paris, stand outside the French tradition. Their work is distinct from that of the other French artists in that it shows no French origin and its influence upon subsequent French traditions cannot be traced. They depicted scenes of everyday life, of interiors, of working people and peasants, in the manner more akin to Velásquez, the Dutch, and the Flemings than to anything French. The chalky color and texture of the flesh is perhaps the only affinity with the early French tradition. The best of their pictures show an ability to portray human character, and a fine

[4] Cf., e.g., "Francois, the Dauphin" (10) and "François I, on Horseback" (93).
[5] Cf., e.g., "Pierre Quthe" (306) and "Diane de Poitiers in the Bath" (414).

sense of composition which is carried out in an individual manner: pyramidal formation is replaced by a lateral alignment of masses attractively arranged in a variety of spatial groupings. Paint is used with facility and distinction. The absence of positive colors and a rather limited range of expression make most of their pictures grayish, dull, monochrome color-ensembles which partake more of the nature of illustrations than of creative plastic achievements.

CHAPTER XI

FRENCH PAINTING OF THE EIGHTEENTH CENTURY

FRENCH painting of the eighteenth century appears in its most completely characteristic form in Watteau, Lancret, Pater, Boucher, and Fragonard, and is cheapened and vulgarized in the work of their academic imitators. Chardin's form, though typically French and of the eighteenth century, stands apart from that of any of his contemporaries in character and quality.

The work of Watteau, Lancret, Pater, Boucher, and Fragonard owes its French character to its concentrated delicacy and grace, and to the emphasis upon decorative charm of color, surface, texture, pattern, drawing, compositional rhythm, and subject-matter. The decorative quality is distinctive in its lightness, dainty elegance, feminity; in its lyric, allegorical form of expression; and in the masquerade of exquisite triviality which represents the court life of the period—a period of pastoral comedies, *fêtes galantes*, and elegant aloofness from the affairs of everyday life. The form had its roots in the innate French feeling for decoration, daintiness, grace, delicacy, gentleness, which we have already observed in the French tradition in its primitive form as, e.g., in the illuminated manuscripts and in such an early painting as the Louvre "Entombment" (324). Its plastic qualities were mainly derived from the Venetians, Rubens, and the seventeenth century Dutch painters, as well as from the sculpture of the Goujon and Girardon type. All the members of the group, though their use of the traditions was more eclectic than that of Poussin or Claude le Lorrain, were more typically French than these two painters. They drew constantly and often mechanically upon the plastic devices of the Italian Renaissance, but retained little or nothing of the grandeur or mystical quality of its effects. Poussin's classic figures reappear in Boucher, retaining their grace but divesting themselves of majesty or even essential dignity; the landscape-form developed by Claude from the Venetians recurs in Watteau, but its epic sweep is replaced by an idyllic romanticism, much less moving but more characteristically French. Illustration and decoration have made extensive inroads upon expression of essentials, and the change is accompanied plastically by a weakening of organic color.

Specific features from Titian and Tintoretto constantly appear, particularly in the rendering of textiles and in the compositional movement of masses in space, but it is more directly the form of Paolo Veronese, together with Rubens' modification of it, that establishes the essential Venetian basis of this eighteenth century painting. From Paolo and Rubens come the spectacular, pageantlike subject-matter, as well as the general decorative design, color, and drawing, the compositional swirl and general rhythm. More specific resemblances occur in the tendency to light tones in the color-scheme, the pearly-rose tonality and comparatively one-piece modeling of women's flesh, and the emphasis upon sheen of textiles and surface-pattern of folds. The texture of the flesh tends toward that of porcelain or ivory, with faces sometimes like daintily chiselled cameos or like figures of Sèvres china. The drama and the sweep of the Paolo-Rubens form lose nearly all their flamboyance, are greatly reduced in scale, and assume a suavity which harmonizes with the much lighter and daintier French form; but correspondingly, except in the best work of Lancret and Pater, vigor and animation are replaced by pose, stilted movement, and sentimental artificiality.

The debt to the seventeenth century Dutch school appears both in genre-painting and in the treatment of landscape. The first shows the Dutch influence in the intime, small-scale type of subject-matter, the attention to exact detail, local color, and contrasts of light and shadow; the second, in the compositional grouping of houses and trees, and in the use of focalized light, dramatically contrasted with dark, both of which landscape-effects recall Hobbema. In landscape as in genre, the Dutch weight of color gives place to the inherent French lightness and delicacy.

Drawing is characterized, in the group as a whole, by daintiness and fragile, often miniaturelike, delicacy. Contours are usually clean-cut, with crisp accents of color, or oppositions of light and dark. There is a pervasive glow of color, but, in contrast to the glow in the Venetians, it rarely adds depth to color; usually it merely enhances the surface-appeal of the color, and creates a sort of fairyland atmosphere. Color and light are frequently used to make a dramatic compositional focus in open-air figure-groups. In landscapes, one of Claude's characteristic features reappears: masses of deep, dense foliage alternate with contrasting areas of subdued light, against which are set the figures and objects in the foreground, but instead of Claude's central open space enframed by bilaterally balanced masses, two or more dramatic space-vistas (*éclaircies*) are created by placing the masses both in the center and at the sides of the setting. The compositional distribution of masses follows, in general, the Italian types, with the French graceful flow often transforming the conventional pyramid-formation into a more fluid, fanlike, oval organization, or into a fluid serpentine frieze.

Most of the characteristics of the tradition, including drawing, technique, surface-quality, type of subject-matter, compositional use of masses and of light and dark, are repeated in different pictures with so little variation that the mechanically formulated treatment is itself an earmark of the form of these painters as a whole.

Watteau (1684–1721) in his few good pictures successfully re-embodies features from Titian, Tintoretto, Rubens, and Claude in an essentially new and French form.[1] The juicy color lends enhanced surface-charm to the drawing; enough glow of color is retained to produce a circumambient atmosphere which expresses the mysticism of space; and enough solidity is preserved to give conviction to the new delicacy. At times Watteau also skilfully adopts the technical methods of Titian, Tintoretto, El Greco, and Rubens in the drawing of textiles, and obtains a charming, crisp, and lively feeling of silk materials, in which the power of Venetian light-patterns in folds gives way to daintiness and graceful, miniaturelike surface-ornamentation. Usually, however, Watteau's use of the traditions and of his own devices is repetitive to the point of academicism, and his facile, superficial technique leaves out too much of the substance of things to give adequate plastic and expressive support to the decorative pattern of color, light, and line.

Lancret (1690–1743) is more important by far than any other member of the group. His work falls into two general types. The first is solid, of a weighty delicacy, with sharp outlines formed by clean-cut junction of color-areas; the second is distinguished by a color-ensemble of very decidedly pastel or water-color quality, and by exceedingly light, delicate, floating figures and objects,

[1] E.g., Watteau's "Game of Love" (160).

Watteau (160)

Analysis, page 459

Chardin (208)

Corot (182)

Longhi (217)

Courbet (308)

with contours less accentuated than those of the first type. He resembles Watteau in his general design, but is superior in his use of color and color-relations, in subtlety of light, in individuality and expressiveness of drawing, in compositional range and variety, and in the more consistently high-grade quality of his work.

Lancret departs further from the Venetians and Rubens than do Watteau and Fragonard, and he retains more of the intime charm and surface-richness of the best of the seventeenth century Dutch genre-painters, de Hooch, Vermeer, van der Heyden, and Berckheyde. His color is more solidly structural than that of his eighteenth century compatriots, while his adaptations of the Venetian glow and his blending of contrasting tones and hues are richer in color-chords, more subtle, and more individual. He added ingenious new effects to the conventional styles of drawing, modeling, and composition of the period. His figures, often elongated, have a pert, graceful rigidity, and clean-cut contours are obtained without Watteau's or Boucher's specious recourse to actual independent line. Modeling of flesh and textiles is usually executed by finely blended modulations of delicate colors, with no undue accentuation of either light or dark areas. The quality and character of the light, and its degree of accentuation, vary with and are adapted compositionally and expressively to the specific type of design, whether it be interior scene, open out-of-door episode, or *sous-bois* group. The light, so adapted, blends harmoniously with color and thus pervades the whole picture with a gentle, uniform glow, even when deep masses of trees in the shade are contrasted with lighted vistas or with lighted spots on figures or garments as, for example, in "Manhood" (140).

Lancret's grouping of figures and objects, in either open-air or interior scenes, varies from the fanlike or pyramidal to a horizontal friezelike alignment. By subtle changes in the arrangement of masses or spaces, and in the position and direction of the individual components both on the same and on different levels, a variety of subsidiary groupings is created. The relation of these groupings to one another communicates a rhythmic, graceful, unifying, compositional flow to the total organization. Lancret thus steers clear of the banality of Watteau's oval and pyramidal schemes, the stylistic and exaggerated movement of Boucher's specious in-and-out thrusts of volumes in space, and the traditional clichés of Fragonard.

Pater (1696–1736) at his best [2] ranks with Lancret in expressive drawing, structural color of fabrics and flesh, and merging of technique with form. His contours are slightly blurred, less clean-cut than Lancret's; the shadows in his textiles are more accentuated and produce a characteristic quivering pattern; his color, less rich and deep, with less pronounced contrasting accents of light, has a slightly greater and more uniform tonal mellowness; and his composition is less varied. His paintings may be divided into two general classes, the first and larger of which is represented by small, colorful, episodic scenes which, in spite of their very close resemblance to Lancret, show Pater at his best. The second includes the large *fêtes galantes*,[3] and are merely academic versions of the conventional eighteenth century subject-matter represented by Watteau's "Embarkation for Cythera" (402). Compositional unification is feeble because the maladjustment of overaccentuated focuses of light and dark makes the pattern of the picture disjointed. The form as a whole is little more than illustration, with no distinction in drawing, color, or composition.

Boucher (1703–1770) stands apart from the relatively homogeneous group formed by Watteau, Lancret, and Pater. His pictures deal more often with mythological and allegorical subjects treated on a large scale; the color is drier, the surface smoother; a somewhat different set of traditional forms is utilized, and the manner of their adaptation is changed. His large compositions are in essentials highly decorative, tapestrylike boudoir-panels, much inferior in quality to his small landscapes with subsidiary figures. The inferiority is due mainly to the dry, arid color, which is scarcely more than a surface decoration, and to the overaccentuation of contour-line in figures.

The style of the large compositions is closely allied to that of Tiepolo. Their general drawing owes more to the classic form of Raphael, Correggio, and Poussin, and to the sculpture of Goujon and Girardon, than to Titian and Tintoretto. Boucher's painting of flesh, with its pearly rose-cream complexion in cupids and women, its one-piece type of modeling, and its use of reflected light and accents of pink at contours, is a modification of the form of Paolo Veronese, Rubens, and Tiepolo, from which he adopted also his broken swirl and independent line of contour.

[2] E.g., "Comedians in a Park" (356).
[3] E.g., Pater's "Camp Scene" (167) and "Outdoor Fête" (357).

His figures are much lighter than either Paolo's or Rubens'; they resemble Tiepolo's in their more decorative movement, their appearance of tinted porcelain and glasslike fragility, the floating, bubbling rhythm of their enveloping draperies, and in the diminution of light-and-shadow pattern in the modeling. Also, as in Tiepolo, the one-piece effect of the volume and surface is more pronounced than in Paolo Veronese and Rubens, and often gives to a profiled head the appearance of a cameo. At times, however, Boucher availed himself also of Rubens' modeling of flesh by means of parallel bands of varied delicate color, which follow more or less the rhythmic swirl of the contour of the volume. In large canvases the men's figures are often reminiscent of Poussin's in general form, in clean-cut drawing, in type of movement and attitude, in the brownish-red flesh with accentuated highlights, and in the color of textiles with patterns of large areas of light and shade. His treatment of landscape in these large pictures shows the influence of Claude in the use of atmospheric haze; but instead of Claude's golden glow, a steely blue tone, cool and dry, pervades the atmosphere and usually dominates the color-scheme of the entire picture. It is this tone, akin to certain color-effects in Tiepolo, which differentiates Boucher's color-schemes from those of the Venetians, Claude and Rubens, and also from most of the work of Watteau, Lancret, and Pater. Not unfrequently in Boucher's large compositions there appears a resemblance to Dutch still-life painting in the miniature type of literal drawing in flowers, fruit, and similar details.[4] Boucher's execution is less heavy, however, and the Dutch influence probably reached him by way of the French flower-painters of the seventeenth century.[5]

Boucher's landscapes with small subsidiary figures[6] are closely allied to the Dutch tradition, especially to Hobbema, in the drawing and placing of masses; and to Vermeer, Berckheyde, and van der Heyden, in the treatment of small figures by juxtaposed contrasting areas and spots of light and dark. These small figures recall also Guardi in the structural quality of color and in the manner of execution.

With very few exceptions, Boucher's whole manner and use of the plastic means is superficial, mechanical, stylistic. His surface

[4] Cf., e.g., Boucher's "Rape of Europa" (161) and Huysum's "Fruit and Flowers" (166).

[5] E.g., French seventeenth century "Flowerpiece" (197) and "Flowerpiece" (198).

[6] E.g., Boucher's "Bridge" (290) and "Mill" (292).

and texture are dry, and so too as a rule is his color, which is mat and without internal glow. His effects of light are artificial, and with no real feeling of out-of-door illumination, and his deliberately concocted decorative light-patterns suggest stage-scenery. His technique—whether of smooth, even finish, or of slightly curved parallel hatchings—is indiscriminately applied to flesh and textiles alike, so that the uniform surface-quality of paint fails to conform to the specific texture of individual objects. His composition is likewise banal and limited in scope: Tintoretto's diagonal type of organization, for example, with compactly placed masses on one side balancing open space on the other, becomes a mere cliché. The rhythm of the component masses in his elliptical and pyramidal formations is usually artificial, and is produced by literally rendered movements of figures, arms, legs, tilted heads, and rumpled floating draperies, all calculatedly set at sharply contrasting direction with each other. Sky, clouds, distance are rendered representatively, never by subtle relationships of color and light. There is constant resort to Tiepolo's vertical organization of rhythmically moving figures and draperies, exaggeratedly projecting in and out of the shallow foreground space.[7] It is this formalistic use of represented movement, perspective and *repoussoir* compositional thrusts, coupled with the general emphasis upon merely decorative aspects of color, light, and line, which gives to Boucher's works, particularly to his large compositions, their quality of stage-settings.

Fragonard (1732–1806), a facile painter, borrowed from various sources without adding anything new to them or achieving a distinctive style of his own. For example, "Happy Mother" (136) and "Schoolmistress" (163) repeat the conventional Dutch interior scene with its characteristic light- and dark-contrasts and subdued color-scheme, in which brownish tan predominates; but the form is Italianized and made lighter by loose drawing, free technique, fluid color, and generally light execution. "Young Woman and Child" (320) is mainly Lancret's delicate type of picture tempered with characteristic Boucher traits. "Fancy Figure" (318) is Rubens parodied by flashy, flamboyant technique, a greater parade of showy brush strokes than any ever perpetrated by Hals, Manet, or Sargent. "Bathers" (316) with its swirl, porcelainlike coloring of

---

[7] The sources of this Tiepolo-Boucher style is in Paolo Veronese's composition of the type represented in "Jupiter Destroying the Vices" (401).

flesh, mechanistic modeling, and sprightliness of movement, is an obvious and specious combination of drafts upon Rubens, Tiepolo, and Boucher. The flashy light-and-dark contrasts in "Bacchante Asleep" (315) repeat the Leonardo-Luini manner and add flabby drawing and ostentatious brushwork, forming the particular type of eighteenth century painting which Prud'hon reduced to academicism. "Blindman's Buff" (317) repeats Hobbema's characteristic use of dramatic contrast of light and dark in composition. Even Fragonard's best work, "Music Lesson" (319), when compared with, for example, Rubens' "Hélène Fourment and her Children" (382), reveals his unscrupulous use of Rubens' color, tone, drawing, and, to some extent, composition. In a number of paintings, Chardin's drawing of figures is also obviously followed but never in a successfully creative manner.

Fragonard, like Watteau, Lancret, and Pater, depicted numerous intime open-air scenes representative of the milieu of the period, and obtained the familiar compositional effects of the tradition, with large dense masses of dark color surrounding areas of diffused light against which smaller masses appear silhouetted *à contre jour*.[8] His rhythms are, in general, more turbulent than Watteau's, Lancret's, and Pater's, his technique is looser, his use of light-and-dark contrasts or chiaroscuro in modeling and composition is more dramatic and closer in effect to that in the Italians and Dutch. He leans more heavily upon these sources than any of his contemporaries, and is of less importance not only as an artist but also as a personality.

With Coypel, Le Sueur, Greuze, Moreau, and Prud'hon the French tradition of the seventeenth and eighteenth centuries degenerated rapidly into academicism. The characteristic French grace and lightness remained, but attenuation of the plastic means made the delicacy feeble and spongy. **Claude Joseph Vernet** (1714–1789) is the only painter of this group who attained distinction as an artist. He utilized Boucher's drawing and modeling of figures, and his cold blue-green atmosphere, and developed a form reminiscent of both Poussin and Claude. His figures are as a rule extremely graceful, with very skilfully rendered active and delicately poised movement.[9] **Louis Gabriel Moreau** (1740–1806) was

[8] E.g., Fragonard's "Gardens of the Villa d'Este, Tivoli" (162) and "Souvenir" (164).
[9] E.g., Vernet's "Bathers" (397), "Landscape" (398), and "Port of Marseilles" (399).

scarcely more than a skilled academic follower of Joseph Vernet. **Pierre Paul Prud'hon** (1758-1823) carried to the extreme of academicism the overdramatic contrasts of light and dark that Fragonard took over from Leonardo and Luini.[10] His drawing is soft, flabby, and amorphous, his color banal, and his composition usually theatrical.

Chardin (1699-1779), one of the most important painters of any time or tradition, has all the basic charm and delicacy of his race and epoch, but he far excels his French contemporaries in the individuality and vigor of his expression and in the originality of his use of traditions. With him the characteristic French grace, daintiness, and delicacy cease to be primarily decorative and are organically embedded in the substance, structure, and meaning of things. Everything is done simply and subtly, and the degree of attention given to each element and aspect of the painting is accurately proportioned to its importance in the design, so that each unit strikes the eye with a sense of rightness as to its individual contribution to the form as a whole. The general effect of Chardin's pictures is of dignified grace and poetry, masterly use of technical means, and full conviction of reality, free from tawdriness, over-accentuation, or melodrama. He restored to French painting the dignity of the great Venetians, which the other eighteenth century painters had lost.

In contrast to most of his contemporaries, Chardin makes no use of the tradition of Rubens. His form is based chiefly upon the Venetians, Velásquez, and the Dutch painters of still-life and genre; what he derived from each of these is enriched by his own extraordinary sense of values and feeling for plastic relationships, and is executed with very great technical ability and sensitive control of the medium of paint.

Chardin did for Dutch genre-painting what Watteau did for Rubens, and what Poussin had done for the Italian tradition—he gave it a French quality and thereby created a new form which became a source of inspiration for many important later French painters. In transforming the Dutch tradition he added strength as well as delicacy, eliminating its tendency to literal representation, and reworking it into a much more appealing and original design. His interior scenes, for instance, creatively reconstruct the forms of Vermeer, de Hooch, and Terborch, by a more ingenious

[10] E.g., Prud'hon's "Justice and Divine Vengeance Pursuing Crime" (366).

and subtle use of the plastic means. His "Grace before Meal" (299) and "Industrious Mother" (300) far excel, plastically, any figure-composition by Vermeer or de Hooch; and "Child with Teetotum" (298) is more solid and convincing, richer in plastic content than any Terborch.

No small part of Chardin's superiority is due to his thorough assimilation of what he learned from the Venetians in the use of color and from Velásquez' subtle rendering of appealing spatial relations. His color is not only more solid and structural than the Dutch, it is also richer, finer in sensuous quality, and more delicately varied and harmoniously related. Unlike that of the Dutch and his French contemporaries, it is not obviously or superficially patterned or peppered with light: light, free from all overemphasis, merges with and reënforces color, drawing, modeling, and space, in individual units as well as in the total compositional form. Modeling is solid without being heavy, and is effected by relationships between color, light, and shadow, as well as by the texture of the pigment itself. Shadows usually fall in well-defined, relatively clean-cut areas, but their color and tone are so subtly adjusted to those of adjacent areas that in the passage from dark to light there is no abrupt transition or overdramatic pattern. The shape, degree of accentuation, and general character of the shadows are so modified in different units and designs that they have variety as well as subtlety. There is no suggestion of the mechanical, accentuated pattern of light and shadow which appears in Watteau, Pater, and Fragonard, and even in so good a painter as Lancret.

Again departing from the usual practice of his contemporaries, Chardin's modeling has no emphatic or isolated highlights. The areas of strongest illumination, even when accentuated as highlighted spots,[11] blend organically with the color and the form of the total unit: the middle tones in the modeling are usually more on a par in light-content with the highlighted portion of the unit than with the shaded area, so that the light spreads gradually and subtly over the surface and through the color and texture of the whole mass.

The surface of the paint in Chardin's pictures is sometimes slightly pitted or grainy, an effect which adds to the rugged delicacy of his modeling and often imparts to the surface of the object a texture like that of ceramics. This surface is not a result of tricky technique but a masterly and distinctive achievement in the qual-

[11] E.g., Chardin's "Bottle of Olives" (297).

ity of the paint itself, which in its inherently appealing texture, has never been excelled, even by Titian at his best.[12]

Chardin's drawing owes its superiority to the fact that it is achieved specifically by means of color, with no reliance upon independent contour-line. His shapes are clean-cut, defined by contact of areas in contrasting color or tone, without being either incisively outlined or dramatically set off from each other. The meticulous effect, the miniature-character of Watteau's, Lancret's, and Pater's drawing is replaced by well-controlled simplifications—a broad treatment which yields an effect of convincing, unostentatious gentleness and simplicity.

Chardin's sense of composition is as personal and unstereotyped as are his color and quality of surface. His plastic organizations are full of unexpected notes that give variety, picturesqueness, and piquancy to presentations of very simple subject-matter. Like Renoir, Chardin put poetry into the smallest and most commonplace object, and was able to render plastically and pictorially the essential charm of everyday life. His, like Renoir's, is a convincing realism, in contrast to the specious portrayal, the obviousness, in the other eighteenth century painters in France. Unlike the latter, Chardin's expression, though very much of his time, is undated as regards the fundamental life-values embodied in his form. His pictures are as meaningful now as they were in his own period and country, whereas much in the work of his contemporaries had an appeal only to their own time and milieu, and has withered in interest with the death of the society in which they lived.

The combination of real but homely poetry, a delicacy which is never weakness, and a full masterly use of all the means of his craft, represent Chardin's form—a contribution highly important in itself, and also of vital meaning to many subsequent painters, of whom Goya, Courbet, Corot, Cézanne, and Renoir were the most distinguished.

[12] Cf., e.g., the loaf of bread in Titian's "Disciples at Emmaus" (391) with the similar unit in Chardin's "Bottle of Olives" (297).

CHAPTER XII

FRENCH PAINTING OF THE NINETEENTH CENTURY
PRIOR TO IMPRESSIONISM

TOWARD the end of the eighteenth century there was an abrupt change in the tradition of French painting. The new movement was characterized by a revival of classicism in which the Renaissance forms of Raphael and Mantegna were used as a basis by the new leaders, David and Ingres. In what is conventionally termed "classic" there is a tendency toward accentuation of line at the expense of most of the other elements of the picture, and that influence taken over by the French led to a cold formalism which dominated the academies at the time of David and Ingres.

David (1748–1825) adopted the technique of the Renaissance classic period as a whole, and in spite of great technical proficiency he created nothing new. His shallow color, his general attenuation of all the plastic means, and his repetition of academic clichés, furnish a conclusive demonstration of the futility of mere talent in a painter.

In **Ingres** (1780–1867) also, there is the clear-cut, cold formality characteristic of classic painting. He had, however, the artist's creative ability to make extremely interesting plastic units which reveal a fine feeling for the function of line, space, and mass. The distinctive feature in his design is the personal and extraordinarily skilful manner of using line in the formation of sharp and clear-cut arabesques and angular patterns, which often unify in a total form that arrests and holds the attention. As a colorist Ingres's sole claim to distinction resides in his ability to use color as a re-enforcement of linear effects. His color has usually a pleasing sensuous quality and is used skilfully in a rather literal reproduction of textures and stuffs with agreeable surfaces, but it is superficial and has little or no structural quality or compositional function. When compared with texture-painting by Renoir it suffers greatly, because Renoir adds significance to the object by

[265]

making color an essential part of it. Ingres's color and form are separable upon inspection, while Renoir's are not; the result is that Ingres's textiles are much the less convincing of the two: we feel the semblance, not the substance.

In all good paintings the background is an integral part of the picture. In Ingres's portraits the background is usually an unrelated, academic arrangement of parts, in an almost monochrome tone, and is scarcely more than a conventional setting of little or no intrinsic interest except for great skill in the handling of paint. The point may be illustrated by a comparison of Ingres with his follower Chassériau, whose backgrounds are more a part of the picture as a whole, though he was in general infinitely inferior to Ingres.

Delacroix (1798–1863) broke away from the neo-classicism of Ingres and David and found inspiration in the Venetians' color, drama, and pageantry, as transmitted through Rubens and modified by Constable's brush strokes and divided color. His color is deeper, richer, stronger than that of his immediate predecessors. It enters into the structure of objects and functions powerfully in composing the picture. Although he had a strong feeling for composition, his habitual overuse of some of the plastic means, especially a swirl derived from Rubens, to achieve dramatic effects often creates a disbalance which breaks down the design. For example, in "Death of Sardanapalus" (311), the dramatic clouds are felt in terms of line, light, and movement, rather than of color, thus asserting themselves as unrelated entities, rather than as harmonic units in the total picture. The tendency to softness in the painting of flesh is often excessive, and the leaning toward histrionics has no proportionate plastic equivalent, so that the dignity which results from a balanced economical use of the plastic means is lacking. Delacroix is an important figure in the history of art principally because his use of color influenced such first-rate artists as Renoir and Cézanne.

Corot's (1796–1875) figure-painting is, in general, much stronger than his rendering of landscape, but in both forms the plastic means are handled with such consummate skill that his best work represents a balanced creation, containing in solution the finest traditions of painting. His landscapes vary greatly in quality; the early ones, especially those done in Italy, rank in lyricism and strength with the best work of all time, while in many of his later landscapes, the romanticism degenerates into softness. Both Corot and Courbet made legitimate use of the great Dutch and Spanish traditions and converted them into new forms by means of personal vision and great technical skill. Corot's work is more delicate and subtle than Courbet's, and is more appealing by virtue of the human values intrinsic to these qualities.

Courbet (1819–1877) made a radical break with the romanticism of Delacroix by building upon essential elements in the forms of Velásquez and the seventeenth century Dutch painters. He turned for subjects to the world of everyday objects and events, which he painted with force and in stark reality. He started the so-called realistic movement, which has dominated much of the important painting since his time. In Corot, there is a glamour and romance, a reminiscence of the Watteau-Fragonard tradition, freshly conceived and executed; Courbet supplants this obvious lyricism by a naturalism which is a rare combination of power and poetry. His firm drawing and hard waxy surfaces offer a striking contrast to the general softness of much of the Barbizon painters' work. He knew better than the majority of these how to distribute his masses, lights, and shadows, proportion his intervals, render space more subtly, put quality into paint, and compose an organic ensemble. Furthermore, his vigorous use of the brush endows his best work with solidity and strength. Color is an integral and pervasive part of his design, but it is often rather poor in sensuous quality, and his lack of control of tonal relations results in occasional effects of muddiness. He was, however, a masterly painter and a superb artist in his feeling for the relation of things. He gives a rather subtle abstract of the deeper meanings of the great traditions, stripped of their external appendages and welded in a new and vigorous form which has had a revolutionary effect upon all important painting since his day.

Daumier (1808–1879), by the emphasis upon design at the expense of subject-matter, profoundly influenced the movement in modern art which started about the middle of the nineteenth century. Combining the influences of Michelangelo, the Venetians, Bosch, Rembrandt, Velásquez, and Goya, he succeeded in condensing in a small space the effects that Michelangelo and Rembrandt rendered only on a large scale.

As a colorist Daumier ranks with Rembrandt in achieving maximum results with the greatest economy of means and in obtaining profound mystic effects by a modified use of chiaroscuro. In the deep, rich color-harmonies that result from the use of somber colors, he obtained color-values superior to those of many important painters who used a great variety of bright colors. He worked principally in large areas of contrasting colors or tones formally related to each other and unified in a powerful design which determines the general character of the picture. The color-effects obtained by means of chiaroscuro are well illustrated in "Water-Carrier" (183), in which the monumental solidity of the figure is set in fine spatial relations, and made to stand out from a background very closely related to it in color-values. Its modeling, by subtle tonal variations, yields the convincing three-dimensional solidity that gives grandeur and nobility to a finely executed marble statue; its power recalls Michelangelo, but Daumier's rendering of figures in space is decidedly more pictorial than Michelangelo's, which is largely conceived in sculptural terms. When Daumier used brighter colors—red, blue, orange—there results a deep, penetrating quality that makes the painting glow with a richness approaching that of Titian or Giorgione.

His successful use of light is implied in what has been said concerning his use of chiaroscuro. When the light is used both for general illumination and for chiaroscuro, the disposition of spots of light in the various areas of the canvas makes an appealing pattern that contributes greatly to the esthetic effect of the form as a whole.

Daumier's superb control over space by extraordinarily subtle means rivals that of Velásquez. Better than any other man except Cézanne, Daumier knew how to select from the literally innumerable planes that build up objects in space, and to reconstruct them in units expressive of power and force. Of the moderns, Cézanne alone excelled him in ability to make color function structurally in simplified planes. The utilization of so few planes makes Daumier's work appear sketchy, but that is so only when compared with its counterpart in nature: the sparse lines and the comparatively few color-accents impart to the essential characteristics of the objects a more forceful convincing feeling of reality than exists in the natural scene.

Daumier's ability to employ space in a successful union with line and color has seldom been surpassed; indeed, the solid three-dimensionality of his figures owes much to his superb use of space: his massive solid figures are always surrounded with a space which is actually apprehended as a reënforcement of their solidity. Spatial intervals enter in harmonious relations with the colors and tones, so that even when only somber tones are used his pictures are literally space-decorations of the highest grade; in other words, decoration is an integral part of the structural form. Like Rembrandt, he succeeds in giving that mysterious feeling of awe, sometimes tinged with gloom, which comes from our contemplation of space successfully used in the hands of a great creative artist. By comparison, Raphael's accentuation of space appears obvious and trival.

Daumier's greatness as a painter was for a long time obscured by the strength and expressiveness of the drawing in his illustrations. He was almost unique in the ability to use a terse line to express convincingly psychological states, as well as actual and poised movement. His line is rarely sharp and incisive, but appears generally as the broad line of color so frequently used by Titian and Tintoretto. Sometimes it is made up of irregular strips of color and is divided into short wavy lengths which, however, maintain adequate continuity. This character of the line is responsible for the feeling of dynamic movement, the sense of actual life, that Daumier puts into his slightest sketch. By the juxtaposition of a few lines he conveys a degree of conviction and force to essentials that no detailed painting could possibly render; it is this terse, expressive drawing which is the foundation of simplifications and distortions that produce forms of tremendous power. In the merging of line with color and light to render movement, Tintoretto and El Greco are his only serious rivals. He is, in this respect, superior to Michelangelo, Goya, and Degas. Michelangelo's resort to muscular accentuations to express movement and power are means less intrinsic to painting. Delacroix's drama is inferior because the drawing is less simple and terse, the expression is tawdry, and there is no comparable utilization of space.

Daumier's influence has been immense. His technique in various degrees of detail was used to new ends by such important artists as Courbet, Corot, Manet, Cézanne, Renoir, Degas, Glackens, Pascin, Rouault, Matisse, Soutine, Biagio Pinto—to mention only a few. These influences, though sometimes subtle, are nevertheless present in the work of nearly all subsequent important painters who have utilized simplification and distortion in realizing design.

CHAPTER XIII

PORTRAITURE [1]

IN PORTRAIT-PAINTING, an artist is much more rigidly limited than in such fields as landscape or dramatic figure-composition, and he is compelled to get his effects with a minimum of means; consequently, his ability to use these means is severely tested. His problems are: to make the figure seem to live, to distinguish it clearly from its background, and to unify figure and background in a design which is itself esthetically moving, apart from physical resemblance to the sitter.

Among numerous examples of supreme triumphs in portraiture are Dürer's "Self-Portrait" (313), Rembrandt's "Hendrickje Stoffels" (373), Titian's "Man with Glove" (394), and Velásquez' "Infanta Marguerite" (396). All these show spaciousness in the design as a whole, aliveness in the figure, and a clear differentiation between figure and background, accomplished by means so simple and subtle that they almost escape detection. In each case, the effect is of convincing reality achieved by a design of great esthetic power. These painters were the great masters of portraiture; hence the qualities in their work may be taken as standards with which to compare portraits painted by other men, of less distinguished excellence.

Antonello da Messina's "Condottiere" (355) is an early example of portraiture at a high level in which the effect is one of literalism rather than of charm. The means employed are primarily contrasts of light and shadow, with the light used in an obvious way. The background is simply a dark mass, but by slight shadings in tone it is given separate existence, so that the head is clearly defined against it as an independent, solid, real object. In the neighboring "Man's Portrait" (288), by Giovanni Bellini, there is greater variety of means, used less subtly, but the picture is more organically unified and therefore of higher quality. In the portrait attributed to Franciabigio, "Young Man" (322), also

[1] See also discussions, as well as analyses, of van Eyck, Petrus Christus, Rembrandt, Velásquez, Dürer, Strigel, the Clouet School, and Goya.

hanging in the immediate neighborhood, the figure is flat and lacks reality, the whole painting is thin, soft, and unconvincing. In still another painting hanging near by, Raphael's "Young Man" (372), the figure is made to stand out by the facile means of bright light, realistic detail, and striking contrasts in color. Skilful utilization of traditional technique replaces imaginative power, and the effect is tawdry: with no opportunity to use his gifts for elaborate space-composition and dramatic movement, Raphael is compelled to resort to what is essentially virtuosity.

In Tintoretto's "Artist's Portrait" (386), linear distortion makes the face striking, dramatic, and interesting in pattern, without loss of essential strength. His characteristic swirl plays an important rôle: it gives animation and power to the features and to the general expression; it also permits duplication, reënforcement, and harmony of rhythms, all of which add interest to the design. As a work of art it is inferior to Titian's "Man with Glove" (394), in which the means are simpler, more restrained, and more organically merged.

In portraiture, as in other subjects, no painter's achievements are uniformly equal. In Titian's "Alfonso da Ferrara and Laura di Dianti" (389), the drawing and light are over-illustrative in the Raphaelesque manner, so that in spite of the Venetian color there is a cloying sweetness. In Rembrandt's "Self-Portrait, as an Old Man" (375), the light is not used with uniform success and it obscures rather than illuminates the hand of the figure. In his "Man with Stick" (374), the very sharp contrast between the dark side and the light side of the face produces an impression of tricky melodrama, which very seriously impairs plastic unity.

An instance of striking, picturesque, and skilfully executed portrait-painting which rarely reached the heights of great art, is that of Frans Hals. His figures are well placed against the background, and they have an attractive sense of animation in posture and expression; but they are usually theatrical instead of solidly human or plastically convincing. His defective grasp of deeply moving human values is only emphasized by his superb technical skill. The minutely detailed stuffs, for example, in "Laughing Cavalier" (165), have a positive intrinsic value in their extraordinarily skilful execution, and intricacy of decoration, and they contribute to the general design by adequate sense of relationship to the contrasting broad painting of the flesh; but we see how extraneous to art is such painting when we compare it with Rembrandt's or Velásquez' less showy but more convincing rendering of textiles. The heraldic device in "Nicolas van Beresteyn" (333), and "Wife of Paulus van Beresteyn" (334), which is used to animate a background lacking in intrinsic interest, is another instance of Hals' cheap strain. Hals' influence upon subsequent painters has been enormous: his technique of brushwork was creatively used by Manet and Cézanne and, to a less extent, by van Gogh. Unfortunately it became the chief stock-in-trade of a host of painters who, mistaking virtuosity for art, turn out portraits that are clever exercises in brushwork.

Rubens falls far below the standard set by the greatest portraitists. His color, brighter than that of Titian or Rembrandt, is put to facile and obvious use in differentiating figure and background. While this method adds decorative quality, the obviousness cheapens the effect. Furthermore, while his greater wealth of detail and the skilled adaptation of swirling line and color lend additional interest to the design, these obvious technical procedures seem to be superfluous baggage that prohibits simplicity and dignity. Rubens' omnipresent dramatic sense appears in his treatment of the figures, and in the merging of light, line, color, and shadow to realize a distinctive form in his dynamic backgrounds. In "Baron Henri de Vicq" (380), the red drapery of the background sets off the head by vivid contrast of color, but functions merely as a screen instead of carrying the volume of the head into encompassing space.

After Rubens, portrait-painting tended, in the main, toward mere surface-prettiness. This is strikingly evident in van Dyck, who is an elegant, feminine edition of Rubens, with essentially nothing of his own to show, in spite of his great skill with the brush. He exaggerated Rubens' decorative quality and transmitted it to the English portrait-painters, Reynolds, Gainsborough, Lawrence, and the lesser men of the English school, in whose work it became mainly mere prettiness and virtuosity. An exception is Bonington's "Old Housekeeper" (289), in which thick impasto, with slight reminiscences of Hals in the brushwork, is successfully used in the manner of Rembrandt and gives an expressive and dignified effect. Romney's portraits display skilful execution but are for the most part attenuated repetitions of what has been said by artists who were creators as well as skilled technicians.

In the nineteenth and twentieth centuries, portrait-painting, as a distinct type of plastic art, was relatively neglected by artists of

Dürer (313)   Analysis, page 440

Rembrandt (373)   Analysis, page 451

Velásquez (396)   Analysis, page 435

Goya (204)   Analysis, page 436

the first rank. Professional portrait-painters have, as a rule, been mere traffickers in the methods of other men. Although great artists, such as Corot, Courbet, Daumier, Manet, Renoir, and Cézanne, painted numerous portraits, they treated them as pretexts for imaginative creations rather than as subjects for the attainment of likeness of particular persons. The gradual decline in portraiture was interrupted, however, by one very important painter, Goya. His psychological acumen and his command of the means of his art combined to make him the last great portrait-painter. After him, portrait-painting becomes chiefly an aspect of the new traditions, and presents no special or distinctive features.

CHAPTER XIV

LANDSCAPE [1]

PRIOR to Claude le Lorrain, landscape was an incidental setting for the life of people, sometimes done skilfully and with poetic insight and charm, but always secondary to the human story. In the early Renaissance painters, Giotto, Piero della Francesca, Mantegna, Carpaccio, the landscape proper was varied by architectural features, and in Mantegna and Carpaccio these architectural features are more important elements in the effect than the natural landscape. Perugino approaches nearer to modern conceptions of landscape in his airy spaciousness, and in Titian and in Giorgione the actual sense of a living world surrounding human beings is very strongly felt. In Leonardo, even when the natural scene is very well done, as it is in his "Bacchus" (341) and "Mona Lisa" (343), its essential function in the picture is to heighten the interest in the human beings portrayed.

In **Claude le Lorrain** (1600–1682) the primacy has passed to nature and, although the human interest remains, the figures are, as a rule, executed perfunctorily and are unconvincing. Hills, valleys, trees, sea, sky, light, and atmosphere are really the chief actors in a drama in which nature dominates man, instead of being dominated by him. Claude paid little attention to naturalistic detail in particular objects and concentrated his efforts on the situation as a whole: the effect is a feeling of place which is epic in its scope. The life is in the whole, not in the parts, and is deep and impressive. He paints a romantic, Virgilian epic in which nature is felt animistically, pervaded with qualities that make a direct human appeal. It is charged with the emotions that come from natural landscape in its vastness, in its glamour, mystery, grandeur, majesty, solemnity, as we feel these in the Grand Canyon or the Valley of the Tarn. Judged as an independent entity, his most successful work, as represented in the London National Gallery pictures, ranks with the best landscape-painting. Claude con-

[1] See also chapters "The Dutch Tradition" and "Impressionism."

verted the Venetian glow into a brilliantly lighted and colorful atmosphere that gives the sense of a livingness in nature, a warmth and charm. He imparted a French feeling to the Italian tradition while retaining the placidity of classic myth.

Claude achieves his results chiefly by means of composition and especially of space-composition, by which he created a plastic design of high order. The color has a pervasive effect, attained through the use of diffused color-harmonies, atmosphere, and light that make powerful contributions to the plastic form. Color itself, as well as the structure of individual objects, were matters of secondary importance to Claude. Detail in objects is lifeless and unconvincing. This, however, is strictly in accord with the requirements of his design—any great interest in particular things would militate against the total effect which it was the purpose of his design to give. For the same reason, the drawing is without the terse, expressive character that it has in Daumier or Goya or Degas. Even the drama of the story in the subject-matter is toned down in individual interest and made contributory to heightening the appeal of the design. In many of Claude's paintings there are glaring evidences of his neglect of technical problems raised by the introduction of the story; but it is a proof of his genius that he could let the subsidiary technical omissions take care of themselves while he confined his attention to the chief purpose of realizing an effective total design of power and magnitude of conception. To censure him because of his particular sins of omission and commission, such as the woodenness of his figures, or the perfunctory rendering of his trees, and other natural objects, is to apply a technical rule and to forget the essential rôle and purpose of design. Unfortunately, many of Claude's paintings do show an overaccentuation of light which creates specious melodrama.

Rubens (1577–1640) was, as a rule, inferior to Claude as a landscape-painter, because the animation and movement which are intrinsic to Rubens' technique are not adapted to the placidity so often characteristic of landscape. Except when he depicts a storm or other manifestation of turmoil in nature, his landscapes suffer from the attempt to adapt his technique to an unsuitable purpose. Although they are often rendered in luscious color, strong line, and fine spacing, all unified in an animated and rhythmic design, these intrinsic merits do not alter the inappropriateness of the form itself. Sometimes, however, as in his "Autumn, the Château de Steen" (150), or in the incidental landscape in "Judgment of Paris" (151), the characteristic Rubens swirl is so toned down that it really accords with the spirit of tranquil nature.

Constable (1776–1837), of all landscape-painters, made the best creative use of Venetian color, in highly individualized interpretations of the forms of Claude, Rubens, and the Dutch landscape-painters, especially Hobbema. His rich juicy color is handled somewhat in the manner of Rubens but he added a jewel-like quality of his own, and he achieved greater power and drama than Hobbema, by plastic means less obvious and of greater esthetic strength. Color in Constable is deeper, richer, and more solid than in the Dutch, and it is handled in quite a special way: it is broken into small units and tinged with spots of lighter paint, so that no one spot is all of the same color, but is a mosaic of colors in itself. This is obviously the source of the color-technique of Delacroix and Claude Monet. The resemblance to Delacroix is greater, because Monet's spots are smaller, more frequent, brighter, and better adapted to give the composite effect of one color when seen at a distance. Constable attains this effect also in considerable degree, but his spots of color are not played upon by light as are Monet's. His light is used as the traditional general illumination with local accentuations rather than, as with Monet, to take the chief rôle in the picture. Constable's method gives a more naturalistic effect and firmer structural solidity to ground, trees, buildings, and other details, such as one would see in ordinary life, without special appeal to the effect that sunlight actually gives to objects, as we see it in Monet.

Constable's luscious, unctuous color is highly structural in quite its own way. There is a richness, a depth, somewhat reminiscent of the Venetians, but the color is used in small areas, patterned by brush strokes of thick, rugged impasto, which merge well in a unified design. His feeling for landscape is akin to Claude's but it is for landscape on a far smaller scale, and is so changed in the manner of presentation that Claude's influence is pervasive rather than apparent in any specific use of technique. Instead of Claude's grandeur, majesty, deeply moving mystery, Constable offers the charm of simplicity, of the intime, the quietly mystical feeling of the countryside; there is an appealing, rugged, this-world solidity, while in Claude an airy, other-world delicacy is found. Constable's spirit is that of local place, but is deeply tinged with Claude's

Claude le Lorrain (180)

Corot (181)

Constable (133)

Analysis, page 463

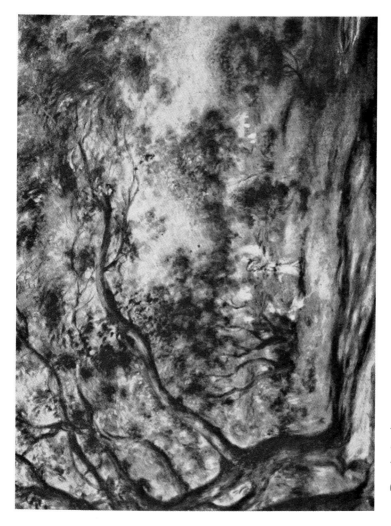

Renoir (242)

Rousseau, *le douanier* (243)

Kane (215)

vision of general landscape. Because of his better sense of color and a more balanced use of the plastic means, Constable produced results that are on the whole superior to those of Claude.

The painting of Constable is best appreciated by a study at close quarters. In his "Hay-Wain" (132), for instance, every small area reveals an exquisite quality obtained by light, line, color, and brush strokes; the surface is enhanced by color-chords which have a sensuous quality sometimes closely akin to that of fine ceramics marked from accidents of firing. This color-form as a whole has a marvelous strength and reality, plus a depth and richness which can only be compared with that of the Venetians and Rembrandt.

Constable's method of drawing is as broad as that of the impressionists: a face, an arm, a hand, when the figure is in a landscape, is rendered by one or two brief touches or strokes. Wagons, houses, trees, are depicted with a greater degree of naturalistic detail than in the impressionists, with more attention to outline, and less to the play of light as a constituent in these large masses. The shadows are dark but rich, and the broad drawing enhances the general decorative quality of the canvases.

Constable's composition is of the highest order because it is organized by means of color, as in all the greatest painters. The masses are distributed in an original manner with little in the way of symmetrical arrangement about a central unit. In general, he is as free from the use of obvious technical devices as any other great painter. His technique of color-division and patterns of light is so merged in the general quality of the landscape that there is a strong composite effect attained without perceptible emphasis upon means. The plastic units are harmonized throughout, and blend into a rich, deeply moving general design.

Constable influenced subsequent landscape-painting very profoundly, and, more than any other single individual, he was the father of impressionism. It was chiefly his example and method that stimulated Delacroix and his successors to turn again to color after the colorless neo-classicism of David and Ingres.

Turner (1775–1851) began as a skilful imitator of the surface-aspects of Claude, which he diluted and made meretricious by an infusion of tawdry melodrama and irrelevant literary baggage. He never escaped from indulgence in cheap contrasts of calm and storm, in garish color and exaggerated light. His pictures are striking because of their superficial colorfulness and patterns. When they are analyzed, nothing substantial emerges: everything is on the surface, even the constant effort to do something for which the requisite grasp of plastic essentials is lacking, as, for example, in his imitations of Claude. Turner's form is that of flashy illustration united with virtuosity. His pictures have no place in art.

The first important landscape-painting in France in the nineteenth century is that of the **Barbizon School.** These painters derived from Claude, the Dutch, and Constable. They made Claude's atmosphere lighter, more silvery, sometimes more delicate, but they lost much of its plastic significance. They did the same with the influence of Constable, from whom, as well as from the Dutch, they got the intime small-scale quality of their style. The skies sometimes suggest Tintoretto's, but are without his quality or force. In **Théodore Rousseau** (1812–1867) the resemblance to Claude in composition, in glowing atmosphere, is most obvious. **Corot** (1796–1875) is the most important member of the school. His early work, done mostly in Italy, is stronger and far superior in every way to his late landscapes which are more delicate, silvery, lacy, and show the influence of the eighteenth century French painters in their lightness. His form lacks Claude's grandeur and Constable's power and richness, but it is essentially genuine and dignified in spite of its lightness and the obviousness of its romantic appeal.

Courbet's (1819–1877) landscapes, like his work in general, are episodic rather than epic, but his power largely compensates for this episodic character. Even at their best, however, his landscapes rarely attain to the high esthetic quality of Corot's.

Millet's (1814–1875) paintings are scarcely entitled to serious consideration as landscapes, because he sees nature as a setting for a human story essentially sentimental. His outstanding characteristic, the portrayal of movement by linear effects, is basically a repetition of Daumier's style, but it lacks Daumier's simplicity, directness, and power, and is employed so monotonously that it amounts to an academic cliché. Millet's preoccupation was with the life of the lower classes, the dignity of labor, the pietism of the masses. This is done well enough as illustration, but is of little plastic interest. He lacks good color, uses light speciously, has no ability to put quality into pigment, and has no feeling for comprehensive designs of his own. He is essentially a story-telling painter whose shoddiness of technical methods is matched by the blatant sentimentalism of his subject-matter.

BOOK IV
MODERN PAINTING

CHAPTER I

THE TRANSITION TO MODERN PAINTING

THE LINE of demarcation between painting which is and which is not modern is difficult to draw with exactness, but it is clear that impressionism made a sharp break with the traditions that preceded it. For practical purposes, contemporary painting may be said to date from the age of Courbet, Manet, Monet, and Pissarro. In the work of these men, the motives of the later men are present, although not disengaged from the traditions which went before. The chief point of difference between the old and the new may be said to be that the moderns exhibit greater interest in a design which depends more upon its plastic content than upon subject-matter for its esthetic value.

In order to show the development of this interest, it will be necessary to trace the evolution of plastic design as something in itself, apart from the question of subject-matter. Criticism of any work of plastic art is valid in so far as it concerns itself with the form the artist has created out of the means at his disposal, namely, line, color, light, and space. That is as true of the work of the Renaissance painters as it is of Cézanne or Matisse, and there can be no reasonable doubt that what makes the art of Giotto great is not the religious subject-matter, but the plastic form, the design, by which deep human values are conveyed. A variety of circumstances prevented the early Italian painters from making a sharp distinction between their interest in design and their interest in illustrating a religious or historical narrative. The spirit and state of culture of the early Renaissance required that painting fulfil definite public functions. It was necessary that church frescoes should illustrate religious motifs, that portraits should reproduce their originals, that pictures ordered by states or guilds should portray specific occurrences of interest to their purchasers. The general conditions were such that books were accessible only to the few, and their function was largely taken over by painting. All these circumstances made it impossible that properly plastic or pictorial motives should operate without constraint. The history of the transition to modern painting consists of an account of the removal of all such irrelevant compulsions, and of how the employment of the various plastic means came to be more and more directed to the realization of pure design. Such an account will make clear the essential continuity between painters apparently as diverse as Piero della Francesca and Picasso, Tintoretto and Cézanne.

Design, as it is found in modern and contemporary painting, appears in the work of the early Italians whenever literal reproduction is so modified that the arrangement and handling of objects make a more esthetically moving plastic form. Giotto is, in his way, as far from literalism as Renoir. If we compare Giotto with his inferior contemporaries, we see at once that a large number of his simplifications must have been conscious departures from photographic representation. These departures are of the very essence of the appeal of his themes, and are clearly expressive of an interest in plastic form for itself. Even though his designs are always accompanied by a narrative, they embody more the spirit than the details of the narrative; in other words, they express a human interest of essential value in terms truly plastic, and such expressiveness is inevitably an enhancement and not a distraction. In this sense Giotto seems far more modern than such painters as van Dyck, Reynolds, or David, in whom the rôle of painting is instrumental to such cheap human activities as personal flattery or surface imitation.

In the early Florentines, Uccello and Fra Filippo Lippi, interest in design was so paramount that academic critics propagate the obvious misconception that Uccello was principally an experimenter in perspective. But considered from the plastic standpoint, his work is a striking illustration of the value of a design which discards an imitative presentation of the spatial relationships of objects in favor of one which has greater intrinsic worth. Fra Filippo Lippi distorted perspective in still another manner, and achieved a design which is akin plastically to that used by many important painters since Courbet.

Design is the animating motive in drawing whenever there is simplification or deliberate distortion directed to heightening of esthetic effect; this is clearly discernible in Andrea del Castagno, in Michelangelo, in El Greco, and other great painters. In all of them drawing is only partly representative and more esthetic or expressive in intent. In the fifteenth century Florentine, Masaccio,

Manet (218)

Greek Sculpture (209)

Michelangelo (421)

Analysis, page 408

The Greek tradition and its

Delacroix (185)

Cézanne (175A)

transition to modern versions.

[295]

Byzantine Mosaic (413)

Analysis, page 470

van Gogh (203)

the deliberate distortions of line, light, and color produce an appearance that is both naturalistic and infinitely more moving esthetically than any literal or photographic representation could be. The paintings of these great artists prove the absurdity of those ultra-modern writers who contend that plastic form is an absolute creation of the artist, in which no attempt is made to render the quality of anything in nature. We maintain that such form can be no more than decoration, that plastic form at its best does seek to give an equivalent of something real—of fundamental aspects, of essences, though not of insignificant detail. In fact, at all stages in the history of painting, from Masaccio to Manet and Matisse, the departures from literalism by which a more satisfactory design is secured, accomplish *also* a convincing effect of reality: we have not receded from the human significance of scenes and events but approached nearer to it.

Another form of modernism is anticipated in Botticelli, in whom design concerns itself chiefly with decoration. This inferior order of design has its modern counterpart in those cubistic paintings in which design is reduced to the level of mere pattern; this is in the same category, esthetically, as the pattern in a rug.

When a painter uses color which departs from the observable color of an object, that also constitutes distortion. Such distortion has been constantly practiced to enhance the value of design, notably by all the great Venetians. The Venetian glow, a circumambient atmosphere of color, is obviously a color-distortion introduced to modify, harmonize, emphasize, and set off the colorful aspect of things, so that the effects are richer than those found in nature. The most original element in the work of Matisse, that is, his interest in color-combinations for their own sake, is thus clearly foreshadowed in the Venetians. But this similarity is overlooked because of the great differences in perspective, solidity, and the quality of the colors used by the Venetians and those used by Matisse.

Light is also distorted from its naturalistic effects in the interest of design. When used naturalistically, light accomplishes some degree of modeling and sets off color; but these are only a few of its functions in contributing to great effects in art. In Leonardo, for example, it does much more than this. Its modeling function is strongly accentuated and the way it falls upon surfaces is not always in accordance with physical laws, but is so modified that it makes a pattern cognate with the general design. It would be manifestly absurd to accuse Leonardo, one of the most advanced scientists of his day, of ignorance of the physical laws that govern the incidence and reflection of light; it is more reasonable to suppose that his distortions of light were used deliberately, with the esthetic motive of forming a specific pattern. Both Leonardo and Raphael used light in the same manner, even to the extent of an accentuation that disturbs the balance of plastic means. A better use of light as an independent pattern that unifies in the total plastic form is found in Piero della Francesca, in most of the painters of the Venetian school, in Poussin, and in most of the important moderns and contemporaries.

Line, light, and color are all highly distorted in El Greco, partly to heighten the effect of religious mysticism, but mainly to achieve a form of intrinsic interest which adds to the direct moving power of the picture without going through the circuit of appeal to the emotions aroused by religious imagery. Rembrandt's chiaroscuro is distorted light employed for two distinct and obvious purposes, first to show an objective fact, such as the three-dimensional solidity of a head; second, as a means of giving to a particular arrangement of color and line a specific quality more moving than that yielded by ordinary illumination. Even in Velásquez, where the effect of the picture as a whole is apparently realistic, the realism, like that of Masaccio, is attained by many departures from exact reproduction, all of which contribute directly to the creation of a form far more effective than any distribution of objects literally depicted. In all these painters there is interest in illustration, but the purely plastic interest is also present, though it has not yet appeared in isolation.

The actual process of transition is to be seen in the impressionists, in whose work literal representation is scarcely attempted; the drawing is very broad, and much greater liberties are taken with the actual coloring of objects than in the earlier painters. With the impressionists it is the mode of presentation and not the object presented that counts. For example, in Manet's "Olympia" (348) it is apparent that the interest lies in the composition and that the story is unimportant. The strangely modeled and proportioned woman placed in just that position and in just those relations with surrounding objects, creates something speaking its own language and more moving than any literally depicted story. This picture represents an advance toward abstract plastic form when compared with, say, Rubens' "Judgment of Paris"

(151), in which it would be much easier for the spectator to lose his way in the narrative.

One of the most important practices of the impressionists, the distortion of perspective, is clearly apparent in the fifteenth century Florentine, Uccello. The impressionists varied the effect by rendering foreground, middle distance, and background as a homogeneous area of light-and-color which serves to unify the composition.

This relative freedom from literary or photographic interest, that is, from the interests which are not plastic, recurs in all the impressionists. Their very technique, the use of divided color, is itself a departure from literalism, since it replaces a merely imitative rendering of colored surfaces by one in which the colorfulness of objects is more imaginatively realized. In Monet, the sense of design is less vigorous than in Manet or in Pissarro, and he sometimes falls victim to an interest in the effect of sunlight on color, which interest is more photographic than plastic. But the greater artists of the group, Renoir and Cézanne, used sunlight and divided tones only as means to the achievement of a design which is purely plastic. Their forms are richer, more powerful, more convincing than those of any of their predecessors in the nineteenth century. They not only sum up the painters who preceded them in much the same way as Poussin and Rubens summed up the painting of the Renaissance, but they created new forms that stimulated their followers to the creation of still other and different plastic forms. From impressionism has been developed most of what is best in contemporary painting. It may be said that in Renoir and Cézanne, design is more completely realized in terms of color than in any of the early great painters, and that this would not have been possible without the researches of Monet and those who followed him. To these pioneers is due the credit for forging the instrument by means of which the effects characteristic of modern art at its best were achieved. To these achievements we may now proceed.

CHAPTER II

IMPRESSIONISM

THE MOVEMENT known as impressionism was more deeply revolutionary than any preceding movement except the departure by Giotto from the traditions of the Middle Ages. However, like all other important developments in either science or art, impressionism was not of sudden birth, a bolt from the blue; it was a natural evolution of methods which had their origin in various traditions including the Florentine and the Venetian; and it was also foreshadowed in certain aspects of drawing and technique in the work of Velásquez, Constable, Daumier, and Courbet. As we have seen, one of the most important contributions of the Florentine tradition was the development of aërial perspective by Masaccio, who portrayed an actually visible atmosphere by means of light and color, blended into a veil or haze. To this atmosphere, the Venetians added overtones of color and achieved the distinctive Venetian glow. Masaccio was also apparently the first to render realistic perspective, by which objects remote from the eye are blurred in outline. This atmosphere and aërial perspective, the blurred outlines of distant objects, and the glow were all utilized in a specific manner by the impressionists.

Their method of using light also evolved from some of the best traditions. The bathing of the whole atmosphere with light in such a way that its various points of contact with masses, spatial intervals, and color, form a definite pattern, was used by Giotto and by important painters of all succeeding centuries.

Another essential feature of the impressionistic method, the use of pure and contrasting colors applied side by side in small brush strokes, was already a characteristic of the work of Constable, and the method had been taken over in the French tradition by Delacroix with scarcely any modification. To Daumier and Velásquez, the impressionists owe much of the character of their simplified drawing and modeling and also the use of a large area of single color so applied that at a distance it gives a greater feeling of reality than could be achieved by the painting of details.

[300]

The major features of the impressionistic technique and method are as follows: (1) Spots of pure color applied side by side in all parts of the canvas. (2) Obvious brushwork in the application of color. (3) Variation in size, shape, direction, and degree of perceptibility of the individual spots of color or brush strokes. (4) Use of light in connection with color in three ways: (a) as a series of concentrated focuses that bring out the glow, intensity, and degree of saturation of the color; (b) as a general illumination by which the canvas is flooded with sunlight; (c) as colored light so distributed all over the canvas that a homogeneous color-and-light mass replaces the representation of aërial perspective theretofore employed by painters.

The originators of impressionism, as represented by particular effects of color, sunlight, drawing, and technique, were Edouard Manet and Claude Monet, each of whom contributed something definite to the tradition which has persisted, with varying degrees of modification, up to the present time. Among the participants were a number of important men including Renoir, Cézanne, Pissarro, Sisley, and lesser artists who worked with essentially the same method.

Manet's (1832–1883) art was founded principally upon the Velásquez and Hals traditions but offered a still greater simplification of means, and his method became, as technique, more obvious than Velásquez'. He abolished dark shadows and supplanted them with color, or sometimes even omitted shadows where they would naturally fall.[1]

The impressionistic technique in its most complete form was developed chiefly by **Claude Monet** (1840–1926), who made a still greater use of light than Manet, and especially adapted it, in combination with bright color, to the recording of the local effects of sunlight at various hours of the day.

With this method certain results can be obtained that are not possible by other means, just as certain other individual effects can be best rendered by the special technique of Tintoretto, of Rubens, or of El Greco. Conversely, it is equally evident that the indiscriminate use of the impressionistic form would yield results as inadequate as, for example, those ensuing upon the application of Rubens' technique to the essentially tranquil aspects of nature.

[1] See also chapter "Manet," p. 305.

This is an instance of the general principle already emphasized, that there are no rules for choice of technique except the intelligence of the artist and his feeling for the essential plastic qualities of whatever is depicted. Monet erred seriously in making his technique the means of portraying objects or situations to which it was manifestly ill-adapted. He was so preoccupied by the particular and evanescent effects of sunlight upon objects at various hours of the day, that the result was very often a too literal reproduction of the superficial appearance of things, and not enough of either the feeling of essentials or the esthetic effect which results when plastic means are coördinated with the larger ends of design. Greater artists, namely Pissarro, Renoir, and Cézanne, used the method with more discrimination, through adaptations of their own better suited to express their individual vision. In the hands of Renoir and Cézanne, the modified impressionistic method reached the stage where the technique as such became generalized, went into solution, and is recognizable only by a careful study of the transition from the original to the finished manner.

The technique, as Monet used it at times, is responsible, however, for some paintings which combine light, line, color, and space in varied and unified plastic forms of esthetic power. In Monet's "House Boat" (225) and "Madame Monet Embroidering" (226), for instance, there is great skill in the use of each of the plastic elements, and sensitive adaptation of them to the rendering of the essential quality of the subject-matter, so that the technique is felt as a means and not as an end. Even at its strongest, however, his form is never of the highest grade. His composition is far from that of the greatest men in originality and moving power, and his drawing is without the expressiveness of Degas' or Daumier's or Renoir's. Compared to Renoir's, his design is much less enriched with subsidiary units, so that the component parts in his paintings have neither the individual richness of Renoir's nor their functional power. Monet's chief deficiency is in color. When compared with that of the great colorists, such as Renoir and Cézanne, it is inferior in sensuous appeal, in structural quality, and in its function in organizing the total composition. The result is that his form as a whole is weaker and thinner.

From the standpoint of the skilled use of the technique, **Pissarro** (1830–1903) is by far the most important purely impressionistic painter. His feeling for the sensuous character of color was finer than that of Monet, he had greater ability to use it in composing the painting, and he had a finer sense for design in its larger aspects. A fine Pissarro, compared with the best Monet, impresses us with its more powerful and expressive drawing, its color of greater variety and finer quality pervading the whole canvas, and its more forceful, unified organization. Pissarro's ability to make the juxtaposed colors more dynamic by the use of brush strokes gives effects comparable to those of Renoir's early landscapes: there is a deep, lustrous glow that enriches the surface and strengthens the design. His juxtaposed color-units are judiciously varied by the application of nearly uniform color in broad areas which reënforce and bring out the rich texture-effects of the various objects in the landscape. This general method of using broad areas in single color was taken over by Gauguin and made the main feature of his best work. It was adopted also by Cézanne who used it in practically all his work, from the earliest to the latest, but who enriched its effects by juxtaposition with differently treated and contrasting color-areas.

Pissarro's early work leans heavily upon the forms of Corot and Millet; after the advent of impressionism he adheres closely to the technique and style of Monet. At a later point in his career, he originated the method known as pointillism, which consists in the application of color in very small spots all over the canvas. His work of this period is less convincing than that done in his typical broad impressionistic manner. It constitutes an obvious over-accentuation of a plastic means, with inevitable disturbing effect upon the general power of the design.

Seurat (1859–1891) made of pointillism an effective instrument through his great mastery of color and space-composition. Each volume and its adjacent clean-cut spatial intervals form dynamic units which are tied together by means of superbly lighted color in a composition of great individuality. His obvious and stylistic technique does not interfere with artistic creation of high rank. Not only does he render the essentials of people, objects, textiles, and landscape, but often, as in "Models" (247), he achieves a classic form akin to that of the old masters; and, as in his "Port of Honfleur" (248), he far exceeds any of the impressionists in the colorful and luminous realization of the lyric charm of landscape. His work, however, is uneven, made so by color which is occasionally glary and lacking in structural quality.

[303]

It is the habit of a few of the writers on ultra-modern art to state that the impressionists left nothing except a series of convincing pictures of sunlight-effects on outdoor objects. The absurdity of the criticism will be revealed if one compares in points of design, a landscape by **Sisley** (1839–1899) with one by Claude le Lorrain. Design is always a reflection of the extent to which an artist has used the means—line, color, light, space—to achieve an expressive form, regardless of the particular technique employed. Claude le Lorrain's design expresses certain human values, while Sisley, in another type of design determined by a different technique, embodies other but just as genuine human values. Claude emphasizes the grandeur and majesty of landscape, while Sisley conveys a delicacy, a lyric charm, and an intime feeling that are comparatively lacking in Claude. In other words, Claude's expression is epic while Sisley's is episodic, but each embodies the general feeling of landscape. The appealing sensuous quality intrinsic to bright colors, combined with Sisley's special technique, is clearly responsible for an effect which is absent in the Claude. It would be manifestly as absurd to condemn Claude for his failure to avail himself of the sensuous quality of color as it would be to condemn Sisley because he obtained special effects, which represent his own personal vision, through the medium of a technique which happens to be that of impressionism.

CHAPTER III

MANET

MANET (1832–1883) was the link between the traditions represented by Rembrandt, Hals, and Velásquez, and the movement known as impressionism, which Manet himself started, and to which he contributed much of its artistic significance and vitality. His influence upon the great impressionists, upon Renoir and Cézanne, and upon most subsequent painters of importance, was fundamental.

His early work is close to Velásquez' form in general treatment, and especially in color and in manner of using paint to obtain convincing effects by very subtle means. This is seen in his "Boy with Sword" (274), in which the color-scheme, the contrasts of light and dark areas, the treatment of the figure in its relation to the background, the subtle spacing, and the manner of application of the paint to effect simplicity of detail, are all in the style of Velásquez. Yet the painting is original and contains a real and individual rendering of essentials.

From the Velásquez manner Manet developed rapidly a style of his own, and his contributions started the movement which revolutionized the whole of subsequent painting. The change was not in one of the plastic elements but in all of them: light, color, line, space, drawing, modeling, conception of design, manner of applying paint. He put color and light to new uses, devised a system of brushwork somewhat reminiscent of Hals', and achieved a new design in comparatively flat painting, which carries an esthetic appeal independent of, indeed, in spite of, subject-matter. He put new meaning into Courbet's demonstration that the simplest objects and situations in life can be made esthetically moving. He replaced the crude, hard matter-of-factness of Courbet's style by a lightness, delicacy, and richness, which came from his use of color, light, and pigment.

An important factor in Manet's form was his marvelous ability to apply paint; by his method, the simplification characteristic of Velásquez is carried to the extreme: drawing is reduced to a broad generalization which portrays the essential quality of objects and obtains an added appeal from the very manner of its execution by visible brush strokes of rich, deep, often lustrous, but seldom very bright, colors. He substituted for Courbet's waxy smoothness simple flat areas of richer color and greater charm of surface. This point is exemplified in the Metropolitan Museum where Courbet's "Village Maidens" (271) hangs not far from Manet's "Woman with Parrot" (276); and in the Louvre where Courbet's "Wounded Man" (309) may be compared with Manet's "Olympia" (348). Courbet's naturalism loses little of its significance but gains much in esthetic value through Manet's modifications of line, light, color, and brushwork.

Manet was a great colorist—a fact that is overlooked in an age in which the color of Renoir and Cézanne has established new standards; and his greatness in this respect is determined by an ability to make color fulfil its most important function, that of composing a canvas. In his "Dead Christ with Angels" (275), an early work much in the Velásquez manner, the broad color-areas serve to integrate the units as a tightly knit, solid, firm composition, which has some of the dignity and grandeur of the old masters. The color is in some places dry and brittle, but it shows how color of comparatively little sensuous appeal can be made organic and, therefore, of fundamental significance: the color and light are the foundation stones of a series of compositional units yielding new, striking, and individual effects, in a well-balanced ensemble. Richer, more solid, and better illuminated color in one of Manet's later pictures, "Olympia" (348), also functions as the primary agent in unifying a design which speaks its own language relatively independently of subject-matter. It was this picture that was responsible for much of the important developments of painting since his time.

In Manet's depiction of objects, representative details are reduced to a minimum, contours are broken and not sharply defined, lines are never long and are related to color and light, and the pigment is applied in broad flat brush strokes. This extremely simplified type of drawing is highly expressive of the essentials of what is portrayed, and it is a determining constructive factor in the total form. He abandoned the usual method of modeling by color, light, and shadow, but attained a degree of three-dimensional solidity with a quality of flatness that enriches the design. It is not the flatness of the early traditional two-dimensional painting: a varied and masterly use of planes, which enter into the drawing of individual objects and of the total composition, is responsible for a solidity and three-dimensional quality, of the kind and degree that became a basic part of most of the subsequent important painting.

It was Manet's recognition of the functional power of light that made possible also some of the principal developments of impressionism and of later modern and contemporary movements. After about 1870 he used light in connection with color as the chief agent in his design: it became a means of creating new compositional units of vitality and force, and of tying these units together into an organic whole. He made light an element in the color which he substituted for the dark shadows theretofore used to emphasize the three-dimensional qualities of objects. Sometimes he omitted the shadows entirely and made light function, although not naturalistically, in their stead. It is generally used in broad areas in combination with broad areas of color, it endows color with depth and especially with internal luminosity, and effects color-contrasts novel in character and of great esthetic power. Indeed, the luster of his color, especially the blacks, has scarcely been equaled in the whole domain of painting up to that period.

Manet's technique—color and light used in broad areas, together with drawing simplified to the point of extreme generalization, and the application of paint with obvious brush strokes—was a very flexible instrument adapted to a great variety of uses. With it, he obtains the large and massive effects of active color-contrasts, as in "Woman with Parrot" (276), and the quite different results seen in numerous others of his paintings in which the brush strokes are used as the chief agent in making the other elements of his technique so active. Brush strokes occur in varying degrees of breadth, in different directions, in variety of quality, content, and thickness of color, and always effect interior patterns of line, light, and color. In some areas there are the juxtaposed color-spots like those which Claude Monet used as the basis of his technique, while in others color is applied in accentuated broader brush strokes.

Manet's actual productions and the developments for which he is responsible, entitle him to high rank as an artist. His "Boy with Fife" (347) shows how superior he was to Hals, how much stronger than Goya, how much more substantial than Degas, and especially how he transformed Velásquez' technique into a new instrument, with an increased range of power. His revelation of the possibilities of light converted Constable's juxtaposed contrasting color-units into the very foundation stone of the characteristic work of Renoir and Cézanne. His technical contributions and his skilful painting added a new grace and charm to the essentials of objects. Indeed everything that Manet painted has an exquisite quality that depends upon the paint itself; it is doubtful if anybody ever excelled him in this respect. The luminous quality which he put into paint was a contribution of epoch-making significance, as is readily seen by how much practically every subsequent artist of importance—Renoir, Cézanne, Matisse, Picasso, Modigliani, Soutine—owes to Manet in that respect. There is present in Manet's best work a grasp of human character, of the essentials of objects; there is also a feeling for the music of space, subtly used, that compares with Rembrandt's and Velásquez'. In his most successful work one feels the technical dexterity, but it is buttressed by so many substantial qualities that it does not appear as virtuosity. Unfortunately, as with many skilled technicians, Manet's vanity prompted him to "show off," and the frequency of that exhibition of weakness bars him from the class of the highest artists.

Monet (226)   Analysis, page 466

Renoir (240)

Modigliani (223)

Degas (184)

CHAPTER IV

RENOIR [1]

RENOIR's (1841-1919) work, at all stages of his career, was as personal, and his use of the plastic means as original, as that of any painter since the Renaissance. His earliest painting was done under the influence of Courbet, Corot, and the Velásquez-Goya tradition, but even at that stage Courbet's naturalism is freed from its heaviness and the influence of Velásquez and Goya is endowed with a new delicacy and charm reminiscent of the eighteenth century French painters, though with an added note of strength.

From the very start Renoir's mastery of color and extraordinary facility in the use of paint are his outstanding characteristics, and in the late 1860's and early 1870's his work compares in these respects with that of any by his great predecessors. His painting of figures and interiors at this period has deep reality with a strength, delicacy, and charm comparable to Chardin's, Vermeer's, and Velásquez' at their best. Goya's superb rendering of the light, diaphanous quality of stuffs is carried to greater heights by Renoir's finer feeling for color: a piece of filmy material is so painted that the individuality of both the textile and what is seen through it is reënforced by a rich, transparent glow.

These early pictures by Renoir were painted before the development of the impressionistic use of divided color. Both before and after the appearance of the impressionists' technique in his work, he made use of Manet's simplifications and broad brush strokes, but in conjunction with more and richer color and with none of Manet's ostentation. About the middle of the seventies, he developed his first fully distinctive form, the most important characteristics of which were the frequent use of perceptible technique, a color-scheme dominated by blue, green, and ivory, and a patterned arrangement of contrasting light and dark areas. These areas are so saturated with color, and the boundaries between them are so

[1] For a comprehensive study of Renoir's form, see Barnes and de Mazia, *The Art of Renoir*, Minton, Balch & Co., New York, 1935.

fluid, that often a continuous succession of color-chords embraces the whole canvas and gives rise to a delicate and charming color-suffusion, which is also an important agent of compositional unification. The loose drawing, done chiefly with color, is as successful as Manet's in rendering the essential nature of subject-matter, and is plastically much richer. Modeling is effected by a union of color, light, and shadow, in which color plays an important part, even though it does not yet operate so powerfully as in Renoir's later pictures. Three-dimensional solidity and deep space are not emphasized but are achieved subtly and with a degree of conviction akin sometimes to Vermeer's or Corot's, sometimes to Velásquez'. The keynote of the whole form is subtlety, delicacy, charm; it breathes the essential spirit of the French eighteenth century tradition at its finest, but with a fidelity to essential realism and a power of color which Watteau, Lancret, and Fragonard never equaled.

In the pictures painted in the late seventies, there is an increasing reliance upon impressionistic technique and the color-scheme is broadened to include a much larger admixture of reds and yellows. Perceptible technique is rarely obvious to the point of overaccentuation, and is usually varied by areas more uniformly painted. At its best, this method causes the colors to melt into each other, and gives to the surface a quality sometimes of cream or velvet, sometimes of delicate mother-of-pearl. In the early eighties, the color and light become more vivid, and especially much hotter: instead of the cool, subdued greens and blues of the seventies, often brilliant, dazzling reds and oranges dominate the color-scheme. Together with much sharper line they make up pictures very striking decoratively and illustratively, but less well integrated plastically than the best of the previous decade. An extensive incorporation of features from the French eighteenth century tradition—notably a smooth, mother-of-pearl surface, one-piece modeling, fluid, ornamental linear rhythms, and non-realistic painting of flesh—intensifies the decorative aspect of Renoir's work at this period, but also makes it less natural and distinctive of him.

In the early eighties, the influence of Cézanne upon Renoir appears in the drawing and modeling by hatchings of color, and in the accentuation of the dynamic relations between three-dimensional volumes and spatial intervals. But the most significant and lasting Cézanne influence was the technique of brush strokes organized in patches which function as planes. After 1884, Renoir had so thoroughly modified these influences and assimilated them as an integral part of his form that they are no longer separable as entities.

About the middle of the decade, Renoir's experiments culminated in a form which, for him, was definitely exotic. The sharp line, hard surface, and dry pigment of this period give the figures a distinctly sculpturesque character, while backgrounds of landscape are endowed with a tapestry-quality in which modified impressionistic brush strokes are used. Color is of fresco-quality, dry, and sometimes acid. The very pronounced linear aspect of this form has been attributed by many critics to the influence of Ingres, but the resemblance is extremely superficial. Ingres's line constitutes the basic plastic structure of his paintings, and his color, which is comparatively perfunctory, thin, and unreal, is a mere decorative addition; Renoir's color is at this period, as always, fundamental, and the sharp line is merely a particular way of bringing colors into relation. It compels the eye to follow the rhythms of color as constituting volumes in deep space, not the movement and direction of the line itself. The real significance of the form is that it achieves a more definite solidity of masses and dynamic space-composition, and the important influences which it shows are those of the Renaissance frescoes, classic sculpture, and the French eighteenth century painters, especially Boucher. As soon as this dynamic space-composition was achieved, Renoir abandoned the form as a whole, and set about attaining space-organizations more specifically by means of color.

In the late eighties, Renoir turned his attention to a similar type of composition in landscapes, and by 1889, in "Mount Ste. Victoire" (241), he achieved an extremely convincing and powerful expression of the movement of solid color-volumes in deep space. These volumes are so free from minute detail or obvious realism that to an experienced observer they often seem to be scarcely solid at all, but plastically they realize the essence of massiveness, while the compositional rhythm is made more pervasive and powerful by the continuous flow of structural color over the whole surface of the canvas, as well as by a suffusion of luminous color which recalls the Venetian glow. Gradually, as Renoir perfects his individual form, the masses become less clearly defined, more floating and vaporous, but not less convincing. The impressionistic technique has become more and more generalized, and the individual brush strokes appear subtly, and only in restricted parts of the canvas. By this time, Renoir has succeeded in giving the large-scale effects of landscape with an impressiveness worthy of Claude, to which he added the spirit of local place, the intime charm, of Constable. The combination of epic grandeur, of lyric charm, of dramatic quality, appears in Renoir's landscape-painting throughout the rest of his life.

In figure-painting of the late eighties and early nineties, Renoir gradually merged the sharp outlines, the exotic surface-quality, and sculptural solidity of his mid-eighties' form with more organic color and more essentially realistic texture, at the same time refining his technique to such a perfection of flexibility that he could paint the same subject over and over and produce in each version a different and distinctive delicacy, charm, and reality. Drawing, primarily by means of color, has become exceedingly fluid, and the characteristic quality and feeling of things is rendered without the least reliance upon literalism, but with a fidelity to essentials worthy of Velásquez. Distortions become more obvious, and the interest in relatively abstract design becomes more and more dominant. Recognizable objects never fully disappear, but they are very freely rendered and conceived chiefly as elements in the design. In "Bathers in Forest" (238), painted about 1897, the design becomes fully Venetian in its general form of organization and in the structural and compositional function of color, but it contains also a decorative surface-quality derived from the French eighteenth century tradition, a wealth of fluid linear rhythms, and an iridescent union of light and color, which neither Giorgione nor Titian, neither Watteau nor Fragonard, ever equaled. It is the ability to unite expressive and decorative values with no loss of conviction, no degradation of form to the status of mere pattern, that makes Renoir an artist of the first magnitude. His design is created out of so many subsidiary designs that every part of the canvas has an intrinsic as well as a functional interest, and the whole form acquires a monumental effect as varied and harmonious as a fugue by Bach or a symphony by Beethoven.

The period after 1900 is that of Renoir's supreme plastic achievements. In his figures there is an increasing use of strongly assertive reddish tones, and a more voluminous and voluptuous three-dimensional solidity. In landscapes there is often a major theme of emerald, ruby, or lilac-blue, around which there is rose melting into violet, blue into shimmering green, with a pearly, luminous atmosphere, giving an effect of deep quietude, serenity, majesty, peace. In everything he painted there is a more convincing solid reality, and a powerful three-dimensional rhythm; and a swirl, not unlike that of Rubens, but of larger compositional scope and much more substantial, lends activity and vitality to the design as a whole and to all its details. Color has become paramount—both space and volumes are built out of structural color, and made a single whole by the continuity of the color. Contour becomes looser than ever before, and color itself, with less aid from the conventional means of modeling and perspective, seems to draw out the quintessence of things, both in their massiveness and in their textural quality; at the same time the color-suffusion floods every area of the canvas, builds up all the space, and gives to it a substantial reality as rich and convincing as that of the volumes. By these means Renoir meets the Venetians on their own ground and transcends their greatest achievements. He recaptures the essential spirit of classic sculpture, rendering it perfectly in the terms of painting, and further adds the grace, lightness, delicacy, and charm of the French eighteenth century. His ability to combine what is essential in these traditions with the realism and impressionism current in the early years of his career in a new form completely distinctive of himself, shows how profoundly he had assimilated what was valuable and living in both past and present. More than that of any other artist his work constitutes an epitome and rounding-out of the whole history of painting.

We may now summarize Renoir's characteristics as they appear in all periods of his work. The foundation of his form is color, derived from the Venetians partly through Rubens and the French eighteenth century tradition, partly through Velásquez and Goya. His technique owes most to the impressionists, but everything in theirs which suggests formula or mannerism is discarded, and it is used for plastic purposes of which they had little or no conception. To the Dutch, to Velásquez, to Courbet and Manet, he owed the interest in everyday life and reality which made him immune to Rubens' flamboyance and grandiosity, or to Fragonard's triviality and artificiality. His temperament made him love and observe attentively the commonplace people and incidents of life, so that in his hands they cease to be commonplace and are suffused with poetic charm. His imaginative discernment makes them living people for him, and he delights in surrounding them with the wealth of sensuous quality, the voluptuousness that came from his own rich endowment.

His delight is that of an artist, not an animal, for his voluptuousness is free from sensuality. His nudes are symbols, not naked women; and a group of them, seen as an ensemble, resembles a bouquet of variegated flowers; commonplace scenes and persons lose their vulgarity in his work. He had an unerring eye for essentials; hence the truth and naturalness of his drawing, the success with which he made his people reveal themselves in some ordinary act, such as taking hold of a cup or handling a needle, and in the unpremeditated play of their features. His sense of the dramatic in ordinary everyday events is comparable to Degas', but unlike Degas Renoir never despises the people whom he shows acting. His pleasure in the beautiful things of the world is revealed in the freshness and delicacy of textiles, flowers, and the natural scene in general, and in his rendering of human beings pulsating with life and glad to be alive. Nobody ever painted more spontaneously, freely, with more improvisation than he. The sensuous charm and the general decorative quality of Renoir's work are achieved by luminous color-chords of a wealth never before paralleled. Rubens' color is less bright and real, and he lacked the characteristic French delicacy of Renoir, which refined and made more subtle the elements of decoration. In Renoir, everything is fluid, light, resplendent; the flesh is glowing, the atmosphere pearly; when the surfaces are hard, their color is jewel-like. This decorative opulence is not bought at the expense of form, of reality, for the rich, juicy, varied, effulgent color is also structural and compositional. It reënforces drawing and perspective, and heightens every rhythm and contrast. His line is not only a rhythmic constituent of pattern, it also expresses the character of personality, of drama, with a conviction equal to that of Degas. He can give the grandeur and majesty of nature in a degree comparable to Claude's, and he advances upon Claude in that he secures these effects to a vastly greater extent by means of color. In landscape on a smaller scale he rivals Constable, and in his sense of the intime character of interiors he is the equal of Chardin. He has the poetry of Giorgione, but it is a more homely poetry, less Arcadian, with less of the pathos of distance. As a plastic artist, he has greater command of means, greater variety of effect, and certainly a more lavish and richer decorative quality than any other painter. It is because of the subtlety and power of Renoir's effects, and the practical impossibility of reproducing or expanding them, that he has had so few disciples even among the intelligent and talented generation of young painters.

CHAPTER V

CEZANNE

CEZANNE (1839–1906) worked at the time when impressionism was at its height but it had little if any influence upon his earliest paintings, which were mainly melodramatic interpretations of Tintoretto, El Greco, Ribera, Rubens, Delacroix, Daumier, and Courbet. His work of that period is characterized by sharp contrast of areas of light and dark, the dramatic effect of which is reënforced by pronounced linear effects with abrupt changes in direction. The composite result is a series of emphatic rhythms which convey a feeling of swirl and turmoil, and the individuality of the composition is emphasized by the bizarre and picturesque distribution of the components of the subject-matter. The pictures are essentially illustrative, a sort of exaggerated literary romanticism, executed in heavy impasto, often with the palette knife, and the line unsupported by light and color. Light-and-dark contrasts are outstanding and often to the degree of converting the color-ensemble into a black-and-white effect. With all their crudities, the pictures are, nevertheless, striking, very individual, and often convey a feeling of power.

In the early seventies, Cézanne came under the influence of impressionism and it was his modification and development of certain phases of its details that culminated in the form characteristic of his work throughout his subsequent career. Indeed, almost immediately after his start with impressionism he attained to the artistic vision which he never outgrew, although he did advance in achieving greater facility in technical execution. In the course of his own development of the impressionists' technique, he made creative use of what interested him in the work of numerous earlier painters. From Chardin, he took part of the method of making volumes solid and weighty, the hard surfaces, and a manner of applying brush strokes; to Daumier, he owes the accentuated lines of contour and the method of simplified drawing which tends toward grotesque distortion; from Courbet, he absorbed the simplifications and vigorous painting of naturalistic objects; from El

[319]

Greco came, probably, the dramatic contrasts of light and dark colors and the occasional use of the swirl; his distortions of the human figure resemble closely those in the work of Michelangelo, Tintoretto, and El Greco; a type of brushwork in Cézanne's painting of the nineties is very similar to that of Hals. His mature form as a whole goes back ultimately to the Florentines and the Venetians: to Uccello in the manifold distortions of perspective, and to Carpaccio in the architectonic plan of composition. But for an explanation of Cézanne's epoch-making achievements, we must understand the fundamental changes wrought by him in the impressionists' technique.

Cézanne's first steps in impressionism were made under the tuition of Pissarro and his paintings of that period could almost pass for Pissarros of extraordinary vigor: they have the same quality and kind of color, the same use of juxtaposed color-spots varied with broad areas, and a similar manner of using light; but Cézanne's pictures are stronger and more expressive of power, the masses are more solid, and the composition is more firmly organized by means of color. His paintings of this period are interesting chiefly because they serve as points of reference in a study of his development and of his reorganization of the impressionistic technique as a means for a more profound expression of nature and of human values.

The first fundamental change perceptible in Cézanne's advance toward his mature form is the vastly more important rôle played by the perceptible brush strokes. These are organized in more definitely shaped areas, usually angular, which function compositionally like the units in a mosaic. The areas take the form of planes which intersect in deep space and, when they are successfully interrelated, convey the feeling of the dynamic movement so characteristic of Cézanne's best work at all stages of his maturity. The difference in treatment, color, position, and direction of the areas adds a sense of drama to the movement, and the combination of these effects seems to create the feeling of power. The rigidity so common in Cézanne's work is obviously due to the sharp impact of one area or object upon another.

Cézanne's very individual method of modeling is also clearly an evolution of the impressionistic technique, and the different effects at various stages of his career are obtained by modifications in the way the contrasting colors are applied, and in the size of the individual areas. The basic principle of the method is the application of small overlapping patches of color, and these color-hatchings function in the modeling. Each of these colors is mingled with light, so that close examination reveals not one solid color, or a one-piece effect, but a series of tones of similar general tint. This method is quite individual to Cézanne, and it produces a pattern which contributes to the total esthetic value of the form.

Cézanne's evolution into his own distinctive technique was a slow process because he was deficient in natural facility in the use of the brush: even his most mature work lacks the finish and mastery of medium which is to be seen in Renoir from the start. The sense of effort and strain nearly always remains, so that his style rarely attains to Renoir's unconscious ease and naturalness. Although Renoir's career also represents a gradual progress toward his final form, his early pictures are much more complete in themselves than Cézanne's and do not so clearly represent experimental and tentative stages. Cézanne's difficulty in control of his medium, and his ultimate triumph in this respect, are attested by the fact that the main difference between his early work and that of his latest phase is that the actual brushwork becomes more and more combined with the effects of color and color-relations, the pigment is less often heaped up in layers, and the individual planes are better related in the total space-composition. In other words, the technique is more flexible, more subtle, less monotonous, and the effect of solidity of volumes is obtained more directly by incorporation of color in the substance of the object.

One striking result in Cézanne's technical progress is an increasing ability to render the effects of solidity in terms free from the sculptural tendency of his earlier thick paint. The fewer coats of paint and the diminution of emphatic brush strokes transformed the roughness of his early work to a more polished effect that involves no loss of strength. As his command of paint grows, his technique builds up color, line, light, shadows, and space into units which belong organically to the composition; for example, brush strokes which make a pattern also create volumes and set them in space; and line which contributes to three-dimensionality is itself usually a brush stroke of color. By means of the technique, color pervades the composition organically, and the separate units are chiefly stages in the organization. Thus did Cézanne carry the impressionistic technique to supreme heights. His line loses to a large extent its earlier tendency to hardness and comparative isolation from light and color, although seldom is there that complete fusion characteristic of Renoir's drawing. Cézanne's inability to draw, model, and define the spatial position of objects without recourse to accentuated linear contour is often perceptible in even the latest and best of his work.

As he reaches his later stages of development his composition departs from conventionality and flows rhythmically throughout the whole of the canvas. The shapes of the objects become more arbitrarily subordinated to the requirements of the design. This distortion of shape, the ruthless sacrifice of recognizable detail, has always been the quality in Cézanne which arouses the scornful wonder of the inexperienced observer, and is chiefly responsible for the effort which is required to appreciate his painting at all.

Cézanne can be appreciated only after all considerations of naturalistic accuracy have been dismissed. His distinctive achievement was to establish a series of relationships in deep space between solid three-dimensional objects, so that their ensemble is a unified plastic form of great esthetic power. This feeling for the dynamic relationships between objects and the ability to coordinate the resulting units in a design, involved a specific genius which often resulted in compositions as original and as esthetically moving as those of Giotto. To achieve these effects he violated all conceptions of probability or possibility. Colors, shapes, and outlines of objects are treated as planes which become motifs to be worked with as the purpose requires; objects appear suspended in the air, in complete defiance of the law of gravitation, figures and faces are sometimes distorted into monstrosities. These distortions are to be found not only in the faces and other parts of the human body, but also in all the plastic constituents. They are fundamental to the planes themselves, which are changed from the normal in every conceivable way, and the new forms are built up by the interpenetration of these distorted planes. In all of his work there is a perceptible, definite idea, which he himself called the *motif:* it was always governed by the desire to make lines, perspective, and space so fuse in planes of color that all the factors come into equilibrium. In other words, objects, deprived of their resemblance to real things, were merely the means used to integrate the plastic elements in distinctive and tremendously powerful forms.

His primary purpose was to make color the essential material of all his forms, and he strove to build up everything with color. In his expansion of the compositional function of color to its supreme degree, he carries the Venetian tradition to its consummation. Perspective, drawing, composition, and the creation of solid structure are all done chiefly by color. Even in his distortions, the line itself is usually color which so enters in a formal relation with adjacent colors as to make the drawing more powerful. The distorted planes in his best work consist of an equilibrium of colors fused into new forms which are Cézanne's very own. In these, color assumes rhythmic relations with all the other plastic elements, and organizes the painting as a series of distinctive units. This rhythmic interplay of color-forms is one of Cézanne's great achievements, and was never realized with greater power by any other artist. In his mature work color animates everything. Through new technical means Cézanne succeeded in giving that sense of profound fidelity to the deeper aspects of things which is the characteristic of all great art.

Cézanne's forms are essentially abstract, but they are achieved through the medium of subject-matter that has sufficient point of contact with the external world to establish relation with our funded experience of real things. His figures or objects are static, but not inert or dead. The drama in which they take part is the interplay of abstract tensions and forces, not one of human incident and personal emotion: they are active as a tower, a pier, or a buttress is active. His form is architectonic, its attributes are weight, equilibrium, and the balance of forces, just as one finds in a systematically planned architectural structure, impressive by its monumental character and dignity. His latest work, "Nudes in Landscape" (177), has the massiveness and cumulative power one finds in the frieze of the Parthenon. In his ability to give the feeling of the basically essential while avoiding literalness, Cézanne vies with Rembrandt and Velásquez although he was by far a lesser craftsman.

Cézanne ranks with the greatest painters of all ages because, by the use of means purely plastic and by a new use of the most difficult of these means—color—he realized a form of the highest degree of conviction and power. In his utilization of everything necessary to attain a personal design, he followed in the footsteps of Michelangelo, Tintoretto, and El Greco, whose distortions he applied to new purposes. From Velásquez, through the intermediation of Manet, he learned to simplify. But in him the whole tradition of simplification and distortion, merged with the impressionistic technique, became something radically new in the history of painting. His power is more expressive than Michelangelo's, and it is achieved by means more intrinsic to painting, instead of the suggestions derived from sculpture to be found even in the best of Michelangelo's work. Cézanne's landscapes have the majesty of Claude's, combined with a more austere, rugged force; they have an added purity because he dispenses with anything of even the degree of obviousness of Claude's atmosphere. His perception of the significant enables him to put into a simple still-life a monumental quality that makes Raphael's "Transfiguration" (427) seem trivial.

Cézanne's shortcomings arise partly from the same source as his greatness and partly from his never wholly-perfect command of his medium. His ability to control paint rarely rises to the greatest heights; his laborious efforts to force and coax paint to express his ideas and feelings are usually perceptible even in his most mature achievements. Another disadvantage is that his resolute adherence to essentials left him comparatively little interest in the sensuous charm that accompanies a specific decorative quality. In this respect he is inferior to all the great Venetians, to Renoir, and even to Rubens. This does not mean that his surfaces are at all bleak or barren, but there is not the wealth of decorative quality throughout every area of his pictures that there is, for example, in Giorgione. In Renoir there is also a strong plastic form made up of solid masses rhythmically ordered in deep space, but in addition there is a greater variety and richness of color-chords and a more ingratiating charm, superior even to that in Giorgione and Titian. The examples of these artists also show that it is possible to have strength of plastic form in combination with a greater variety of human values than Cézanne presents to us, so that his purification of plastic form is not attained without loss. This defect is offset to a certain extent by the rich expressiveness of color thoroughly integrated in the form.

Cézanne was the equal of the greatest artists in making his forms embody the abstract feelings and the human values, that the objects and events of everyday life communicate. He rendered the essential qualities of these feelings stripped of the irrelevant and accidental, and endowed them with the pervasive mystery, strength, and power that make them uniquely moving and vital.

CHAPTER VI

DEGAS AND PUVIS DE CHAVANNES

Degas (1834–1917) was one of the most active and potent figures in the art-life at the time of the impressionists, although he never shared their chief interests nor adopted in its entirety their technique. Practically the only developments of impressionism that Degas employed to any extent are the distortion and simplification of objects by which they are rendered in their broad general terms, with comparatively little attention to detail. To a lesser extent he employed also the impressionistic method of using lighted color-areas.

Degas' drawing resulted in such distortions of the parts of the human body that facial features are obliterated and the general effect sometimes is that of grotesqueness or monstrosity, but the distortions enhance the plastic ensemble. His attention was centered upon the events of everyday life, in which he saw and emphasized the ironic and sardonic. Nearly all of his pictures are trenchant, biting, sarcastic comments upon such subjects as ballet-girls, laundresses, women getting into or out of bathtubs, people at café-tables, race tracks. The situations involve acts of life that most people have to perform, but Degas accentuated the essential triviality of the acts. However, when we abstract the plastic means from the subject-matter and turn our attention to their use, we find that he had a fine sense for the relationships between objects and was able to create personal expressions. His sense of relationships, however, was limited to individual units, a group of dancers, for instance; but he lacked ability to unify several groups in a composition which should be plastically whole.

His design owes its strength to the infinite variety of patterns produced by the meeting of various objects or parts of the body, posed in unusual attitudes, generally tending toward the dramatic. The weakness of his form lies in the fact that the predominance of line relegates color to a comparatively subsidiary position. His picturesque patterns, attained as a rule by the skilled use of arabesque, owe much to the influence of Japanese prints.

The color in his oil-paintings is usually dull, drab, dry, and he seems unable to attain harmonious combinations, particularly between bright colors. His own consciousness of that fact led him to work mostly in pastel. In this medium, he sometimes rises to great heights as a colorist: scintillating, iridescent, bright colors used harmoniously occur frequently, but he rarely succeeded in using color successfully in composing a picture of uniform color-strength. In some parts, the color is weaker either in quality or in carrying-power than in other parts, so that the general effect is rather of spots of color than of a strong rhythmic flow which embraces all of the picture. His pastels have an animation and a sparkle which are totally lacking in the majority of his oil-paintings. His modeling in pastel is also generally more successful: the three-dimensional quality, while slight, is of sufficient solidity to go well with the general lightness that pastel-effects require.

These disadvantages in the use of color are offset to a considerable extent by the many good results obtained by the skilled utilization of highly expressive line. The many and diverse uses to which he puts the line give rise, in almost any unit selected, to a series of formal relations, so rich that these areas compare favorably with similar units in the work of men who used color more successfully. In pastel, where he could control the color better, he used it in connection with line to get a composite effect in which the color-function contributes much to the general appeal of the particular form.

Degas' high place in art is determined chiefly by the character of his line and the great variety of specific effects which he was able to produce with it. It is rarely continuous, sharp, or incisive; is sometimes heavy in defining contour, and often consists of ragged edges of color which determine the character of the drawing. His line was especially adapted to the representation of active movement, and in that he is not excelled by any other artist. But a still finer and more subtle use of line is that which portrays poised movement, and in this respect Velásquez is Degas' only serious competitor. The poised movement of Velásquez is much more important as an artistic creation than that of Degas, because the means by which it is accomplished are more comprehensive and more subtly used. In Degas, it is usually possible to see the very bend of line or the combination of lines that renders the poised movement. The result is felt as somewhat of a *tour de force*, which would be virtuosity in any man to whom it came less naturally and who could render it in less variety of forms than could Degas.

Degas created nothing that can be compared, in wealth of plastic forms or in depth of human values, with the work of either Renoir or Cézanne, but he did create a series of forms which are his, and in which there is an airy, light delicacy, a grace and a power that reveal him as an artist of high rank. His linear patterns and his interest in the episodic were a perfect combination for the production of illustrations that penetrate to the essential psychological significance of the events of daily life. Indeed, no follower of Degas, not even the very skilled and sensitive Toulouse-Lautrec, has ever succeeded in attaining the plastically expressive strength of his linear drawing.

Puvis de Chavannes (1824–1898) lived at the time of the impressionists, but his work was free from their influences. The spirit and style of his painting is based upon the frescoes of Giotto and Piero della Francesca, and he succeeded in putting into his work in oil considerable of the charm of those early Italian frescoes, but in a weaker form.

Puvis's work is distinctive in pattern, drawing, quality of color, and ability to bring the compositional units into harmonious relations. His feeling for space and his suave, smooth, skilful use of paint have rarely been excelled. In all of these respects his models were Giotto and Piero. His form is closer to Piero's in that the individual units partake of a static quality, and the color-ensemble is cool and often dominated by a pervasive blue-and-ivory tonality. He makes extensive use of a delicate deep blue in combination with other delicate colors, notably a fluffy white and shades of lilac, that have the fundamental feeling of blue. His large mural decorations are usually well-balanced, fluid compositions with a feeling of a processional flow of one group-unit into another. His drawing is light, delicate, and graceful, but academic rather than strongly individual and expressive. His contour, which at a distance may look sharp and incisive, is seen upon close inspection to be irregularly defined by color instead of by sharp line as division or contact of areas. His modeling of figures into a light three-dimensional solidity is well adapted to the delicacy of the general design. The best of his work has the classic, delicate quality of Poussin.

CHAPTER VII

THE POST-IMPRESSIONISTS [1]

Gauguin's (1848–1903) earliest pictures are very much in the impressionistic manner of Pissarro, under whose tuition he started his career. Later he gave up the divisionistic method and used color in broad areas which he modified by means of Cézanne's parallel hatchings, slightly modulated with light and varied with occasional accents of contrasting colors. This is the method of his Tahitian pictures, which represent his most characteristic form.

The essential features of his perfected method are a skilled use of broad areas of single colors placed in contrast with each other, a quite individual color-scheme of an appealing sensuous quality, and a good organization of planes in space. The formal relations established constitute composition of a high order, but the general effect partakes more of the nature of decoration than of a successful merging of the structural and decorative elements into a substantial plastic form. Much of the popular appeal of his Tahitian pictures is due to the exotic character of subject-matter, in which the romantic surroundings and the facial expressions are instrumental to a facile mysticism. His drawing is predominantly linear; that is, line does not fuse with color to produce fully expressive drawing. His modeling is accomplished usually by almost a repetition of Cézanne's planes or facets of color; to Cézanne also he owes much of his effective use of planes as compositional framework, even though Gauguin injects into their ordering a quality suggestive of the Orientals. His whole composition is accomplished by rather obvious use of flat planes of color so that figures and objects have very little three-dimensional feeling. His figures appear static even when they are supposed to be in movement, an effect attained intentionally, in the interest of design. This general treatment enters well into the decorative nature of his form and provides a fitting embodiment for the subject-matter of primitive, dark-

---

[1] "Post-impressionism," a term more arbitrary than rational, is usually extended to include such diverse painters as Cézanne and Seurat.

Gauguin (199)

Seurat (248)

Glackens (201)

Analysis, page 471

Cézanne (175)

skinned, semi-nude people. He makes an effective use of the dark natives garbed in bright and gayly patterned sarongs, the colors in which have an appealing sensuous quality. In his drawing of figures and objects, there are distortions of color, line, and light that give them positive values as plastic entities but differentiate them considerably from naturalistic appearances.

Gauguin's paintings may be considered essentially as decorations which attain a considerable degree of artistic significance through the successful use of masses, planes, color, and space. His forms are rather slight and there is a suggestion of affectation in both the nature of the subject-matter and its plastic treatment. His influence has been mostly upon those painters interested primarily in decoration, for example, van Gogh, Matisse, and Maurice Denis.

Van Gogh's (1853–1890) earliest paintings and black-and-white drawings are scarcely more than thin versions of the sentimental academicisms of Mauve, Israels, and Millet. His mature work is based upon the impressionistic technique, which he modified chiefly in matters of detail: he enlarged and greatly elongated the spots of color used by Monet, he applied paint in visible brush strokes somewhat in the manner of Manet and of Hals, and he also used Manet's broad areas of color. These diversifications of the technique he adapted to a form which is basically akin to that of the Dutch tradition and that of the Japanese prints.

Van Gogh's method of placing a figure or mass against a background contrasting vividly with it in color and usually in manner of treatment, is obviously derived from Japanese prints. The figure or mass is almost always greatly simplified and distorted, and the accentuated ribbonlike brush strokes of bright color, much varied in size and direction, help make of the total picture a striking pattern of line and color. The contrasting background may be comparatively a monochrome containing a light-pattern or an ornamental motif in other colors, or it may be animated by a swirl or by contrasting areas of color. In any case, the contrast between the foreground and the background produces a dramatic effect, to which the very dynamic quality of the ribbonlike streaks of color, the strikingly vivid and unnatural hues employed, and the character of the distortions, all contribute. The generally wavy, rhythmic line and the frequent sudden transitions from minute color-divisions to broad areas of unbroken color further heighten the dramatic contrast. With these facile means, van Gogh infuses a spirit of emotional tenseness into themes ordinarily placid, and a feverish, almost delirious, quality into situations intrinsically dramatic. Emotion thus rendered by almost literal sign-posts evocative largely of associated values is far removed from the esthetic emotion produced by values intrinsic to a truly expressive plastic form.

His color is bright, often exotic, and usually employed in daring contrasts but it lacks structural quality; it does not often function effectively in organizing the painting, and rarely adds anything expressive to the form. His pictures are always rhythmic, but the rhythms are obvious and usually mechanical. The result is that the total compositional activity of the color is chiefly decorative, and the technical means of achieving animated effects and striking patterns are rather specious and overaccentuated. His compositions are generally flat, his drawing and modeling are relatively unvaried and not very original; his latest work, that of the Arles period, for example, follows closely Gauguin's drawing and use of color-areas.

Van Gogh's influence upon subsequent painters has been considerable, especially in the employment of daring color-contrasts and accentuated brushwork. Matisse and Soutine owe much to him in these respects, even though they used his technique as a point of departure and not as a model for imitation.

Bonnard's (1867–1947) most distinctive form is that of his early work: it is impressionistic, more in the manner of Renoir than in that of Monet; that is, juxtaposed color-spots are used only as an incident to serve a particular purpose and do not dominate the entire canvas. These color-spots are used in connection with broad areas of nearly uniform color modified by streaks of light which give a rich and varied effect. His color-forms are enhanced in both their structural and decorative functions by linear patterns made up of the various objects in the scenes represented, but his color has never the depth nor the rich, sensuous quality of that of Renoir, Monet, Sisley, or Pissarro. Sometimes it tends toward the garish, but it usually has a delicacy and a force that make him, at the most individual stage of his career, an important, though minor, colorist. His drawing is done by ragged, irregular lines of color that indicate rather than define the parts of the body or object portrayed. His

[334]

deceptively attractive

Having the ring of truth or plausibility but actually fallacious (misleading, deceptive) best results are in small compositions representing interiors, and to these he succeeds in giving an intime feeling which has both power and charm. His late work represents too often unsuccessful attempts to emulate Matisse's use of bright and exotic colors in daring contrasts.

CHAPTER VIII

AMERICAN PAINTING

PERHAPS the only painting done in America that might claim to have an identity of its own is that done in the early part of the nineteenth century by the "Pennsylvania Dutch" peasants and by some of the itinerant painters of portraits and romantic scenes. Practically all other painting in America has followed so closely the European traditions that a distinctively American form of painting does not exist. It is equally true that a number of American painters have achieved a personal expression, even though it has been chiefly a version of one or the other of the European traditions. Much of the early work in America was under the influence of the great Dutch and Spanish painters; but even the best of these Americans—Benjamin West, Gilbert Stuart, the Peales, Thomas Sully—were skilled craftsmen utterly uninspired. In our own day the Dutch-Spanish tradition, in the version given by Manet, has been followed chiefly by painters of no artistic importance, virtuosos such as Sargent, Henri, Seyffert, and Bellows, whose brilliance in the use of a borrowed technique covers an esthetic vacuum. Of all these it may be said that their pictures, when analyzed, show scarcely a vestige of authentic plastic quality. Poor line and color, stereotyped composition, drawing subordinated to illustration, a plastically illegitimate appeal through superficial picturesqueness and adventitious subject-matter, are glaringly apparent in the work of all of them.

George Inness (1825-1894) took over the van Goyen - Claude - Corot conception of landscape, overdramatized it, and added nothing from the standpoint of creation. His pictures are pleasing renderings of the theme of landscape in a language which has been spoken practically in its entirety by great masters of the past. Almost their sole claim to attention is the fact that Inness had a feeling for landscape and the ability to reproduce it in a familiar language.

Whistler (1834-1903) leans heavily upon traditions, to which he adds too little to take high rank as an artist. The daintiness and grace of his work are generally used to render poses; one feels it is not only the pose of the subject, but also the pose of the artist in the effort to make an impression. Occasionally, as in the portrait of the "Artist's Mother" (403), he also renders character in honest art-terms. His synthesis of various traditions—the Japanese, Velásquez', Courbet's—is clever rather than imaginative or creative. While he undoubtedly had a pictorial sense and a feeling for life, neither seems to have been very deep or original. Whistler's status as an artist becomes immediately apparent when a picture of his is put beside one of its prototypes. For example, his "Théodore Duret" (280), when seen by itself has a definite appeal; but when compared with Manet's "Woman with Parrot" (276), in the same museum, the Whistler seems an adroit *tour de force*, a specious utilization of the technical means by which Manet created an original and profoundly moving work of art.

Winslow Homer (1836–1910) was important as an artist in that he was able to portray situations and objects in a good pictorial setting, with objects effectively related in space and thrown upon a background of striking general pattern. His work, in the main, is rather illustration than plastic realization of the essence of what is presented, and even as illustration it suffers from an overdramatic use of obvious technical means. His pictures are honest but ineffective attempts to give authentic plastic quality to drama. His style is related to impressionism only in the accentuation of light, the use of bright colors, and in simplifications somewhat in the manner of Manet. Unlike the impressionists he cannot organize his pictures by the use of illuminated color, nor has he any real gift for feeling the sensuous quality of individual colors and relating them in small color-units. Thus his large color-areas, arranged in striking patterns, are unsupported by minor color-harmonies. The colors themselves are usually raucous, and there is no reënforcement with light to give them depth and internal luminosity. In almost all parts of his pictures light is overaccentuated and made the chief agent in the drama. This excess of light converts drama into melodrama, and what is left of plastic organization is merely light-and-dark pattern and color-pattern, though these are of undeniable decorative power. Homer also lacked sufficient command of his medium, sufficient ability to put quality into his paint, to relieve his pictures of their overload of narrative, drama, and decoration. How thin, plastically, his drama is, is revealed when it is compared with

Constable's more subdued, yet colorful, painting of nature. Constable gives the essence of drama without either overemphasis or deficiency, while in Homer the effort and the means are so apparent that the pictures seem as superficial as tinsel. Homer was undoubtedly an artist, but his artistic conceptions were greater than his power to realize them in paint.

Thomas Eakins (1844–1916), though essentially a school-painter, had so considerable a command of his medium, and so fine a feeling for the relations of objects in space, that he achieved at his best a genuinely personal expression. His "Dr. Agnew" (187) illustrates well his skill in rendering effective space-relations, solidity, poised movement, and the essentials of human character. The general run of his work, unfortunately, is much inferior: for example, while his limited palette in "Dr. Agnew" gives the effect of subtlety and economy of means, in the general average of his work it seems a sign of poverty of resources, just as his tight drawing, his inadequate feeling for color, and the banality of his themes stamp him the skilled academician. His work is, in the main, an echo of the Velásquez and Dutch traditions and also sometimes of Whistler.

Albert P. Ryder (1847–1917) was primarily a poet who gave dramatic setting to his feelings in good, but not very original, plastic terms: his forms are usually too close to those of Tintoretto, El Greco, the seventeenth century Dutch landscapists, John Crome or Daumier. He renders the spirit of the place, of landscape, of the sea, with an imagination suffused with mysticism. His kinship to El Greco and Daumier is very close both in spirit and in technique. His mysticism differs from El Greco's in being pagan rather than Christian, and from Daumier's in being more universal than episodic. He was inferior to both as a painter and in the creative adaptation of the great traditions of painting.

Ryder was a successful colorist in the manner of Rembrandt and Daumier: with economy of means and without resort to bright hues, he achieved great color-power. He is not their equal, however, because his color-forms, though rich and deep, are relatively lacking both in variety and in originality. His work is so profoundly moving in itself that the unoriginality of his technical methods is likely to be overlooked; for example, the general theme and manner of treatment in his "Curfew Hour" (278) are found in Jacob van Ruisdael, van Goyen, Claude, and other landscape-painters; his handling of color in general is Venetian, especially as that was modified by El Greco and Daumier; his "Toilers of the Sea" (279) repeats Tintoretto's dramatic contrast of light and dark colors, but the color-chords in Ryder's surfaces are less rich and less varied in hue and tone.

Much of Ryder's drama is due to his use of light both as pattern and as illumination of color, though the light is usually rather over-accentuated and the color-illumination inadequate. His relative inability to fuse light and color may be appreciated by a comparison of his surfaces with Berckheyde's. In the latter, color-chords are greatly varied, rich, and many-hued, while in Ryder they are rather uniform and often monotonous. Another fall from the highest standards is Ryder's comparatively unsatisfactory fusion of light and color to achieve atmosphere or what is known as the Venetian glow. It is less successful than Claude's glow; it is rather in the manner of the painters of the Barbizon school, especially of Rousseau, and there is a tendency to concentration and emphasis of the glow in areas of sunset-color. The effect is very dramatic though there is a taint of speciousness in it. His composition is interesting but often unoriginal.

Ryder is an important artist, primarily because of the profound and pervasive mysticism which makes him a great poet. This mysticism, in its all-embracing sweep, is undeniable, but appreciation of it is tempered with regret at its failure to find a more individual plastic realization. Unfortunately, because either of the thick paint or of its application in repeated coatings, many of his pictures are rapidly going to ruin.

George Luks (1868–1933) worked mainly in the Dutch tradition, and most successfully in the realm of genre. When his palette is restricted largely to shades of gray and brown, these few colors are skilfully handled to yield harmonious combinations and to contribute to the effect of reality and power. His line is expressive and his organization of compositional masses is good, particularly in the relation of figures and objects to a background near in tone. He owes much to Manet in his use of broad brush strokes to express essentials. Although his command of the plastic means suffices to give him, at his best, a certain vigor and strength, his work is very uneven. His attempts to use bright colors, or those outside the range of his habitual Dutch tradition gamut, are disastrous: they reveal his lack of any far-reaching grasp of immediate color-quality, of the compositional values of color, or of its structural function. As with many other painters, Manet's influence often led him into mere virtuosity, and he further compromised the plastic quality of his work by frequent recourse to cheap sentimentality.

Of the Americans who worked in the impressionistic tradition, Prendergast, Glackens, and Lawson will serve as examples.

Maurice Prendergast's (1862–1924) technique is derived from the impressionists, from Cézanne, and from the pointillists' application of color-spots all over the canvas. These color-spots are the most immediately obvious characteristic of his work, but his use of them is more varied than anything to be found in the work of his predecessors. The richness and harmony of the color itself give rise to a great variety of formal relations which constitute his individual note. His drawing is extraordinarily broad and free: contours are ragged, details are constantly blurred, simplification and distortion are often carried to such a point that particular objects can be identified vaguely or not at all. Yet these indistinct masses are effective because of their striking and multiple functions in the ensemble. This also is true of space: the intervals between the masses are clear and convincing to the point required by the exigencies of his design. Though the manner of accomplishing it is totally different, the infinity of distance is rendered by Prendergast as subtly as by Titian or Velásquez. The most important factor in his form is color. Few painters ever had as fine a feeling for pure color, both in its direct sensuous quality and in the possible variety of its uses. It is rich, juicy, glowing, alive, and harmonious. The sharply contrasted areas, spotted with light, give an effect of staccato color-movement throughout the whole picture, not unlike that sometimes achieved by Renoir. This color-movement is one of Prendergast's chief means of welding his composition into an organic whole. Quite particular and outstanding characteristics of his work are the freshness of his resplendent color and the vigor of his rugged pigment—qualities which give to his best pictures, sometimes, the glowing vitality of the great mosaics and, at other times, the charm and delicacy of the finest of early tapestries and frescoes. Another claim to distinction is that the composition in his easel pictures often yields the effect of murals to a larger degree than the work of any mural painter since the Renaissance. Prendergast's form expresses the vision of a childlike mind, seeing simply, naïvely, yet

Biagio Pinto (406)

Demuth (186)

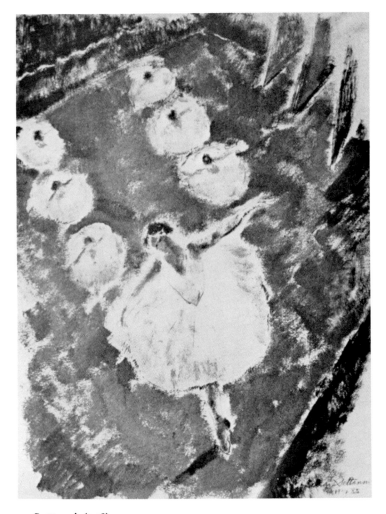

Settanni (246)

Pennsylvania Dutch (231)

penetratingly, the esthetic aspects of everyday life, and rejoicing in them.

William J. Glackens (1870–1938) is notable for his ability to make bright color and a very individual and expressive style of drawing the media for rendering a fine sense of the drama of the events of ordinary life. His early painting derives from Manet, but subsequently his form came to resemble more closely that of Renoir, especially in the general effects of color. Glackens' color has less sensuous appeal, is less solidly structural, and is less well fused with the technique; it is used in broader areas, in more daring, even exotic, contrasts, at times suggestive of Matisse's.

Glackens' best black-and-white work is as individual, as strong, and as expressive as that of Goya, Daumier, and Degas, and like theirs, his illustrative powers do not depend upon adventitious literary or sentimental sources of appeal. The individual quality of his line arises out of simplification to the point of epigrammatic terseness, and it is so set in a context of other qualities that there is no loss of either plastic reality or feeling of completeness. His work is impersonal in the sense that Velásquez' is impersonal: he selects the picturesque and significant and renders them without comment of his own.

Ernest Lawson (1873–1939) took over the impressionists' technique in all its phases—color-division, atmosphere, and the direct effects of sunlight. Although he introduced no important modifications into the impressionistic technique, and is therefore justly chargeable with lack of originality and with a certain monotony, he nevertheless uses his means effectively in rendering diverse qualities in nature—the fresh bloom of early spring, the hot haze of summer, the cold steely blue and white of winter. He achieves the natural lyric quality of landscape, but neither so deeply nor so delicately as the great French impressionists.

The most recent painting in America is based chiefly upon the work of Cézanne, Matisse, and Picasso. There exists among the young generation of American painters a great deal of talent and much well-directed effort to attain a form that represents their own reactions to the American scene.

Charles Demuth (1883–1935) was one of the most capable of these Americans. He worked mostly in water-color, and his command of this medium is equal to that of any other contemporary painter. His early work is chiefly illustrative and in it the essence of the situation is portrayed in a vivid and personal manner. Figures and objects set against backgrounds of contrasting color-areas yield a succession of rhythmic color-units related to each other in a harmonious and strong design. His line is sensitively expressive both of movement and of psychological states, he had a fine feeling for the sensuous quality of color, and possessed the ability to make color act in knitting the picture together. Like many of the moderns he emphasized planes, and he had such control over his medium that the planes themselves, and the intervals between them, function as charming color-forms.

In his later work the representative elements in subject-matter are simplified and distorted by his adaptations of the cubistic technique, with, however, sufficient retention of representative matter to indicate the identity of the subject portrayed. Planes are still further emphasized; their bright, delicate, and varied colors are modulated with light, and there are perceptible separate patterns made up of each of the elements—the planes, the color, the light, and the spatial intervals. These units fuse into a total design that is comparable in plastic strength to the best cubist pictures of Picasso and Braque. Demuth's method of using interpenetrating planes and angular surface-patterns derives from Cézanne's; but the resulting forms are much slighter. In the work of his latest period the influences of Cézanne and of cubism are very much less perceptible and the form as a whole is more like that in his early pictures. His paintings at all stages consist of a series of rhythms of light, line, color, and space, which have a delicate, fluid charm sometimes reminiscent of the Chinese in general effect.

John Kane (1860–1934) was modern in the sense that his usually trite, romantic, or commonplace subject-matter is incorporated in a patterned design which is both ingenious and forceful. His sketches and unfinished paintings reveal that he was primarily concerned in constructing a firm framework of patterns consisting of a well-balanced interrelation of units of line, space, light, and color. Upon this framework he depicted scenes imbued with the spirit of romance and poetry which recall, variously, the fifteenth century Italians, the seventeenth century Dutch landscapists, the Barbizon painters, le douanier Rousseau, and the early American "folk-lore" group. He was not, however, either a plagiarist or an eclectic, for in whatever style he adopted, there is strength, naïveté, and charm in a form which is quite personal.

The work of **John Marin** (1870–1953), **Georgia O'Keeffe** (1887–1986), the three **Pinto** brothers—**Salvatore** (1905–1966), **Angelo** (1908–   ), and **Biagio** (1911–1988)—**Settanni** (1908–1984), and a few other painters is entitled to respect because it represents personal visions embodied in individual plastic forms.

Unfortunately for the intelligent appreciation of art in America, certain painters have been persistently exploited in the public press as the producers of what has been termed creative inter-pretation of American life. Among this group are **Thomas Benton** (1889–1975), **Grant Wood** (1892–1942), and **John Curry** (1897–1946). The work of these painters consists of illustration rendered in technical practices which have been the stock-in-trade of academic painters since the time of the Renaissance. One looks in vain for a form that is genuinely creative or that furnishes anything more moving esthetically than does illustration, flagrant sentimentalism, photographic literalism, or the specious use of facile rhythms imposed upon subject-matter to effect symmetry and balance of composition.

BOOK V

CONTEMPORARY PAINTING

CHAPTER I

THE TRANSITION TO CONTEMPORARY PAINTING

In the chapter "The Transition to Modern Painting" is mentioned the fact that the distinctive note in the painting of our own day is the development of interest in design as something comparatively independent of the ostensible subject of the painting. Almost all modern painting of any importance shows the influence of impressionism, especially as that movement was shaped and brought to its consummation by Renoir and Cézanne. In the work of both of these artists, the interest in achieving design primarily through the medium of color is paramount, but the interest in color takes a different form in the two men. Renoir's color is brighter, more sensuously charming, more decorative, and its effects are more varied, in spite of the fact that his palette consisted of nine colors, Cézanne's of seventeen. In Cézanne, color is used more directly in the interest of solidity or mass. But in both artists, color assumes a functional power to effect composition in a degree unexcelled in the history of painting. The emphasis upon color as the most potent of all the instruments of design is thus due chiefly to the researches of these two men.

In the evolution of their techniques, Renoir and Cézanne adopted methods that came, through Manet, from the Venetians, and from Velásquez, Hals, Rubens, Goya, and Courbet. Their simplifications and generalizations were achieved principally by the broad brush strokes that enabled Manet to give the essential quality of things, stripped of adventitious matter, in a form that added a new note to the tradition of painting. The concentration on the essential visible reality, which was the distinctive contribution of Velásquez, was revived and made a part of the living tradition of the time, but with the addition of an independent non-naturalistic design, which also reveals penetratingly the nature of things. Manet's method of using his brush had much influence upon Renoir and Cézanne; his contribution as a whole was in solution in most of the painting of the time, and it constantly reappears in the work of subsequent painters. Unfortunately, his brushwork survives also as an academic cliché, while his form as a whole is caricatured and commercialized by numerous portrait-manufacturers.

We have already summed up the details of the advance made by Renoir and Cézanne upon the impressionistic painting which constituted their point of departure. In their forms, impressionism was further fertilized by their use of the great traditions of the past, and, together, Renoir and Cézanne represent the highest development of plastic expression. Simplification and distortion are more obvious in Cézanne's work than in Renoir's, and this fact has led to the view, at present much in vogue among superficial critics, that Cézanne represents a stage further in advance than Renoir in the progress toward the goal of a pure art. Such a view is due partly to an assumption which is false, and partly to insensitive observation. The assumption is that which has been given currency by the advocates of cubism and other ultra-modern art-forms, namely, that pure art involves a complete breach with reality, that plastic values are totally detached from human values. We have already seen the falsity of this assumption, and it will be further indicated in the discussion of cubism. The critics' fault in observation is that of failing to see in Renoir a more complex and profound originality than in Cézanne.[1] The obvious surface-characteristics of Cézanne's work lend themselves to detection by academic critics, and imitation by academic painters, more readily than do the complex fundamental characteristics of Renoir. Cézanne's distortions, the simplicity of his compositions, and the comparatively limited effects of his palette—all these are easily seen and mimicked, but are far from explaining his power. Cézanne's greatness depends upon the use of color to achieve his peculiar effects of convincing massiveness, spaciousness, and compositional relations. To appreciate these, it is necessary to be able to abstract color and discern its function, its structural and organizing power; alleged appreciation not based upon such discernment is plain illusion and self-deception. But where the ability to grasp such color-values exists, there will also be ability to see in Renoir's paintings greater wealth of color-relationships, based upon the use of an infinite variety of shades and modulations with light. Color-chords in Renoir's canvases are far richer and more numerous than in those of any painter before or since his time. The difference between Renoir and Cézanne is this: Cézanne concentrated his efforts upon

[1] See Barnes and de Mazia, *The Art of Renoir*, pp. 216–221, Minton, Balch & Co., New York, 1935.

a much narrower range of problems; he attained a quite individual strength, but he became something much nearer a specialist than Renoir. The specialist is, of course, more advanced in his particular province than a man of broader activities, but he is not therefore more original. It is true that Cézanne was extraordinarily original in his own sphere, but Renoir's originality was the more universal, subtle, and inimitable. Critics desirous of showing Renoir as at a disadvantage compared with Cézanne, point to Cézanne's more numerous imitators among the painters of the last decade or two, and assert that he has had more influence upon subsequent artists than Renoir. To any one with the slightest knowledge of history, the fallacy of judging the fertility of a man's work by its influence on the members of the generation just following his own will be apparent. The truth is that any profound or far-reaching originality requires for its understanding and use more than the very few years that have elapsed since Renoir's and Cézanne's activities.

The art of painting as it emerges from the hands of Renoir and Cézanne demonstrates as never before two all-important principles: first, that of relatively abstract design, embodying the values of human experience but not tied down to a literal reproduction of the situations in which these values are found in ordinary life; second, the principle of color as the most essential of all the plastic elements, the means most entirely intrinsic to the medium of paint. This latter principle means, pragmatically, that effects of mass, composition, space, drawing, are most moving esthetically when rendered in terms of color. Upon this foundation rests all that is truly significant and important in contemporary art.

Factors contributing to the development of modern design are found also in the work of Gauguin and van Gogh. Other very important sources of inspiration are Negro sculpture, in the case of Picasso, Modigliani, and Soutine; and the art of Persia, Byzantium, Egypt, India, China, and Japan, in the case of Matisse and his disciples.

In Gauguin, there reappear, with a different effect, the broad areas of color which are to be found in Manet. The areas are broader, more purely decorative, and do not show Manet's characteristic brushwork. In Manet the design is intended much more to render the essential natural quality of what is depicted, while in Gauguin the forms are less expressive and they function more obviously as means to a design which is much more nearly mere pattern. This undoubtedly makes Gauguin a less important artist,

[353]

but it also made his pictures fertile in suggestions for the painters who followed him. In Gauguin's general exotic quality and in his unusual color-contrasts, there is an anticipation of the color-scheme which is used by Matisse with more subtlety, variety, and power. Van Gogh's exaggeration of the impressionists' spots of color into ribbonlike streaks gives a general animation to the canvas and a brightness to the color itself, in addition to making a specific design in which line reënforces color. In this respect, van Gogh's painting is more literally expressive, less merely decorative, than Gauguin's; but a similar step is taken toward the emphasis upon design, and the decorative motive is also strongly felt. The strikingly unnatural shades of color and the distortions of line and mass are steps in the same direction, and these, together with the other characteristics of van Gogh's work, have been utilized freely by contemporary painters.

Negro sculpture has enriched contemporary painting to a great extent. In the early periods of Greek sculpture figures were conceived as combinations of back, front, and side bas-reliefs. Design was too often encumbered by representation, so that the arrangement of masses—head, trunk, and limbs—which would have made the most effective esthetic ensemble, is rarely found. Literature, in other words, stood in the way of plastic form. With Negro sculpture, the literary motive is submerged in the artist's distribution of masses in accord with the requirements of a truly sculptural design. There is no suggestion of bas-relief: the figures are three-dimensional through and through. Freedom from the adventitious or meaningless gives Negro art a sculptural quality purer than that of the majority of the best Greek work or of Renaissance sculpture, which is Greek in another guise. In this respect, Negro sculpture is quite the equal of Egyptian sculpture of the best periods.

Greek and Græco-Roman statues have had an enormous influence on the whole course of painting since the Renaissance, and the pictures in which this influence is most apparent, for example, those of Leonardo and Michelangelo, represent in a double sense a mongrel art. They are imitations, in painting, of another art and this other art is in itself hybrid, a cross between pure sculpture and flat representation. Hence the confusion of values in Leonardo and Michelangelo, and in all who showed the influence of their examples. This confusion was not incompatible with considerable achievement, since Giorgione, Renoir, and Cézanne are clearly within the classic Renaissance tradition, but it has unduly limited the range of possible pictorial effects.

Negro art, in exhibiting a form which is in the fullest sense sculptural, has enforced a sharper distinction between the possibilities inherent in painting and sculpture, respectively, and it has also put at the disposal of painting a new source of inspiration. It is not a confusion of values when a painter finds inspiration in another art: the confusion arises when he directly imitates the methods of that art. Michelangelo's stonelike masses and Leonardo's rounded forms are such an imitation, but the use of Negro motifs in the work of Matisse, Modigliani, or Soutine is not. The latter do not attempt to re-produce the three-dimensional qualities of Negro statues: what is taken over is rendered in terms proper to painting, and so has nothing of the mongrel quality which is found in the present-day revivals of Renaissance art. Matisse, Modigliani, and Soutine avail themselves of the essential feeling, the spirit of Negro art, and give it force in a new setting.

The attempt in painting to use sculptural motifs or suggestions may either be quite unsuccessful, or produce an effect entirely other than that intended, as in cubism. Cubistic pictures, far from possessing the characteristics which the word "cubistic" would properly imply, often tend to go toward the opposite extreme of utter flatness. The great success of Lipchitz in applying the cubistic principles to sculpture suggests that the peculiar type of emphasis upon selected planes, advocated by Picasso, Braque, and their followers, is a valid procedure in its proper sphere, however much of a fiasco it has been in painting. When suggestions supplied by sculpture are employed with due consideration for real and fundamental problems of painting, especially with an eye to the possibilities of color, as in the work of Soutine, the result is a very strong plastic form of which nothing in the previous history of painting is an anticipation. The achievement is of epochal importance.

CHAPTER II

CONTEMPORARY PAINTING

In 1904 a group of Cézanne's followers established in Paris the *Salon d'Automne* and thereby started a movement which has determined much of what is vital and important in contemporary painting throughout the world.

What interested the insurgents of the early years of this century was Cézanne's development of a form that had freed itself to an unheard-of extent from the representative values of subject-matter. The foundation of his form was the impressionists' practice of using colors different from the natural tones of the objects portrayed: color combined with light was so distributed all over the canvas that a homogeneous color-mass replaced the old-fashioned representation of foreground, middle-distance, and background; and color became the most active compositional agent in the plastic organization. In Cézanne's hands the method attained to the color-power which only a few great artists of the past—the great Florentines and Venetians, and El Greco, Poussin, Delacroix—had possessed.

Cézanne's treatment of subject-matter led some of his followers to believe that painting could be purified and refined into abstract forms by abolishing all representation of natural objects. Picasso went to the extreme of conceiving objects as a series of planes which revealed only sections of objects in angular and cubic formation. The practice spread rapidly and was defended by a system of absurd psychological and metaphysical doctrines that impressed unreflecting painters and critics.

In 1913 cubism invaded America through the Armory Exhibition in New York. Its advent was brilliant in the sense of Goethe's remark that "there is no great art in being brilliant, if one respects nothing." Its intrinsic capital consisted of the fact that the paintings offered a fresh, vivid impression in the name of art, at a time when creation was at its lowest level. The combination of circumstances influenced most of the young and a number of the older unstable painters to the extent that cubism in varying degrees of

[356]

purity flourished in independent exhibitions for a number of years. The practical result was that a new academy, cubism, supplanted the one which the impressionists had maintained for the previous twenty years.

Sufficient time has passed to view cubism in retrospect and to evaluate it as an art-form and as an influence. Picasso and Braque put considerable esthetic power into cubistic paintings, but it is doubtful if that power is not due to something independent of both the principles and the technique. The idea of abstract form divorced from a clue, however vague, of its representative equivalent in the real world, is sheer nonsense. In cubistic paintings that move us esthetically there are always sufficient representative indications, as well as reliance upon traditional resources of painting, to stir up something familiar in our mass of funded experience. In these cases, the cubist technique functions psychologically precisely as do the distortions of El Greco, Renoir, or Cézanne; that is, the representative element in the distortions contributes to the total esthetic effect. The great majority of cubistic paintings fail in this respect and, as a result, they have no more esthetic significance than the pleasing pattern of an Oriental rug.

A more important and constructive influence that came from the insurgent group in France is that of Matisse. He was never tempted to seek the metaphysical abstract that led Picasso astray. Matisse, like Cézanne, has always been interested in the real world as the source of a plastic instrument that would enable him to recombine selected aspects or phases of human experience into a form which is something new, a thing in itself, with its own independent existence. He used distortions and also certain technical devices, which Cézanne invented, and he carried them to extremes in making them constructive factors in his own designs. Subject-matter was further minimized: it remained merely as the foundation stone upon which to build lines of extraordinary plastic power, and color-forms of unusual compositional significance. In other words, Matisse followed Renoir's and Cézanne's practice in creating plastic forms of structural integrity. Where Picasso abstracted an element in a situation, Matisse dealt with the whole situation as it exists in reality. The error in Picasso's cubistic excursions is that he ignored the fundamental psychological fact that *continuity* is the essential feature of perception. It is absurd to say that planes or sections of cubes represent the reality of objects as—to quote an observation of William James—to contend that our perception of a river is of spoonfuls or bucketfuls of water. In short, Picasso dealt with irrational abstractions that led him into a cul-de-sac, while Matisse dealt with concrete realities that expand continuously into unlimited fields.

The tendency in present-day painting is away from the abstract and toward the utilization of situations of everyday life as a means of individual expression of universal human values. The impressionism of Claude Monet is scarcely in evidence, but the influences of Renoir, Cézanne, Gauguin, van Gogh, and Matisse, all of whom had their origins in impressionism, are almost universal in one or more of their phases. To these influences have been added the decorations and distortions found in the arts of India and Persia, China and Japan, and especially in Negro sculpture. Certain practices of cubism—for example, the accentuation and interpenetration of planes—have been generalized in the new manner of emphasizing spatial relations of naturalistic objects. The primitive element which reappeared in *le douanier* Rousseau is also evident in the work of some of the contemporaries. These various influences have determined the exotic, the distorted, the primitive effects which have stirred the wrath of our fetish-worshiping academicians. What they have urged against contemporary painting is duplicated in every essential point in what their prototypes of 1875 published about many paintings now considered to be among the best in the Louvre.

The canvases of the important contemporary painters are filled with units actively constructive in the general design, and representative elements are distorted for obviously specific purposes. The fresh and bright colors which cubism tabooed are almost universal, color composes the painting, and all the plastic means are employed to emphasize decoration as a reënforcement of the expression of the human values intrinsic to the scenes and events of everyday life. In the limited space of this book, only a few of the many good contemporary painters can be mentioned. An attempt will be made, therefore, to select for discussion some of the artists whose work may be considered as representative of the tendencies that make up the new tradition.

CHAPTER III

MATISSE [1]

MATISSE's (1869–1954) form is fundamentally determined by his primary interest in the decorative aspects of both the objective world and the traditions of painting. Throughout his whole career this interest has dictated his choice of subject-matter, his drafts upon the traditions, and his employment of all the plastic means. His immediate point of departure was naturally provided by impressionism and post-impressionism, and he first attained his artistic maturity when these influences were fused with those of Oriental art. His subsequent growth consisted in an ever-increasing assimilation of the Oriental traditions, which greatly extended both his command of his means and the variety and complexity of his effects.

At the start, and indeed at all times, he made extensive use of the impressionistic technique, bright illumination and pure colors, and especially of Manet's simplified drawing, flattened volumes, and luminous quality of paint, but all of these are employed with basically decorative intent. Elimination of detail is carried further and contributes to formal pattern rather than to the natural quality of what is presented; brush strokes are less perceptible and their function is ornamental elaboration rather than realistic drawing and modeling; brighter and more vivid colors are disposed in broader, more sharply contrasted areas, which are frequently enclosed by marked linear contours to heighten the effect of pattern. Of the other modern influences by far the most important is Cézanne's, which appears in distortions of many kinds, in compositional color-patterns and distribution of subject-matter, in linear emphasis of contour, and in modeling by hatchings and accentuated planes of color.

The importance of the Oriental influence upon Matisse is due to the fact that Oriental art has always been decorative rather than expressive in both conception and execution, and hence pre-

[1] For a comprehensive study of Matisse's form, see Barnes and de Mazia, *The Art of Henri-Matisse*, Charles Scribner's Sons, New York, 1933.

eminently adapted to his purposes. The outstanding feature of Matisse's painting is his bizarre, exotic color in daring contrasts and patterns; and the relationships of this color as well as its framework of pattern are derived from Japanese prints, Chinese paintings, Byzantine mosaics, Persian miniatures and tiles, and Oriental textiles of various types. The pattern of color-compartments of which he makes such constant use is common to all of these and is definitely Oriental in origin; even when the small vibrant color-units of the impressionists and the modulations of the post-impressionists occur in his work, they are secondary to the pattern of broad contrasting color-areas. It is by this compositional device that Matisse gives his own distinctive form to what he borrows from Manet and Cézanne, and the results are nearer to the Orientals than to the Western prototypes. He also adopts extensively such other Oriental means of subordinating expression to decoration as the flattening of three-dimensional volumes into broad compactly wedged planes; equalization of foreground and background in a single, all-inclusive, rhythmically organized surface; and general accentuation of line, in the form of either broad ragged stripes of color or continuous arabesques. All of these practices render pattern even more emphatically than in the source of derivation.

Among the Oriental sources it was the Japanese prints which influenced Matisse most strongly and directly. In addition to the general Oriental traits just referred to, his work reflects the Japanese use of stripes and bands, vivid contrasts of bright and light colors, and extensive use of black in lines and areas. His color, brighter, more vivid, more superficial than the impressionists', without the fluidity that produces color-chords, is in all these points especially close to the Japanese, but it is even more vivid than theirs, more animated and brightly lighted within, more patterned, and more dramatically contrasted. His line is heavier and terser, his decorative arabesques are fewer and less clear-cut, and he has none of their miniature-quality. In the comparative looseness of his drawing, he is more akin to the Chinese, from whom he took his islands of color and light and a number of technical devices, such as the use of areas of bare canvas, but his pattern and color are more vivid and striking than theirs. In his treatment of space as a series of closely placed planes, moving toward a high horizon, he is especially indebted to the Persians, as he is also in his decorative union of foreground and background. The small brush

Negro Sculpture (227)　　　　　**Egyptian Sculpture (188)**

Design characterized by distortions from naturalistic appearance.

Hindu-Persian Miniature (211)

Shows distortion of perspective to achieve design.

Matisse (221)

Similar in the use of perspective to the Hindu-Persian miniature on
the opposite page.

Hindu Sculpture (212)

Matisse (222)

The effect of quasi-detached rounded volumes in this Matisse establishes a kinship with the Hindu sculpture above.

strokes by which his broad color-areas are patterned are an echo of Byzantine mosaics, as are also the parallel bands and stripes and irregular patches of color of which he makes extensive use in modeling. Other of his linear effects and decorative devices have their source in Negro sculpture and in Egyptian art, especially in Coptic textiles and Egypto-Roman funeral portraits.

In spite of the great diversity of traditional sources upon which Matisse draws, every borrowed element is so adjusted to his individual purposes, fused with elements taken from other traditions, that his form is an organic unity, never an eclectic patchwork. This fusion of traditional themes is personal in every aspect: whatever their prototypes, their color, light, line, and space are recast in a manner distinctively Matisse's own. Each traditional form and each plastic means is adapted with the utmost ingenuity to drawing out the decorative qualities of the subject-matter, usually with extensive distortion. In his disregard of natural appearances when the design requires it, Matisse is exceedingly audacious. Solid objects become flat color-areas, their natural color and shape are often entirely disregarded, space is at times expanded, at other times compressed in the extreme, and often reduced to projection on a single plane. The texture of materials is almost never reproduced with naturalistic fidelity, psychological characterization is not attempted, and there is little or no representation of action: the movement and drama, of which his canvases are full, are wholly plastic.

Color is by far the most important element in Matisse's design: he himself has said that the world presents itself to him primarily and most forcibly in terms of color. In his paintings not only is the impact of color the most striking effect, but it is by color that the other plastic elements are chiefly rendered. His individual colors are frequently harsh and strident; their combinations are daring and often repellent to the conventional sensibilities; but they are related with such consummate skill that harmony, delicacy, and charm are achieved, as well as drama and power. The variety of his color-schemes is extraordinarily great, as is the variety of color-relationships, and both the individual hues and the ensembles are practically always vivid and exotic. Even more important than the immediate qualitative color-relations is the function of color in organizing the form as a whole. As we have already seen, Matisse's characteristic type of organization is a pattern of color-compartments, almost always with strongly accentuated linear divisions between the broad areas, so that line is an element second in importance only to color. His subject-matter is often chosen for the sake of its richness in linear pattern, and this aspect is constantly emphasized by his distortions. The line is scarcely ever the mere meeting-place between colored areas, and it is never conceived in isolation: it is itself color, and it works in the closest conjunction with the color-areas to bind together the pattern as a whole. It is largely responsible for the modeling of volumes, which are rarely very solid, but to which added weight is lent by broad and heavy line; it also does much, especially in the form of stripes and bands, to render space.

Matisse's color-pattern largely determines also his use of light, which is seldom naturalistic, and plays a relatively minor part in modeling. Its chief function is to make color more vivid and luminous, and, by its distribution in patches or islands, to reënforce the pattern. Its placing in the compositional pattern is also an important means of rendering space, and when in addition it forms an enveloping radiance, the radiance is itself highly colorful. The same color-pattern is what chiefly determines the treatment of space, its frequent compression, and the use of a high horizon; it is also the most important agent of composition, regarded either as the distribution of masses or as the unification of the entire design. The organization is achieved by repetition of particular colors and color-areas, by continuity of linear pattern, and by a general rhythmic movement of all the plastic elements over the canvas as a whole.

The general decorative quality of Matisse's design is greatly enhanced by the fact that it effects the transfer of values from one realm of experience to another. In even such subject-matter as landscapes or human beings his pictures constantly recall the qualities of cretonnes, tapestries, tiles, posters, mosaics, rosettes, and fireworks; the process often involves extreme distortion, but the result is a greatly enriched picturesqueness, and a bizarreness which carries further the general exoticism of his form. In spite of the enormous liberties which he takes with natural appearances, his objects always preserve recognizable identity, remain an authentic part of the real world, and he can present with a high degree of essential realism, though never in representative detail, such subject-matter as a bourgeois interior, a still-life, a figure picturesquely clad and posed. To this essential realism his transferred values add a further expressive effect: they invest the most prosaic objects with the attributes of tapestries or banners, flowers or jewels.

Matisse has the defects of his qualities: his limitations spring from the same decorative emphasis to which he owes his distinctive personal form. His work lacks the deeper values, plastic and human, which arise from concern for the substance of things as well as the surface. In the work of the great Venetians, and of Rembrandt, Renoir and Cézanne, there is a profound conviction, a monumental character, a moving humanity, of which Matisse has little or none. His painting presents a world bathed in light and color, full of movement and drama and unsuspected possibilities of embellishment; but it reveals little of its depths. His portraits, for example, are of human beings only in a superficial sense; essentially they are pretexts for exercising his ingenuity in devising patterns of line and color and other ornamental arrangement; rarely do they show any realization of the sitter's personality. The poignant, the epic, the deeply mystical, are all absent from his work. This dearth of profound human values is accompanied by a lack of complete plastic conviction. So encyclopedic is his erudition, so complete his command of his medium, that he seldom fails to accomplish what he sets out to do, but the intense realization of the greatest painters, based upon structural color and dynamic space-composition, lies almost wholly beyond him. Correspondingly his form, personal as it is and free from the taint of plagiarism, is not of really profound originality. What he borrows from the traditions is not reorganized in a form of revolutionary novelty, such as Renoir's or Cézanne's; his growth, in the course of his career, is an advance in range, not in depth of insight or essential esthetic stature. Even in his own chosen sphere of decoration, the absence of rich color-chords impoverishes his surfaces, which are often arid and unappealing; his pictures are great as decorative organizations, but they lack the textural richness of the great artists whose expressive form flowered naturally and inevitably into a decorative charm not deliberately planned for and contrived.

Matisse, in a word, is a painter definitely limited in the range of his interests, but within his limits he displays sensitivity, skill, erudition, and intellect of a very high order. He seems never to be carried away or deeply inspired; each of his pictures represents the execution of a highly intelligent plan of campaign, upon which are brought to bear an extremely resourceful and discriminating technique and fund of knowledge; and it is a part of his intelligence, the sobriety of his judgment, that he undertakes nothing to which his powers are inadequate. His great natural sensitiveness to color, his ability to organize a painting and to render every plastic element in terms of color, enable him to realize his designs plastically with superlative success. He is not only the most important living painter, but he has achieved a range and variety of decorative forms second to none in the history of painting.

CHAPTER IV

PICASSO

Picasso (1881–1973) ranks second only to Matisse in the importance of his achievements in contemporary painting, and his influence upon young painters has been greater than that of any other artist of his epoch. His indebtedness to the traditions and his ability to give them an original setting are evident in his work of all periods.

In his earliest paintings, the influences most apparent are those of Degas and Toulouse-Lautrec. From them he took over the expressive character of line, the quality and manner of application of color, and the illustrative type of subject-matter in which psychological expression predominates. Later, in what is known as his "blue period," his work shows the influences of Cézanne, El Greco, and the fifteenth century Italian, Piero della Francesca. The Piero-school picture "Marriage of St. Catherine" (15) shows the kinship in general expressive use of color, line, light, and distortion. Also like Piero, Picasso made a strong and very resourceful use of color, and more particularly of a single color, blue. Blue was the foundation of his "blue period" color-scheme: amply varied and modulated with light, it gives diversified color-effects, it works through the whole expanse of the picture, makes direct color-contrasts, and aids in the general composition and in the construction of the masses themselves. Compared with the color of Renoir and Cézanne, it is lacking both in richness and in depth; but it is often very subtle, gives the effect of great economy of means, and is in keeping with Picasso's form, which is slighter than that of the greatest artists.

His line at this period shows the influence also of El Greco as well as of Cézanne: its distortions give a heightened degree of psychological expressiveness, and the use of the line in connection with light in modeling is also El Grecoesque. In the less successful pictures of the "blue period" the separate influences noted are more or less perceptible in isolation, but in his best work, as represented by "Girl with Cigarette" (233) and "Harlequins" (234),

[369]

they are very well fused into a characteristic Picasso form. The treatment of subject-matter displays Picasso's marked tendency to illustration, but on the whole the pictures of both the "blue" and the so-called "rose" periods represent successful integrations of color, line, modeling, and space-composition, in picturesque ensembles which are fully expressive plastically.

In 1907 Picasso became interested in Negro sculpture to such an extent that his paintings of that period are really pictorial reproductions of the sculptural values of Negro carved figures and masks. This part of his work was only fragmentary and transitional, but the increased technical resources remained at his command and paved the way for his later work, in which the sculptural forms are more fully assimilated in terms proper to painting.

About 1909 the sculptural influence began to be paramount, and naturalistic appearances gave place almost completely to the rendering of abstract forms. In his still-lifes of this period, several objects are often placed so close together that the whole group functions as a single mass. His former suave, curved lines have become sharp and heavy, and the objects outlined are angular and blocklike. The pinks, blues, and yellows of his earlier work have changed into a somber combination of slate gray, drab green, and dull brownish-red. These new shapes and colors are the distinctive mark of Picasso's form at that period and constituted the point of departure for cubism.

The roots of cubism can best be seen by an examination of the distortions in Cézanne's work, in which a single element or aspect of an object is often exaggerated out of all reasonable proportion to the other elements. This distortion represents an imaginative analysis of the dissociation of an object into its plastic elements and their recombination in a new form differing in appearance from the original object, but constituting a more forceful embodiment of its plastic qualities. All painting which makes any pretense to artistic significance involves some measure of this selection and emphasis. This principle is precisely the principle of cubism, with the difference that in cubism, as in other contemporary painting, it is carried much further. Every object in the real world, as viewed from various angles, may be regarded as a multitude of planes which so melt into one another that their participation in the construction of three-dimensional quality is not in evidence. Cubism is an effort to bring this three-dimensional feature into clear relief by abstracting and showing only a certain number of the planes.

These experiments in pure design are obviously closely related to Cézanne's similar interest, but in Cézanne, there is much more of the direct resemblance to real objects; and the distortions, produced by the interpenetration of planes at angles departing from the normal, result in both an increase in degree of three-dimensional solidity and a heightened sense of design.

In Picasso's cubism, the process departs so far from naturalism that what is shown is of little or no assistance in identifying the object as it exists in nature. Distortion of this type is consistent with the imaginative purpose of art, provided the created design is more moving esthetically than is the naturalistic aspect of objects. There is no doubt that such resolution of masses into their constituent planes does sometimes produce a pattern much more interesting than a naturalistic rendering could hope to achieve. However, pattern is not synonymous with design constituting great art. Many cubist pictures do not sufficiently anchor the patterned forms to the real world to make possible a transfer of the many echoes and reverberations of feelings which objects gain by their multiform relationships in ordinary experience. In short, the cubist principle, if carried to its logical conclusion in wholly abstract design, is as much an overaccentuation as is Botticelli's line or Leonardo's light-and-dark contrast; that is, one of the plastic factors—pattern of planes—is made to do the work which should be done by the unified action of all the elements: it is only by the merging of *all* the elements that all the resources of our experience can be brought into play to give emotional force to the form presented. The appeal of pure cubism is, therefore, due to the same psychological factors which are responsible for our pleasure in a decorative rug or wall paper. Nevertheless, this fact does not prevent the imaginative and resourceful use of cubistic technique from producing pictures of a high degree of esthetic value. In fact, many of Picasso's cubistic paintings achieve this value by their harmonious interplay of line, color, and space, and produce unified designs embracing a wide variety of effects. If an observer cannot appreciate such paintings, and at the same time professes to enjoy art-values in Titian, Velásquez, or Renoir, we are justified in questioning whether he is not really deceiving himself. This means not that Picasso is as great as Titian, Velásquez, or Renoir, but only that he has created a plastic form the essential value of which, although not different in principle, is less in degree than theirs. To sum up: Picasso's cubism made dominant what was merely a by-product in Cézanne's work, that is, one of the surface-effects incidental to the rhythmic movements of solid objects in deep space. Picasso's followers attempted to give a rationale of the procedure; psychologically considered, such reasoning is nonsense, and it has brought discredit upon the whole movement.

After a number of years of experimenting with the cubistic technique, Picasso resumed his interest in painting in which the representative element is more in evidence. His line became finer and more in the manner of Ingres, though by no means an imitation of Ingres's line. The figures and objects assumed a solidity and blocklike effect which constitute decided distortions from the naturalistic viewpoint. They have a monumental sculptural quality that was lacking in his early period, and it seems that the influences of Negro art, of El Greco and Cézanne, have been more or less supplanted by the influences of ancient Greek sculpture and of those painters of the Italian Renaissance who were themselves preoccupied with the three-dimensional solidity characteristic of Greek statuary. He attains a personal plastic form of considerable power, but much of this painting represents such an accentuation of heavy voluminous masses that it savors strongly of virtuosity. These pictures, while always of considerable esthetic value, show a decided retrogression when compared with the balanced use of plastic means in the best of his earlier work.

About 1920, Picasso again departed radically from his form of the years immediately preceding and began to use bright, exotic colors in daring contrasts, in conjunction with accentuated linear patterns and semi-abstract units based upon his adventures in cubism. During the four years, 1929–1933, he used these abstract units as distorted representation of the human figure in color-ensembles often almost monochromatic.

In perhaps the majority of his pictures painted between 1921 and the present time, his colors and their manner of use are obviously imitative of Matisse's. Picasso's lack of feeling for relationship of such colors makes them seem so incongruous with the usually attractive patterns of lines and shapes, that the end result is a hybrid and unconvincing decorative concoction. Intermittently during this period, he further experimented with novel, extremely distorted representations of the human figure and with spatial constructions of bonelike structures, in delicate pastel-like color-schemes or in gray-tan monochromes, usually with very bizarre and striking effects of space-composition.

Psychologically considered, Picasso's art represents a great natural sensitiveness and a fertility of resources and ideas rather than a reflective, resolute, and well-directed search for an individual esthetic conception. In men like Cézanne, Renoir, or Matisse, it is possible to see a constant struggle for a form which will express all that the artist has to say. This sense of a deeply purposeful effort toward a style adequate to carry a profoundly personal and original vision is absent in Picasso. The successive styles seem less cumulative, less like stages on the way to a goal which has been foreshadowed all along, than they do, for example, in Renoir. In this sense, Picasso is unreflective, as is shown by the fact that his later work does not always show an improvement in the fulness and strength of his plastic form. In his latest periods, for instance, the distinctive traits do not seem a real augmentation of his resources, but rather a reversion, since it suggests that a new interest had intervened which was in the nature of a distraction rather than of a fulfilment of his earlier and more natural interests. In the same way, his cubistic paintings are in most respects less satisfactory than those of his "blue period." Such veerings marked with partial retrogression suggest an impulsive temperament, going off at a tangent from the line of maximum advance rather than using every new element of technique to deepen and enrich a fundamentally organic grasp of the world of plastic forms.

CHAPTER V

OTHER CONTEMPORARIES

Soutine (1894–1943) occupies a distinctive position in modern painting because of his achievements in the use of solid, deep, rich, juicy, and variegated color. The paint is laid on the canvas very heavily, much in the manner of van Gogh, with ribbonlike strokes which are longer than van Gogh's, more varied, more dynamic, and more suggestive of power. There are few areas of simple homogeneous color: everywhere there is animation, motion, heightened by variety in the direction in which the color-strokes run. The color is diversified and intensified by light and it creates extremely vivid, intense, and dramatic rhythms. The drama is strongly suggestive of Tintoretto's, but is more striking and it pervades the entire picture.

His technique is closest to that of van Gogh, whom he resembles also in the fervidness of his style and the general surface-quality of his effects. His color-chords compare in richness with those of Renoir and Cézanne, though they are less uniformly active in organizing the picture. His modeling by the use of contrasting areas of color in connection with light, suggests Cézanne's, but the color-areas are larger, the brush strokes much more obvious, and the masses are less solid and convincing. From Daumier he took the method of so simplifying and distorting objects as to make them appear monstrous or grotesque, but without loss of essential reality. This exaggeration is carried much further by Soutine and is modified by his use of many of the characteristic simplifications and distortions of Negro sculpture. With the extensive omission of detail involved, the simplification is strongly contributory to primary emphasis upon color and to increase in the power of rhythm.

Soutine's drawing is almost exclusively executed by means of color. The streaks of color defining outlines of masses are duplicated by or related to similar streaks within the masses or in the neighboring background. No attempt at naturalism is made, and it is often only after considerable study that the identity of the

[374]

object drawn can be discovered. The indications of space are slight and incidental to the color-design. The equivalent for distance is usually rendered simply by the elevation of the more remote objects toward the top of the canvas. Light is used chiefly to vivify and diversify color, and is rarely naturalistic. Although thus subordinate to color, the light, the line, and the space are well coördinated with color, and sufficient contact with nature is preserved, to assure plastic reality.

No contemporary painter has achieved an individual plastic form of more originality and power than Soutine. But extreme preoccupation with color, absence of the deep space required for monumental effects, and his habitual inability to organize the plastic units, exclude all but a few of his best pictures from the highest range of art. The bulk of his work is very uneven—excess of intensity prevents synthesis of all the parts of the picture into an organic whole, even when individual units are effectively done. It is nevertheless true that, at his best, he compares in strength and dramatic power with important painters of the past and present.

Pascin (1885–1930) is kin with several important artists: with Rubens in activity of swirling rhythms, and in modeling of flesh by contrasting parallel bands of color; with Daumier and Degas in expressive quality of drawing; with Renoir and Cézanne in general technique; and with the cubists in his use of angles and planes. Cézanne's influence is seen in Pascin's color-effects, and in his distortions of figures to enhance design. At times, whole color-forms and color-areas in his pictures closely resemble those of Cézanne. From Renoir, he absorbed chiefly the lightness, delicacy, and fluidity of color. His wavy contour is an actual line as in Cézanne but the delicacy of its effect is more reminiscent of Renoir; it imparts a graceful and rhythmic flow to his drawing of masses. His modeling of flesh combines the patches of Cézanne, and the parallel bands of Rubens with Pascin's own relation of light and shade: the shadow is usually placed on the foremost area of the volumes and is flanked on each side by a band or area of light. After 1914 the influence of cubism upon Pascin became apparent in the extensive use of geometrically shaped color-areas which, by the interpenetration of their planes, form a pronounced angular pattern and give a block-like character to houses, trees, and other objects.

Pascin's outstanding plastic characteristic is a short and wavy line which, in most of his work, evokes a sense of drama and a feel-

[375]

ing of extremely animated movement. These short wavy lines, reënforced by light and color, create a complex series of active, almost quivering, rhythmic units which continuously flow into and link up with each other. The result is a sort of swirl which, though less colorful than Rubens', and less powerful and convincing than Tintoretto's, is akin to both. The number, variety, and activity of Pascin's rhythms have rarely been equaled by other painters. His line is not only highly decorative, but also as free, as terse, as varied in expression as that of any of the great illustrators. The distortions in his painting increase the expression of the natural, essential quality of objects or episodes as they are perceived by a vision highly sensitive to every type of thing or activity. The dynamic qualities are especially felt: his ability to represent movement is extraordinary; even when a figure is motionless, the effect is not of inertia, but of suspended movement ready at any moment to be resumed. Every unit in his canvas is alive, and so, thanks to the pervasive, delicate, graceful rhythms, is the composition as a whole.

The lightness and freshness of his color contribute a quality of pastel which heightens the pervasive delicacy of all his work in oil. His manner of applying color is a triumph in economy of means: a minimum of pigment yields a fully adequate color-effect. In his sense for the compositional relation of masses, both in two and in three dimensions, Pascin ranks with the greatest of contemporary painters. His light is well used to diversify his compositions. His slight degree of modeling, together with the lightness of his color and the mode of its application to the canvas, diminishes the weight and carrying power of his pictures, and tends to emphasize the patterns at the expense of the solidity of volumes. Pascin's travels have taken him to every part of the world, and given him an unlimited store of experiences to draw upon and reduce to good plastic form.

The greater part of **Modigliani's** (1884–1920) paintings consist of single figures which have the distorted, elongated, oval faces, and the very long slender necks characteristic of Negro sculpture. These figures appear to be stiff and static, devoid of movement and psychological expressiveness. The facial expression is so nearly identical in all of them that they are to be viewed as focal masses in a plastic design rather than as representations of the human body. A basic feature of Modigliani's form is a very graceful, clean-cut, and marvelously effective line, which not only clearly defines contours, but is the major factor in imparting an adequate solidity to the volume enclosed between the contours. This ability to model with line is apparent in Modigliani's black-and-white drawings, in which there is a minimum of recourse to obvious shadows; in his paintings, it is the line quite as much as the color and the light which renders three-dimensionality of volume. This furnishes a fine example of what we term the plastic quality of line.

Modigliani's compositions are simple, harmonious, and distinguished. His color is rarely bright, and it is neither juicy nor greatly varied, but it is rich, delicate, light, and structurally solid; and it is so admirably coördinated with line that variation in line is paralleled by variation in color. His superb command of the subtle use of space is apparent in his manner of relating figure and background: each is clearly distinct from the other, even when their color-values are very close. The background is never a mere setting: in it are echoed, by subtle and ingenious rhythmic units, the shapes, colors, and patterns of the figure, thereby making of the composition an organic entity.

In the best of his work, painted after he had attained his individual mode of expression, there is a resemblance to Picasso in the color-schemes and in the decorative appeal of the surface, and to Cézanne in the solidity and surface of flesh. Occasionally, as in "Red-Headed Woman" (224), Modigliani modifies Manet's pattern of broad brush strokes by a strikingly decorative stippling effect, due to suction of the wet pigment by paper applied upon and pulled away from its surface. In a number of his paintings the influence of cubism appears in the division of surfaces into multiple angular and cubic patterns. The resulting complexity of units is in strong contrast to the uniformity of color and the simplicity of pattern usually characteristic of his best work.

Henri Rousseau (*le douanier*) (1844–1910) is not strictly a contemporary painter, but the vogue of his work began only a few years after his death in 1910. His form is an odd combination of an archaic literalism with distortions inspired by that interest in patterned design which is the mark of all contemporary painting. It unites almost photographically detailed drawing with color that is sometimes naturalistic, sometimes untrammeled by any consideration of accuracy in reproduction. His canvases are packed full of masses, arranged in intricate spatial relationships, with complete disregard for literary or scientific plausibility. The result is a strange, naïve, exotic quality of great appeal. Such is his command of space that his congregated masses never get in each other's way or encroach on each other's room, and the intervals between them are so varied as to create a rhythmic, melodious spatial symphony. With this structure of plastic essentials, the often disproportioned objects and figures, and the fantastic distortions of their color and shape, yield a genuinely naïve, very personal, and very effective design. His pictures have the charm of a child's fairy-tale, but there is nothing childish or untutored in the skill with which they are executed.

Utrillo's (1883–1955) very individual form reveals a delicate sense of the picturesque, an ability to portray it in distinctive color-forms, and a fine feeling for quality of paint. His best work, that of his early years, known as the "white period," renders the spirit of place with the sensitiveness, delicacy, and lyric charm that one finds in Corot and Renoir. His use of architectural features, related harmoniously to each other in space and bathed in an atmosphere of crystal-clarity, is reminiscent of the Corots of the Italian period.

Most of Utrillo's work portrays street-scenes or landscapes in which details are often painted with considerable fidelity to naturalistic appearance, but with the broadening inevitable in the use of the impressionistic technique. The literalness of subject-matter is completely submerged in the powerful esthetic feeling of design, the successful merging of color, light, line, and space. Perspective, also rendered almost naturalistically, is an important means of establishing and revealing finely harmonious spatial relations between objects as these move from the foreground toward the remoteness of infinity. This feeling of infinity Utrillo achieves with a rare degree of success by a subtle blending of color and light in space.

Much of the distinction of his form is due to the sensuous quality of his bright, rich, and deep color, applied in a manner resembling Manet's, and productive of an exquisite choiceness of surface and a solidity of structure much like Daumier's. The foundation of the color-scheme is often a rich ivory, modulated by delicate blues, pinks, and greens of great charm. Upon this foundation are laid broad areas of bright color, varied in size, direction, content of color-chords, and degree of lighting, and enhanced in esthetic value by linear patterns and harmonious spatial relations. His work is very uneven; but the best of it is characterized by a rich, glowing delicacy and poetic charm.

Rouault's (1871–1958) drawing follows Daumier's, but Rouault's line is broader, becomes more nearly a color-area, and is more economically used in defining contours. As a result of these variations, the psychological characterization of Daumier is replaced by vaguer representation and a greater emphasis upon pattern. Lines frequently go off at a tangent from the mass to which they originally belonged, meet other lines which have similarly wandered afield, and their union often forms a general swirling pattern embracing all objects or figures. Sometimes the lines are as broad as adjacent color-areas; sometimes the color-areas representing the surface of objects are indistinguishable from those representing background; contours usually show extensive gaps and are often defined simply by areas of bare canvas. The result is a strong plastic form made up of swirling line and color. The principle involved, that of breaking up contour and eliminating some of its elements while retaining and accentuating others, is an old one in the history of art. It remained for Rouault to carry it further, and adapt it to a form, the general effect of which is not unlike that of stained glass windows. It is quite natural that with Rouault's accentuation of line, color, and pattern, his failure to coördinate these factors should often result in pictures which are either glaring or somber in color and overdramatic in movement.

Derain (1880–1954) has a real pictorial sense, an eye for the picturesque; his compositions are well ordered, and his figures and backgrounds are related effectively. Moreover, by the sheer quality of superb painting, he can produce skilful imitations of the rich surface-effects of Chardin, Daumier, and Cézanne. Indeed, his skill and his acquaintance with the great art of all periods, enable him to paint in the manner of any one, and this is substantially all that can be said for him, for his work as a whole is nothing more than a compendium of excerpts taken from his predecessors and his contemporaries. In these fragments there is little if anything of his own that is of any value, and since the forms are borrowed, they are also lifeless: they constitute the shadow of art with none of the substance. To name the painters after whom his work is modeled would be to call the roll of nearly all the great, and many of the small, painters in the history of art. Giotto, Bronzino, El Greco, Chardin, Corot, Courbet, Manet, Renoir, Cézanne, van Gogh, Picasso, can all be identified in his paintings, but the significance of the originals is lacking, and superficial aspects alone have been rendered. Derain's superb craftsmanship, his acquaintance with the art of the past, and his contact with contemporary movements have done nothing to make him an artist, though they have made him one of the cleverest eclectics of all time. He is to our age what the Carraccis were to the Italian Renaissance.

Chirico's (1888–1978) design is attained by modifications of old and new traditions. His massive architectural elements in composition are reminiscent of Masaccio's, and his use of space recalls the Umbrians, but these factors are given a new meaning by their merging with a framework of geometrical patterns in which color-contrasts and linear contour are emphasized. Broad areas of relatively uniform color, usually exotic in quality, enter into harmonious relations with each other, with patterns of equally broad areas of accentuated light and shadow, and with bizarrely shaped masses picturesquely arranged in clean-cut and greatly varied space. The exotic quality of the color-relations, his strange and extensive distortions, and his fine feeling for the compositional organization of masses, combine to evoke a mystic feeling such as one finds in El Greco. His extremely versatile and skilful use of space—his ability both to emphasize space and to make the spatial relations between compositional units an element of great power—stands comparison with that of the great artists of all time.

Chirico is perhaps the most original of contemporary painters in the individuality of the creative use he makes of the essentials of the great traditions of painting. In his own idiom he has rendered— in different pictures—the spirit of Velásquez, Rubens, Poussin, Claude, Ingres, and the great Italians. He has made a new use of the linear patterns and geometric forms of cubism, and he is often the equal of Matisse in making daring contrasts of exotic colors a strong factor in his very personal design. He has embodied, in good plastic terms, the spirit of the classics of literature with a degree of romanticism and classicism that compares favorably with the finest achievements of Poussin and Claude; this is accomplished in an atmosphere as clear as crystal, that is, without the adventitious aid of the haze so constantly used by Poussin and Claude. Chirico's

Chirico (179)

Smyrna Sculpture (249)

Soutine (250)

Utrillo (252)

Hugo (214)

best work is the plastic equivalent of mystical poetry. It is this ability to render the essence of the metaphysical which was responsible for the development of the movement termed surrealism.

The best known of contemporary painting in Germany, usually termed expressionism, attains typical forms in the work of **Nolde** (1867–1956), **Hofer** (1878–1955), **Klee** (1879–1940), **Marc** (1880–1916), **Lehmbruck** (1881–1919), **Pechstein** (1881–1955), and **Kokoschka** (1886–1980). With the exception of the delicate form of Klee, the work of the contemporary Germans has a certain rugged force and drama due, chiefly, to bizarre distortions and violent contrasts. What they have of positive plastic value is based upon the contributions of Cézanne, van Gogh, Gauguin, Matisse, Picasso, and the impressionists. The discussion on the derivations of Soutine, and on his manner of using the plastic means [1] applies to a considerable extent to the work of the most important of the expressionist group.

[1] See p. 374.

APPENDIX

ANALYSES OF PAINTINGS

THE ARRANGEMENT of the succeeding analyses follows in the main the order of the discussion in the text. However, the correspondence is not exact: a number of painters whose pictures are analyzed are not mentioned in the general discussion, and the order of arrangement of these has been determined chiefly by convenience. Since the discussions in this Appendix are intended to be illustrative and not exhaustive, no attempt has been made to deal fully with all the pictures referred to. Many pictures which would in themselves repay extended comment are dismissed with only a few words, by which attention is called to either their more important or their less obvious characteristics.

GIOTTO

THE ASSISI FRESCOES (18)

The color is fresh, rich, free from stridency, and constitutes, through harmony and contrast, an infinite number of rhythmic patterns. A subtle glow permeates the color-ensemble and adds greatly to its richness, delicacy, and charm: this glow is made up principally of reds and golden yellows, contrasted and yet merged with a pervasive light-blue which, by its very blueness, provides a unique sensuous experience.

Line is terse, simple, powerful, and in the highest degree expressive and personally distinctive. The figures are rhythmically grouped and their drawing portrays movements which are easy, graceful, and individually characteristic; the expressions are intent without being melodramatic. Each object or group of objects functions rhythmically, both as a part of the group in which it is a unit, and as a unit coördinated with other groups; this use of design within design contributes variety to unity and helps establish balance and harmony of contrasts.

The finely coördinated three-dimensional solidity of the objects is achieved not only through light and shadow, but through marvelously expressive line brought into a linear pattern of intrinsic value, and also through color which is in itself charming. Perspective, indicated rather than rendered in detail, is fully adequate to give the necessary degree of depth to the plastic organizations; indeed, Giotto's simplicity in the treatment of space and his economy of resources offer an illustration of the basic difference between artistic power and technical competence or repertory of means. His comparatively limited and primitive methods secure effects which equal or surpass those achieved by later men with much more elaborate means.

Background-units seem to float ethereally, in a pervasive atmosphere of silvery crystalline delicacy which greatly heightens the mystical effect, and attests to Giotto's consummate power of adjusting plastic to narrative and human values. This subtle mysticism is akin to that in the best of the early Chinese paintings. Giotto was a supreme master in the use of light. Both in the modeling of figures and in the vivifying of atmosphere, the light is reënforced by the color; that is, color, instead of being confined within the contour of objects, filters into space and permeates the atmosphere in conjunction with the light. When his light is accentuated, it achieves very appealing and convincing dramatic effects; in **Miraculous Production of a Spring of Water** (19), for instance, the dramatic pattern of light conveys a feeling of fleecelike fluffiness which expresses, at one and the same time, great delicacy, force, and dignity.

In composition, Giotto makes free use of architectural features which are very effective as masses in relation to the total design and interesting in themselves as patterns. The conventional arrangement of central mass with balancing features on each side seldom occurs; more often, an obviously decentered main figure or mass is brought into relation with the other parts of the picture by a series of rhythmic lines, colors, or masses which save the organization from being one-sided or disjointed. In Giotto, in other words, a decentered object neither arrests the attention nor frustrates the demand for balance. Indeed, Giotto can so handle the plastic elements that a rhythmic unit of line, of light or of color often plays the part of a balancing mass in composition. This use of color in composition seems to have been overlooked by the critics: its recognition illustrates the need of making design the central idea in the analysis of pictures, and of judging each of the means by the part it plays in the design.

In **Saint Francis, Supporting the Lateran, Appears to Pope Innocent III** (23), the narrative is presented in two distant groupings which occupy, each, an approximately same expanse of wall-surface, but contain an unequal amount of illustrative detail. The striking contrasts, in the two parts of the composition, in the direction of the masses and the differences in the plastic treatment—color and rhythms of masses, planes, and spaces—are masterfully brought into a unified totality by ingenious relationships of linear rhythms, the key to which is supplied by the flow of the curtain from the right-hand side of the composition over into the linear pattern made by the figure at the left. To this organizing function of line, the color, light, space, and degree of massiveness are very appropriately adjusted. This is a supreme triumph of line-composition of a novel character: the unexpected is also the inevitable.

In the fresco just discussed, the use of line in mass-composition is particularly well illustrated; in **Saint Francis Restores His Apparel to His Father** (22), color plays a similar rôle: the compositional problem again involves the tying together of two main parts, each of which occupies about half of the total surface, and the continuity of the two sections is attained not by a central mass but by color. The color in the foreground, apart from its function of tinting the garments, acquires an independent value by creating a color-atmosphere that fills the space between the main figures. This color, slightly modulated with light, flows through the center of the composition, extends to the far-away horizon, and from that point it carries our attention upward to the distant sky and then forward to the upper-foreground vertical plane. This unifying function of color, effective in a degree rarely approached by other painters, gives with admirable success a sense of infinity. The fact that color is not solidly structural is not disturbing in Giotto: color is so related to the other plastic factors that it blends with them harmoniously, and is separable only when abstracted and analyzed.

Another point to be emphasized with reference to these frescoes is the use of the plastic means for expression of the basic spiritual values of what is presented. Giotto's realism is far from photographic, for he renders essentials rather than details. This is true even in pictures in which details are shown. What is felt as paramount is the solemnity, mystery, truth, humanity of the events depicted. For example, in **Saint Francis Clothing the Poor** (21), the epic power and the strikingly realistic effect are due in great part to the simplicity of the means used and to the judicious selection of a minimum of representative units. Giotto portrayed the grandeur and majesty of nature in landscape, in a manner worthy of Claude, at a time when the esthetic aspect of nature was so generally overlooked that only a man of the most original genius could have become aware of it. In **Saint Francis Blessing the Birds** (20),[1] the spirit of place is manifested in a lyric vein, not unlike Sisley did later. The design is achieved by all-pervasive effects of color, atmosphere, and glow, working in unison with drawing, modeling, and space.

In all of these frescoes the realization of form and movement attains the highest degree, an achievement due to such consummate blending of the function of all the plastic means that the form embodies a sense of tranquillity, peace, reality, and of the dignity, infinity, and mystery of religion. In short, Giotto's genius lies in the universality of his message.

THE PADUA FRESCOES (284)

The intrinsic value of these frescoes is great, but their general impression is not so overpowering as that of the frescoes at Assisi. While in general effect the Padua frescoes are more suave, fluid, and dainty, they are less powerful, and the relatively stereotyped character of their compositional organizations diminishes the feeling of novelty. In contrast to the Assisi frescoes, architectural elements do not function as main masses on a compositional par with figures, but are relegated with landscape-units to a position of secondary importance as part of the setting or background. The

[1] Illustration, p. 120.

loss in boldness and originality, thus produced, may be easily perceived by comparing the Padua **Entry into Jerusalem** (282) or **Flight into Egypt** (283) with the Assisi " Flight into Egypt " (17).

Though less simple than the Assisi paintings, the Padua frescoes show nevertheless Giotto's ability to secure powerful effects with simplicity of means. The compositional units themselves are not really very varied, but they owe their strength to the infinite variety of their interrelationships. In **Lamentation over Christ** (287), the composition focuses in the oval made by the body of Christ and the five immediately surrounding figures; in **Joachim's Vision** (285), the framework too is based upon a circular organization of units, yet in their entirety these two pictures are radically different.

Color in the Padua frescoes is less jewel-like than in those at Assisi and it is not so combined with atmosphere to give that pervasive effect which contributes so much to the charm as well as to the effect of mysticism in the Assisi pictures. The Padua frescoes do, however, offer a successful integration of subject-matter and plastic means: a spectator sensitive to plastic values is able to experience, without a detailed knowledge of the story related, the drama of the narrative.

This plastic expression of human values is supremely illustrated in **Joseph and Mary Returning after Their Marriage** (286). The specific and forceful feelings intrinsic to a dignified solemn procession are rendered by the spacing of the individual figures and of their groups; the relationships of line, color, and light converge toward a central idea: the abstract meaning and feeling of procession. No element is overdone: one perceives a measured orderly movement that progresses rhythmically from one side of the picture to the other. The pervasive effect of color, characteristic of the Assisi paintings, is retained: a swimming, silvery light-blue aura gives a sense of infinity to space and particularly to the background-sky, with no obvious accentuation of perspective. This color-effect forecasts the aërial ambiency of Masaccio. The fresco is a perfect example—one of the best in existence—of a painting in which all the plastic components of the representative matter converge toward and unify about a central psychological idea, in this case that of procession.

Christ Bearing the Cross (281) is highly expressive of that deep sense of mystic power, grandeur, majesty, characteristic of religion in its broadest conception. Every relevant detail of the narrative receives adequate plastic embodiment in the expressive color and drawing of the figures and architectural elements. The same story depicted in Simone Martini's " Ascent to Calvary" (351), evokes a sense of turmoil tending toward melodrama; its only appeal is the sparkle of bright vivid colors that reënforce the linear depiction of movement; that is, decoration reënforcing illustration. A similar comparison is that between Tintoretto's and Delacroix's treatment of subject-matter: like Giotto, Tintoretto tells the story in genuinely plastic terms, but Delacroix habitually resorts to adventitious aids.

ANALYSES OF PAINTINGS

In **Lamentation over Christ** (287), a wall extends transversally across the picture as does the hill in Botticelli's " Incidents in the Life of Moses " (418). In the Botticelli the wall-like hill interrupts the continuity of conception; the wall in the Giotto merges organically with the total plastic organization besides fulfilling several individual activities in the design: it functions as a balancing and integrating unit in the mass-composition and contributes vital elements to the expressive organization of rhythms. Because of the purposiveness of these activities the wall is free from the disturbance and distraction that the corresponding unit exercises in the Botticelli.

PIETRO LORENZETTI

Scenes from the Life of St. Umiltà (99). The architectural settings show how the Sienese school utilized the Byzantine tradition. Perspective is taken over at about the stage reached by Giotto. The color is dry, laid on, and the feeling for color is poor in general, except in the lower-right outer panel of the ancona.

ORCAGNA

Coronation of the Virgin (145). The influence of Giotto's contribution is shown in the color and in the manner of attaining three-dimensional quality. The picture falls short of Giotto's standard because of too great a reliance upon illustration at the expense of plastic units harmoniously blended in a genuinely expressive form.

LORENZO MONACO

Virgin and Child, with Four Saints (101) exemplifies the Florentine tradition at a marked stage of retrogression. The design, built around religious themes, is speciously reënforced by Gothic architectural features. This use of adventitious means and non-integrated detail is paralleled in music by Tschaikowsky's symbolic employment of familiar melodies in his *Overture, 1812*. The effect in each case constitutes unassimilated decoration. A successful use of linear rhythms and an unconventional attractive setting of three contrasting bands of color make up the chief appeal of the painting. Color throughout has no expressive power and the picture as a whole reverts in plastic value to a stage before Giotto and near to Cimabue.

PISANELLO

Vision of St. Eustace (148). The outstanding characteristic of this picture is the very attractive effect obtained by practically abolishing literal perspective and replacing it by an upward succession of compact vertical planes. This representation of perspective by substitutes, or what French critics have termed *équivalents*, recalls the method in use by the Orientals, es-

[393]

pecially the Persians in their miniatures, and also by many of the modern painters such as Gauguin and Matisse.

Figures and animals detach themselves in a pattern of light against the dark browns and greens of the landscape; their extremely dainty drawing partakes of the grace and delicacy of that in Italian and Flemish miniatures and, more particularly, in French miniatures of Pol de Limbourg's type and period.

FRA ANGELICO

The Florentine school began with Giotto, but it was not until the work of Masaccio that a fully developed Florentine " form " can be distinguished. Florentine painters of earlier date than Masaccio represent the transition from medieval art, and Fra Angelico's work is typical of the transition period subsequent to Giotto.

Deposition (81) suffers throughout from a dearth of originality. The composition, drawing, and general feeling suggest the Sienese form. A reminiscence of Giotto in the linear drawing produces, because of inadequate plastic support, an effect of perfervid pietism and affectation. The color is that of Lorenzo Monaco; in isolated units it is fresh, delicate, and well related, but as an ensemble it is garish, superficial, and compositionally inert. Perspective is accentuated and conventionally rendered, and the landscape is merely a patterned setting for the religious foreground-theme. The spacing is mostly uninteresting: groups play a part in the composition but their individual units have little distinction and no great variety in compositional function. The appeal of the picture is due chiefly to the decorative quality of a staccato rhythm of color-areas, contained within simple, linear contours. The total effect is banal and monotonous.

Mystical Crucifixion (82), because of its comparative freedom from Fra Angelico's usually overloaded sentiment, is more convincingly expressive than the majority of his pictures. A graceful rhythmic wave starts at one end of the group of figures and extends, with well-proportioned breaks in continuity, to the other end of the picture. The grouping is varied and excellently spaced. The modeling, recalling Giotto's by its unobtrusive contrast of light and shadow, gives a successfully rounded three-dimensional form. In some of the faces the manner of modeling is reminiscent of Domenico Veneziano and Piero della Francesca. The pleasing shades of various, harmoniously related colors are organized in diverse patterns. Line, light, color, and space work in unison and create an effective plastic ensemble. Fra Angelico here rises above the level of eclecticism, although it would be difficult to find any single element that cannot be referred to a prototype. The color is relatively juicy, and it is less acid than usual in Fra Angelico, and the faces are realized as three-dimensional forms with no outstanding evidence of the means of accomplishment. It is probable that a good deal of the charm of this picture is due to its restoration by an artist who was more gifted than Fra Angelico.

ANALYSES OF PAINTINGS

MASACCIO

Masaccio represents a much greater advance upon Giotto than does any of his predecessors. He departs from Giotto in color, drawing, spacing, the use of light, and in compositional organization.

In comparison with the earlier painters, Masaccio's figures look more like actual people and his drawing is more expressive of natural movement. There is a tendency to dramatic expression, but it is intentness rather than melodrama. His drawing is simple, terse, and expressive, and his line, unlike Giotto's, is not clean-cut; that is, color-relations between objects and their immediate setting temper the sharpness of the outlines. The resulting blurred effect, together with the use of shadow along contours, forecasts the method of the later Venetians, particularly Titian. Masaccio's draughtsmanship is realistic in the best sense, that is, imaginatively so; he had the ability to render convincingly the essence of an object or situation.

His color and light contribute much to the individuality and expressiveness of his drawing. The color is rich and subtly powerful, and it is active in organizing the composition; moreover, its combination with light renders a pervasive effect of atmosphere. This atmosphere, much heavier than that in Giotto, assumes the aspect of a haze akin to the glow of the Venetians, or to the swimming atmosphere of the impressionists, and it also suggests Rembrandt's chiaroscuro. Masaccio's chiaroscuro is less intense than Rembrandt's but it conveys a similar feeling of mysticism.

Masaccio's depiction of distance is much more naturalistic than Giotto's. The aërial perspective created by the atmosphere is reënforced in feeling of naturalism by a blurring of objects as they recede in space. The method is not far removed from that of the impressionists, and it further contributes to the general realistic aspect of Masaccio's form.

Masaccio's accentuation of light is a new step taken toward naturalism. Besides its part in the rendering of atmosphere, light both forms patterns and gives a degree of solidity and three-dimensional character in modeling greater than in Giotto. Giotto's figures are also perfectly real, in the sense of being esthetically and plastically convincing, but they are more other-worldly.

Saint Peter Healing the Sick (85) well illustrates Masaccio's dual use of light to make a pattern and to aid in unifying the composition. Light is subdued at the right of the group of figures, it increases in intensity as it moves toward the left, and it finally concentrates upon the two sitting figures, which are illuminated as by a spotlight. This powerful dramatic effect has no taint of melodrama. Light bathes uniformly the larger of these two figures, while on the smaller it is so focused that it produces an effect of chiaroscuro approaching Rembrandt's. Throughout the picture, the light merges with the color and thus enlivens the otherwise rather somber and uniform brown color-scheme. Light bears direct relationship to the color itself as well as to the combined unit of color and light that creates the atmosphere and thus helps to organize the space-composition and determine its character. Light also participates actively in the modeling and in the plastic expression of the subject-matter. In the latter, it aids directly by singling out the important figures, and indirectly through the feeling of dignity and religious mysticism derived in great part from the all-pervasive atmosphere. The light, therefore, besides forming its own pattern, reënforces every other factor. Its use in this fresco illustrates what is meant by that perfect merging of factors which constitutes plastic form at its best.

Saint Peter Raising Tabitha (86). The standing figures outside of the canopy form a group subdivided into three groups of two figures each. The variety in activity, attitude, position, direction, and spacing of these figures adds interest to the rhythm of their space-organization. A compositional movement flows slowly upward from the sloping figures at each end of the picture, and unites all the individual groups in a wide pyramidal curve which is both contrasted with and related to the angular framework of the buildings. The ensemble embodies a well-lighted rhythmic interplay of these two contrasting motifs.

The most important of the frescoes in the Brancacci Chapel is Tribute Money (87).[2] Its great dignity and its deeply mystic character depend primarily on the effect of an all-pervasive floating atmosphere. There is a lightness of touch everywhere: the figures seem to float in the air, though their feet are firmly planted on the ground. The supernatural character imparted to the entire design is achieved by a perfect coalition of the activities of all the plastic means. This harmonious correlation of factors precludes the feeling of unreality to be noted in Cimabue and Fra Angelico, for example.

The picture shows the futility of the academic dictum that composition should be balanced by the use of bilaterally symmetrical masses. Here, a house and two life-sized figures on the right are balanced on the extreme left by a very small kneeling figure and by a landscape of the same general color-tone as that of the house on the right—an instance of composition through the medium of color—which adds to the sense of equilibrium the charm of a beautifully achieved atmospheric milieu, and thus increases the esthetic satisfaction. The central figures are so placed that the intervals between them function eloquently as colorful space filled with a veil of atmosphere. The total space-composition, without being in any way overaccentuated, conveys a sense of roominess and contributes very much to the esthetic quality of the general design.

The color lacks the sparkle and freshness of Giotto's or Piero della Francesca's, but it is reminiscent of Giotto's in its ubiquitous compositional function; the difference is that in Masaccio it is the filmy color-light atmosphere rather than definite color that contributes to the merging of figures and landscape.

[2] Illustration, p. 118.

ANALYSES OF PAINTINGS

The drawing, broad and simplified, recalls that of Rembrandt, Goya, and Daumier; though less terse than in these men, it attains to an extremely convincing degree of solidity. For example, the legs of the central figure, shown with his back toward the spectator and his face in profile, have a monumentally solid character of a more legitimate pictorial quality than the sculptural modeling in Michelangelo's painting. Garments and draperies are filmy, though not so much so as in Giotto, because Masaccio's touch was not so light, and his color lacked Giotto's jewel-like quality. The light is generally well distributed; in the sky and background it produces a succession of dramatic effects which harmonize with the dramatic actions in the group.

The picture is as satisfactory a rendering of a story as is possible through the use of the plastic means. Like Giotto, Titian, Renoir, and Cézanne, Masaccio was a great artist because he had *something to say*—that is, something of universal human value—and because he said it in plastic terms individual to himself and comprehensible to others.

DOMENICO VENEZIANO

Madonna and Child, with Saints (106). The composition, simple and conventional in its distribution of masses, is unusually effective, chiefly because of the color-scheme. A series of light cool tones of pink, green, blue, and ivory, punctuated with bright red and deeper tones of blue and green, blend in a harmony of pastel-like freshness and delicacy.

Space-composition is exceptionally well realized; linear perspective, although accentuated, remains unobtrusive as such because it participates actively, with numerous other linear elements, in an all-over, clean-cut, and delicate pattern, of a decorative appeal commensurate with that of the color. The subtle adjustment of color, light, line, and space results in a well-balanced plastic expression of religious sentiments embodied in a decoratively attractive form.

In its drawing and modeling of figures, the picture represents various effects and methods characteristic also of several other Italian painters of the period, namely Uccello, Andrea del Castagno, Piero della Francesca, Verrocchio, and Giovanni Bellini. The clean-cut cameolike profile on the right, for example, modeled by subtle suggestions of light, shadow and color into a one-piece volume, has its counterpart, with individual variations, both in Uccello and in Piero della Francesca; the graceful linear drawing and the fluid light-and-shade modeling of the Madonna and the Child, together with the spatial organization of their delicately rounded volumes, represent a form into which Bellini, later, injected solid color and greater plastic force. The modeling of the flesh in the bishop, the monk, and particularly in St. John, with its pronounced pattern of light-and-shadow in planes and related to sharply linear outlines, is in the same tradition as the chiseled type of sculptural modeling achieved by Verrocchio, and it is somewhat

[397]

similar to the patterned effects in Andrea del Castagno. A pervasive coolness and a static impassive feeling of quiet deep contentment also recall Piero della Francesca, but Piero's color, even in its light and delicate tones, is much more deeply felt and convincing. Domenico Veneziano's color is far from that of any of the above-mentioned painters in degree of solidity; it has great decorative charm but very little textural quality; the flesh is non-naturalistic, the columns, walls, and pavement are like cardboard, the draperies are papery, and all the surfaces tend to be dry and brittle. This absence of color-depth, however, does not materially detract from the total quality of the picture, because the design calls essentially for decorative color-and-line units, and upon that score, the picture is, indeed, very finely organized.

PIERO DELLA FRANCESCA

Discovery of the True Cross (11) [3] well illustrates Piero's typical treatment of space-composition and his unconventional plastic organization. With no dominating central mass between them, the right and left sections, into which the total narrative is divided, are held together by an interplay of rhythms and contrasts, as well as by the pervasively cool, pleasantly varied and animated color. Much as in Giotto's frescoes, the buildings and landscape enter into the drama and unification of the design almost on a par with the groups of figures. For instance, the up-and-down rhythm, made by the sequence of houses, temple, hill, and village, establishes a feeling of continuity in the setting, in keeping with the pattern in space made by the varied grouping of the foreground figures. The unit of the village at the upper left, with its intersecting planes and its strongly lighted crystal-clear atmosphere, balances, with adequate elements of contrast, the well-lighted group in front of the temple. Similar plastic relationships exist between the unit of space-composition made by the buildings at the upper right and that made by the figures in the left half of the foreground.

Each group of figures is rhythmic in itself and its constituent masses are charmingly and subtly spaced; the figures are quietly dramatic, dignified, finely realized in plastic terms. Even though attitudes appear sometimes stiff or rigid, the groupings are fluid and merge with each other and with the setting. The keynote of the ensemble is Piero's cool, impersonal, plastic interpretation of a religious scene, in which naturalism is simplified and non-photographic in its total effect.

The color increases in decorative, compositional, and expressive quality as one continues to observe: it owes much of its harmonious effect to its uniform dryness and coolness; as usual in Piero, it is well reënforced by light and interestingly punctuated by bright areas in the vital parts of the composition.

Exaltation of the Cross (12). The pervasive color-tone of harmoniously blended, varied units, and the unification by color of the two separate halves

[3] Illustration, p. 132.

of the story, again recall Giotto's manner. The landscape carries space back to the horizon and then forward again through the sky to the upper part of the foreground.[4] Compositional relationship is further established by the cross and the tree at the center which, besides forming a striking pattern of planes in contrasting angles, throw a sort of bridge between the right and left parts of the picture. Each group of figures is rhythmic in line and color, but the kneeling group, on the right, is not quite successfully spaced and functions rather as a single mass. This disturbing feeling, however, is diminished by the fine quality and skilful variation of the color.

Reception by Solomon (13). The fresco is sharply divided into two parts, the interior scene on the right and the figures-in-landscape on the left, each section being in itself a plastic organization of masses in space. As in Giotto's compositions similarly divided into halves,[5] there is no conventional use of a central mass as connecting link; plastic unity results from the pervasive quality of the color and from the continuity of rhythms—of line, space, light, and mass—from one half of the picture over into the other. In other words, the picture is divided by the illustrative facts depicted, and is integrated by judicious use of their plastic constituents.

By the alignment and grouping of the figures, the elements of the subject-matter are divided also into an upper and a lower section, throughout the entire length of the fresco, and the plastic as well as the illustrative factors are concentrated all along the lower half. At the right, the varied rhythms of the space-composition formed by the grouping of the figures are carried upward by and into the enclosing spatial organization of the vertical columns, the horizontal and oblique sections of the ceiling, and the patterned, colorful areas of the wall. The left side of the picture likewise functions as an interior scene in its compositional value: the landscape, like the architectural features on the right, is a setting of relatively subdued color for the quietly brighter figures in the foreground. The shapes, the linear patterns, the voluminous character, and the quality of light and color in the landscape carry upward the pyramidal, undulating, vertical, horizontal, and oblique three-dimensional rhythms that are concentrated in the lower left half of the picture.

Piero's mastery of space-composition is particularly well illustrated in the rhythmic in-and-out and up-and-down sequence of the principal masses, and in the placing of the figures with the intervals between them combining also into a series of compositional rhythms. The figures, though close together, are easily separable into masses: they are grouped, not jumbled together. Worthy of notice are such ingeniously unobtrusive, active, compositional links as, for example, the kneeling figure in blue near the center of the picture; the figure of Solomon and the leaning woman at his left, in the interior scene; and the small, eighteenth century-like girl in the left-hand part of the fresco.

The whole picture is cool in feeling as well as in color. Piero's distinctive

[4] Cf., e.g., Giotto's "Saint Francis Restores His Apparel to His Father" (22).
[5] E.g., Giotto's "Saint Francis Restores His Apparel to His Father" (22) and "Saint Francis, Supporting the Lateran, Appears to Pope Innocent III" (23).

blue in the sky is finely tempered and modulated by light, so that the tonal variations increase the moving power of the color and reënforce its service as a mass, as one of the bonds that hold the picture together compositionally.

Drawing and modeling of faces are broadly done with light and color often merging into a continuous one-piece effect, particularly noticeable in the clean-cut cameolike profiles. Heads have a feeling of three-dimensional fulness and a firm, often hard, solidity. Delicately treated textiles and diaphanous materials alternate with draperies of ample, weighty folds, the rhythms of which are active agents in the paradoxically static movement of the entire design—a personal adaptation of the processional theme in Giotto's " Joseph and Mary Returning after Their Marriage " (286).

Victory over Maxentius (14) is another instance of plastic effects realized without undue reliance upon illustration. The drawing of the figures, although ostensibly indicating movement, is static, and there is no feeling of turmoil or even of the activity suggested by the narrative. In short, the subject-matter has been transcribed into a plastic form that functions chiefly as a rhythmic organization of units—a pattern in three-dimensional space. The eye travels from the left group of figures to the background and sky, along an oblique direction, and comes down and forward again to the group at the right, completing thus a very effective pyramidal pattern. The small tree in the center—not unlike that in Cosimo Rosselli's " Pharaoh's Destruction in the Red Sea " (423)—actively contributes to the pulling together of the entire composition. The sky is superbly lighted and is made interesting by the rhythmic succession of its variously shaped clouds. A slight effect of haze in the otherwise clear space vaguely recalls the feeling of Masaccio's atmosphere. The pronouncedly patterned space-composition suggests Uccello's, in a form simplified by broader drawing and modified by Piero's characteristic, cool, dry, and quietly bright color, which, while lacking great depth, is sensuously appealing because of the harmonious juxtaposition of contrasting yellows, reds, blues, and browns.

The dignified, poised movement results from an impersonal, detached, unemotional rendering of a story, told simply and with perfect control of the plastic means. The contrast afforded by the simplicity of statement in this picture and, for example, Delacroix's overemphasized drama, or Raphael's profusion of literal detail, shows that control of the plastic means makes it possible to give the essence of drama without recourse to accentuation of narrative of essentially sentimental appeal.

Baptism of Christ (146) is inferior in general quality to the Arezzo frescoes. The color, however, has a peculiarly charming surface: a multitude of delicate hues subtly intermingle and produce a series of smooth color-chords resembling mother-of-pearl.

Nativity of Our Lord, with Angels Adoring (147). The color lacks the convincing quality of that of the Arezzo frescoes, and the light is treated more realistically—more like actual sunshine—than in Piero's frescoes in which it was used either as a general lighting or as a compositional pattern, rather

Upper- or Middle-Rhine Master, active c. 1410 (109)

Chirico (256)

Pollaiuolo (102)   Analysis, page 410

Pollaiuolo (103)   Analysis, page 410

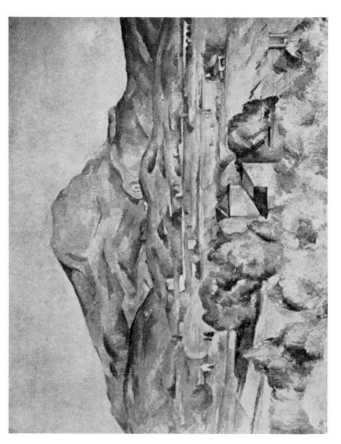

Cézanne (176)

Analysis, page 468

than as sunlight. The extremely cool detachment and the individuality of the Arezzo pictures are not so pronounced here. Figures are light in weight, and are treated more nearly in the conventional Greek-like style of the fourteenth and fifteenth century in Italy. The landscape, likewise of the traditional type of the period, acquires distinction by a striking pattern of small dark tufts of grass and foliage set against the light ivory-toned color of the land itself. This effect—a natural, local characteristic of the country around Arezzo—is adapted quite effectively by Piero as a light-and-dark punctuated setting in this and other paintings.

SCHOOL OF PIERO DELLA FRANCESCA

Marriage of St. Catherine (15) [6] is interesting chiefly because of the compositional use made of color at the upper left of the background to balance the tall figure at the right; and also because of the obvious relations the drawing and distortions of that figure bear to El Greco's drawing and to Picasso's form in his pictures of acrobats or circus-scenes.

BOTTICELLI

Allegory of Spring (90). [7] The especial feature of the design is its highly decorative character brought about chiefly by the successful use of linear rhythms in the unification of the total space-composition. The complexity and activity of the pattern on the right, for instance, adequately compensate this half of the picture for the fact that its number of figures is smaller than that in the area at the left. Linear rhythms extend harmoniously from side to side of the composition with extremely fluid grace; they are carried upward by the patterns of the tree-trunks, foliage, and fruit which balance in the background the various decorative motifs of the legs, draperies, grass, and flowers in the lower part of the foreground. The figure of the cupid at the upper center and the effectively related curves in the main units of the design are specious factors in the integration of the composition; they supply focal centers and transform the lateral bandlike grouping into a large horizontal oval, a variant upon the conventional pyramidal type of organization.

Planes and volumes are clearly defined in space; the pattern of light is effective, particularly in the contrast of the light figures and the dark quasi-screenlike setting, and between the latter and the lighter sky. The color, sufficiently varied and harmoniously related, is nevertheless drab and superficially laid on. The figures, like Mantegna's, have a feeling of stone, but are dead compared to his. Chiefly because of the deficiency in color and textural quality and the lack of imagination in composition, the essential effect of the picture is that of a facile type of decoration, feebly felt plastically, and somewhat overcrowded; even as linear and compositional motifs it is banal and threadbare. Resort to illustrative elements—graceful figures in a

[6] Illustration, p. 22.   [7] Illustration, p. 161.

landscape setting, cupid, trees, flowers, fruit—brings the appeal of the picture largely into the realm of sentimentality and day-dreaming.

Birth of Venus (91). Subject-matter and obvious linear rhythms again constitute the chief appeal of the picture. The simplicity of the bilaterally balanced composition is detracted from by the stridency of the accentuated linear arabesques in the figures on each side of the central mass. The line itself, as always in Botticelli, is very skilfully used, but it functions as a distraction, not as an integral part of the design. This fact, coupled with the thinness of color, the superposed streaks of gold, the unintegrated highlights, the hardness of the surface, the porcelain or eggshell-like textures, and the coldness of feeling, illustrate once more Botticelli's general esthetic poverty.

Incidents in the Life of Moses (418). As usual with Botticelli, the design is founded on obvious and fluid linear rhythms, the striking character of which is accentuated by a pattern of colors which in themselves have little sensuous appeal. The form as a whole is defective, because of the disbalance between the right and the left halves of the design, in color quality, rhythm of line, lighting, and space-organization of masses. The slanting hill and the vertical tree-trunks in the center sharply divide the picture into two sections, each of which remains practically independent of the other. The mass-composition at the right is organized upon a radiating motif around the central angular pattern made by the path and dagger. The accentuated, curvilinear units in each figure or group of figures pull strongly away from this center and form a series of diverging rhythms, which are overaccentuated in terms of line and remain unsupported by quality of color. The upright rhythm of the columns and tree-trunks counterbalances the curvilinear rhythm of the figures, but it is a specious balance obtained chiefly by linear pattern.

The area to the left of the dividing hill is a mass of relatively small, curvilinearly accentuated units which, by their grouping, radiate cross-wise from a central point—the tree-trunk that rises at the base of the slanting hill. That is, the slant of the two figures at the upper left is carried diagonally across to the two girls in the foreground on the left of the well; similarly, the contrasting linear direction of the group of figures at the lower left is continued upward by the hill and figures at the upper center of the total picture. Botticelli fails in his attempt to unify the two halves of the fresco because the linear pattern and directions that bear the burden of compositional integration—that is, the row of trees, the converging curvilinear figures around and above the well—are outbalanced in their action by the disrupting effect of the color and the light. Color is superficially laid on; it is either drab, or flashy and tawdry; its patterns and rhythms throughout are obvious and mechanical; and the light-and-dark relationships are dramatic surface-contrasts, for the most part ununified and therefore meaningless.

In short, the plastic disproportion between the two main sections of the picture is so great, and it is revealed in so many of its vital elements that, through this conflict, the effort to grasp the design precludes esthetic satisfaction.

VERROCCHIO

Baptism of Christ, with Two Angels (107) is less a work of individual genius than a utilization of extraordinary talent. It is essentially academic; composition is conventional, color is superficial, textures are wooden, drawing relies upon incisive line, and modeling upon sculpturesque light-and-shadow contrasts and pronounced muscular accentuation. It is successful in effects of space, in the unification of figures and setting, and in the intelligent variation of the linear drawing to form rhythmic patterns; moreover, in the central figure and the one on the right, the incisive linear contour is expressive and its relationship to the muscular modeling contributes a feeling of movement.

The picture is of interest as showing one of the sources of Leonardo and Raphael, and as revealing the fact that these painters were drawn under the influence of an academician. It contains the germ of Raphael's incisive contour, though Raphael gave greater fluidity and a more unbroken continuity to his line; he also discarded much of Verrocchio's muscular accentuation and increased the feeling of space. The two angels on the left forecast Raphael's sweetness and sentimentality, and their facial expression is of that type that became Leonardo's stock-in-trade. Indeed, the legend that one of these two figures is said to have been actually painted in by Leonardo is credible because the method of modeling is very close to his in its tendency toward accentuated contrasts of light and shadow. The fact that the drama is not entirely rendered by the plastic means makes the picture fall short of greatness.

LEONARDO

Lucrezia Crivelli (342) is, on the whole, a successfully rendered plastic form, but it is not free from Leonardo's characteristic accentuations. A good Bellini, in contrast, would offer a correspondingly well-realized expression with no accentuation of any of its constituents.[8]

Mona Lisa (343). A fine harmony exists between the three-dimensional figure and the spacious landscape: modeling in the former and perspective in the latter are convincing and not overaccentuated. There is also an organic relationship between the deep and rich brownish-red tones of the landscape proper and the color of the woman's sleeves; and between the curvilinear motifs in the background and the pattern of folds in the woman's garment. A better use of color than is usual in Leonardo and a finer adjustment of color to light free the picture from Leonardo's familiar, spotty pattern of overdramatic contrasts. Shadows are not muddy and the high-

[8] Cf., e.g., Bellini's "Doge Leonardo Loredano" (127).

A corresponding disparity is felt in the total organization of the space-composition. The group of men, boy, and woman, on the right, for instance, is a fine spatial arrangement of masses, with expressive movement, a powerful upward rhythm, and a nice gradation of color from the light blue of the foreground to the deep red of the man's drapery at the upper left of the group. This group is well balanced and pictorial in itself but does not link up organically with the other groupings, principally because color-relations are bad throughout the composition. The bright colors stand out from their context, and the darks sink in and appear as holes; there is therefore no feeling of continuity or of flow of color from area to area.

Pattern of light, reënforced by the directions of gestures and attitudes, is the principal agent of unification; it is organized as a pyramidal succession of sharply accented lighted areas of varied degree of intensity; and it culminates at the apex in the bright suffusion which surrounds the figure of Christ. The picture is overdramatic, obviously because the plastic and narrative elements are not successfully coördinated. An equally dramatic subject-matter treated by El Greco, for instance, carries conviction because the human elements of the story are given plastic equivalents by well-balanced relationships of color, light, line, space, mass, and movement.[12]

ANTONIO POLLAIUOLO

Hercules Crushing Antæus (102); **Hercules Overcoming the Hydra** (103).[13] The outstanding characteristic of these pictures is their extremely intense expression of movement, emotional states, and of power in action, in forms of almost miniaturelike size. The drama of the episodes and the pictorial technique are well coördinated. Bosch, Goya, Daumier owe much to this type of drawing, in which the highly expressive linear contour is organically related to the other plastic elements.

In " Hercules Crushing Antæus " the powerful intertwining masses in the foreground make up a well-balanced and compact upward-rising pattern, which is forcefully set off by the miniature-effect of the detailed screenlike setting.

In " Hercules Overcoming the Hydra " the rhythms are more elaborate, less concentrated, more pronouncedly linear in effect, and more obviously used as compositional arabesques to bring foreground and background together. The use of this decorative pattern is exceptionally skilful and novel, and it contributes much to the expressiveness of the total form.

The use of linear patterns in drawing, decoration, and composition recalls Raphael, and the muscular accentuations in both of these pictures are suggestive of Signorelli and Michelangelo. The linear drawing is more powerful than in any of these other painters, and it is also more varied in its expression of movement and strength.

[12] Cf., e.g., El Greco's "Assumption" (429).
[13] Illustration, p. 403.

ANALYSES OF PAINTINGS

COSIMO TURA

Pietà (395) [14] is a very great achievement in painting. The composition is replete with rhythmic convolutions of draperies and muscular accentuations, the use of which is much more expressive and convincing, as well as more decorative, than Michelangelo's and Signorelli's use of similar means. A powerful compositional rhythm flows from side to side of the picture and involves combined units of line, color, light, mass, and space. The body of Christ is a very effective central unit around and back of which the other figures are organized. The spacing of the main and subsidiary masses is particularly distinctive in its clean-cutness, and in its charming compositional variety and feeling of continuity. Legs, arms, hands, fingers, heads, halos, folds, are each clearly distinct from the other, and all are greatly varied in direction, size, and color. Each of these volumes occupies its place in space like a finely chiseled piece of ironwork, and the course of their rhythms, interlocking with that of the space-intervals, is chiefly responsible for the charm and power of the total design.

In the emphasis upon space-composition, Cosimo Tura recalls both Uccello and Poussin. The kinship with Uccello is made more evident by the general greenish-brownish color-scheme; but Cosimo Tura, both in color and in space-composition is much more alive. His linear rhythms in space are indeed astounding in their variety; they are more intricate even than those in Poussin's " Blindmen of Jericho " (361) with which this " Pietà " compares favorably in point of charm and intensity of expression realized by fluidity of line in space-composition, and by the way color—subtle and non-brilliant—becomes part of the spatial intervals and adds to the power and appeal of their rhythms.

The emphatic, emotional expressions are born legitimately of the variety and individuality with which each of the plastic means is used; in other words, the narrative is embodied in an integrated plastic form.

PERUGINO

Combat of Love and Chastity (358) is superior to Perugino's religious pictures, which are usually academic, soft, and sentimental. Here, the delicate colors, comparatively superficial, blend well with the dainty drawing of the lacy trees and the general lightness of the picture. The pervasive feeling of delicacy is reënforced by the very successfully rhythmic space-composition.

GHIRLANDAIO

Scenes from the Life of the Virgin and from That of John the Baptist (88). The esthetic offense of these frescoes is not only plastic, but it is also moral: it offends the intelligence that such an important work should have been attempted with so limited a use of the technical means.

[14] Illustration, p. 60.

APPENDIX

SIGNORELLI

Four Episodes in the Life of Moses (424). A very effective contrast is achieved between the upper and the lower half of the picture which represents respectively the background and the foreground of the composition. The entire lower half is practically filled with a compact horizontally wavy succession of curvilinear volumes; the upper part is organized as a rhythmic alternation of three large masses (one in the center and one at each extreme side) and two relatively large windowlike openings of space each of which in itself is a particularly fine unit of space-composition (the landscape-scenes on each side of the central rock). Plastic integration of the design is attained partly by a rhythmic interplay of directions between the upper and the lower half and chiefly by the rhythmic quality of light and color. Light blends very effectively with color, and their modulations are well adapted to the varied linear flow of the masses and the quality of the diverse types of space represented. The activity of the light is one of the striking features of the fresco: its pattern increases the rhythmic feeling of movement in the sequences of masses, intervals, and lines; and its suffusion at the right and left in the distant background contributes a very charming, dignified, placid, and lyric quality to the landscape-scenes, at the same time as it helps to establish a feeling of balance and continuity between their respectively different content of masses and space. These very appealing decorative, expressive, and compositional activities of the light are particularly commendable, because color as a whole is neither bright nor glowing, it is punctuated with dull areas, and its structural function is relatively limited. Color, nevertheless, is so blended with the other plastic elements and the dull units so participate in organizing patterns that a harmony pervades the ensemble and is felt to be a properly proportioned factor in the plastic design. Indeed, in point of proper adjustment of elements for pictorial unity, this fresco ranks very high.

COSIMO ROSSELLI

Pharaoh's Destruction in the Red Sea (423) is interesting chiefly for its solution of a familiar compositional problem: the integration of a picture centrally divided into a right and a left section. The remarkably fine landscape-background is made up of a series of powerful continuous rhythms which function compositionally on a par with the dramatic patterns and units of space-composition in the foreground. The unifying function of the background is greatly increased by the linear pattern of spears that tends from the lower right masses in the foreground obliquely toward the upper left trees and rocks in the background; and also by the location of the small tree slightly to the left of the picture's center. This tree, somewhat Chinese in the character of its pattern, leads the eye across from the group of figures at the lower left to the group of clouds at the upper center and upper right

[412]

Pacino di Bonaguida (228)

Masaccio (83)

Daumier (183)

Grünewald (55 and 56)   Analysis, page 440

of the background. A more specious means of unification is the vertical column, rising from the water at the center, which carries downward and forward, in a sort of triangular formation, the rhythm of upright trees and rocks at the upper left, and of towers and buildings at the upper right. Another obvious but less facile device is the repetition by the pyramidal cloud at the upper center of the inverted triangular opening of space between the two groups of figures in the foreground.

The area of landscape in the center, with its diffuse effect of volumes in space, and its fine realization of the feeling of distance is reminiscent of Chinese landscape-painting and, in a measure also, of Giotto's.

In spite of all ingenious compositional practices, linear movement is excessive, particularly in the foreground to the right of the water; and the depiction of the story is obvious, literal, and somewhat overdramatic.

MANTEGNA

Parnassus (349) and **Wisdom Triumphing over the Vices** (350). Mantegna is essentially an illustrator. His stories are told in terms of the Roman antique, and the illustration is seldom properly welded into art. In these two paintings, the subject-matter is conveyed with marvelous ability by clean-cut linear contour, and active movement results principally from the very rhythmic relations of line. Architectural buildings or masses of landscape are practically equal to the figures as compositional units, but landscape, as such, is merely incidental, and the figures seem built of stone. Color has but slight structural quality and its relationships are inharmonious; its inadequate content of plastic value in relation to that of the linear rhythms and mass-composition, militates against unified plastic expression. This applies in a lesser measure to " Parnassus " than to the other picture, but even in " Parnassus " color is superficial and non-organic.

ALVISE VIVARINI

Madonna Enthroned, with Saints (436). Sharp, clean-cut line is used as a means for literal expression of sentiment, and its pattern, duplicated on each side of the central unit, is a monotonous rhythm, unrelieved by color. The same lack of color-support applies to the pattern of light which in itself is well organized, but stands alone. Color, indeed, hardly functions in the design; it is without distinction either in the individual tones or in their combined effect. In short, this is essentially the work of an academician, who owes the characteristics of his form, including the expression of excessive pietism, to the conventions common to the Sienese and Florentines of the fourteenth and fifteenth centuries.

APPENDIX

GIOVANNI BELLINI

Allegory of Purgatory (89) [15] represents a transition from the austere form of the Middle Ages to the rich, full-blossomed painting of the Venetian tradition. A kinship is retained with Bellini's contemporary, Mantegna, in the drawing of the nudes and their three-dimensional character, in the general patterned compositional organization of masses in space, and in the dark browns and greens of the landscape. Mantegna's classic, tight drawing is modified, here, by a more naturalistic, looser definition of contour, and Bellini's more structural color and finer relationship of light to color give a new, stronger, and more full-bodied pictorial significance to modeling, composition, and color-harmony in general. The tendency to render aërial perspective by tonal gradations and atmospheric effect recalls Masaccio, but Bellini's outlines of objects in the distance are not so blurred in relation to those in the foreground, and the haze acquires the quality of a color-glow. This glow is a forerunner of Giorgione's, Titian's, and Tintoretto's, but it still lacks the density and richness of the fully developed Venetian atmosphere: it is relatively subdued and not yet all-pervasive.

Further evidence of the beginning, in Bellini, of the Venetian tradition is given by the constructive function of the color, particularly in the landscape; by the expressive drawing, light-and-color modeling, and dramatic rhythmic swirls of the figure in yellow near the center; and by the grouping and distribution of the figures in relation to the landscape—an anticipation of Carpaccio's and later Venetians' pageantlike presentations of the outdoor-life of ordinary people. The landscape, with its feeling of profound lyricism and poetry, is obviously the source of Giorgione's similar effects. Perfect unity exists between the figures and the setting. A natural unstereotyped series of rhythms flow gracefully from side to side of the foreground, involving in their course pyramidal groupings, and volumes and space-intervals of varied size, color, direction, and location in depth. Pattern, color, and spatial rhythms function about equally in the integration of foreground and background, but light is the most active factor. The general illumination is superb, and the relationship between dark and lighted areas achieves a pronouncedly rhythmic all-over pattern, which moves unobtrusively through space and makes all near-by and distant objects plastically kin.

Madonna of the Little Trees (430) [16] is the source of much of Raphael's effects in his Madonnas, but, in contrast to Raphael's sweetness, an appropriate expression of sentiment does not compromise dignity and reality. The brightly lighted distance, on each side of the yellowish-green screen, is a novel and picturesque note in the compositional use of color, light, and space, and is far superior to Raphael's stereotyped use of light and landscape in settings for his Madonnas. Leonardo's debt to Bellini is apparent in the general fluidity of the drawing and in the use of light to model and form patterns. In Bellini, light more subtly permeates the color and texture

[15] Illustration, p. 80.　　　　　　　　　　　[16] Illustration, p. 426.

[418]

of the mass, its pattern is thus less pronounced, and modeling is achieved without calling undue attention to the means of execution.

The color-organization is particularly appealing: the cool green area, back of the Madonna, sets off with distinction the rich blue drapery, the warm color of the flesh, and the red sleeve. Volumes are set in a rhythmic sequence of receding planes, and distance in the landscape is ingeniously accentuated by the dark trees silhouetted against the lighter sky. A compositional interplay of oval motifs further contributes to the individuality of the picture by varying the traditional type of pyramidal organization.

Madonna and Saints (437). Dignity and strength characterize the drawing, especially of the Madonna and Child. Facial expressions are free from softness, sentimentality, or excessive piety. The two angels at the foot of the throne, for example, are two happy children of this world.

The color is not bright, but rather subdued; in some units, for instance, in the Madonna's robes and the heads of the Saints, it is used structurally in a manner anticipating that in Titian's modeling; indeed, the faces and hands of the Saints on the right are already quite Titian-like in color and general form and have a fairly well-developed Venetian glow. In the robes of the Saints, especially in the painting of the folds, the color is more conventional in tone and manner of use.

The large area occupied by the Madonna's robes functions as a background that sets off the pattern of light. Color, light, and line are satisfactorily unified, and the form as a whole is charming in its dignity, conviction, and great simplicity.

CARPACCIO

Dream of St. Ursula (431). [17] The effect is one of deeply felt, all-pervasive, charming gentleness and peace embodied in a well-organized series of plastically constructed compositional rhythms. The points of interest in the narrative—the sleeping figure and the angel—effectively coincide with the pictorial centers of interest, chiefly because of the organization of the pattern of light. The light-focuses here are not to be confused with objectionable overaccentuation of light, for they are successfully used to help realize the spirit of the scene and also integrate the design. The light-pattern, in fact, enters so deeply into the network of the other organizing factors, that the pyramidal formation of the three main units of light—angel, figure in bed, and window—seems spontaneous and inevitable rather than calculated.

The general composition is unconventional and extraordinarily well balanced. Equilibrium is attained by an orderly variation in the distribution of masses and in their rhythmic progression through space, in which line, light, and color participate. The enclosed three-dimensional space is admirable in its simplicity, naturalness, and airy roominess and also in the fluid continuity of the subsidiary units of space-composition. These units

[17] Illustration, p. 425.

exhibit a great variety of effects: for example, the space underneath the bed, the corner of the room compactly punctuated with still-life objects, the pattern of planes around and beyond the open door, the effective distinction in space of objects placed against the wall, and the plants silhouetted in dark against the lighted outside-space with a patterned effect recalling Baldovinetti but with a subtlety of space-relationships akin to that of Rousseau *le douanier*.

The color-ensemble is rich, mellow, harmonious, and its effect of variety is derived from the contrasts of lighted and shaded broad areas rather than from a use of many colors. The color-pattern is anchored upon a strong framework of geometrical shapes formed by a very ingenious interplay and ordering of lines. Linear pattern is active in all parts of the design and contributes to every aspect of it. Its pronounced activity in the rendering of perspective is matched by its composite decorative organization, its variety of internal decorative motifs, its compositional network of relationship to color, light, and space, and its achievement of simplicity, subtle directness, and clarity of statement.

The spirit of place, the mysticism, peace, and serenity of the scene, owe much of its feeling of reality to a wonderful realization of texture. The painting of the bed-covers, for instance, yields a charm of soft textural quality akin to that in Vermeer but free from the Dutch preoccupation with minute detail. Textural effects in objects where highlights are relatively active suggest the work of the early Flemings, but the form, here, is unmistakably Italian because of its delicacy in the use of line and color, and the subtlety in spatial relationships, which is worthy of Chardin, and which, with the possible exception of van Eyck, the Flemings rarely possessed.

GIORGIONE

Madonna, with St. Francis and St. Liberal (50). The general compositional plan is the traditional pyramidal organization of the main constituent units arranged in bilateral symmetry. All feeling of banality or monotony is banished by the consummate skill in the use of the plastic factors, the ingenious elaboration of decorative detail, the imaginative treatment of the setting in both foreground and background, and by the inventive power in composition. An organized network of internal compositional rhythms of color, light, line, space, mass, pattern, and decorative motifs is powerfully active throughout the picture; and these rhythms contribute variety, subtlety, and a highly distinctive identity to the general pyramidal plan to which they are subordinated.

The upright pyramidal arrangement of figures, throne, and draperies, consists of a compact grouping of masses and planes which recede as they rise from the bottom to the top of the picture at steplike intervals. The setting to this majestic and monumental upward-moving construction is made up of three main units—floor, wall, and landscape—each of which is in a contrasting plane to the other, and also leads both backward and upward in space. Moreover, the pattern of the floor, the color of the wall, and the light of the landscape, being only partially interrupted by the figures and throne, conveys a feeling of lateral extension of these units across the total width of the composition in a pattern of three juxtaposed broad bands of contrasting color and degree of illumination, in keeping with a similar motif of contrasting vertical and horizontal oblongs in the throne and its draperies.

Another picturesque compositional feature is the inverted pyramid formed by the oblique staff on the left, and the oblique direction of the monk's right leg, continued by the tilt of his head and the location of the bush and tree at the extreme right of the landscape. This triangular arrangement opens up into an inverted pyramid of light, extremely rich in content of colorful plastic units: the graceful figures of the Madonna and Child, with their dignified poise and naturalness of expression and their interesting pattern of color, line, and light; the textiles covering the throne, with their varied colors and decorative medallions and stripes; the throne itself with its own medallion and rhythm of planes; and the two views of airy light-bathed landscapes at the top. The open-window effect of these two distant views of landscape, provides a picturesque, dramatic note of contrast between the open-air feeling of space that recedes to infinity and the more distinct and compact units of space-composition in the quasi-interior scene in the foreground. Worthy of particular notice in this foreground composition is the distinction in space between the lower textile covering the throne and the part of the throne back of it; between the figure of the monk and his immediate setting; and between the different volumes composing the Madonna, the Child, and the upper part of the throne. Equally subtle and convincing is the realization of a gentle and calm, wide space-ambiency in the landscapes: both landscape-views are permeated with the idyllic charm and majesty of nature, but the effect varies in each. On the left, the atmosphere assumes a rather yellow sunny glamour, while on the right it is lighter and more silvery, though the golden light extends far enough into it to tinge it also with that tone. The denser golden glow in the landscape on the left is ingeniously balanced in that on the right by the light-mottled blue mountain. Bellini's influence is clearly apparent in these landscapes but the light is more generally diffused, has no especial tendency to form intricate patterns, and its glow is slightly more silvery than golden. Though as yet lighter than it became in Giorgione's later pictures, the feeling of landscape has already his individual and unmistakable character, his lyric and Arcadian charm.

Color throughout is well illuminated, is rich and harmonious, and it functions powerfully in the integration of the composition. Linear perspective is pronounced, but, like color, light, space, and pattern, it participates organically in the rhythm, expression, and compositional integration of the design.

The total impression of the picture is one of gentle delicacy, grace, peace, dignity, majesty, and convincing reality, for the achievement of which land-scape and figures are brought into perfect plastic accord. The influences of Mantegna, of Bellini and, in general, of the painters of the thirteenth and fourteenth centuries, are synthesized in a form which is not only novel, but stronger, richer, more solid, and more graceful than the prototypes.

Concert in the Open Air (330) [18] is one of the greatest achievements in the history of painting. Nothing is academic either in composition or in any of the plastic means. Masses are distributed unconventionally in deep colorful space, and are compositionally held together by wonderful rhythms of color, line, space, mass, and light, and by the mellow, warm, all-pervasive golden glow that participates in the fluidity of all these rhythmic relationships. The composition, in short, is one of color-masses gracefully set and moving in colorful space. The ensemble is extremely rich in pictorial and human values; but with all the abundance of plastic qualities no element is over-active at the expense of others; each seems to contribute its utmost, com-mensurately with what is required by the design, and in harmonious accord with the activities of all the other factors. Color is fully structural; it is deep, rich, glowing, resplendent; by its relationship to light and to space, its ensemble is evocative of a profound sense of mysticism. The light appears as a natural illumination; its patterns and its rhythmic contrasts with areas in shade recall Bellini's "Allegory of Purgatory" (89) in their organizing function, but they are less accentuated: Giorgione's light blends more organically with the color and the structure of the objects, and pervades more thoroughly the colorful space and glow.

Every compositional grouping is a pictorial entity in itself: for example, the three central figures; the woman at the well with the green mound and tree-trunk as immediate setting; the opening of distant landscape at the left of the center; the area of sky, patterned with light and silhouetted trees; the rolling large masses of foliage in the middle distance; and the group of small figures and animals in the illuminated area on the right, which suggests Rembrandt in its chiaroscuro. The ensemble of these units offers an infinite variety in all their plastic aspects; yet, because of the un-interrupted flow of organic relationships throughout the picture, the com-posite form is one of balance, peace, and simplicity.

The charming Arcadian quality, the power, majesty, peace, splendor, and deep mysticism conveyed, are legitimate values because the attendant emotions are rationally anchored in the objective features of the picture.

TITIAN

Bacchus and Ariadne (155) is inferior to Titian's best work: the individual units differ greatly in plastic strength, and there is less simplicity of means, and a diminished degree of compositional and structural activities of the color. The very effective rhythmic movement is attained mainly by linear

[18] Illustration, p. 98.

pattern indicating gestures, attitudes, and directions of masses and draperies. Spacing and grouping of masses are, on the whole, not successful, partly because of the lack of balance on the left with the drama and detailed numerous masses on the right, and partly because of the failure of color to support composition. The mass-organization, for instance, might not appear so overconcentrated in one side of the picture, if the landscape at the left were conceived in better terms of color. As it is, this portion of the landscape seems perfunctory and uninspired, the color in the background has a hard, quasi-metallic quality, and in the sky it serves chiefly as superficial and literal representation of patterning clouds which remain detached from the rest of the composition.

Parts of the canvas, however, are superbly rendered; notably, the texture of the drapery under the jug in the foreground at the left, the feeling of movement, aliveness, and reality, and the subtlety of space-relationships in and around the hind legs of the leopards, and the marvelous fluidity, grace, and charm of some of the figures—those in the center in particular and also Ariadne on the left. These units, even though by no means equal to Titian's best work, emphasize the poor or indifferent quality of their context; this precludes the feeling of congruity which is characteristic of plastic integration. The drapery of the young satyr, for instance, conveys no feeling of textural reality and no solidity: its color is deficient in structural quality when compared with the units above-noted. Other shortcomings appear in the accentuated pattern of light, in the absence of Titian's poetic charm and grandeur in landscape, and in the intensified gestures, even though these might be said to be intrinsic to the nature of the subject. Titian, at his best, is subtle in all these respects, and adapts and merges his means in a composite, unjarring ensemble.

Christ and the Magdalen (156) is of a much higher grade of painting than " Bacchus and Ariadne " (155). Drama is restrained, composition is smooth, evenly flowing, and picturesque; color is rich, deep, and subtly glowing; drawing is graceful; light is fluid; and textures are sensuously appealing and convincingly real.

In both the landscape and the figures, the space and masses create, in unison, a series of gently curvilinear rhythms which in their continuous, graceful sweep from the foreground to the extreme distance as well as from the lower right to the upper left, and from the lower left to the upper right, integrate figures and landscape in a charming ensemble full of lyric grace, peacefulness, and Arcadian poetry. Everything is gentle, nothing seems forced or overdone; even the contrasts afforded, for instance, by the angular planes of the buildings, or by the counterthrusts in space of figures, arms, draperies, staff, and tree-trunk, have no savor of abruptness or clash; their vivid drama is tempered by the pervasive gentleness and fluidity of the total form into which it enters with perfect accord.

Unlike " Bacchus and Ariadne," there is no feeling of compositional discrepancy in the distribution of the masses. Color functions in the distance on the left in plastic proportion to the group of buildings on the right; distance and clouds, moreover, are reënforced compositionally by the large tree at the top and the upright figure in the foreground. Counterbalance on the right is achieved by reversing the proportionate relationship of mass and space: the background of hill and buildings is a group of compact masses, and the foreground a relatively large unit of space, enriched by the patterns and the glowing deep color of the Magdalen's draperies.

This picture, although superb in itself and a supreme achievement in painting, represents a skilful adaptation of the ideas, technique, and effects of Giorgione and Bellini rather than an original creation.

Disciples at Emmaus (391).[19] The various attitudes and movements are rendered by highly expressive drawing, and are harmoniously organized in a single " plot " by a compositional series of fluid linear rhythms that encompass the entire design. From each area a linear flow, broken in continuity of direction by the varying height of the masses, is met and carried onward by other graceful linear rhythms coming from and going into all directions in two- and three-dimensional space. The linear motif formed by the table as a whole is paralleled above by the more varied movement of the group of figures which flows smoothly from side to side. Starting at the man on the right, for instance, the linear rhythm rises up to his neck and flows on over his head to the figure of Christ, and similarly downward and upward on through the individual figures of the group on the left. The folds in the tablecloth form a rhythm that echoes the linear pattern in the Christ's robe.

Color throughout is rich, deep, and subtly varied; and space is masterfully adjusted to the rhythm of the composition: the diversified intervals of space, with their subtle feeling of depth, atmosphere, and color, seem to regulate the orderly, graceful, gentle beat of all the figures and objects. In other words, masses and units of space succeed each other in an uninterrupted fluid space-composition of color-volumes in colorful space. The feeling of circumambiency around the entire group is equally well realized, and the effect of deep space under the table is admirably yet unobtrusively achieved.

The rhythmic organization of color, line, space, pattern, volumes, planes, without emphasis upon adventitious effects of facial expressions or gestures, constitutes a form which holds in solution the deepest human and mystical values. The impression is one of profoundly satisfying rhythm, harmony, grace, and deep peace.

Jupiter and Antiope (393). From the group at either side of the dividing tree-trunk in the foreground, the eye is carried upward to the well-lighted cupid and then down to the group at the opposite side. This pyramidal organization of the masses is strongly supported by the pattern of light, particularly by the focus of light upon the cupid; this pattern unifies a composition which would otherwise tend to be separated into two parts by the foreground tree near the center.

[19] Illustration, p. 150.

Carpaccio (431)   Analysis, page 419

Bellini (430)

Analysis, page 418

Raphael (369)   Analysis, page 409

Titian (394)

The essence of the form is a pictorial rendering of figures living in a pleasant landscape. The spirit of place is superbly grasped; the typical Venetian glow is present; and the landscape sets off effectively the activity in the foreground. The influence of classic antiquity is embedded in a form that renders more naturalistically the feeling of lyric poetry. This picture illustrates some of Poussin's derivations from Titian's form, notably the drawing of the figures, the painting of the flesh, and the compositional focus of light at the upper part of the organization.

Saint John the Baptist (434) shows how even the mightly fall before Leonardo's example in the use of line and accentuated light-and-dark contrasts. The form lacks Titian's usual solidity and tends toward the stilted drama of Verrocchio, which had been taken over and refined by Leonardo.

Assumption (438) [20] illustrates a successful solution, on a large scale, of complex plastic problems. The framework of the composition consists in a grouping of figures at three different levels. Each group greatly varies from the others in number and character of the masses, in degree and kind of drama, in compositional form of organization, and in pattern, color, light, and line. These greatly varied elements, which give a distinctive identity to each group, are rhythmically related to each other with the result that a continuous and powerful upward rhythm of plastic units casts a bridge between the separate groups and integrates the entire design. Therefore, the point of paramount interest in the compositional problem is the relationship of the subsidiary units to the character of the general design.

The group at the bottom forms a solid, firm, massive basis for the whole composition; drama in this lowermost area is strongly accentuated by thrusts and counterthrusts of relatively large color-masses, compactly ordered in space. Directions and patterns are the most active agents in the organization of this group: they yield a surging movement that converges from both sides and culminates in the striking pattern made by the two upward-pointing arms around the central man's head. This unit, dramatically set off by its background of lighter sky, is very active in carrying up to the central large group of figures, the general upward movement of the design. The effect of continuity with the central group is further increased by the pyramidal convergence of the figures below toward the figure of the Madonna which functions as the apex, and rhythmically counterbalances, by the direction and pattern of her arms and head, the sweep and drama of the above-noted head-and-arms unit in the group below.

The central group is made the point of chief interest in the picture by its colorfulness, its great variety of rhythms in space, its patterns of light and of line, and the structural quality of its color. The Madonna, a tall, colorful and highly patterned mass, is flanked on each side, first, by a large unit of space, then, by a quasi-pyramid of compact small color-volumes (the angels and clouds). These two lateral pyramids are joined at the base, and thus enframe the Madonna in a semicircular or crescentlike formation. The

[20] Illustration, p. 447.

numerous arms, legs, wings, bodies, heads, and clouds in this complex garland of angels intertwine in all directions, but their composite rhythm moves slightly backward and decidedly upward. Indeed, their short rolling movement in compact planes is actually continued, on a diminished scale and degree of accentuation, by the clouds and angels' heads indicated all around the upper part of the picture, together with which they form a circular frame around both the central and the uppermost group.

At the top, the figure of God and two angels make up a strikingly picturesque pyramid of which the apex, God's head, comes forward, and the broad base is deeply set in space. The pattern of this pyramid extends, through numerous planes, into three-dimensional space, and repeats again, in a different direction, the pyramidal formation of the two other groups. The slant of this pyramid across the upper part of the picture gives a novel, almost bizarre, effect to its pattern. The relations of its components to the rhythms below ingeniously bring to rest the total movement of the composition. The forward and downward tilt of God's head rhythmically contrasted by the upward and backward thrust of the Madonna's and the counterthrust of the head of the man in the lower foreground on the right, is only one instance of the numerous rhythmic contrasts that carry on the feeling of continuity throughout the three main motifs.

The use of light is another vital factor in the plastic expression and in the total unification. Light-and-dark contrasts in the modeling are pronounced in the Leonardo manner, but are not overaccentuated, and their pattern contributes much to the drama. Light, moreover, depicts the sky, functions as atmosphere, as the setting for the entire composition, and, consistently with the general design, it is also organized in a relatively upward-developing mass. It rises from the calmly assertive blue-and-silver sky that divides and connects the lower and middle groups; it expands around and above the Madonna and the uppermost group into an enveloping atmosphere, and it reaches a fitting climax in a nicely tempered, strongly dramatic golden glow, which gradually deepens around the upper circular edge of the picture toward a characteristic Titian red. This glow is Venetian in essence, but is more like Bellini's in its lightness, less weighty than the typical Venetian glow. It is used superbly in the upper part of the design, conveying thereto the sense of infinity in that supreme degree attained only by painters of the first magnitude.

To sum up, the complex compositional problem is solved by an intricate network of relationships between all parts of the design, and the powerful drama is incorporated in a form of great dignity and simplicity; each group of figures plastically supports the other groups; color is variedly but adequately solid; drawing is proportionately detailed and simplified, even broadly generalized, as the emphasis is demanded or rejected by the particular motif of the general theme; there is complete freedom from softness, sentimentality, or melodrama; and the execution is free from virtuosity. The unified and infinitely varied plastic elements blend so organically with the values of the subject-matter, that the objective content of the picture admits of a wide range of symbolic interpretation.

TINTORETTO

Paradise (387). The framework of the design is a concentric arrangement in deep space of large, sweeping, rhythmic bands of color, light, line, and masses; and each band is in itself a complex organization of plastic units in movement. The colors—chiefly blue, silver, ivory, and reddish-brown—are as harmoniously rhythmic in themselves as are the individual figures, the groups, the draperies, the clouds. Indeed, all the plastic and representative factors enter into the general fluid movement and the all-pervasive whirl. The lack of variety in the drawing of the individual units detracts considerably from the plastic status of the picture.

Calvary (433). The striking drama and effects of animated movement are obtained by expressive drawing, muscular accentuations, color-contrasts, and an all-pervasive swirl of masses in space, which swirl varies greatly in direction, size, and degree of activity and forcefulness. A serious compositional defect appears in the failure to harmonize the light and the dark colors: the latter, for the most part, appear to sink into the canvas, as in holes, and thereby destroy the feeling of color-continuity between the contrasting areas.

PAOLO VERONESE

Burning of Sodom (400).[21] The narrative, a flight from a burning city, is very successfully embodied in the plastic form: line, color, pattern, as well as masses, all flow away from the fire. The design is fundamentally one of movement, and, because of the balanced use of color, line, light, space, and modeling, this movement is equilibrized and rhythmically organized. The pronounced linear effects are the result of well-coördinated activities of line, light, and color: an example of drawing in its best estate. Textures and surfaces are firmer, more lustrous, and more convincing than in the general run of Paolo's pictures.

Banquet in the House of Levi (435). The spirit of pageantry is achieved with power and in a degree approaching grandeur, in a space-composition on a large scale with none of the specious exaggerated effect or the overaccentuated linear perspective of, for example, Perugino's similarly vast composition, " Christ Giving the Keys to Peter " (422). The organization opens up into Paolo's familiar V-shaped grouping, and the compositional masses, varied and convincingly rendered by a skilful fusion of the plastic means, are characteristically set at sharply oblique angles to each other, and form a highly effective series of contrasting rhythms. There are no inactive areas of space in the superb rendering of the vastness and infinity of distance.

[21] Illustration, p. 79.

PIETRO LONGHI

Dancing Master (432). The Venetian tradition is successfully modified, and is adapted to a charming intime form which recalls the Dutch genre-painting of the seventeenth century and the French eighteenth century tradition, especially Lancret and Chardin. Simplifications and distortions endow the somewhat rigid figures with naïveté and charm. The spirit of place and the story are rendered in good plastic terms, with fairly good structural color.

CANALETTO

Grand Canal and Church of the Salute (296). Canaletto caught the Venetian glow and Claude's feeling for the grandeur and majesty of land-scape. He had a sense for space-composition and panoramic effects, for the use of architectural details, and for the pictorial function of light-and-dark contrasts—all of which, in their ensemble, constitute his form. Canaletto is important because he told his story in plastic terms; he is not of the greatest importance because his means are not original, and nothing he says, only his manner of saying it, indicates a fertile imagination.

GUARDI

Doge Embarking on the Bucentaur (332) exemplifies Guardi's version of the Venetian form. The color is less structural than Titian's or Tintoretto's, and the brownish-red tones of the glow are replaced by a clear silvery at-mosphere. Guardi's extraordinary feeling for space-composition enables him to render, in a small canvas, the sense of a vast outdoor space filled with a multitude of finely related objects expressively rendered by broad generalized drawing. This picture illustrates also Guardi's great sensitivity to the picturesque and his ability to render the spirit of place in good plastic terms and in a very individual style.

CORREGGIO

Danaë (415). Correggio's mastery of the means, in this picture, shows that a tendency to sweetness is compatible with a successful use of the plastic factors. Light and linear flow, as the main motifs of the design, are particularly effective. The pervasive, rhythmic linear elements form numer-ous and varied patterns, and convey grace and fluidity from figure to figure, and from figures to draperies and background. The contrast of the lighted figures against the dark setting is very well rendered in the terms of a modi-fied chiaroscuro, with adequate sense of space. The subtly structural color is commensurate with the general delicacy of the form.

RUBENS

Autumn, Château de Steen (150). The rich, deep, juicy color and its use in comparatively small touches indicate that Rubens inspired some of Constable's best effects.

Judgment of Paris (151) [22] is an extraordinarily fine version of the Venetian form at its best. It is very close to Giorgione and Titian in the structural use of color, in the feeling for landscape, and in the richness of rhythms. Rubens' characteristic swirl is very much diminished, the nudes are graceful and majestic, and their contour, restrained in its curves, is extremely rhythmic. The flesh lacks Rubens' usually pronounced pinks and reds; it recalls Giorgione's " Sleeping Venus " (73) in its solidity and depth of color, but the texture is more natural than in most Venetian painting. The pattern of light-and-dark in the modeling of the nudes derives from Titian, and the general golden-yellow tone of the flesh, with pinkish light tinging the pink-orange shadows, is allied to Paolo Veronese. The fluid drawing and compositional grouping of the figures stem from Raphael's classic themes, but the line is less sharp, it is broken in shorter curves, and enters into forms that are infinitely more solid and richer in color-values. The figure seated at the tree has a grace and charm akin to Poussin's, but its color is more Venetian, and its solidity more pronounced.

A quite distinctive feeling of charm and delicacy is produced by a general simplification of Rubens' technique in the treatment of textiles and in the landscape. The draperies are rich in color and in pattern, and the graceful and gentle flow of their folds, enters unobtrusively in the series of rhythms which intertwine and expand throughout the composition. Color is entirely free from the suggestion of stridency so often present in Rubens' work. Its structural quality is tempered by a delicacy which makes it less solid than in the best of the Venetians, though it functions decoratively and compositionally much as in Giorgione and Titian. A warm color-glow pervades and helps unify the entire organization; it contributes a feeling of placidity and Arcadian lyricism strongly reminiscent of Giorgione, but interpreted with less subtlety, delicacy, and majesty.

Peace and War (153) represents Rubens' skilful use of the Titian-Tintoretto tradition, particularly noticeable in the painting of the figures and the sky. The textures in the animal and in the still-life of fruit are rendered in the realistic Flemish manner but with the color-solidity of the Venetians, so that the composite effect is distinctly Rubens' own.

Country Fair (381). The total effect is one of rhythmic animation. The landscape is Venetian in general feeling, but the grouping, movement, and drawing of the figures are more akin to the Dutch.

Tournament (383). The Venetian influence is more in evidence than it is usually in Rubens, especially in the union of suffused glow and color, which resembles also Claude's. Linear effects, secured largely by the succession of

[22] Illustration, p. 97.

the masses in space, are very fluid and participate actively in the general rhythmic swirl.

POUSSIN

Cephalus and Aurora (149) furnishes a good example of Poussin's interpretation of Venetian landscape, his version of the classic Greek profiles and figures, his fine porcelainlike surfaces, and his adaptation of Titian's fluidity of mass-composition.

Blindmen of Jericho (361) is a fine example of Poussin's fusion of Florentine and Venetian traits in a highly expressive and characteristic form. The space-composition is essentially that of Raphael; the color has the Venetian characteristic of functioning as a rhythmic, structural, and decorative factor, but is less rich, and its effect is thus delicate rather than effulgent. Light also is used in the Venetian manner, both in the form of patterns and as atmospheric glow. The Raphaelesque line, coördinated with the more substantial Michelangelo type of modeling, renders the figures and their activities with a degree of conviction and charm superior to either of the prototypes. The architectural background functions in much the same way as in Carpaccio and Masaccio, and the dark shadows cast by the figures, trees, and buildings further contribute to the strength and intricacy of the design, as do the sequences of light falling upon the various masses. A ubiquitous linear flow imparts variety and unity to the design: line, light, color, and intervals of space participate in the flow, and produce intricate sets of interrelated rhythms in every part of the canvas.

Earthly Paradise (362) represents a greater emphasis upon landscape, as such, than is usual with Poussin. The landscape is also more modern in feeling and treatment, but the most interesting feature of the picture is the marvelous compositional arrangement of the two figures. These form a simple, rhythmic, well-unified pattern which fits perfectly into the landscape-setting, and is reënforced by the other compositional unit, the angel in the cloud, with which it is inseparably connected by fine plastic relationships of light, line, color, and space.

Holy Family (364) is interesting chiefly as an example of Poussin's rendering of classic themes in a form which draws upon both Venetian and Florentine traits. The light, while resembling the Florentine as a constituent of the drawing, has a suggestion of the Venetian glow in its use as atmosphere. The color is nearer to the Venetian than to the Florentine in sensuous quality and structural solidity. The linear element in the depiction of movement is close to Raphael's and, as in Raphael, the effect inclines toward the sentimental and theatrical.

VELÁSQUEZ

Don Baltasar Carlos in the Riding-School (169). The simplification characteristic of Velásquez at his best is superbly illustrated in the painting of the horse and, especially, of the figure in all its details. The technique and general style reveal the origin of Goya and Manet, while impressionism is forecasted in the blurred outline and broad drawing of the small figures in the background. The black horse makes a striking contrast with its subtly rich gray background interspersed with figures in various colors, including a slight note of red. The vague aërial atmosphere is slightly reminiscent of both Masaccio and the Venetians. A pervasive general richness gives to the entire picture the feeling of quiet dignity, subtlety, peacefulness.

Lady with a Fan (170) tends toward surface prettiness, and is more interesting as an example of skilful execution than as a plastic embodiment of human character. The painting of the various units differs greatly in quality. The head and flesh are more literal than expressive; the gloved hands, rendered broadly in rather thick strokes of richly illuminated light blue, make an interesting note in the composition, but the gloves do not seem to fit the hands; the shawl and the ribbons are less rich than the gloves; and the color of the dress is less appealing in sensuous quality and in light-content than are the other parts mentioned. The dark gray background conveys the effect of a wall, and, in contrast to the corresponding area in Velásquez' " Infanta Marguerite " (396), it does not function as an integral part of the composition.

Infanta Marguerite (396) [23] represents Velásquez' form at its very best. The figure is finely and delicately rendered as a convincing three-dimensional volume set off by a background of relatively uniform color; the head is fully surrounded by space and the background conveys the feeling of infinite distance. This organization of mass and space is matched in subtlety and expressive power by the treatment of the garments, chair, and other details. Figure and chair, each subdivided into subsidiary units, are related to each other in space, and form an intricate series of compactly arranged units of space-composition, tied together by their space-to-volume relationships to the child's arm and hand. The complex series of relationships existing between the components of the child's dress with its various trimmings, differing in color, direction, spacing, and degree of three-dimensionality, form an appealing, decorative pattern which merges harmoniously into the basic compositional color-pattern made up of the background, figure, and chair.

The colors are rich, deep, and alive, and they blend harmoniously in the design. The whites have the quality of old ivory, the blacks are like ebony with a patina, the pinks are like roses, the red fabric on the chair has the dull richness of old velvet. This sensuous appeal, inseparably bound with structural solidity, illustrates Velásquez' masterly and personal use of the color-values intrinsic to the best Venetian painting. The solidity of the objects shows how tactile values can be rendered superbly by such diminution of perceptible methods of modeling that a feeling of flatness to the volumes adds an appeal of its own without detracting from the feeling of solidity and reality of structure. Similar subtlety in the use of perspective, light.

[23] Illustration, p. 275.

and line, prevents overaccentuation of any of the plastic elements, and the decorative and expressive factors fuse organically in a form which reflects the universal human values of simplicity, balance, dignity, peace, charm, mystery.

GOYA

Royal Family of Charles IV (171) is interesting mainly as an example of illustration of high order, in which Goya comments upon the essential ugliness and stupidity of his royal patrons. As a plastic form it achieves some distinction by its patterns of line, light, and color, which blend in a harmonious ensemble, but the compositional organization is rather conventional.

Don Galos (204) [24] illustrates Goya's close adherence to Velásquez' style and at the same time his modifications of essentials to create a personal expression. The relationships of the foreground to the background recall the delicate, subtle space-composition in Velásquez' " Infanta Marguerite " (396), but the drawing, quality of color, and manner of using light are individual to Goya. The drawing renders a more commented-upon expression of the sitter than does Velásquez' impersonal detached treatment. The light is more active as pattern, as general illumination, and as a constituent of color. The color is more solidly structural, it has more internal glow than in the average Velásquez, and its surface is less arid. The fine three-dimensional solidity of the figure is attained by modeling in which the chief agent, light, is reënforced by an effective and varied use of line and color. The painting of fabrics is very much in the manner of Velásquez but, due to Goya's departures in the use of line, light, and color, the stuffs are more solid, and the surfaces have less of that feeling of paint so common in all but the best of Velásquez' work. This portrait has a ruggedness which marks it off from any picture by Velásquez; indeed very few of Goya's paintings attain to its plastic strength.

MASTER WILHELM

Kaiser Karl IV, and Heads of Prophets (71). These frescoes reveal clearly the influence of the Byzantines and of Cimabue and Giotto upon the Cologne school in its early period. They are notable for their color and for their vividly expressive linear drawing. The line is sharp and swirling in much the manner of certain French and German thirteenth century illuminated manuscripts; in conjunction with many distortions, it conveys a sense of movement, convincing in itself and successfully integrated in a plastic form which anticipates Andrea del Castagno's. The color lacks sparkle and transparency but it is rich, deep, sensuously pleasing, and free from any suggestion of garishness. Its application is of the general Byzantine compartmental type, but its planes are sufficiently differentiated in space to

[24] Illustration, p. 276.

ANALYSES OF PAINTINGS

convey an impression of depth. Modeling of volumes at times reaches a considerable degree of solidity. The reworking of antecedent traditions is original, and the form is convincing, deep, and expressive of static dignity.

COLOGNE MASTER OF THE BEGINNING OR MIDDLE OF THE FOURTEENTH CENTURY

Crucifixion, and Four Scenes from the Life of Christ (58).[25] The design, of extraordinary individuality, is conceived chiefly in terms of color and striking linear patterns. The colors by their brightness and delicacy recall Fra Angelico's, but are free from the latter's stridency; they have also a tonal quality somewhat resembling Ugolino's, but are fresher, more richly varied, and more delicate. Indeed, seldom has a painter equaled this subtle pastel-quality: it is pale yet colorful, and not unlike the delicacy of French miniatures, in spite of the radical difference in execution and general effect.

The gold background precludes any extensive or precise representation of depth, but the space-composition, within its limits, is very effective, and the conventional distribution of masses is redeemed from banality by the individuality in the use of the other plastic features.

The thin, black, inklike line, so often used by the Germans, appears in some parts of the picture. Numerous distortions which amplify the linear pattern contribute to an appealing sense of movement. These patterns assume geometrical shapes which resemble those in cubistic pictures, but differ in that the patterns, here, tend to flow instead of being static. The feeling of rigidity and other-worldliness is tempered by a sophisticated naïveté that gives the painting a peculiar force.

COLOGNE MASTER OF "SAINT VERONICA"

Six Scenes from Christ's Passion (66) (attributed to the Cologne Master of "Saint Veronica"). In these panels, the Sienese form, as represented by Simone Martini's religious narratives, is enriched by color of structural solidity and great sensuous charm. The background is extraordinarily attractive: an area of blue, deeper than the blue of Piero della Francesca and of astounding carrying-power, is studded with small golden stars, and the light, blending with the blue, yields varied series of color-chords. The designs are further enriched by fine space-compositions and by numerous distortions which extend and diversify the effective linear pattern, and introduce the familiar note of the grotesque. These pictures are incomparably superior to Simone Martini's treatment of similar subject-matter: they supplant his fragile structure and superficial brilliance by the weight of solid appealing color.

Saint Veronica (258). In distribution of figures and in color-scheme, this picture bears a strong kinship with the work of the Master of Flémalle.

[25] Illustration, p. 182.

The color-scheme resembles also that of Lorenzo Monaco and Fra Angelico, but the ensemble is decidedly heavier than in these Italians and even heavier than in the Master of Flémalle.

STEFAN LOCHNER

Last Judgment (67) conveys a sense of movement, vivacity, and turmoil in legitimate plastic terms, and is executed with great technical skill. Mass-composition is much varied in number and character of its components and in the manner of their grouping. The spacious pyramidal formation of the three large figures in the upper half of the picture contrasts in color, in patterns of line and light, and in diversity of space-intervals with the varied compact groups of small and actively moving numerous figures in the lower half. The architectural units on each side, in relation to the focus of plastic activity at the lower center of the picture, establish a counterbalancing pyramidal factor to the upright pyramid of Christ, Madonna, and Saint. The flying angels carry to the upper part of the painting the active movement and pattern, which are concentrated below.

Space throughout the composition is particularly well handled, and the clean-cut intervals between the masses participate, on a par with the masses themselves, in the rhythm and movement of the entire organization.

The color-scheme, while somber in general effect, has a richness and a depth rarely attained in the early German tradition; the structural quality of the color approaches that of Bellini's; light and color are finely adjusted to each other; drawing is very expressive; textiles are solid; and the flesh, in numerous instances, has the feeling and surface-appearance of translucent old ivory. The highly decorative character of this picture is due to an ingenious use of color and space, allied to the patterns of line, light, and masses, and to the setting of gold.

Madonna in the Garden of Roses (69) [26] well illustrates Lochner's modification of the Florentine tradition. The bright and delicate blues, pinks, yellows, and greens are enriched by subtle modulations of light, and strengthened in plastic function by a feeling of depth and solidity somewhat akin to Bellini's. The color-ensemble is a charming harmony of rich, vivid, and delicate color-forms, enhanced in decorative value by the dainty, almost miniaturelike, execution, and by a variety of curvilinear patterns which convert Florentine rigidity into delicate grace.

The pyramidal arrangement of the main masses, in spite of the almost exact bilateral duplication of units, takes on a fluid character that relieves the form of fixity or monotony. The pattern is varied and well correlated: it is chiefly curvilinear in the figures, with a decidedly circular motif in the faces and halos; it partakes of both the curved and the angular in the drawing of the angels' wings and musical instruments; the trellis of roses is an arrangement of small, variedly circular color-areas upon an angular linear

[26] Illustration, p. 181.

framework, set off by the gold background; both the circular and the angular motifs are repeated at the upper part of the composition, in the unit of figure-and-ruffled-clouds at the center, and in the angel-and-drapery at each corner. The immediate foreground of daintily depicted flowers and leaves balances the pattern of the rose-trellis and the Madonna's crown; its horizontal band together with the pattern made by the angels around the Madonna follows a generally square arrangement that repeats the square framework of the trellis. The pattern of all these units involves volumes and planes in three-dimensional space; indeed, the composition recedes as it ascends, and forms a varied series of well-defined delicate volumes, set in relatively compact planes, with adequate intervals of space. The fine integration of all the plastic means adds to the highly decorative appeal of the picture a very successful expression of gentleness, grace, and joy.

The presentation of the subject-matter—the Madonna and Child in a highly decorative setting—although treated occasionally in other traditions,[27] was a favorite theme in the Rhine region: Lochner himself gave other versions of it;[28] in " Madonna and Child, Three Saints and Donor's Family " (29) by the Cologne Master of "Life of Mary," the subject is embodied in a heavier form; in Schongauer's " Madonna in the Garden of Roses " (54) the feeling and treatment are decidedly Flemish of the Memling type; and in the typical Rhine pictures of the period, for example, " Madonna and Child, with Female Saints " (41), " Mary with Female Saints " (72), and " Garden of Paradise " (109), the miniature character and the decorative qualities are accentuated at the expense of expression. In contrast to all of these, Lochner's version in this picture and also in " Madonna in Paradise Garden " (68) retains a greater kinship with the Italians, represents a more original adaptation of the traditions, and offers a more thorough and organic integration of decorative and expressive values.

COLOGNE MASTER OF " LIFE OF MARY "

Crucifixion (61). The debt to the Flemings, particularly to Bouts, is no less obvious or striking than is the individuality in the interpretation of the prototype.[29] The space-and-mass organization is finely rendered and extraordinarily attractive. The distribution of the masses offers an unusual departure from the conventional central-unit idea; light permeates the entire composition and also forms a rich pattern related to the well-marked patterns of color and of line. Light so enriches both the dark and the bright colors that no dull spot exists, even in the deepest shadows. There is a pervasive richness to the color-ensemble, even though the only bright notes are the red gown on the left, the blue in the sky, and the small touch of

[27] E.g., the French diptych panel "Madonna in Garden" (75); Memling's "Marriage of St. Catherine" (353).
[28] E.g., "Madonna in Paradise Garden" (68).
[29] Cf., e.g., Bouts' "Deposition" (295).

green on the kneeling figure. The ensemble has grace, fluidity, and a delicate charm; it embodies, by a fully plastic use of color, line, light, and space, the feelings of repose, placidity, dignity, and deep religious mysticism.

GRÜNEWALD

Crucifixion (55),[30] which is Grünewald's masterpiece, offers a simple but marvelous composition: the horizontal bar of the cross relieves a large space from emptiness and makes a perfect balance to the figures in the lower part of the picture. The stiff body of the Virgin, in a nun's white veil, acts both as a foil and as a reënforcement to the light and graceful figures of the Saint at the left and the kneeling woman. The light colors of the figures make a very dramatic contrast with the dark-green, vague, deep distance in the background. This deep distance is related to the foreground by a strip of subtle lighter green, representing a river. This lighter area in the setting also plays its part in the unusual and striking pattern of light, which varies in intensity through the different sections of the picture and merges into the subtle and greatly powerful color-pattern. The figure of Christ—somewhat El Grecoesque—is of a general dark-green interspersed with brown and with ivory light, and presents a series of mottled color-chords. The face and legs of the Saint on the right are reddish-brownish yellow, they are modeled with light and shade, and have a rather wooden stiff solidity. One does not feel the lack of structural color: stuffs and flesh are slight but very adequate; the figure of Christ, especially, is convincing and solid. The distinctive trait is that color is used creatively: in each of the figures the actual hues as well as the manner of handling are different. The headdress, face, and hair of the kneeling figure are rich in color-chords of green and ivory-pink shot with light, and her salmon-pink gown is enhanced by flowing, rhythmic, linear patterns.

The contours are sharp in all the figures and objects. The somewhat El Greco-like swirling patterns, which are achieved by a wonderful fusion of line, color, and light, are arranged in deep dark space, and yield an effect like that in Titian's " Disciples at Emmaus " (391), plus something of Giorgione's peaceful drama. From a distance, the finely realized space-composition is most impressive. The psychological expressions are vivid and alive, and the spirit of the mystic sorrowful scene is powerfully and convincingly rendered.

DÜRER

Self-Portrait (313).[31] *Color:* The color-ensemble, dominated by grayish-green and ivory tones, is rich, powerful, smooth-surfaced, and wonderfully glowing. A few accents and contrasts are given by the red cap and cuff, the golden-yellow hair, and the green-tinged spray of foliage in the hands. The color of the face is a subtle merging of nuances of ivory, rose, and lavender,

[30] Illustration, p. 416.   [31] Illustration, p. 273.

with no one color paramount; in the hands, the general tone varies by admixture of another shade of rose. The complexion and texture of the flesh throughout have a kind of lurid, ethereal, ghastly quality, slightly reminiscent of some of the figures in Lochner's " Last Judgment " (67).

The pervasive color-power is akin to that which Rembrandt and Daumier attained by their particular blending of light with deep golden-browns. In the Dürer, color-power also results from organic and subtle relationships between color and light, but the linear factors contribute more directly to the character and individuality of the color-form than they do in Rembrandt, and with different effect than they do in Daumier. Indeed, by its relationship to line, Dürer's color assumes a particular fluidity and a graceful charm.

Line: The extraordinarily rhythmic organization of a multitude of delicate linear factors would offer a quasi-competitive element to the color-effect, were it not that line and color harmonize perfectly and thus reënforce rather than combat each other. The motif of the linear design is a graceful downward flow with cascade effect: the tassel on the cap, the hair, and the folds of the sleeves, coat, and shirt-front, all stream downward in rhythmic fluid sequences of delicate and variedly curved vertical and oblique linear units. They are brought to an equilibrium by the upward movement of the spray of foliage, and by the subsidiary pattern of oblique-horizontal rhythms formed by the hands, the colored braids across the shirt and the areas of the shirt between them, the outline of the jaw, the general direction of the facial features, and the cap. All of these linear rhythms involve color, light, and space, so that both the variety and the subtlety in the linear motif are further increased by the relationships of line with all the other plastic constituents. For instance, the relative lack of linear pattern on the outer area of the man's left sleeve is compensated for by the note of red that extends along the inner side of that sleeve. Another illustration of the organic function of the linear pattern is the series of triangular solids in three-dimensional space; these are built of line working in conjunction with light and color, and the line is largely responsible for their fluid grace. The cascade-effect so pronounced in the tassel and hair, for instance, is as much one of variedly illuminated slightly voluminous color-masses and of intervals of space, as of lines and shapes.

Light: The light is not so striking a pattern as is the color or the line, but its use is just as creative and subtle, and its function as vital to the design as that of any of the other constituents. Light pervades the color, creates a variety of nuances in the otherwise uniform color of the face, and contributes both to the general effulgence and power and to the particular complexion and texture of the flesh. Its subtle modulations in the face and neck, together with the scarcely perceptible shadows, are the chief agents in the modeling. Moreover, the fluid tonal gradations throughout the figure and the relationships to the pattern of shadows, work in conjunction with the profuse linear color-rhythms to vary and reënforce their decorative, expressive, and compositional activities. From the subtly illuminated area in the cap, light increases in degree of intensity as it flows downward over the hair, face, neck, and upper part of the shirt; its glow gradually diminishes in the lower area of the garments and is again intensified in the hands and in the ivory and gray-green portions of the shirt showing through the man's right sleeve. In short, light is used creatively, it organically supports the other factors, and it actively shares in the achievement of the design.

Space: Space surrounds the entire figure, recedes to infinity in the background, and enters into very eloquent and subtle relationships with the subsidiary component masses and patterns. In other words, the cascade of linear color-and-light units is transformed into a graceful interplay of volumes in space. Particularly extraordinary effects of space-composition occur in the ripples of the hair, in the folds of the garments, and in the unit formed by the spray of foliage, the two hands and the portion of the background from which they stand out. The unit of hands-and-spray is comparable, in moving esthetic quality, and in subtlety of effect, to the corresponding unit in van Eyck's " Man with a Pink " (36), to Cosimo Tura's " Pietà " (395), and to the best still-life compositions by Chardin. The deep space of the background and the varied intervals between the stems and leaves of the spray, between the spray and the hands, and between the fingers and thumb of each hand, are wonderfully realized, and their relations to each other and to the delicate color-volumes of hands and spray are a master-stroke of ingenuity, creative sensitivity, and technical ability.

Composition: The generally pyramidal mass-arrangement of the figure against its background acquires novelty by its becoming part and parcel of the main constructive motif of the entire design—the cascade rhythm of color-and-light volumes in space. The triangular or pyramidal formation recurs in practically every unit of the composition; it varies in size and direction, in degree of precision, and in the character of its plastic constituents; but it continuously reappears throughout the picture, as for instance, in the cap, the tassel, the face, the individual locks of hair, the intervals between them, the parts of the garments and their folds, the area of the shirt-front, the spray of foliage, each hand, and the composite unit of hands-and-foliage. Indeed, the total movement of the plastic organization owes its cascade-effect to the graceful rhythmic interplay of the variedly triangular and pyramidal units.

Summary: The individual patterns of color, light, line, and space are so interrelated that they merge in an all-inclusive form which is highly rhythmic and organically unified. The rhythmic character of the ensemble is like that of a musical symphony: the contrasting movements are deployed and then brought together in a harmonious whole.

Although the drawing of figure, garments, and spray of foliage renders considerable detail, the form of the picture emerges as a correlation of plastic units and not as photographic representation; the form has the dignity, the placidity, the solidity, the profound grasp of character, found in the best portraits of van Eyck, Titian, and Rembrandt. Even if Dürer, here, owes much to van Eyck, the early Italians, and the Cologne school, he has recast the traditional features and rendered a distinctly personal creation.

HOLBEIN

Merchant Georg Gisze (38) represents essentially an intricate space-pattern made of the almost literally reproduced details of a man and numerous objects around him. Space is very successfully handled in itself, but its complex rhythms stand out as an overaccentuated motif, because of the lack of adequate support from the other plastic elements. Plastic integration is compromised by Holbein's mechanical use of paint, by his lack of feeling for color-relationships and for grasping the essentials of texture in flesh and stuffs. The feeling of textile in the shirt-front, for instance, is submerged in the feeling of paint; this is true also of the rendering of the red sleeves, of numerous accessory objects in the setting, and of the face and hands, although the flesh partakes slightly less of a wooden character than is usual in Holbein. The black of the coat is dead compared, for example, to the quality of the blacks in Dürer; and the portion of the coat on the man's right arm appears more like space back of the red sleeve than it does a piece of material covering the body and part of the sleeve.

Dürer's portraits in the same gallery, " Hieronymus Holzshuher " (32) and " Jacob Muffel " (33), facilitate a relative classification of the two painters: Holbein is the skilled technician with but shallow vision and limited sensitivity to plastic values; Dürer, equally able in the technical handling of the medium, reaches a far higher rank as an artist, because his technical proficiency is allied to grasp of essentials and feeling for relationships, and it serves as an instrument in the creation of well-integrated plastic expressions.

VAN EYCK

Jan Arnolfini and Jeanne de Chenany, his Wife (134) [32] has the polish and charm of the miniature-effects seen in the best of the Dutch genre-painters, and was probably one of the sources of inspiration for what is best in the work of Vermeer, Pieter de Hooch, Terborch, and other great Dutch painters of family-life. Here, van Eyck plays upon the effect of sunlight in a room; the light does not stand out in isolation, but becomes the most active means in the organization of the picture: the light-pattern serves as a reënforcement and as a foil to the dark element which takes the form of an organized set of rather somber but deep, rich, glowing colors that carry the effect of color-power. As in van Eyck's " Crucifixion " (35), the color is infinitely varied with light, and a series of rich color-chords are thus created in the most vital parts of the picture. In objects of the setting, the variety of these

[32] Illustration, p. 445.

color-chords is not so pronounced as in the figures and objects in the foreground, but there is no drabness anywhere, nor any dull surface or monotonous color-area.

The pattern of light is focused in the joined hands, near the center of the composition; additional active elements in the pattern occur on the other hands and in the lighted area of the window, which latter is balanced on the right by the vertical areas of light upon the deep-red bed-curtain back of the woman. The light on the mirror in the background, and on the faces is a subdued glow and it is repeated in smaller areas and in lower tones in the highlighted spots of the chandelier. At the lower part of the picture, the white fur edging of the woman's dress is another small area upon which light is concentrated; it is balanced on the left by the illuminated color of the sandals on the floor. Similarly, the highlights on the mirror at the upper part of the back wall, are echoed in the dog's body in the lower foreground. The light ascends and recedes from back of the dog, through the green of the floor, up to the chair, continues through the red cloth on the chair, through the cushion and joins the light-pattern of the mirror.

The light from the window descends on the man's cloak and forms two parallel rhythms with the two lighted areas in the red curtain and the bed drapery. This vertical motif in the pattern is brought into equilibrium by the curve at the bottom of the man's robe and the horizontal and oblique folds in the woman's dress. All the above-mentioned units are but the high notes in the pattern of light; moreover, while functioning as light, they are tinged with color and participate in all the color-, line-, and space-relationships into which enters the particular area or object which they illuminate. Minor notes in the light-pattern, such as the highlights on the still-life near the window, the light-suffusion in the woman's dress and fur-edged sleeve, the man's cloak, the headdresses, and the back wall, offer subtle variations upon the motif. In short, the pattern of light is an integral part of the entire picture.

The color and the space, no less than the light, are compositionally integrated in the form and are organized with as much subtlety and distinction; and an equal degree of completeness of plastic relationships exists in the use of the linear elements.

Van Eyck's delicate and very expressive sharp line forms a subtly varied pronounced pattern: the generally vertical linear rhythms in the figures, draperies, chair, and window are balanced by the oblique and curved linear motifs in the woman's headdress, the man's hat, the sleeves, the mirror, the chandelier, the sandals, the dog, the draperies, and the folds and zigzag white edging of the woman's dress.

While the predominance of vertical rhythms gives a static quality to the ensemble, the varied curvilinear and angular formations add the needed note of variety, and translate the essential rigidity into a feeling of placidity rather than of stiffness. This picture is as patterned as a cubist composition, but in the patterns of color, of light, of space, and of line, and in their

van Eyck (134)   Analysis, page 443

Raphael (427)   Analysis, page 409

Titian (438)   Analysis, page 429

Westphalian Master, active c. 1400 (255)

interrelationships, everything is subtle: no factor is accentuated at the expense of another. Space, for instance, is genuinely colorful everywhere, and the color-organization, while containing an active theme of light-and-dark contrast, is just as much a rhythmic ensemble of color-, line-, and space-patterns as of light-units. In short, the picture represents a triumph of integration of all the plastic elements in a form in which the pattern of light functions as a basic agent of unification. It thus differs radically from the Dutch genre-pictures in which pattern of light-and-dark is also an active factor in composition, but in which story-telling so often outbalances plastic qualities.

PETRUS CHRISTUS

Edward Grimston (129). The ingenuity of the artist appears in the organization of figure and setting in a form which gives vivid characterization and which is also extraordinarily striking as a well-illuminated multicolored pattern.[33] Line and space are also active in giving individuality to the picture. The framework of the composition is a pattern of color-areas, sharply outlined, related to each other through space, and as modern in that respect as a cubistic organization by Picasso or Demuth.

As appealing and striking as are certain color-relations in German portraits such as Bruyn's and Baldung's, they seem tame in comparison with this color-organization in which every part is rendered with equal strength. No drab spots are apparent, even in the shadows, and rich color-chords are obtained by the reënforcing action of light.

DIRK BOUTS

Deposition (295). The first general impression is of a striking color-pattern dramatized by sharp contrasts of light. Light is concentrated upon the body of Christ, the Madonna's face, and the headdress of the Saint to the left; sunlight illuminates the ground occupied by the figures and cross; it shines also upon the paths and buildings in the middle ground, and it lights up the distant sky. These illuminated units alternate with areas of brown in the landscape proper and of blue in the sky and in the hills at the horizon. The browns and blues are shot with light but they do not impair the predominance of the organizing motif of light-and-dark contrast.

The Flemish color-scheme is effectively modified by an almost total elimination of the usual greens from the landscape and by an accentuation of the browns. In richness and degree of conviction Bouts' brown approaches a similar shade used by Rembrandt in " Hendrickje Stoffels " (373), but the comparison reveals a glow, a structural depth, an organic effulgence and a rugged surface-quality in Rembrandt's color, and a relative shallowness, a

[33] Viz., green coat, red sleeves and collar, white shirt-front with red braids, black hat and streamer, grayish-brown lower paneling in the background, light olive-green upper paneling, grayish-brown rafters, and still another grayish-green shade in the wall on the right.

superficial illumination, an enamel-like surface tending to waxiness, and a lack of subtle tonal variations in Bouts'. The bright blue in the sky and distant mountains saves the picture from a general monotonous somberness. The color, however, is richer than van der Weyden's and its compositional function is reënforced by the patterns of line and the rhythmic distribution of masses in space. Line defines contours sharply and its pattern merges with that of the color. Space in all its aspects is finely rendered, and the appeal of its organization rivals that of the pattern of color, of light, and of line. The strongly rendered background makes an appropriate setting for the figures; all parts and patterns of the composition are nicely coördinated and yield a well-balanced picturesque and expressive ensemble.

MEMLING

Saint Benedict (100). The successful relationships between the landscape, the figure, the staff, the hands, the book, the wall, the column, and the parapet, form an organic ensemble which is convincingly real and esthetically appealing. All the plastic means are employed with variety and great skill. Spatial distribution of objects is very eloquent, particularly in the foreground. Light bathes the entire composition naturally and without accentuation. Modeling, achieved by light and shade blended with color, gives a satisfying degree of weight and solidity to the figure. The picture would suffer in comparison with Titian's " Man with Glove " (394) because color is less structural and there is less simplicity in the use of the plastic means; in comparison with Raphael's " Count Baldassare Castiglione " (367), it is painted with a finer feeling for color-values, and its dignified solid character is far more appealingly human than the sentimental softness typical of Raphael, even in his best work.

LUCAS VAN LEYDEN

Saint Jerome (39) shows a design based upon the interplay of planes in space. The picture is highly patterned by contrasting areas of color and of light which divide the space-composition in a continuous sequence of receding planes. The treatment of the halo illustrates a remarkably ingenious adaptation of subject-matter to design: three concentric bright color-bands—ivory, gray, and pink—replace the conventional uniform area of color or gold, and are set one behind the other in three parallel strata or planes. Similarly, the color-relations and the dark-and-light contrasts in draperies, trees, foliage, and clouds convert a composition of voluminous objects into a fluid rhythm of solid planes receding in deep space.

REMBRANDT

Unmerciful Servant (168). An extremely difficult mass-composition is so skilfully handled that an effect of simplicity is achieved: the three figures on the right seem to be fused into a single mass which balance the single figure at the left, and the disposition and directions of the various parts of the different bodies cause all the figures to join in a continuous compositional flow. Each of the plastic elements—line, light, color, and space—participates in this flow, each with a special appeal of its own. Space between the heads of the three figures to the right is varied in each of the intervals by the lines which determine the different position and direction of each of the heads. Very active as reënforcing factors in this uniquely subtle and powerful unit of space-composition is the varied use of color and light. Color proceeds from dark to lighter tones through many gradations, and then, by a reversed order of the gradations, back to dark color, the process taking place in a graceful fluid movement. The light contributes drama to this movement by its variation from spots of emphasized light to subtle gradations which merge with the color and illuminate its depths. A similar harmonious inter-action of line, light, color, and space is perceptible in the single figure at the left, but without that emphasis which gives the three figures at the right their distinction as a powerful unit of space-composition. This method of treating differently the two main and balancing masses of the composition gives the keynote of the plastic drama so characteristic of the picture; and this drama is echoed in every part of the picture by variations in contrasts in the use of line, light, color, and space to attain varying degrees of lighting, of effulgence, of three-dimensionality of volume, and a diversity of space-effects. The colors in the single figure, for instance, are brighter and more effulgent than those in the three figures, while in the latter, a large expanse of light makes a contrast with the larger area of the more uniformly lighted dark robe of the single figure. The outstretched hand which ties the two main masses into a single composition, forms a striking contrast with the vast area of space in which it is placed. It is because this series of dramatic contrasts is attained legitimately by plastic means, that the drama of the story as revealed by the meaningful gestures, the intent facial expressions, the expressive poses, is so powerful and convincing. The whole picture has power, charm, and dignity; its delicacy is born directly of its lightness and subtlety of execution; its fluid, floating quality is the natural result of the harmonious dovetailing of the activities of all the factors in a graceful, rhythmic, and unified compositional flow.

Hendrickje Stoffels (373) [34] represents not only Rembrandt at his best, but perhaps the finest achievement in the whole domain of portraiture. The design is simple and arresting, and it displays a new variation in every area, the source of which variety is at first elusive. The solid, rich, golden, glowing figure melts into the darker background which is felt as infinite space. There is no visible contour to the figure, and the background seems as if there were nothing physical in it at all. Even within the figure, linear effects are few and extremely subtle, and color is there only in the form of tones. The golden glow of the head and chest gradually merges into the deep, gold-tempered

[34] Illustration, p. 274.

brown of the garments, and reappears in the hand in a slighter degree of intensity. Rembrandt's unique ability in the subtle use of light-and-shadow modulations yields an infinite variety of tonal effects within the golden-brown ensemble, and a great diversity of color-units and patterns, which impart an extraordinary richness and strength to the general simplicity of the form.

The simplicity of statement, here, is not especially directed, as for instance it is in Velásquez, to the physical representation of objects; the method indeed is far removed from that of Velásquez' clean-cut unemotional detachment: every area in this painting is a source of wonder and mystery, we *feel* the wonder and mystery—we see only the objective fact that calls them up in a way that we cannot explain. Simplicity and mystic power result from a very particular use of technical means that are extremely simple in themselves and loaded with the emotion-provoking power of the object portrayed, rather than with Velásquez' physical essences. Physical values are rendered, nevertheless, with great command of paint; but no flesh ever looked like that in this picture, and yet no flesh ever showed more clearly its origin in the supernatural in which we all believe in our mystical moments. Conversely, in all parts of this painting, in the unreal-real hair, face, garments, hand, and background, there is that pervasive, indefinable something which ties our mystic religious nature to this world by a definite, specific, visible, objective fact. Neither the mouth, nor the total facial expression, is at all sentimental; their drawing renders the individuality, the feeling of the person herself, and calls forth a like feeling in us as we respond to the plastic values embodied in the painting. The entire form is noble and sublime; it is saturated with profound mysticism; and the experience it represents and re-creates in the sensitive observer, is truly and genuinely religious, with no adventitious reference to story-telling or to religious symbols. Rembrandt, here, is the supreme magician who paints in terms of the broadest universal human values.

Woman Bathing (149A). The chiaroscuro comes to a focus in the form of an emphatic pattern of light on the chest and the broadly drawn shirt. The drawing of the figure is particularly charming and almost Renoiresque in its grace and expression of poised movement.

VERMEER

View of Delft (113) [35] *Pattern:* A series of horizontal irregular broad bands, counterbalanced by smaller varied vertical units, map out the general framework. Practically all the horizontal elements extend across the picture: the band of dark clouds at the top, two bands of lighted clouds below alternating with strips of blue sky; the area of buildings-and-trees; the canal as a whole and the reflections in it; and the triangular bank in the foreground. None of these areas is rigidly horizontal, each is varied by an internal pattern of

[35] Illustration, p. 221.

preponderantly vertical units. Thus, the clouds form a series of undulations, or sequences of triangular areas or pyramidal masses. The row of buildings-and-trees is rhythmically subdivided by a more pronounced and varied pattern of upright elements, the gables, steeples, towers. The reflections in the water carry the subsidiary vertical element of the pattern to the area of the canal; and the figures, the posts, and the prow of the ship function like-wise in the foreground bank.

Color: Each of the broad bands of the pattern has a general color-note which contrasts with that of the band with which it comes in contact; and the pattern of shapes is thus accentuated by the contrasts of color: the gray-white sky sets off the solid and compact blue-red-green masses in the center, which in turn contrast with the gray-brown water; and the latter comes in contact with the tan-yellow bank in the foreground. There is no really bright color anywhere, nor a great number of individual hues, yet the color-ensemble is rich, varied, and subtly glowing. No color is used uniformly over a large area without being so mottled with light that the effect is one of richly-varied color-chords, or color-modulations, reminiscent of Tintoretto's or Cézanne's, with the difference that Vermeer's nuances result from an internal pattern of light within each color-area, sometimes amounting to a series of superposed spots, rather than to actual change of hue. An effect of color-variety is also due to tonal modifications by light of a basically same color used in different areas of the picture. In the row of buildings, for instance, blue and red are deployed as a theme, varied with minor motifs of gray and green. A blue of extraordinary sensuous and structural quality is the key-note in this part of the color-design, and indeed is so powerfully eloquent as to be chiefly responsible for the individuality of the entire picture. Yet, what functions as a rich symphony of different blues is in reality a har-monious interplay of variedly illuminated blue units which have all a basic similarity in actual color and in structural activity. In other words, besides the color-variation attained by relationship to different context, the blue in the various gables, roofs, towers, and trees, appears as a contrasting factor in the color-theme as the degree of illumination varies its general tonality, or as the pattern of spots of light alters its local aspect. The brownish reds are likewise played upon by light, and supply a strong, rich, and well-integrated secondary rhythm in the color-design.

The composite color-pattern of the picture is focused in the row of build-ings, in which color is the richest, the most varied and personal, and the most structural. In this area, to a greater extent than in the rest of the painting, the colors and nuances are so integrated in the form that the individuality of the different tones is submerged in an essential feeling of texture.

Light: True to the Dutch tradition, contrast of light and dark is an essen-tial characteristic of this landscape. The general pattern of broad horizontal color-bands, above noted, is also one of contrasting light and dark areas: the dark and lighted clouds at the top; the central deep-toned mass of houses, trees, and boats; the dark reflections and the lighted water; and the contrastingly illuminated foreground-bank. In consonance with the internal variations in the theme of color, the dramatic motif of light-and-dark is likewise very ingeniously exploited as an internal pattern in each area, and is particularly rich in variety of effects in the row of buildings-and-trees. At the extreme right of this row, for instance, an area, about five inches high by four wide, is flooded with sunlight; and within this sunlit expanse, rich reds and reddish-browns function as the element of dark in a pattern, in which the ivory part of the wall, subtly modulated with a relatively bright red, acts as light. In the immediately adjacent section of this wall, the relation of light to dark is reversed: the ivory is at the top and the brownish red below. Again, the area of the ground bathed in sunlight, in this part of the picture, is of an ivory tone tinged with red and blue, which creates a striking note of contrast with the adjacent area of the ground which is modulated with grayish bluish-green. In the part of the house immediately to the left of the boats on the right of the picture, the wall and turret function as the dark element in contrast to the sunlit, modulated, yellow-and-red roof; and each factor in this light-and-dark relationship also contributes to the continuity of color-contrasts and rhythms which particularly abound in this central band of the total organization. In each of the above-noted units of light-and-dark contrast, there is a succession of rich color-chords, of which the essential characteristic is light; that is, even the color of the shadows is also permeated with light, and no disrupting drab spot occurs anywhere.

Drawing: The drawing, throughout, is a successful merging of color, light, and line. Contour appears as a sharp outline, for example, in some of the roofs; as a loose boundary in some of the boats, and also as a linear color-area, or a broad line of color, such as Tintoretto, Daumier, and Cézanne have used. The charm of the drawing lies in the ingenious versatility of the subtle variations of the quantity of each of the plastic elements. For instance, the first blue gable to the right of the yellow spire, and also the yellow roof immediately to the right of this blue gable, are each drawn by almost equal proportions of light and color, with a slight preponderance of light over color in the yellow roof and a slight preponderance of color over light in the blue gable; in the second tree to the left of the large yellow church-spire, the drawing is chiefly by means of light. The drawing of the wall of the viaduct is a rich symphony of color, light, and irregular contour, all functioning as color and organically integrated in the structure and form of the unit. The same is true of the drawing of the boats at the extreme right; in fact, drawing everywhere is rendered by greatly varied units of structural color-forms, the sensuous quality of which increases the appeal of the essential feeling of each object depicted.

The small kiosklike structure with black roof, to the left of the towered building in the center, illustrates a successful use of simplifications in drawing. The wall of this structure, from the window to the ground—a red area mottled with ivory-white spots—is subtly rendered, loosely drawn, yet convincingly solid and real. Contour, surface, texture, color, melt in a single composite mass, of which the general effect preserves the distinctive essential nature of the object, with scarcely any indication of detail. This type of drawing represents Vermeer's version of Velásquez' interpretation of the Venetian form, particularly Tintoretto's.

The figures in the foreground, notably the two on the right, are also broadly and simply drawn, much as in Velásquez or Manet, and are as real and solid as some of Guardi's and Corot's small figures, which they also resemble in that general type of execution that draws out essentials and eliminates details. Simplication and generalization of another sort, are very effective also in the drawing of the blue tree, just to the left of the large yellow church-spire: lines as such are non-existent; the contour of the individual bunches of foliage and branches, is drawn by a merging of color and light, and the linear effect results from contrasts between the high spots of blue light on the leaves and the darker blue which is used to draw out the spatial intervals.

Drawing, in short, is varied and is of a high degree of expressiveness in every area of the picture, with the exception of the clouds; these, the weakest part of the picture, are rendered in typically Dutch manner by tonal patterns of light and dark.

Composition: Composition is represented in its best estate, because its constituents are drawn with color, and their rich glowing color-forms intermingle and pervade the entire painting. The plastic organization of the subject-matter is one of colorful units that recede in deep space and attain a degree of three-dimensionality commensurate with the exquisite character of the painting as a whole. Space-composition is particularly attractive but not overemphasized. In the foreground, for example, the boat and group of figures on the left form a very fine unit of space-relationships, and participate in the larger space-organization that includes the posts and the two figures on the right, the bank itself, and the background of water. Further examples of very appealing space-distribution of masses abound in the row of buildings-and-trees; for instance, the entire area to the right of and including the yellow church-spire is a succession of variedly shaped, colored, and illuminated gables, walls, towers, chimneys, set at intervals which also vary in expanse, depth, and content of color and light.

The treatment of certain areas is reminiscent of other Dutch painters; the sky, for example, is such as van Goyen would have given, and the foreground boat and figures tend toward the quasi-precious miniature-effects of van der Heyden and Berckheyde. The picture is, indeed, Holland itself, and its form embodies a creative use of traditional features and represents Vermeer and the Dutch tradition in their highest estate.

[455]

APPENDIX

TERBORCH

Concert (385).[36] The painting of stuffs is particularly well done: the table-cloth, for instance, has just enough elaboration of detail and brightness of color to enable it to function harmoniously as a mass with the other units in the picture, and to help achieve a high degree of integration.

FRENCH MASTER OF END OF FOURTEENTH OR BEGINNING OF FIFTEENTH CENTURY

Entombment (324) [37] exemplifies the joint influence of the miniaturists and early Italians upon French primitive painting. Like nearly all other French primitives it is an organization of compact color-planes. The color has the delicacy of miniatures in the illuminated manuscripts, but the actual hues, the patterning with light, and the organization of the planes in compressed space, indicate a close relationship to the successors of Giotto, especially to Daddi. " Entombment " is distinguished from these Italian sources by greater subtlety in general, less sharp linear divisions between color-compart-ments, less solidity, and by a more intimate union of light and color, which produces a rich variety of color-nuances in spite of the absence of color-chords. The dynamic, varied rhythm of planes in compressed three-dimen-sional space, makes a type of space-composition which, together with the subtle relations of light and color, and the general finesse of execution, estab-lishes the essentially French character of the form.

Drawing and modeling, as well as color, composition, and technical execu-tion, testify to the confluence of Italian and miniature influences, but the derivations are all modified and set in new contexts. For example, the Sienese droop is conjoined with typical French color; the painting of flesh has sources in Daddi, Lippo Memmi, and the Lorenzetti school, but the flesh has the characteristic non-naturalistic French tone, and the pattern of light on which the modeling largely depends is more fully integrated with color than in the Italians, more free from accentuation of any kind. The whole picture is a strongly integrated plastic creation, a form both authen-tically French and of high intrinsic excellence.

FRENCH MASTER OF ABOUT 1400

Altarpiece of the Virgin (326) is essentially a decorative pattern of deep, rich, and bright colors set against a tooled gold background. The pattern is highly rhythmic in itself, and the rhythms are reënforced by flowing ara-besques in the ornamental setting; the relation of the colors to one another and to the gold are subtle and at the same time organic; and all the plastic components of the picture are organized in a form of expressive conviction and great decorative charm.

[36] Illustration, p. 224.　　　　　[37] Illustration, p. 243.

Germanic influences appear in the execution of faces and hands, in the vivid alert facial expressions, and in the short, squatty, almost grotesque, figures. The drawing, by juxtaposed areas of color and light, is of the type which originated in illuminated miniatures of the Ingeburge Psalter (52), but was given a more definite form by the Cologne and Bohemian painters; the modeling, by a pattern of streaks and spots of light, is also derived from the Germans, though its ultimate source is Byzantine. Another Byzantine feature employed in this as in other French primitive paintings is a subsidiary pattern of very fine ridges of paint, which blends with the pattern of light to draw out the solidity of the flesh and to contribute to the rendering of facial expressions. The line is in general Florentine, with very little actual line, and there are also echoes of the Sienese droop, especially as modified and made more weighty by the Bohemian school. The linear pattern as a whole is varied, fluid, rhythmic, and graceful, and it enhances the expressiveness and vivid power of the color-ensemble. The debt to the miniaturists appears chiefly in the use of an indented ornamental gold background; to the Italians, in the color-scheme and graceful Sienese drawing and composition; to the Germans, in the weight of the color, the distortions, and the manner of execution, as well as in the modeling and drawing.

None of the derived elements remains unaltered: the general textural quality, the pervasive use of ivory, the subtlety of relationships, and the delicacy and essentially decorative quality make the form as a whole unmistakably French.

FRENCH MASTER OF THE FIFTEENTH CENTURY

Salome (1) exemplifies the Franco-Flemish type of early French painting tempered by Italian elements. Flemish drawing, modeling, distribution of masses, and light-pattern are organically merged with Italian color, in a form which is completely French. The most distinctive feature of the painting, its ensemble of bright harmonious colors, is indubitably Italian in origin. A few areas of somber Flemish brown serve mainly to set off by contrast the vivid, bright, and brilliant colors, which are nuanced and blended with light to form rich color-chords and a subtle irridescent glow. The surface of the picture has a lustrous enamel-quality which shows the influence both of the Italians, and of van der Weyden, and Bouts.

The pattern of light has also an important compositional function. Organized in bands, it embraces the whole surface of the picture in a series of subordinate patterns, which unify in a single comprehensive design and thus bind every area to every other in a single rhythmic whole. This light, chiefly Flemish in origin, is so enriched by the vivid color that the whole light-organization becomes also a composition of luminous color. No less effective is the rhythmic, dynamic, varied, organically integrated composition of volumes and spatial intervals. Space is for the most part rendered literally as in the Flemings, but its organization acquires a very distinctive French character from the unusual colors and color-relations.

The linear drawing departs from the Flemish by the looseness of facial contour, a tendency usually characteristic of paintings of the Franco-Flemish type in which Italian influences are pronounced. Flesh is painted with rose-ivory tones, typically French, and sometimes approaching the peachblow of the Gréolières " Altarpiece of St. Etienne " (110); the modeling of the flesh, by patterns of light and shadow, is much more subtle than in the Flemings.

The traits which make the picture French are: the quality of color and the subtlety and variety of the relations of color to light, line, and space; the graceful rigidity of the figures, which show a number of highly decorative distortions; the pervasive naïveté of the drawing and composition; and the simplicity and delicacy which distinguish the tradition in all its forms.

FRENCH MASTER OF THE FIFTEENTH CENTURY

The Gréolières **Altarpiece of St. Etienne** (110),[38] the most individual and one of the most important of all the French primitive paintings, is a rich and strikingly patterned decorative color-composition, of great simplicity, dignity, and delicacy. Each of the larger panels is dominated by a single color, of which numerous tones give the effect of rich variety, though there are not many actually different colors. In the predella, in contrast, the variety of color is very obvious and striking, though the blue background provides an element of uniformity underlying all the different hues. This blue, of exquisite sensuous quality is very closely akin to that of Piero della Francesca in its lightness and delicacy; its compositional function, however, is entirely different, since it serves chiefly to set off the pattern of multi-colored bright figures.

The comprehensive color-pattern of the altarpiece, comparatively simple in the main panels, elaborate in the predella, is rounded out by the three small panels at the top, in which light pastel tones are organized in an ensemble of great delicacy and charm. The entire picture forms a single design, predominantly decorative, with little depth of space or solidity of masses; but the expressive aspects are adequately realized. The freshness and delicacy of both the colors and their relations make the painting an extraordinary masterpiece of color-composition.

The color in its freshness and dryness recalls that of Italian frescoes. Except for its delicacy, it owes nothing to the Italian panel-painters who worked with bright delicate tones, nor to the illuminated manuscripts, but is most closely akin to the color of some of the Byzantine panels and to Piero della Francesca's. The flesh has a peachblow tone, and a delicate chalky texture. It is modeled with little or no pattern of light or line, but its homogeneity is diversified by subtle color-contrasts.

[38] Illustration, p. 242.

The linear demarcations between color-compartments make up an extremely pleasing pattern, which plays an important compositional rôle and is reënforced by the sensuous charm of the color. In the predella, in which the figures are numerous and compactly organized, the sequence of color-areas produces a continuous flow, an effect of abstract movement, even though there is no represented movement whatever. The contrast between the composition in the different sections of the picture varies the organization, and works in conjunction with the color-relations to increase the harmony and unity of the total effect.

Although this altarpiece has no exact counterpart in the French or any other tradition, it is French in all its plastic characteristics and in its expression of grace, delicacy, and naïve archaic charm.

GILLOT

Scene of the Two Coaches (329) indicates one of the sources of the eighteenth century French form represented by Watteau—a pupil of Gillot—Lancret, and Pater, in the following characteristics: the type of subject, the general treatment, the brightening of Venetian color, the drawing of the heads, and the rendering of the garments.

WATTEAU

Game of Love (160) [39] illustrates Watteau's characteristics at their best. The influences of Rubens and the Venetians are well integrated in a form of essential delicacy typical of the French eighteenth century. Color is rich, solid, and glowing; textures are adequately deep and very decoratively appealing; flesh, particularly the woman's chest, is rendered by a gentle flow of subtle color-chords; composition is a compact graceful sequence of colorful volumes, rhythmically organized, as often in Tintoretto, diagonally across the picture.

Embarkation for Cythera (402). The Venetian feeling in the landscape is modified by the influence of Claude and the use of Rubens' swirl. Both in general effect and in the drawing of the figures and units of landscape, the picture is softer, less solid and robust, and more feminine, idyllic, and romantic, than the form of any of the prototypes.

BOUCHER

Pastoral: Sleeping Shepherdess (293). The idyllic character of the subject makes for an appealing charm which, however, remains superficial. The execution is crisp, line is fairly expressive, and the figures seem to be alive in their activities, but the movement is obtained speciously rather than by legitimate plastic means.

[39] Illustration, p. 253.

Rinaldo and Armida (294). Features characteristic of Rubens appear in a weakened form, and the general artificiality of the painting is emphasized by the essential triviality of the subject-matter.

FRAGONARD

Music Lesson (319) [40] is a technically skilful rendering, in a delicate attenuated form, of traditional Venetian color-effects, particularly Paolo's, as these were adapted and modified by Rubens and Terborch. This picture represents Fragonard at his best: it lacks his usual ostentatious decorative display of technique, the brush strokes function plastically in the drawing and modeling, and the compact composition is heightened in appeal by the delicacy of the execution and the charming rigid grace of the figures.

GREUZE

Village Betrothal (331). The classic Poussin tradition has gone far on the road to degeneration: composition is stereotyped; color is mediocre in sensuous quality and functionally dead; and drawing, though skilful, gives no more than specious drama.

CHARDIN

Still-Life with Fish and Eggs (301) and **Still-Life with Meat** (302) are good illustrations of how Chardin brings Venetian solidity and dignity, and French subtlety, simplicity, and delicacy to the Dutch type of still-life by structural color, simplified drawing, and exquisite rendering of spatial units.

Various Utensils (303) ranks as a masterpiece in the traditions of art: what is best in the Venetians, the Dutch, and Velásquez, has been recast in a very individual form that conveys a convincing sense of reality with extraordinary subtlety, charm, and simplicity.

The non-symmetrical distribution of the masses is an unconventional variation upon the pyramidal arrangement: the tendency of the compositional elements in the total pattern is toward the rectangular rather than the triangular, and the rhythm of the masses in space is chiefly one of vertical and horizontal units, livened up, but undisturbed by the few contrasting oblique features.

Space, in all the aspects rendered, is marvelously handled and extremely moving esthetically: effects vary from the deep dark space at the bottom of the picture and the shallower broad expanse in the gray background, to the rhythmic interplay of colorful masses and intervals in the still-life proper, the keynote of which is variety, subtlety, and simplicity. There is clarity throughout the organization, with successful unaccentuated atmospheric

[40] Illustration, p 474.

effect and no impression of jumble: space flows gently between and around the individual masses, even between objects placed close to each other, and it unifies with the color, the light, and the pattern in a very harmoniously punctuated space-composition. This charming and highly skilled treatment of space is well matched by the choice, varied, structural, and delicate color, and the extraordinary blending of color and light with technique and the pigment itself in the achievement of textural quality.

INGRES

Madame Rivière (338) is interesting chiefly as a unified ensemble of decorative patterns and linear rhythms. Ingres's coldness is particularly well illustrated by the painting of the flesh. Compared to Delacroix's rich rendering of warm human flesh in, for example, " Death of Sardanapalus " (311), Ingres's painting is like an arabesque on an alabaster wall.

Spring (339). The popular appeal of the picture is obviously due to the charm and grace of the youthful figure; that is, to the subject-matter literally represented and practically devoid of plastic qualities. The color is superficial and drab, the setting looks like painted scenery, and there is neither structural nor textural distinction in any of the units.

DELACROIX

Algerian Women (310) is a conventional composition made interesting by color, a variety of planes, patterns of light and lines, and by solid painting. The color is bright and rich with a tendency to atmospheric glow, and it functions well in unifying the composition. The picture is especially noteworthy because of the method of application of paint in some of its areas: juxtaposed small strokes of contrasting colors, much in the manner of Constable, are associated with spots of accentuated light. This method of broken color-and-light was developed into a characteristic technique by the impressionists.

COURBET

Painter's Studio (308).[41] The space-composition is of outstanding interest. The complex number of figures and objects are organized in three main groups, one on each side of the central unit of painter-canvas-nude-boy chair-drapery. Each of these groups is made up of a number of subsidiary groupings, and offers a variety of individual arrangements of volumes in space. From both the extreme right and the extreme left of the total organization, a rhythmic sequence of masses and intervals recedes into the depth of the room, converges toward the center of the back wall, and is brought forward again by organic relationships with the central grouping, the focal unit in the total composition. While a large triangular volume of deep space

[41] Illustration, p. 256.

is thus created on each side of the center group by the lateral in-and-out main movement of the composition, no inactive space occurs, but rather an uninterrupted continuity in the rhythmic sequence of the masses, with great variety in their individual direction, size, and general character, and in the relationships they establish with one another. All the plastic factors contribute a share to the satisfactory solution of the complex compositional problem, but lines, or rather linear elements, are perhaps the most active agent of unification. From one end of the canvas to the other, a linear rhythm, sweeping up and down and in and out, leads each unit toward the other and helps to tie intervals and masses in an organic entity. A series of upward linear rhythms, for instance, in the woman with the shawl on the right, and in the drapery on the floor, move from the lower right corner of the picture toward the nude and also toward various other linear elements in the background figures and draperies to the right of the nude. From the figure of the nude, the linear element flows downward to the figure of the painter, the little boy, and the strikingly Daumier-like woman sitting on the floor immediately to the left of the easel. From there on, the linear sweep continues to the extreme left of the total composition through a varied series of short units, chiefly curvilinear. The essential difference between this compositional activity of the line and the corresponding factor in Ingres's " Turkish Bath " (340) is that the linear arabesque, in the latter, works practically entirely alone, while in the Courbet it serves to bring into relief a particular character and effect, also contributed to by color and light even though in lesser degree of accentuation. In other words, the compositional linear pattern in this Courbet—as in Renoir's " Bathing Group " (239), as in Poussin's " Blindmen of Jericho " (361), or as in Titian's " Disciples at Emmaus " (391)—is only one aspect of the compositional rhythm of color-masses.

In drawing, modeling, use of color, and surface-quality, the picture holds in solution various effects and methods characteristic of Leonardo, Bronzino, Tintoretto, Velásquez, Goya, Daumier, and Corot.

CLAUDE LE LORRAIN

Seapiece (304) marks a step in the direction of nineteenth century romanticism. Only the painter's admirable use of the plastic means saves the picture from being an illustrated postal-card loaded with romantic and dramatic lyricism and sweet sentimentality.

Village Fête (305). Claude's characteristics are all to be observed here: his preoccupation with and mastery of landscape, the romantic glamour and drama of nature, the classic and Venetian influences, the pervasive French feeling, the faulty drawing of the figures when they are looked at in detail, and the compositional function of the tree in the center, which compels the spectator to join with the artist in giving attention primarily to the landscape.

CONSTABLE

Flatford Mill (131), like " Hay-Wain" (132), reveals Constable's method of color-division, but the rendering of landscape is less original than in " Hay-Wain"; the color is not so rich and juicy, and the compositional relationship between the large trees, on one side, and the pattern of clouds, on the opposite side, results in more facile and obvious drama. Much of the foreground, though not completely destitute of color-quality, is rather brittle and dry.

Hay-Wain (132) embodies all of Constable's characteristics in their highest estate: his feeling for intime landscape and for the spirit of place; his unconventional unification in composition of groups of house-and-trees by open space and color; his juxtaposed small spots of color, forecasting impressionism; his rich juicy pigment and glowing surface; his powerful use of color- and light-patterns to organize the composition; and his ability to merge relatively small figures or objects into the general massive effect of the landscape by impressionistic elimination of details and by adjustment of the simplifications to the compositional importance or function of the unit depicted.

The general feeling of the picture is reminiscent of both Rubens and Hobbema. Indeed, Rubens' " Landscape with Shepherd " (152) is strongly suggested by the treatment of the sky, trees, house, and team, and it is quite probable that it had been particularly studied by Constable. The kinship with Hobbema is less in the execution than in the grouping of masses and, especially, in the dramatic character of the sky and its compositional function in relation to the mass of the tree. Constable's drama, however, is less stylistic, his trees are more subtly active in composition, and the general feeling of the landscape is more placid than in Hobbema's treatment of similar subject-matter. All the traditional elements relied upon have been organically absorbed into Constable's new and very personal form.

Salisbury Cathedral (133).[42] Color is again jewel-like and treated divisionistically, but the touches and patches are broader than in " Hay-Wain " (132). Individual figures and foliage are simplified to the extreme, and the background of sky is rendered practically entirely with light used in spots and areas of irregular shape and size. Throughout the picture, there is so much manipulation of light that the painting could have been done by Jongkind or Monet, had either of them had Constable's feeling for rich juicy color.

TURNER

Calais Pier (157) contains nothing original in conception, composition, color, or method of execution. It merely tells of a melodramatic episode, entirely outside the realm of art.

[42] Illustration, p. 282.

Dido Building Carthage (158) is but a weak imitation of Claude. In his obvious attempt to simplify Claude's form, Turner omits so many of the details, that the effects he was after—the majesty, grandeur, and mystery of landscape—fail to materialize. The non-accentuated representative details in Claude are usually adequate, and their controlled degree of simplification is actually conducive to the pervasive feeling of the majesty and grandeur of nature on a vast scale. In Turner, the technique and the efforts are paramount, and the esthetic effect is nil.

THEODORE ROUSSEAU

Edge of the Forest of Fontainebleau, toward Brôle (379). Compared with Claude—to whose form this painting owes most of its traits—Rousseau's rendering of the glow, and of the feeling of grandeur and majesty in landscape, tends toward plastic disbalance and theatrical effect. The glow, for instance, not so pronounced as in Claude, is felt as something apart from the total form rather than as one of its pervasive qualities: it stands out as an overaccentuation of light which speciously carries the eye to the distant landscape; within this area, the glow, nicely modulated with blue, and the attendant feeling of romantic grandeur and mystery, are relatively circumscribed. The inferiority to Claude is further revealed in the artificially rendered vista-effect in the arching of the foreground trees, and in their realistic painting which competes rather than merges with the effect obtained in the glowing distance.

The appeal of the picture is due to the pleasing distribution of the masses, the well-proportioned relations of planes, and the attractive variety of color-effects, but the obviousness of the means in attaining compositional organization precludes a genuinely mystical expression of nature. The landscape is felt as something painted, not as something impressive and real.

MANET

Olympia (348) is a modern version of Titian's composition in his numerous pictures of a reclining figure with counterbalancing use of a secondary figure, a room-interior, or a landscape.[43] The novel effect in the Manet lies chiefly in the execution, drawing, and modeling, and also in the relatively greater compositional interest given to the secondary figure and objects. Titian's curvilinear rhythms of fully three-dimensional and weighty volumes in the nude are replaced by a strangely graceful angularity, a pert rigidity, and greatly simplified modeling and drawing which flatten the masses and endow the form with daintiness.

Except occasionally in the deepening of tone into a line at contours, dark shadows are abolished, and replaced by lighted color; middle tones are reduced to a minimum, and the resulting flat volumes represent a treatment

[43] E.g., Titian's "Venus and Organ Player" (44); "Venus with Dog" (105); "Venus and Love" (173); "Venus and Music" (174).

and a form which build upon Velásquez' simplifications a novel and very personal creation. With all its flatness, the figure is solid and is alive both as a human being and as a plastic unit. Each area of the picture is replete with pictorial and compositional effects: the decorated shawl and the red and ivory bed clothes paralleling the nude; the vivid black cat wonderfully set in space- and color-relationships with its contrasting white and green context; the delicately colorful compact planes of the simplified bouquet of flowers; the vague pattern of folds in the background draperies; the bold division of the background by a central vertical band; and the extremely picturesque figure of the negress which counterbalances the slant of the upper part of the nude's body and helps incorporate the longitudinal rhythm of the bed and nude in a very picturesque inverted pyramidal formation. The black-ness of the negress' head and hand is accentuated by the pink of her gown with extremely appealing result. Space- and color-values of extraordinary effect, established by the relationship between the negress' figure and its green setting, form practically a complete picture in itself. Another fine pictorial organization on the left of the dividing vertical background-band, is the ensemble of contrasting rhythms created by the color-, space-, and pattern-relationships between the different parts of the nude's head, trunk, and arms, the pillows and bed-clothes, the brown vaguely flowered back-ground, and the green drapery at the upper left. These two subsidiary designs—one on each side of the vertical background-band—are organically tied together by the striking body of the nude which extends across from one section to the other, and also by the above-noted pyramidal formation, by which the nude's legs are plastically continued upward, as it were, by the slanting figure of the negress.

The painting is executed with outstanding technical skill and the entire picture has power, simplicity, terseness, grace, picturesqueness, and feeling for character and essential reality. Its distinctive identity emerges from Manet's transformation and fusion of various traditional features: Titian's composition, Velásquez' simplified modeling and drawing, and Courbet's stark realism—all re-created and organically embedded in Manet's own novel form.

MONET

House Boat (225) reveals Monet's use of a technique derived largely from Manet, and well-adapted to giving pictorial expression to the tranquillity of landscape and a specific effect of light and atmosphere. Simplification of representative detail is carried to the extreme, largely by the use of the broad brushwork of Manet. Light is skilfully employed to bathe the picture in sil-very sunlight, to illuminate color, and to form a pattern. Perspective is ren-dered picturesquely and enters effectively in units of space-composition. Color is admirably adapted in tone and variety to fit in with the simplicity of the design and with the directness of statement. In short, unity of organ-ization is achieved by a skilful balanced use of the plastic means.

APPENDIX

Madame Monet Embroidering (226) [44] represents the Monet technique in its most characteristic form. In the woman's gown, the curtain, the two jardinières, the carpet, in fact in every object in the canvas, a richness of color is obtained by the juxtaposition of spots of contrasting color. It gives not merely the surface-quality of the different textures, but also the abstract quality of richness. The picture is essentially a genre-type of interior scene in which basic human values, especially the feeling of the intime, triumph over the accentuated technique.

RENOIR

Bathing Group (239). [45] Renoir in this picture has taken the classic form as a motif for the elaboration of a symphony in plastic design in which color is exploited to its fullest possibilities. The figures are reminiscent of the Greek statues of about 400 B.C. [46] They also recall Rubens in their voluptuousness and in the use of a swirl made up of line, color, and light; but Renoir uses light in a more organic manner; he reduces the intensity of the movement and drama; and his color not only has a more appealing sensuous quality but is more solidly structural and its compositional range is greatly extended. [47] The influence of the eighteenth century French painters, especially Boucher and Fragonard, is apparent in the general delicacy and in the enamel- or porcelain-quality of the surfaces, each derivation made stronger by Renoir's more powerful drawing into which enters a deeper and richer color. [48]

The transformations achieved by Renoir in all of the sources drawn upon result in a new form which resembles in general structure and plastic expression that of the great Venetians, notably, Giorgione, Titian, and Tintoretto. The general effect is that of the Arcadian, Elysian feeling evoked by "Concert in the Open Air" (330) of Giorgione, but Renoir's form is freer from the influence of classic myth and is tied more closely to reality as we know it: there is a lesser idealization of landscape, and a more this-worldly character in the figures.

Color: Renoir has here attained to supreme heights in the use of color, and has endowed it with an outstandingly individual character in its decorative, structural, and organizing functions. Color-chords are literally innumerable and extremely varied: from one end of the canvas to the other they vibrate, scintillate, dance, move in relation with each other; they are not merely surface-decorations but are solid units of perceptible three-dimensional quality, richer, more varied, more solidly real than those used by any other painter, not excepting the great Venetians; and they help compose, tie together, and unify the various units in a more powerful organic plastic

[44] Illustration, p. 309.
[45] Illustration, p. 163.
[46] Cf., e.g., Greek "Standing Figure" (201).
[47] Cf., e.g., Rubens' "Andromeda" (42).
[48] Cf., e.g., Boucher's "Diana at the Bath" (291) or Fragonard's "Bathers" (316).

whole. Renoir replaces the Venetian glow by a richer pervasive color, of greater appeal, which, in combination with light and line, produces solid color-masses which move through deep colorful space, and evoke a feeling of drama.

Light: Renoir's color is more thoroughly permeated with light than is that of any of his predecessors. Patterns of light, present in every part of the canvas, constitute an important factor in the total esthetic effect: they reënforce both the color and the line everywhere—in the flesh, the draperies, the trees, the bushes, the water, the sky—they are never of equal intensity or solidity, but are graded from their strongest structural quality in the main figures to a lesser degree of intensity in the middle distance, and they diminish to a further degree of lightness in the background-landscape and sky.

Shadows as such are practically absent; their equivalents are given by contrasting colors, which, in relation to the light, yield a firmly modeled three-dimensional solidity as convincingly real in its setting as is the more solid three-dimensional character of Cézanne's figures.

Drawing: The drawing is done by color more than by line: color and line merging with light give a type of drawing which is Renoir's own and which is more expressive and esthetically more moving than is the sharper line of either Raphael or Ingres. The classic influence, as one finds it in the Greek vases of the best period, appears in the graceful linear quality both in the individual figures and in the groupings of units. The linear element is broken into curves that vary in length, and it is therefore less continuously flowing than in the Greeks. Moreover, the Greek line has lost its incisive character and has attained a new quality of strength, due to the organic union of line with the powerfully moving color, and to the consequent freedom from linear sharpness. Throughout the picture, color overflows the contours; even in the figures which at a distance seem to be sharply defined in their outline, the contour is never an isolated line nor a sharp boundary when examined at close range; yet there is never any question of distinction between the various objects. These rich linear rhythms function inseparably with the rhythms of volumes; in other words, line, color, and light blend in the formation of volumes which are related to one another in deep space, in an orderly, linearly fluid manner.

Drawing is far removed from literal representation of subject-matter. The faces and other parts of the bodies are very generalized in their detail: the features are only indicated by broad notes of color, line, or light which not only creatively transform surface-appearances but also give the effect of solid underlying structural form. Anatomical distortions are indeed vital to the achievement of Renoir's design. For instance, in the two standing figures at the right of the canvas, the distorted arms of the nude flow into and become continuous with the arms of the clothed figure, and together they form a rhythm of elongated masses which merge harmoniously with a series of rhythms that include such other units as the neighboring tree-trunk, the nude's legs, and the arms of the seated figure. Distortions in the other figures likewise make them function powerfully as rhythmic units in the composite set of plastic relationships. Each figure has an ease, a graceful fluidity, which extends from one mass to the other in a general rhythmic flow, and ties up the various units in a harmonious ensemble. This compositional rhythmic motif is more of color than of line, but is just as much a rhythm of volumes, and the abstract feeling rendered by the rhythmic relationships is that of grace, delicacy, and charm.

Space: Literal representation of perspective does not exist; that is, neither line nor linear effect is used directly in the production of the illusion of space, yet the center of the canvas gives the effect of great depth, and each of the masses, from the foreground to the background, occupies a plane of its own, moves in a space which is itself subdivided into an infinite number of planes and, like the volumes, is also essentially made of color. Color thus entering into both the masses and the space helps to organize the picture in a space-composition of the highest grade.

Mass-Composition: The mass-composition is fluid with no tendency to the conventional central mass and bilateral symmetry; it may be taken up at any point and carried around in a series of graceful arabesques so as to relate all units in a continuous organic ensemble. In other words, no matter which of the main volumes be selected as focal unit, its relationships to the other elements in the picture always establish a satisfying balance and compositional continuity. As color-volumes set in colorful space, the heads, arms, legs, and bodies enter into rhythmic compositional organizations with the masses made up of the trees and bushes; and differences in their details yield an effect of rich variety. Each of these volumes is reducible to units of color, light, line, mass, and space, which constitute a rich array of rhythmic motifs in themselves. This great variety of compositional elements shows Renoir's fertile imagination and extraordinary versatility in making use of the compositional possibilities of color, line, light, mass, and space. In the compositional use of the plastic means, it is indeed a question whether any painter ever attained an equal degree of ingenuity and range of effects.

The overwhelming richness of the total picture is not only of color but of all the plastic elements; and even though the surface has an extraordinarily rich sensuous appeal, the feeling of richness emerges from the innermost substance of the form. By Renoir's individual use of color, the most potent and at the same time the most difficult of all the plastic means to use, this picture carries the Venetian type of composition to new heights of esthetic expression and to a richer realm of decorative qualities.

CEZANNE

Mount Ste. Victoire (176).[49]   The essential feature of the picture is a powerful rhythmic color-movement of volumes and planes which carries the eye from the immediate foreground to the distant background, interpene-

[49] Illustration, p. 404.

trates in all directions, and comes to rest in compositional equilibrium. The rhythm is slight in the foreground-bushes; it increases in size, power, and degree of voluminousness in the pyramidal group of trees-and-houses immediately back of the bushes; it then drops to a relatively flat, directly receding plane in the middleground, which is patterned by color, light, and line and punctuated at irregular intervals by small upright color-masses; the rhythm rolls on backward and upward in the volumes of the foot-hills, gathers greater power and weight in the larger mountains, and reaches a climax in the mountain-peak. The vaguely modeled area of sky behind this mountain-peak acts as a foil to emphasize and set off the complex symphony of rhythms.

The composite series of these rhythms holds the attention by the variety in color, illumination, linear definition, size, shape, position, degree of massiveness, and solidity of the constituent units, a variety which heightens their decorative, expressive, and compositional effectiveness. All the plastic factors participate in this movement, and the interrelation and piling-up of the rhythms is like a Bach fugue, and is even more complex in the variety of its components.

The space itself is rhythmic because of differences in size of the intervals between the various masses and planes. The perspective is so merged with color that it cannot be separated from it; that is, color gives the perspective its compelling charm. With all the activity of space and perspective, there is no overaccentuation: the distance, the spaciousness, that give grandeur and majesty to nature, are fittingly rendered.

The general mass-composition tends toward a bilaterally symmetrical distribution around central units. The clump of trees-and-houses in the foreground, for instance, functions as a central mass, and the bilaterally balanced units on each side consist of a comparatively flat receding plane and a large expanse of space, which set off the group of trees-and-houses as a large central pyramidal organization of masses in space. From this pyramid, the eye is carried upward and backward to the peak of the mountain in the background. Between the foreground pyramid and the mass of the mountain there are a number of focal points with elements to the right and to the left which achieve symmetrical balance. In no case is there an exact duplication of units: each is so varied from the other that a picturesque variety results.

The modeling, done by Cézanne's usual hatchings of color modulated with light, imparts a convincing feeling of three-dimensional solidity to the individual color-patches which build up the masses and create within each volume a constructive rhythmic series of compact color-planes.

This picture shows that Cézanne was an impressionist in the sense of using light as one of the chief motifs and as an integrating factor in composition. All parts of the canvas are bathed in light, and the pattern made by the light is complex, infinitely varied, harmoniously related to the other factors, and it strongly reënforces the rhythm of color-forms which unifies the total organization. Wherever the eye rests, the canvas is of compelling interest because of the organic fusion of the plastic means.

VAN GOGH

Landscape (202). The design consists of a dramatic contrast between a relatively uniform background of sky and an accentuated pattern of bright vivid color-patches in the foreground; and this drama is intensified by the active movement of broad swirling outlines and brush strokes. Picturesqueness is attained by a contrast of directions: the distorted, diagonally placed houses; the curvilinear upright figure; the foreground bushes arranged in a wavering, horizontal-oblique, linear sequence.

Postman (203).[50] The figure is a series of bright reds, yellows, greens, and blues, making in themselves an interesting color-form. The background consists of a wall paper of pink flowers drawn with the impressionistic brushwork on a background of green, almost monochrome but varied somewhat by the use of light. Distortions in the features are increased by the use of obviously unnatural color-effects. Here again the keynote of the design is contrast—of color, line, pattern, direction, brushwork—in both the figure and the background. The composition is unified chiefly by a rhythmic repetition in the facial features, of the decorative motifs in the background. The general effect is close to that of Japanese prints.

MAURICE PRENDERGAST

Landscape (237) represents Prendergast's personal technique made instrumental to a form of high esthetic content. Spots of light and color function as linear and color elements that enter into harmonious relationships and produce active and appealing rhythms of color and line. The method varies in different parts of the canvas but contributes everywhere to the drawing, to the pattern, and to the general liveliness of the form. In the water in the foreground, for instance, short dabs of color and light, close to boats and figures, function rhythmically with the long vertical and horizontal masses of comparatively uniform color used in the drawing of the main objects. The banks in the middleground are depicted by contrasting horizontal broad bands and wavy strokes of color which undulate across the entire canvas. These masses of color, tending in a generally horizontal direction, are relieved by numerous vertical masses—figures, houses, trees—which contrast in color and direction with the horizontality of the general compositional framework. The entire canvas is a succession of contrasts of line, color, mass, and spatial relations, that produce a series of interlocking rhythms, crisply punctuated at clean-cut intervals. The effect is comparable to that of a Bach fugue: the horizontal lilac-pink river bank in the middleground at the right may be considered as a motif in the fugue; it is repeated

[50] Illustration, p. 296.

with modification in size and color in the various other parts of the landscape and in the bands of clouds; this lilac-pink band gradually changes in color by interspersions of ivory and green, and starts a new unit or motif in the fugue, which in turn is modified by line and color as it glides onward up to the multicolored group of houses at the left. Again, each constituent of this group is so varied from the others and so related to them that their ensemble takes on the character of a succession of rhythms which retains the same general fugue character as in the rest of the composition. In every part of the picture there is an infinite number of minor variations of color, light, line, mass, space, and general treatment, which correspond to the internal variations in contrapuntal music.

GLACKENS

Race Track (201) [51] is as perfect an example of a sun-lighted open-air scene as exists in the work of any of the great impressionists. The hot sunlight is felt as a background to the scene depicted, and the colors are glaring in both their intrinsic quality and their infusion with light. Not any of the objects is naturalistically rendered: no grass was ever so green as that grassplot, no clay was ever so reddish-yellow, no sky was ever of that quality of blue, no roofs were ever so iridescent. Here Glackens uses color creatively: it has an individual sensuous quality, and is the means of organizing the canvas in a color-form totally different from that to be found in any other painter. Individual colors are more reminiscent of Matisse than they are of any of the impressionists, yet their quality and manner of combination are radically different from Matisse's. The drawing is broad and free; it is made up of a successful merging of line, light, and color, and portrays the essential quality of objects at rest and in movement. The painting conveys the very spirit of a race track on a summer day, with the myriads of subtle feelings that charge the event with its intrinsic quality.

MATISSE

Green Dress (219). The picturesque effect of this ensemble is due principally to spatial distribution of color-components and treatment of surfaces. Large areas of green, red, gray, and small units of vivid black are set against each other in a most unconventional pattern of color-contrasts; one tone of green, for instance, against another tone of green, a rose red against a salmon red. Some of these areas are decorated with stripes, others with floral motifs, with curvilinear pattern, or with irregular dabs of the brush. The areas all differ in shape, yet collectively they unite in a bizarre and picturesque pattern. While all of them are basically color-areas, they are also compositional objects; as such, that is as masses and planes, their arrangement in space is equally bizarre, and gives a picturesque character to the entire

[51] Illustration, p. 331.

composition. For example, the rising perspective of the floor, couch, and foot-rest is a distortion that transforms these naturally horizontal objects into oblique planes and masses that counterbalance the vertical planes of figure and background, and form with these an aggregate of odd angular relationships. The two main planes which bring the composition into balance consist of the large salmon-red area of the screenlike background and the still larger area of the green floor. The latter is an oblique-horizontal plane of mottled surface and general triangular shape, and the background a rather smoothly painted horizontal oblong placed vertically in space: the two are thus sharply contrasted to each other in color, position, shape, and surface-quality.

A large part of the distinctive character of the picture is due to the exotic textural quality of the various objects. Color throughout is solid and luminous, and the pigment is applied thickly over what seems to be another layer of paint. However, in each area a different combination between the color, the light, the quality of the pigment, and the brushwork yields various effects of exotic solidity. The floor, for example, seems to be made of the material of ceramics; the red pillow or foot-rest, of painted metal; the face and bust, of heavy china; the green dress, of lacquered wood with flowers applied in gesso on its surface; the gray sleeve is like a transparent stone and its folds seem wired; the salmon-red background resembles wood or hard cardboard; the curtain on the right stands up like a piece of solid wall or a column; the couch shares this general porcelain feeling which reaches its maximum in the tilelike surface of the patterned wall paper in the upper left background.

This play upon the unrealistic structural quality of objects reënforces the dramatic contrasts between the colors, and greatly emphasizes the unconventional picturesque positions of the areas in relation to each other. The contrast between the floor and the foot-rest is not only one of green against red, and of a large irregular plane with a small hexagonal volume, it is also a contrast between the solidity of the green plane, as of porcelain, and the red volume, as of steel. Hardness and solidity of some sort pervade all the color-units and thus contribute to their plastic integration. In this picture Matisse thus realizes not only a unified set of dramatic contrasts of color and a bizarre arrangement of compositional objects, but also a series of transferred values relating mainly to metal and tile.

PICASSO

Girl with Cigarette (233) [52] represents Picasso at his best. It shows a creative use of the contributions of El Greco, Daumier, Manet, and Cézanne, to achieve a design through the medium of distortions which contribute actively to composition and to distinctive expressive form. All the constituents of the subject-matter depart from the normal in color, shape, and relative

[52] Illustration, p. 475.

Pascin (229)   Analysis, page 478

Fragonard (319)   Analysis, page 460

This painting is similar in point of design to the painting on the opposite page.

Picasso (233)   Analysis, page **472**

Picasso (235)   Analysis, page 477

size and position, and are organized as members of a patterned color-design of flattened volumes. The keynote is the bizarre effect resulting from the conjoined activities of the accentuated angular pattern of broad color-areas, the decentered placing of the main masses, the contrasts of the dominating blues with the reddish-orange, the pasty-white and the whitish-green areas, and the quasi-grotesque simplified drawing of the figure. Moreover, the effects of contrast, distortion, and of the bizarre, work hand in hand in all parts of the picture, and embody the expression of the human values of ghastliness, weirdness, the drama and pathos of the subject-matter, in a form individual to Picasso.

The large focus of lurid light on the pasty-white face, the slight greenish shadows, and the various daubs of red in the modeling and drawing of the facial features, together with the surface-pattern of the brushwork in the flesh, represent a very personal creation based upon characteristics of El Greco, Manet, and Cézanne. The hair, a mixture of reddish orange, yellow, green, and brown, emphasizes the whiteness of the flesh; it also helps balance the color-scheme and stabilizes the upward right-to-left swing of the figure. The head as a whole serves as an intermediary compositional unit between the square framework of the arms-and-torso and the square deep-blue area at the upper right in the background.

The drawing of the torso, arms, and hands, with broad outline of dark color, makes up an accentuated pattern of angular areas and volumes which is echoed in the areas of the background and contributes an appealing, naïve, bizarre effect of rigidity to the ensemble. The interlocking rhythm of the arms and hands acquires forcefulness and added distinction from the accentuated space-composition of radiating volumes, which it creates in the foreground. In both the background and the figure, the component parts are varied in tone—if not in color—in size, shape, and direction, and also in the manner of application of the paint. These two entities—setting and figure—are unified in themselves, and also enter into compositional relationships with each other to achieve a strong, well-balanced, and strikingly original plastic form.

In **Still Life** (235),[53] the individual parts of various objects have been separated from their normal relationships to the extent that it is impossible to say definitely what the objects are, but there is sufficient indication to enable one to select some of these apparently meaningless and disparate parts and relate them to one's experience with the real world. Picasso, by an imaginative rearrangement of the individual parts of the objects in a series of new and non-naturalistic interrelations, has created a novel and unified form which carries its own powerful esthetic appeal independent of the representative values of the objects as they are known to us. In other words, the sense of bewilderment and strangeness is supplanted by a new experience which is primarily and authentically esthetic: the parts of the objects, disorganized as such, have been re-organized as units of color, light, space, line,

[53] Illustration, p. 476.

and mass, to emerge as a new form which has the attributes of a work of art, namely, unity, variety, and individuality. The characteristics of the form arise from Picasso's use of line, light, color, mass, and space in such a way that their interaction creates a movement of contrasting compact color-planes which takes place in two- and three-dimensional space as a series of well-related contrasting rhythms integrated as a plastic entity. The lack of appreciation of this painting by any one who supposes himself to understand the work of Titian, Velásquez, Cézanne, and Renoir, is proof that what the person in question likes in the paintings of these great artists is not the art-value, but something else. As a matter of fact, the quality in their work that entitles it to be considered as art is precisely that which gives esthetic value to this cubist painting by Picasso; that is, the interrelationships assumed by line, light, color, mass, and space create a unified and distinctive plastic form embodying the meanings of a real and personal experience. This is not to say that this painting by Picasso is as great a work of art as a picture by Titian, Renoir, or Cézanne, for Picasso is a lesser artist than any of these; it means merely that Picasso has constructed a form which has a positive esthetic value of its own.

PASCIN

Seated Figure (229) [54] is reminiscent of both Renoir and Cézanne. The fluid, delicate, and pastel quality of the color has its parallel in some of Renoir's works, as has also the drawing of the arms, legs, and chest of the figure. The drawing and modeling of the face is much in the manner of Cézanne, and the color-areas in the back part of the canvas are Pascin's own adaptation of Renoir's and Cézanne's methods of obtaining the movement of masses in deep space. The basket and fruit might pass as a sketch by Cézanne. The whole painting has the light, delicate, fluid rhythm of Renoir, with an admixture of Cézanne's influence as above noted. Here, as always with Pascin, the modeling is only suggestive of three-dimensional solidity, but this is not a drawback, because this type of modeling fits in with Pascin's general lightness and delicacy.

Standing Nude (230). The particular use of color, light, line, and space, which gives the nude its identity as a plastic form, is rhythmically repeated in the adjoining table, the wall at the back, the bureau at the right, and in all of the objects upon the table and bureau. The units are similar only as plastic forms of the same general feeling, but differ in all of their constituent elements. Pascin's capacity to diversify these units by varied adaptations of their plastic factors shows great ingenuity and originality.

[54] Illustration, p. 473.

CATALOGUE DATA*

The following list contains the locations, names, and page references of the paintings, sculpture, etc., mentioned or illustrated in this book; the number to the left of each title corresponds to the reference number placed in the text after each name of picture, sculpture, etc. Footnotes are designated by an n after the page-reference number. The dates and attributions are those accepted or given by the author. For the purpose of identification, the museums' attributions, dates, and catalogue numbers are recorded in parentheses, and the titles are given both in English and in the language of the country in which the works of art are to be seen.

AIX-EN-PROVENCE

Musée Granet

FRENCH MASTER, fifteenth century.
    1. Salome. (187—Salomé présentant à Hérode la tête de St.-Jean-Baptiste—Inconnu, Ecole française.) Pages 232 n., 245. Analysis, page 457.

AMSTERDAM

Rijksmuseum

BERCKHEYDE, 1638–1698.
    2. Flower Market. (483—De bloemmarkt.) Page 229.
HOBBEMA, 1638–1709.
    3. Water Mill. (1188—Watermolen.) Pages 217, 219.
RUISDAEL, JACOB VAN, c.1628–1682.
    4. Landscape with Water Mill. (2077—Landschap met watermolen.) Page 219.
RUYSDAEL, SALOMON VAN, c.1600–1670.
    5. Halt. (2083—Pleisterplaats.) Pages 217, 218. Illustration, page 222.
VERMEER, JAN, 1632–1675.
    6. Cook. (2528A—De keukenmeid.) Page 227.
    7. Girl Reading Letter. (2527—Het lezende vrouwtje.) Page 227.
    8. Letter. (2528—De brief.) Page 227.
    9. Little Street. (2528B—Het straatje.) Pages 214, 217, 227, 228.

* The inclusion of page references converts this catalogue into a supplementary index.

APPENDIX

ANTWERP

Musée Royal des Beaux-Arts

CLOUET, JEAN, 1485–1540.
   10. François, the Dauphin. (33.) Page 248 n.

AREZZO

San Francesco, Chiesa di

PIERO DELLA FRANCESCA, c.1416–1492.
   11. Discovery of the True Cross (fresco). (L'invenzione e verificazione della Santa Croce.) Analysis, page 398. Illustration, page 132.
   12. Exaltation of the Cross (fresco). (L'esaltazione della Santa Croce.) Page 127. Analysis, page 398.
   13. Reception by Solomon (fresco). (L'incontro della Regina Saba con Salomone.) Analysis, page 399.
   14. Victory over Maxentius (fresco). (Fuga e sommersione di Massenzio.) Analysis, page 400.

PIERO DELLA FRANCESCA, SCHOOL OF.
   15. Marriage of St. Catherine (fresco). (Sposalizio di S. Caterina— Scuola di Piero della Francesca.) Page 369. Analysis, page 405. Illustration, page 22.

ASSISI

San Francesco, Chiesa Inferiore di

CIMABUE, c.1240 – c.1301.
   16. Virgin Enthroned (fresco). (La Vergine col Figlio.) Page 112.

GIOTTO, 1266–1337.
   17. Flight into Egypt (fresco). (La fuga in Egitto.) Page 392.

San Francesco, Chiesa Superiore di

GIOTTO, 1266–1337
   18. Frescoes. (Affreschi.) Pages 62, 113. Analyses, page 389 *et seq.*
   19. Miraculous Production of a Spring of Water (fresco). (S. Francesco fa scaturire l'acqua da una rupe.) Analysis, page 390.
   20. Saint Francis Blessing the Birds (fresco). (S. Francesco benedice gli uccelli.) Analysis, page 391. Illustration, page 120.
   21. Saint Francis Clothing the Poor (fresco). (S. Francesco dona ad un ricco caduto in povertà la propria veste.) Analysis, page 391.
   22. Saint Francis Restores His Apparel to His Father (fresco). (S. Francesco rinunzia ai suoi averi.) Page 399 n. Analysis, page 390.
   23. Saint Francis, Supporting the Lateran, Appears to Pope Innocent III (fresco). (S. Francesco veduto in sogno dal pontefice Innocenzo III.) Page 399 n. Analysis, page 390.

CATALOGUE DATA

AVIGNON

Musée Calvet (Bibliothèque)

ILLUMINATED MANUSCRIPT, end of thirteenth century.
24. Roman Breviary. (MS. 121—Breviarum Romanum.) Page 238.

Palais des Papes (Chambre de la Garde-Robe)

FRENCH SCHOOL, c.1344.
25. Frescoes. (Fresques.) Page 236.

BAD WILDUNGEN

Stadtkirche

SOEST, KONRAD von, active c.1404.
26. Altarpiece of Crucifixion. (Kreuzigungsaltar.) Pages 188, 188 n.

BASEL

Kunsthalle

HOLBEIN, HANS, the Younger, 1497–1543.
27. Erasmus. (319.) Page 198.

BERLIN

Kaiser-Friedrich-Museum

BROUWER, ADRIAEN, c.1605–1638.
28. Halt. (853H—Der Hirt am Wege.) Page 218.
COLOGNE MASTER OF " LIFE OF MARY," active 1460–1480.
    29. Madonna and Child, Three Saints and Donor's Family. (1235—
    Maria mit Kind, drei Heiligen und Stifterfamilie—Meister des
    Marienlebens.) Page 439.
DÜRER, 1471–1528.
    30. Girl's Portrait. (557 I—Bildnis eines jungen Mädchens.) Page 194.
    31. Head of Woman. (557G—Bildnis einer junger Frau.) Page 195.
    32. Hieronymus Holzshuher. (557E—Bildnis des Hieronymus Holz-
    shuher.) Page 443.
    33. Jacob Muffel. (557D—Bildnis des Jacob Muffel.) Page 443.
    34. Madonna. (557H—Betende Maria.) Page 194.
EYCK, JAN van, c.1385–1441.
    35. Crucifixion. (525F—Christus am Kreuz.) Pages 25, 205, 443. Illus-
    tration, page 202.
    36. Man with a Pink. (525A—Der Mann mit den Nelken.) Page 442.
FRENCH MASTER, active c.1400 or 1410.
    37. Crowning of Mary. (1648—Krönung Mariä—Französische Schule
    um 1410.) Page 231.
HOLBEIN, HANS, the Younger, 1497–1543.
    38. Merchant Georg Gisze. (586—Bildnis des Kaufmanns Georg
    Gisze.) Analysis, page 443.

APPENDIX

LEYDEN, LUCAS van, 1494–1533.
    39. Saint Jerome. (584A—Der hl. Hieronymus in Bussübung.) Analysis, page 450.

MARMION, SIMON, active c.1450.
    40. Legend of St. Bertin. (1645 and 1645A—Die Flügel des Altars von St. Omer: Das Leben des Benediktiners St. Bertin.) Pages 232 n., 245.

MIDDLE-RHINE MASTER, active c.1420.
    41. Madonna and Child, with Female Saints. (1920—Maria mit Kind und Heiligen—Mittelrheinischer Meister.) Pages 175, 187, 439.

RUBENS, 1577–1640.
    42. Andromeda. (776C.) Page 466 n.

STRIGEL, BERNHARD, 1461–1528.
    43. Saint Norbert as Protector. (583A—Der hl. Norbert als Schutzheiliger eines Ordensbruders.) Page 192 n.

TITIAN, c.1477–1576.
    44. Venus and Organ Player. (1849—Venus und der Orgelspieler.) Page 464 n.

VERMEER, JAN, 1632–1675.
    45. Girl with a Pearl Necklace. (912B—Die junge Dame mit dem Perlenhalsband.) Page 227.

WITZ, KONRAD, c.1398–1447.
    46. Christ on the Cross. (1656—Christus am Kreuz.) Page 191.

BONSON

Chapelle St.-Jean-Baptiste

FRENCH MASTER, active c.1517.
    47. Altarpiece of St. John. (Retable de St.-Jean-Baptiste—Ecole niçoise.) Page 233.

BRUGES

Couvent des Sœurs Noires

BRUGES MASTER OF "LEGEND OF ST. URSULA," active c.1465.
    48. Legend of St. Ursula. (La Légende de Ste.-Ursule—Maître inconnu de Bruges.) Page 188.

Musée de l'Hôpital St.-Jean

MEMLING, c.1430–1494.
    49. Scenes from the Legend of St. Ursula. (Scènes de la vie de Ste.-Ursule.) Page 188.

CASTELFRANCO

Duomo

GIORGIONE, 1477–1510.
    50. Madonna with St. Francis and St. Liberal. (Madonna con S. Francesco e S. Liberale.) Pages 103, 147. Analysis, page 420.

CATALOGUE DATA

CHANTILLY

Musée Condé

LIMBOURG, POL DE, and BROTHERS, active before 1416.
   51. Book of Hours of the Duc de Berry. (Très Riches Heures du Duc de Berry.) Page 236.

RHENISH MASTER, active 1170–1200.
   52. Ingeburge Psalter. (MS. 1695—Psautier d'Ingeburge.) Pages 175, 176, 178, 457.

CIMIEZ

Eglise

BREA, LOUIS, active end of fifteenth and beginning of sixteenth century.
   53. Pietà. (La Vierge de Pitié.) Pages 233, 238, 246.

COLMAR

Eglise St.-Martin

SCHONGAUER, MARTIN, 1445–1491.
   54. Madonna in the Garden of Roses. (La Madonne dans le jardin de roses.) Pages 192, 439.

Musée

GRÜNEWALD, MATHIAS, active c.1485 – c.1530.
   55. Crucifixion (Isenheim Altarpiece). (Christ en Croix—Retable d'Isenheim.) Pages 25, 193. Analysis, page 440. Illustration, page 416.
   56. Entombment (Isenheim Altarpiece). (Mise au Tombeau—Retable d'Isenheim.) Page 193. Illustration, page 416.

SCHONGAUER, MARTIN, 1445–1491.
   57. Christ's Passion. (La Passion.) Page 187.

COLOGNE

Wallraf-Richartz-Museum

COLOGNE MASTER, beginning or middle of fourteenth century.
   58. Crucifixion and Four Scenes from the Life of Christ. (1—Triptychon: Kreuzigung—Kölner Maler vom Anfang des 14. Jahrhunderts.) Page 176 n. Analysis, page 437. Illustration, page 182.

COLOGNE MASTER, active c.1340.
   59. Annunciation. (4—Verkündigung—Kölner Maler der ersten Hälfte des 14. Jahrhunderts.) Page 176 n.
   60. Presentation. (5—Darstellung im Tempel—Kölner Maler der ersten Hälfte des 14. Jahrhunderts.) Page 176 n.

APPENDIX

COLOGNE MASTER OF "LIFE OF MARY," active 1460–1480.
  61. Crucifixion. (125—Christus am Kreuz, mit Maria, Johannes und Magdalena—Meister des Marienlebens.) Page 186. Analysis, page 439.
  62. Saint Barbara, with Donor and Seven Daughters. (127—St. Barbara mit der Stifterin und sieben Töchtern—Meister des Marienlebens.) Page 187.
  63. Saint Katherine, with Donor and Eight Sons. (126—St. Katharina mit dem Stifter und acht Söhnen—Meister des Marienlebens.) Page 187.

COLOGNE MASTER OF "LIFE OF MARY," active 1460–1480, Attributed to.
  64. Lyversberg Passion. (143 to 150, inc.—Leidensgeschichte Christi—dem Meister des Marienlebens zugeschrieben.) Pages 186, 187.

COLOGNE MASTER OF "SAINT VERONICA," active c.1400–1420, Attributed to.
  65. Madonna with Pea-Blossom. (10—Die Muttergottes mit der Wickenblüte—Unbekannter Meister des 15. Jahrhunderts.) Page 185.
  66. Six Scenes from Christ's Passion. (38, 39, 40—Altarflügel mit sechs Passionsszenen auf drei Tafeln—Der Kölner Passionsmeister; auch dem Meister der hl. Veronika zugeschrieben.) Analysis, page 437.

LOCHNER, STEFAN, c.1400 – c.1451.
  67. Last Judgment. (66—Das Weltgericht.) Pages 186, 441. Analysis, page 438.
  68. Madonna in Paradise Garden. (70—Die Muttergottes im Paradiesgarten.) Pages 439, 439 n.
  69. Madonna in the Garden of Roses. (67—Die Muttergottes in der Rosenlaube.) Analysis, page 438. Illustration, page 181.

LOWER-SAXONY MASTER, active c.1360 – c.1380.
  70. Altarpiece—Life of Jesus—from the Cologne Laurenziuskirche. (Laurenziuskirche Lebenjesu—Niedersächsischer Meister.) Pages 180, 185.

MASTER WILHELM, active c.1370, Attributed to.
  71. Kaiser Karl IV, and Heads of Prophets (wall paintings). (Vier Köpfe von Prophetenfiguren und die Figur des Kaisers Karl IV—Dem Meister Wilhelm zugeschrieben.) Analysis, page 436.

DARMSTADT

Museum

MIDDLE-RHINE MASTER, active c.1420–1430.
  72. Mary with Female Saints—center panel from the Altarpiece of Ortenberg. (167—Maria im Kreise weiblicher Heiliger—Mitteltafel des Altars aus Ortenberg—Mittelrheinischer Meister.) Pages 187, 439.

[484]

CATALOGUE DATA

DRESDEN
Staatliche Gemälde-Galerie

GIORGIONE, 1477–1510.
  73. Sleeping Venus. (185—Schlummernde Venus.)   Pages 146, 433.

FLORENCE
Bargello, Museo del

FRENCH MASTER, fourteenth century.
  74. Calvary—right shutter of diptych. (Il Calvario—Scuola dell'Ile-de-France.) Page 232.
  75. Madonna in Garden—left shutter of diptych. (La Madonna e Santi nel Giardino—Scuola dell'Ile-de-France.) Pages 187, 232, 439 n.

FRENCH MASTER, second half of fourteenth century.
  76. Adoration—Crucifixion—diptych. (Adorazione—Crocefissione, Scuola francese.) Page 232.

Cenacolo di S. Apollonia

CASTAGNO, ANDREA DEL, c.1410–1457.
  77. Last Supper (fresco). (La Cena.) Page 123. Illustration, page 21.
  78. Pietà (fresco). Page 123.

CASTAGNO, ANDREA DEL, SCHOOL OF.
  79. Saint Eustachius (fresco). Page 123. Illustration, page 129.

Pitti, Galleria dei

RAPHAEL, 1483–1520.
  80. Woman with Veil. (Donna velata.) Page 88. Analysis, page 408.

San Marco (Ospizio)

ANGELICO, FRA, 1387–1455.
  81. Deposition. (Deposizione.) Analysis, page 394.

San Marco (Sala del Capitolo)

ANGELICO, FRA, 1387–1455.
  82. Mystical Crucifixion. (Crocefissione.) Page 25. Analysis, page 394.

Santa Maria del Carmine, Chiesa di
(Cappella Brancacci)

MASACCIO, 1401–1428.
  83. Adam and Eve Expelled from Paradise (fresco). (Adamo ed Eva.) Page 116. Illustration, page 414.
  84. Frescoes. (Affreschi.) Analyses, page 395 *et seq.*
  85. Saint Peter Healing the Sick (fresco). (S. Pietro con la sua ombra risana gl'infermi.) Page 116. Analysis, page 395.

APPENDIX

86. Saint Peter Raising Tabitha (fresco). (S. Pietro resuscita Tabíta e risana uno storpio.) Analysis, page 396.

87. Tribute Money (fresco). (Gesù comanda a S. Pietro di prendere in bocca al pesce la moneta per pagare il tributo.) Analysis, page 396. Illustration, page 118.

Santa Maria Novella, Chiesa di

GHIRLANDAIO, DOMENICO DEL, 1449–1494.

88. Scenes from the Life of the Virgin and from That of John the Baptist (frescoes). (Storie della vita della Vergine e della vita di S. Giovanni Battista.) Analysis, page 411.

Uffizi

BELLINI, GIOVANNI, c.1428–1516.

89. Allegory of Purgatory. (631—Allegoria Sacra.) Pages 65, 145, 422. Analysis, page 418. Illustration, page 80.

BOTTICELLI, 1444–1510.

90. Allegory of Spring. (8360—Allegoria della Primavera.) Pages 17, 128. Analysis, page 405. Illustration, page 161.

91. Birth of Venus. (878—Nascita di Venere.) Pages 17, 92, 128. Analysis, page 406.

CIMABUE, c.1240 – c.1301.

92. Virgin Enthroned. (La Vergine col Figlio.) Pages 112, 113.

CLOUET, JEAN, 1485–1540.

93. François I, on Horseback. (Ritratto equestre di Francesco I.) Page 248 n.

DÜRER, 1471–1528.

94. Adoration of the Magi. (Adorazione dei Magi.) Page 194.

GIOTTO, 1266–1337.

95. Madonna Enthroned. (8344—La Vergine in trono col Bambino.) Page 113.

LEONARDO DA VINCI, 1452–1519.

96. Adoration of the Magi (sketch). (Adorazione dei Magi.) Page 133.

97. Annunciation. (L'Annunciazione.) Page 133.

LIPPI, FRA FILIPPO, c.1406–1469.

98. Virgin Adoring the Child. (8353—La Vergine che adora il Figlio.) Pages 62, 106, 124. Illustration, page 130.

LORENZETTI, PIETRO, active 1305–1348.

99. Scenes from the Life of St. Umiltà. (Santa Umiltà di Faenza, e storie relative alla medesima.) Analysis, page 393.

MEMLING, c.1430–1494.

100. Saint Benedict. (San Benedetto.) Analysis, page 450.

MONACO, LORENZO, c.1370 – c.1425.

101. Virgin and Child, with Four Saints. (468—La Madonna col Bambino e Santi.) Analysis, page 393.

POLLAIUOLO, ANTONIO, 1432–1498.
102. Hercules Crushing Antaeus. (Ercole che soffoca Anteo.) Analysis, page 410. Illustration, page 403.
103. Hercules Overcoming the Hydra. (Ercole che abbatte l'idra.) Analysis, 410. Illustration, page 403.
REMBRANDT, 1606–1669.
104. Old Man. (Ritratto di un vecchio.) Pages 69, 226.
TITIAN, c.1477–1576.
105. Venus with Dog. (Venere del cagnolino.) Page 464 n.
VENEZIANO, DOMENICO, active 1438–1461.
106. Madonna and Child, with Saints. (884—La Vergine col Bambino e varî Santi.) Analysis, page 397.
VERROCCHIO, ANDREA, 1435–1488.
107. Baptism of Christ, with Two Angels. (Il Battesimo di Gesù Cristo.) Analysis, page 407.

FRANKFURT
Städelsches Kunstinstitut
MIDDLE-RHINE MASTER, active c.1340.
108. Altenberg Altarpiece. (S.G. 358 to 361, inc.—Altenberger Altar—Mittelrheinischer Meister.) Page 176 n.
UPPER- or MIDDLE-RHINE MASTER, active c.1410.
109. Garden of Paradise. (H.M. 54—Das Paradiesgärtlein—Mittelrheinischer Meister.) Pages 175, 187, 439. Illustration, page 401.

GREOLIERES
Eglise paroissiale
FRENCH MASTER, fifteenth century.
110. Altarpiece of St. Etienne. (Retable de St.-Etienne—Ecole niçoise.) Pages 233, 234, 238, 246. Analysis, page 458. Illustration, page 242.

HAGUE, THE
Mauritshuis
VERMEER, JAN, 1632–1675.
111. Diana at the Bath. (406—Diana en haar Nymfen.) Page 228.
112. Girl with Turban. (670—Meisjeskopje.) Page 208.
113. View of Delft. (92—Gezicht op Delft van de zijde de Rotterdamsche vaart.) Pages 227, 228. Analysis, page 452. Illustration, page 221.

HAMBURG
Kunsthalle
MASTER FRANCKE, active c.1424.
114. Adoration of the Kings. (493—Anbetung der Könige—Meister Francke.) Page 190 n.
115. Bearing of the Cross. (495—Kreuztragung—Meister Francke.) Page 190 n.

116. **Birth of Christ.** (492—Geburt Christi—Meister Francke.) Page 190 n.
117. **Christ, Man of Sorrows.** (499—Christus als Schmerzensmann—Meister Francke.) Page 190 n.
118. **Entombment.** (497—Grablegung Christi—Meister Francke.) Page 190 n.
119. **Flagellation of Christ.** (494—Geisselung Christi—Meister Francke.) Page 190 n.
120. **Flight of St. Thomas of Canterbury.** (490—Flucht des hl. Thomas von Canterbury—Meister Francke.) Page 190 n. Illustration, page 183.
121. **Martyrdom of St. Thomas of Canterbury.** (491—Martertod des hl. Thomas von Canterbury—Meister Francke.) Page 190 n.
122. **Resurrection.** (498—Auferstehung Christi—Meister Francke.) Page 190 n.
123. **Women of the Crucifixion.** (496—Frauengruppe der Kreuzigung—Meister Francke.) Page 190 n.

HANNOVER

Provinzialmuseum

LOWER-SAXONY MASTER, end of thirteenth century.
124. **Antependium from the Cloister of Wennigsen a. Deister.** (Antependium aus Kloster Wennigsen a. Deister—Niedersächsischer Meister.) Page 180.
LOWER-SAXONY MASTER, beginning of fifteenth century.
125. **Golden Panels, from Lüneburg.** (Goldene Tafel von Lüneburg—Niedersächsischer Meister.) Page 188 n.
WESTPHALIAN MASTER, active c.1400.
126. **Marienkirche Altarpiece from Göttingen.** (Marienkirche Altar von Göttingen—Westfälischer Meister.) Page 188 n.

LONDON

National Gallery

BELLINI, GIOVANNI, c.1428–1516.
127. **Doge Leonardo Loredano.** (189.) Page 407 n.
BOUTS, DIRK, c.1400–1475.
128. **Entombment.** (664.) Page 208.
CHRISTUS, PETRUS, c.1410 – c.1473.
129. **Edward Grimston.** (Lent by the Earl of Verulam.) Analysis, page 449.
130. **Marco Barbarigo.** (696.) Page 206.
CONSTABLE, JOHN, 1776–1837.
131. **Flatford Mill.** (1273.) Analysis, page 463.
132. **Hay-Wain.** (1207.) Page 285. Analysis, page 463.
133. **Salisbury Cathedral.** (1814.) Analysis, page 463. Illustration, page 282.

CATALOGUE DATA

EYCK, JAN VAN, c.1385–1441.
    134. Jan Arnolfini and Jeanne de Chenany, his Wife. (186.) Analysis, page 443. Illustration, page 445.
    135. Man's Portrait. (290.) Pages 200, 206.

FRAGONARD, 1732–1806.
    136. Happy Mother. (2620.) Page 260.

FRANCO-GERMAN MASTER, active first half of fifteenth century.
    137. Holy Trinity. (3662—German school c.1410.) Page 232.

HOLBEIN, HANS, the Younger, 1497–1543.
    138. Ambassadors. (1314.) Page 198.

HOOCH, PIETER DE, 1629–c.1683.
    139. Court of a Dutch House. (835.) Page 228.

LANCRET, NICOLAS, 1690–1743.
    140. Manhood. (103.) Page 257.

LEONARDO DA VINCI, 1452–1519.
    141. Virgin of the Rocks. (1093.) Pages 83, 133.

LEYDEN, LUCAS VAN, 1494–1533.
    142. Man's Portrait. (3604.) Page 213.

MANTEGNA, ANDREA, 1431–1506.
    143. Agony in the Garden. (1417.) Page 88.

MEMLING, c.1430–1494.
    144. Duke of Cleves. (2594.) Page 209.

ORCAGNA, ANDREA, c.1308–1368.
    145. Coronation of the Virgin. (569.) Analysis, page 393.

PIERO DELLA FRANCESCA, c.1416–1492.
    146. Baptism of Christ. (665.) Analysis, page 400.
    147. Nativity of Our Lord, with Angels Adoring. (908.) Analysis, page 400.

PISANELLO or PISANO, c.1397–1455.
    148. Vision of St. Eustace. (1436.) Analysis, page 393.

POUSSIN, NICOLAS, 1594–1665.
    149. Cephalus and Aurora. (65.) Analysis, page 434.

REMBRANDT, 1606–1669.
    149A. Woman Bathing. (54.) Analysis, page 452.

RUBENS, 1577–1640.
    150. Autumn, Château de Steen. (66.) Page 279. Analysis, page 433.
    151. Judgment of Paris. (194.) Pages 280, 298. Analysis, page 433. Illustration, page 97.
    152. Landscape with Shepherd. (2924.) Page 463.
    153. Peace and War. (46.) Analysis, page 433

TINTORETTO, 1518–1594.
    154. Origin of the Milky Way. (1313.) Illustration, page 78.

TITIAN, c.1477–1576.
    155. Bacchus and Ariadne. (35.) Analysis, page 422.

APPENDIX

156. Christ and the Magdalen. (270.) Page 147. Analysis, page 423.
TURNER, 1775–1851.
    157. Calais Pier. (472.) Analysis, page 463.
    158. Dido Building Carthage. (498.) Page 108. Analysis, page 464.
UCCELLO, 1397–1475.
    159. Rout of San Romano. (1432.) Pages 104, 122. Illustration, page 119.
WATTEAU, 1684–1721.
    160. Game of Love. (2897.) Page 252 n. Analysis, page 459. Illustration, page 253.

Wallace Collection

BOUCHER, 1703–1770.
    161. Rape of Europa. (484.) Page 259 n.
FRAGONARD, 1732–1806.
    162. Gardens of the Villa d'Este, Tivoli. (379.) Page 261 n.
    163. Schoolmistress. (404.) Page 260.
    164. Souvenir. (382.) Page 261 n.
HALS, FRANS, c.1580–1666.
    165. Laughing Cavalier. (84.) Page 271.
HUYSUM, JAN van, 1682–1749.
    166. Fruit and Flowers. (207.) Page 259 n.
PATER, 1696–1736.
    167. Camp Scene. (452.) Page 258 n.
REMBRANDT, 1606–1669.
    168. Unmerciful Servant. (86.) Pages 69, 105, 226. Analysis, page 450.
VELÁSQUEZ, 1599–1660.
    169. Don Baltasar Carlos in the Riding School. (6.) Analysis, page 434.
    170. Lady with a Fan. (88.) Analysis, page 435.

MADRID
Prado

GOYA, 1746–1828.
    171. Royal Family of Charles IV. (726—La Familla de Carlos IV.) Analysis, page 436.
    172. Witches' Sabbath. (761—Aquelarre.) Page 170 n.
TITIAN, c.1477–1576.
    173. Venus and Love. (421—Venus recreándose con el Amor y la Música.) Page 464 n.
    174. Venus and Music. (420—Venus recreándose en la Música.) Page 464 n.

MERION
Barnes Foundation

CEZANNE, 1839–1906.
    175. Bathers. (906.) Illustration, page 332.
    175A. Men Bathing. (101.) Illustration, page 295.

176. Mount Ste. Victoire. (13.) Analysis, page 468. Illustration, page 404.

177. Nudes in Landscape. (934.) Page 323. Illustration, part of frontispiece (254).

178. Still-Life with Gray Jug. (94.) Illustration, page 77.

CHIRICO, GIORGIO DE, 1888–1978.

179. Alexandros. (960.) Illustration, page 381.

CLAUDE LE LORRAIN, 1600–1682.

180. Landscape. (78.) Illustration, page 281.

COROT, 1796–1875.

181. Landscape. (586.) Illustration, page 281.

182. Woman in Pink Blouse. (822.) Illustration, page 255.

DAUMIER, 1808–1879.

183. Water Carrier. (127.) Page 268. Illustration, page 415.

DEGAS, 1834–1917.

184. Race Horses. (572.) Illustration, page 312.

DELACROIX, 1798–1863.

185. Triumph of St. Michael. (32.) Illustration, page 295.

DEMUTH, CHARLES, 1883–1935.

186. Negro Dancing. (741.) Illustration, page 342.

EAKINS, THOMAS, 1844–1916.

187. Dr. Agnew. (341.) Page 338.

EGYPTIAN SCULPTURE, XVII Dynasty, 2000 B.C.

188. Figure. (A89.) Illustration, page 361.

FLEMISH MASTER, fifteenth century.

189. Crucifixion. (123.) Illustration, page 203.

FLEMISH MASTER, active c.1480.

190. Man's Portrait. (440.) Illustration, page 201.

FRENCH MASTER, fourteenth century.

191. Crucifixion. (82.) Illustration, page 241.

FRENCH MASTER, fifteenth century.

192. Birth of the Virgin. (863.) Page 232 n.

193. Mary Going to the Temple. (864.) Page 232 n.

FRENCH MASTER, fifteenth century.

194. Circumcision. (869.) Page 232 n.

FRENCH MASTER, active c.1400.

195. Scene in Temple. (797.) Illustration, page 241.

FRENCH MASTER, active c.1480.

196. Saint Roch. (418.) Page 232 n.

FRENCH MASTER, seventeenth century.

197. Flowerpiece. (555.) Page 259 n.

198. Flowerpiece. (556.) Page 259 n.

GAUGUIN, 1848–1903.

199. Landscape: Haere Pape. (109.) Illustration, page 329.

APPENDIX

GIORGIONE, 1477–1510.
    200. Two Prophets. (816.) Illustration, page 149.
GLACKENS, 1870–1938.
    201. Race Track. (138.) Analysis, page 471. Illustration, page 331.
GOGH, VINCENT VAN, 1853–1890.
    202. Landscape. (136.) Analysis, page 470.
    203. Postman. (37.) Analysis, page 470. Illustration, page 296.
GOYA, 1746–1828.
    204. Don Galos. (5.) Analysis, page 436. Illustration, page 276.
GOYEN, VAN, 1596–1656.
    205. Seascape. (843.) Illustration, page 223.
GRECO, EL, c.1541–1614.
    206. Annunciation. (117.) Illustration, page 24.
    207. Vision of St. Hyacinth. (876.) Illustration, page 58.
GREEK POTTERY, 500 B.C.
    208. Vase. (A57.) Illustration, page 57.
GREEK SCULPTURE, 500 B.C.
    209. Figure of a Man (bas-relief). (A86.) Illustration, page 294.
GREEK SCULPTURE, 300 B.C.
    210. Standing Figure (bronze). (A66.) Page 466 n.
HINDU–PERSIAN MINIATURE, sixteenth–seventeenth century.
    211. Interior with Figures. (755.) Illustration, page 362.
HINDU SCULPTURE, Kushan Empire, third–fourth century.
    212. Figure (high-relief). (A235.) Illustration, page 364.
HUBER, WOLF, c.1485–1553.
    213. Man's Portrait. (827.) Illustration, page 184.
HUGO, JEAN, 1894–1984.
    214. Audierne. (1140.) Illustration, page 384.
KANE, JOHN, 1860–1934.
    215. Farm. (947.) Illustration, page 284.
LEYDEN, LUCAS VAN, 1494–1533.
    216. Adoration of the Magi. (443.) Page 213. Illustration, page 204.
LONGHI, PIETRO, 1702–1785.
    217. Interior Scene. (858.) Illustration, page 255.
MANET, 1832–1883.
    218. Washerwoman. (957.) Illustration, page 293.
MATISSE, HENRI–, 1869–1954.
    219. Green Dress. (891.) Analysis, page 471.
    220. Joy of Life. (719.) Illustration, page 100.
    221. Music Lesson. (717.) Illustration, page 363.
    222. Reclining Nude. (199.) Illustration, page 364.
MODIGLIANI, 1884–1920.
    223. Girl in Sunday Clothes. (180.) Illustration, page 311.
    224. Red-Headed Woman. (206.) Page 377.

CATALOGUE DATA

MONET, 1840–1926.
  225. House Boat. (730.) Page 302. Analysis, page 465.
  226. Madame Monet Embroidering. (197.) Page 302. Analysis, page 466. Illustration, page 309.

NEGRO SCULPTURE, Bushongo-Baluba, sixteenth century.
  227. Figure. (A220.) Illustration, page 361.

PACINO DI BONAGUIDA, contemporary of Giotto.
  228. Saint Bartholomew. (833.) Illustration, page 413.

PASCIN, 1885–1930.
  229. Seated Figure. (229.) Analysis, page 478. Illustration, page 473.
  230. Standing Nude. (182.) Analysis, page 478.

PENNSYLVANIA DUTCH PAINTING ON VELVET, early nineteenth century.
  231. Still-Life with Bird. (1172.) Illustration, page 344.

PICASSO, 1881–1973
  232. Composition. (140.) Illustration, page 59.
  233. Girl with Cigarette. (318.) Page 369. Analysis, page 472. Illustration, page 475.
  234. Harlequins. (382.) Page 369. Illustration, page 23.
  235. Still-Life. (673.) Analysis, page 477. Illustration, page 476.

PRENDERGAST, MAURICE, 1862–1924.
  236. Idyl. (113.) Illustration, page 99.
  237. Landscape. (216.) Analysis, page 470.

RENOIR, 1841–1919.
  238. Bathers in Forest. (901.) Page 316.
  239. Bathing Group. (709.) Pages 62, 87, 462. Analysis, page 466. Illustration, page 163.
  240. Mademoiselle Jeanne Durand-Ruel. (950.) Illustration, page 310.
  241. Mount Ste. Victoire. (288.) Page 315.
  242. Noirmoutier. (163.) Illustration, page 283.

ROUSSEAU, *le douanier*, 1844–1910.
  243. People in Sunday Clothes. (570.) Illustration, page 284.
  244. Woman in Landscape. (260.) Illustration, page 131.

RUBENS, 1577–1640.
  245. Holy Family. (849.) Illustration, page 162.

SETTANNI, LUIGI, 1908–1984.
  246. Russian Ballet. (1152.) Illustration, page 343.

SEURAT, GEORGES, 1859–1891.
  247. Models. (811.) Page 303.
  248. Port of Honfleur. (942.) Page 303. Illustration, page 330.

SMYRNA SCULPTURE, fourth century, B.C.
  249. Grotesque Figure. (A93.) Illustration, page 382.

SOUTINE, 1894–1943.
  250. Seated Woman. (271.) Illustration, page 383.

TINTORETTO, 1518–1594.
  251. Woman of Samaria. (823.) Illustration, page 151.

APPENDIX

UTRILLO, 1883–1955.
   252. Church of St. Aignan, Chartres. Illustration, page 384.

VERONESE, PAOLO, 1528–1588.
   253. Baptism of Christ. (800.) Illustration, page 152.

WALL OF GALLERY, BARNES FOUNDATION.
   254. *Reading from top to bottom and from left to right:* **French Gothic wrought iron door-knocker,** thirteenth century; **Pennsylvania Dutch wrought iron hinges** (large pair), c.1750; CEZANNE—**Nudes in Landscape** (934); **Pennsylvania Dutch (Moravian) wrought iron hinges** (small pair), c.1770; **Pair of French keyhole escutcheons,** Louis XIII period; **French Gothic wrought iron motif,** thirteenth century; CHARDIN—**Still-Life** (530); COROT—**Mme. Lemaistre** (895); RENOIR—**Artist's Family** (819); COROT—**Woman in Pink Blouse** (822); FLEMISH MASTER, active c.1480—**Man's Portrait** (440); CEZANNE—**Distant View of Mt. Ste. Victoire** (300); GIORGIONE—**Two Prophets** (816); TINTORETTO—**Two Prophets** (807); RENOIR—**Pourville** (6). Illustration, frontispiece.

WESTPHALIAN MASTER, active c.1400.
   255. Healing of Lazarus. (853.) Illustration, page 448.

Mullen Collection

CHIRICO, GIORGIO DE, 1888–1978.
   256. Horses near a Lake. Illustration, page 402.

MUNICH

Alte Pinakothek

COLOGNE MASTER OF " LIFE OF MARY," active 1460–1480.
   257. Scenes from the Life of Mary. (H.G. 618 to H.G. 624, inc.—Marienaltar—Meister des Marienlebens.) Pages 186, 187.

COLOGNE MASTER OF " SAINT VERONICA," active c.1400–1420.
   258. Saint Veronica. (H.G. 664—Die hl. Veronika—Meister der hl. Veronika.) Page 185. Analysis, page 437.

DÜRER, 1471–1528.
   259. Apostles John and Peter. (545—Zwei Apostel: Johannes und Petrus.) Page 194.
   260. Apostles Paul and Mark. (540—Zwei Apostel: Paulus und Marcus.) Page 194.

LEONARDO DA VINCI, 1452–1519.
   261. Virgin and Child. (7779—Maria mit dem Kinde.) Page 408.

MEMLING, c.1430–1494.
   262. Seven Joys of Mary. (H.G. 668—Die sieben Freuden Mariae.) Page 209.

RAPHAEL, 1483–1520.
   263. Madonna, from the House of Tempi. (H.G. 796—Die Madonna Tempi.) Analysis, page 408.

STRIGEL, BERNHARD, 1461–1528.
264. Conrad Rehlingen and his Children. (H.G. 1065—Die Kinder des Conrad Rehlingen.) Page 187.
265. Sibylle von Freyberg. Page 192 n.

MÜNSTER

Landesmuseum der Provinz Westfalen

SOEST, KONRAD von, active c.1404.
266. Crowning of the Virgin. (Krönung Mariae.) Page 188 n.
267. Outpouring of the Holy Spirit. (Pfingsten.) Page 188 n.

NETZE

Luthernkirche

LOWER-SAXONY MASTER, active c.1360 – c.1380, Attributed to.
268. Altarpiece. Page 180 n.

NEW YORK CITY

Metropolitan Museum

BRUEGHEL, PIETER, the Elder, 1525–1569.
269. Harvesters. (B832–1.) Page 214.

CHRISTUS, PETRUS, c.1410 – c.1473.
270. Deposition from the Cross. (C861–1.) Page 206.

COURBET, 1819–1877.
271. Village Maidens. (C83–52.) Page 306.

DAVID, GERARD, c.1460–1523.
272. Crucifixion. (D28–1.) Page 211.

ISENBRANT, c.1485–1551.
273. Nativity. (Is2–2.) Page 212.

MANET, 1832–1883.
274. Boy with Sword. (M311–1.) Page 305.
275. Dead Christ with Angels. (M311–51.) Page 306.
276. Woman with Parrot. (M311–2.) Pages 306, 307, 337.

REMBRANDT, 1606–1669.
277. Old Woman Cutting her Nails. (R28–11.) Pages 42, 226.

RYDER, ALBERT P., 1847–1917.
278. Curfew Hour. (R97–1.) Page 338.
279. Toilers of the Sea. (R97–4.) Page 339.

WHISTLER, 1834–1903.
280. Théodore Duret. (W57–7.) Page 337.

PADUA

Cappella degli Scrovegni all'Arena

GIOTTO, 1266–1337.
  281. Christ Bearing the Cross (fresco). (Gesù che porta la Croce.) Analysis, page 392.
  282. Entry into Jerusalem (fresco). (L'ingresso di Gesù in Gerusalemme.) Page 392.
  283. Flight into Egypt (fresco). (La fuga in Egitto.) Page 392.
  284. Frescoes. (Affreschi.) Page 113. Analyses, page 391 *et seq.*
  285. Joachim's Vision (fresco). (Visione di S. Giovacchino.) Analysis, page 392.
  286. Joseph and Mary Returning after Their Marriage (fresco). (Ritorno di Maria e S. Giuseppe dal Tempio.) Page 400. Analysis, page 392.
  287. Lamentation over Christ (fresco). (Gesù deposto dalla Croce.) Page 74. Analysis, pages 392, 393.

PARIS

Louvre

BELLINI, GIOVANNI, c.1428–1516.
  288. Man's Portrait. (1158a—Portrait d'homme.) Page 270.
BONINGTON, 1802–1828.
  289. Old Housekeeper. (1805—Vieille gouvernante.) Page 272.
BOUCHER, 1703–1770.
  290. Bridge. (3019—Le pont.) Page 259 n.
  291. Diana at the Bath. (30—Diane au bain.) Page 466 n.
  292. Mill. (3018—Le moulin.) Page 259 n.
  293. Pastoral: Sleeping Shepherdess. (33—Pastorale: la bergère endormie.) Analysis, page 459.
  294. Rinaldo and Armida. (38A—Renaud et Armide.) Analysis, page 460.
BOUTS, DIRK, c.1400–1475.
  295. Deposition. (2196—Déposition de Croix.) Page 439 n. Analysis, page 449.
CANALETTO, ANTONIO, 1697–1768.
  296. Grand Canal and Church of the Salute. (1203—Le Grand Canal. La Salute.) Analysis, page 432.
CHARDIN, 1699–1779.
  297. Bottle of Olives. (107—Le bocal d'olives.) Pages 263 n., 264 n.
  298. Child with Teetotum. (90a—L'enfant au toton.) Page 263. Illustration, page 254.
  299. Grace before Meal. (92—Le bénédicité.) Page 263.
  300. Industrious Mother. (91—La mère laborieuse.) Page 263.
  301. Still-Life with Fish and Eggs. (95—Le menu de maigre.) Analysis, page 460.

CATALOGUE DATA

302. Still-Life with Meat. (96—Le menu de gras.) Analysis, page 460.
303. Various Utensils. (101—Ustensiles variés.) Analysis, page 460.
CLAUDE LE LORRAIN, 1600–1682.
    304. Seapiece. (319—Marine.) Analysis, page 462.
    305. Village Fête. (312—Fête villageoise.) Analysis, page 462.
CLOUET, FRANÇOIS, c.1510–1572.
    306. Pierre Quthe. (1034.) Page 248 n.
CORREGGIO, c.1494–1534.
    307. Jupiter and Antiope. (1118.) Page 75.
COURBET, 1819–1877.
    308. Painter's Studio. (L'atelier du peintre.) Page 104. Analysis, page 461. Illustration, page 256.
    309. Wounded Man. (144—L'homme blessé.) Page 306.
DELACROIX, 1798–1863.
    310. Algerian Women. (210—Femmes d'Alger. Analysis, page 461.
    311. Death of Sardanapalus. (La mort de Sardanapale.) Pages 266, 461.
DÜRER, 1471–1528.
    312. Erasmus (drawing). Page 194.
    313. Self-Portrait. (Son portrait.) Pages 195, 270. Analysis, page 440. Illustration, page 273.
EGYPTIAN SCULPTURE, 2500 B.C. (De Morgan Collection, Mastaba.)
    314. Statues. Page 18 n.
FRAGONARD, 1732–1806.
    315. Bacchante Asleep. (294—Bacchante endormie.) Page 261.
    316. Bathers. (293—Baigneuses.) Pages 260, 466 n. Illustration, page 163.
    317. Blindman's Buff. (Le colin-maillard.) Page 261.
    318. Fancy Figure. (299—Figure de fantaisie.) Page 260.
    319. Music Lesson. (291—La leçon de musique.) Page 261. Analysis, page 460. Illustration, page 474.
    320. Young Woman and Child. (300—Jeune femme.) Page 260.
FRANCESCO DI GIORGIO, 1439–1502.
    321. Rape of Europa. (1640—Enlèvement d'Europe.) Pages 105, 128.
FRANCIABIGIO, 1482–1525, Attributed to.
    322. Young Man. (1644—Portrait de jeune homme.) Page 270.
FRENCH MASTER, active c.1374.
    323. Altar-Cloth of Narbonne. (1342 bis—Parement de Narbonne.) Page 240.
FRENCH MASTER, end of fourteenth or beginning of fifteenth century.
    324. Entombment. (997—La mise au tombeau—Ecole française.) Pages 231, 238, 240, 246, 250. Analysis, page 456. Illustration, page 243.
FRENCH MASTER, active 1390–1410.
    325. Pietà of Our Lord. (3158—Pitié de Notre-Seigneur—Ecole de l'Ile-de-France.) Pages 231, 240.

APPENDIX

FRENCH MASTER, active c.1400.
  326. Altarpiece of the Virgin. (3157—Chapelle portative: Scènes de la vie de la Vierge et de l'Enfant Jésus—Ecole française.) Page 232. Analysis, page 456.

FRENCH MASTER, active c.1400.
  327. Scenes from the Life of St. Andrew. (Scènes de la vie de St.-André; Ste.-Claire; St.-Sébastien—Ecole d'Avignon.) Page 233.

FRENCH TAPESTRY, c.1500.
  328. Concert in the Open Air (Bareiller legacy). (Le concert champêtre—Tapisserie—Art français.) Page 236.

GILLOT, CLAUDE, 1673–1722.
  329. Scene of the Two Coaches. (3092—Scène des deux carrosses.) Analysis, page 459.

GIORGIONE, 1477–1510.
  330. Concert in the Open Air. (1136—Le concert champêtre.) Pages 62, 103, 107, 146, 466. Analysis, page 422. Illustration, page 98.

GREUZE, 1725–1805.
  331. Village Betrothal. (369—L'accordée de village.) Analysis, page 460.

GUARDI, 1712–1793.
  332. Doge Embarking on the Bucentaur. (1328—Le Doge s'embarquant sur le Bucentaure.) Analysis, page 432.

HALS, FRANS, c.1580–1666.
  333. Nicolas van Beresteyn. (2386.) Page 272.
  334. Wife of Paulus van Beresteyn. (2387—Femme de Paulus van Beresteyn.) Page 272.

HOLBEIN, HANS, the Younger, 1497–1543.
  335. Anne of Clèves. (2718.) Pages 197 n., 198.
  336. Erasmus. (2715.) Pages 197 n., 198. Illustration, page 184.
  337. Head of a Man (drawing). (Tête d'homme.) Page 194.

INGRES, 1780–1867.
  338. Madame Rivière. (427.) Analysis, page 461.
  339. Spring. (422—La source.) Analysis, page 461.
  340. Turkish Bath. (Bain turc.) Page 462.

LEONARDO DA VINCI, 1452–1519.
  341. Bacchus. (1602.) Pages 87, 278.
  342. Lucrezia Crivelli. (1600.) Analysis, page 407.
  343. Mona Lisa. Pages 87, 92, 133, 278. Analysis, page 407.
  344. Saint John the Baptist. (1597—Saint Jean-Baptiste.) Page 133.
  345. Virgin of the Rocks. (1599—La Vierge aux rochers.) Pages 83, 133. Analysis, page 408.
  346. Virgin, St. Anne, and the Infant Jesus. (1598—La Vierge, l'enfant Jésus et Ste. Anne.) Page 104.

MANET, 1832–1883.
  347. Boy with Fife. (173—Le fifre.) Page 307.
  348. Olympia. (613.) Pages 298, 306. Analysis, page 464.

CATALOGUE DATA

MANTEGNA, 1431–1506.

349. Parnassus. (1375—Le Parnasse.) Page 88. Analysis, page 417.

350. Wisdom Triumphing over the Vices. (1376—La Sagesse victorieuse des Vices.) Page 88. Analysis, page 417.

MARTINI, SIMONE, c.1285–1344.

351. Ascent to Calvary. (1383—Jésus-Christ marchant au Calvaire.) Pages 88, 392.

MASTER OF MOULINS, fifteenth century.

352. Magdalen and Donor. (1005A—Madeleine et Donatrice—Maître de Moulins.) Page 232 n.

MEMLING, c.1430–1494.

353. Marriage of St. Catherine. (2027—Mariage de Ste. Catherine.) Page 439 n.

354. Woman's Portrait. (2028B—Femme âgée.) Page 209.

MESSINA, ANTONELLO DA, c.1430 – c.1479.

355. Condottiere. (1134—Le condottière.) Pages 213, 270.

PATER, 1696–1736.

356. Comedians in a Park. (690—Comédiens dans un parc.) Page 258 n.

357. Outdoor Fête. (689—Fête champêtre.) Page 258 n.

PERUGINO, 1446–1523.

358. Combat of Love and Chastity. (1567—Combat de l'Amour et de la Chasteté.) Page 87. Analysis, page 411.

PISANELLO or PISANO, c.1397–1455.

359. Princess of the Este Family. (1422A—Une princesse de la famille d'Este.) Page 105.

POUSSIN, NICOLAS, 1594–1665.

360. Arcadian Shepherds. (734—Les bergers d'Arcadie.) Page 62.

361. Blindmen of Jericho. (715—Aveugles de Jéricho.) Pages 104, 160, 411, 462. Analysis, page 434.

362. Earthly Paradise. (736—Paradis terrestre.) Analysis, page 434.

363. Funeral of Phocion. (Funérailles de Phocion.) Page 165.

364. Holy Family. (713—Sainte Famille.) Analysis, page 434.

365. Summer, Ruth and Boaz. (737—L'été, Ruth et Booz.) Illustration, page 164.

PRUD'HON, PAUL, 1758–1823.

366. Justice and Divine Vengeance Pursuing Crime. (747—La Justice et la Vengeance divine poursuivant le Crime.) Page 262 n.

RAPHAEL, 1483–1520.

367. Count Baldassare Castiglione. (1505.) Pages 88, 450.

368. Holy Family, of François I. (1498—La Sainte Famille, dite de François Ier.) Page 104. Analysis, page 408.

369. Madonna: *la Belle Jardinière.* (1496.) Pages 43, 88. Analysis, page 409. Illustration, page 427.

370. Saint Michael Crushing Satan. (1504—Saint Michel terrassant le démon.) Page 136.

371. Virgin with Blue Diadem. (1497—La Vierge au diadème bleu.) Page 88.

372. Young Man. (1506—Portrait de jeune homme.) Page 271.

REMBRANDT, 1606–1669.

373. Hendrickje Stoffels. (2547.) Pages 69, 106, 226, 270, 449. Analysis, page 451. Illustration, page 274.

374. Man with Stick. (2551—Portrait dit: L'homme au bâton.) Page 271.

375. Self-Portrait, as an Old Man. (2555—Portrait de Rembrandt âgé.) Page 271.

RENI, GUIDO, 1575–1642.

377. Deianeira and Nessus. (1454.) Page 68.

RHENISH MASTER, active c.1340.

378. Scenes from the Life of Christ: Annunciation, Nativity, Adoration, Presentation. (Scènes de la vie du Christ: Annonciation, Nativité, Adoration, Présentation—Ecole rhénane.) Pages 175, 176.

ROUSSEAU, THEODORE, 1812–1867.

379. Edge of the Forest of Fontainebleau, toward Brôle. (827—Sortie de la forêt de Fontainebleau du côté de Brôle.) Analysis, page 464.

RUBENS, 1577–1640.

380. Baron Henri de Vicq. (2111.) Pages 106, 272.

381. Country Fair. (2115—La kermesse.) Analysis, page 433.

382. Hélène Fourment and her Children. (2113—Hélène Fourment et ses enfants.) Page 261.

383. Tournament. (2116—Château et tournoi.) Analysis, page 433.

SOUTHERN FRENCH MASTER, second half of fifteenth century.

384. Villeneuve Pietà. (1001B—Pietà, provenant de la Chartreuse de Villeneuve-lès-Avignon—Ecole d'Avignon.) Pages 233, 238, 246. Illustration, page 244.

TERBORCH, GERARD, 1617–1681.

385. Concert. (2589.) Analysis, page 456. Illustration, page 224.

TINTORETTO, 1518–1594.

386. Artist's Portrait. (1466—Tintoret par lui-même.) Pages 153, 271.

387. Paradise. (1465—Le Paradis.) Pages 87, 103, 153. Analysis, page 431.

388. Susanna at the Bath. (1474—Suzanne au bain.) Page 153.

TITIAN, c.1477–1576.

389. Alfonso da Ferrara and Laura di Dianti. (1590.) Page 271.

390. Christ Crowned with Thorns. (1583—Le Christ couronné d'épines.) Pages 75, 148.

391. Disciples at Emmaus. (1581—Pèlerins d'Emmaüs.) Pages 103, 148, 264 n., 440, 462. Analysis, page 424. Illustration, page 150.

392. Entombment. (1584—La mise au tombeau.) Pages 74, 103, 148. Illustration, page 77.

393. Jupiter and Antiope. (1587.) Page 103. Analysis, page 424.

394. Man with Glove. (1592—L'homme au gant.) Pages 65, 85, 88, 104, 106, 148, 270, 271, 450. Illustration, page 428.

CATALOGUE DATA

TURA, COSIMO, c.1420–1495.
  395. Pietà. (1556.) Pages 142, 442. Analysis, page 411. Illustration, page 60.

VELASQUEZ, 1599–1660.
  396. Infanta Marguerite. (1731.) Pages 76, 270, 436. Analysis, page 435. Illustration, page 275.

VERNET, CLAUDE JOSEPH, 1714–1789.
  397. Bathers. (921—Les baigneuses.) Page 261 n.
  398. Landscape. (923—Paysage.) Page 261 n.
  399. Port of Marseilles. (940—Port de Marseille.) Page 261 n.

VERONESE, PAOLO, 1528–1588.
  400. Burning of Sodom. (1187—L'incendie de Sodome.) Pages 75, 93. Analysis, page 431. Illustration, page 79.
  401. Jupiter Destroying the Vices. (1198—Jupiter foudroyant les Vices.) Pages 75, 260 n.

WATTEAU, 1684–1721.
  402. Embarkation for Cythera. (982—L'embarquement pour Cythère.) Page 258. Analysis, page 459.

WHISTLER, 1834–1903.
  403. Artist's Mother. (La mère de l'artiste.) Page 337.

Musée de Cluny

FRENCH TAPESTRIES, end of fifteenth century.
  404. Lady and Unicorn. (La dame à la licorne—Tapisserie française.) Page 236.
  405. Scenes of Seigniorial Life. (Scènes de la vie seigneuriale—Tapisserie française.) Page 236.

PHILADELPHIA

Dreibelbies Collection

PINTO, BIAGIO, 1911–1988.
  406. Checker Players. Illustration, page 341.

POMPEII

MURAL PAINTINGS, before first century.
  407. Frescoes. (Affreschi.) Page 111.

PRAGUE

Museum

BOHEMIAN MASTER, active 1370–1378.
  408. Votive Picture of the Archbishop Očko v. Vlašim. (158—Votivbild des Erzbischofs Očko von Vlašim—Böhmish.) Page 174.

BOHEMIAN MASTER, end of fourteenth century.
  409. Resurrection (part of Wittingau Altarpiece). (Auferstehung Christi.) Illustration, page 183.

APPENDIX

410. Wittingau Altarpiece. (Wittingauer Altar.) Pages 174, 191.

RAVENNA

Mausoleo di Galla Placidia

BYZANTINE MOSAICS, fifth century.
411. Figures of Apostles. (Apostoli—Mosaici bizantini.) **Page 111.**

S. Vitale, Basilica di

BYZANTINE MOSAICS, sixth century.
412. Empress Theodora Makes an Offering to Religion. (L'Imperatrice Teodora fa l'offerta alla Religione—Mosaici bizantini.) Illustration, page 117.
413. Massimiliano (detail). (Mosaici bizantini.) Illustration, page 296.

RICHMOND, ENGLAND

Cook Collection

CLOUET, FRANÇOIS, c.1510–1572.
414. Diane de Poitiers in the Bath. Page 248 n.

ROME

Galleria Borghese

CORREGGIO, 1494–1534.
415. Danaë. (125.) Analysis, page 432.
RAPHAEL, 1483–1520.
416. Descent from the Cross. (369—La Deposizione.) Page 136.

S. Pietro in Vincoli, Chiesa di

MICHELANGELO, 1475–1564.
417. Moses (sculpture). (Mosè.) Page 18 n.

Vaticano (Cappella Sistina)

BOTTICELLI, 1444–1510.
418. Incidents in the Life of Moses (fresco). (Fatti della vita di Mosè.) Pages 105, 128, 393. Analysis, page 406.
MICHELANGELO, 1475–1564.
419. Frescoes. (Affreschi.) Page 134.
420. Last Judgment (fresco). (Giudizio Universale.) Page 134.
421. Original Sin and Expulsion from Eden (fresco). (Il peccato originale e l'espulsione dal Paradiso terrestre.) Analysis, page 408. Illustration, page 294.
PERUGINO, 1446–1523.
422. Christ Giving the Keys to Peter (fresco). (Gesù che dà a S. Pietro le chiavi del regno dei Cieli.) Pages 107, 431.

CATALOGUE DATA

ROSSELLI, COSIMO, c.1438–1507.
423. Pharaoh's Destruction in the Red Sea (fresco). (Il passaggio del Mar Rosso.) Pages 103, 105, 400. Analysis, page 412.

SIGNORELLI, LUCA, 1441–1523.
424. Four Episodes in the Life of Moses (fresco). (Quattro episodi della vita di Mosè.) Analysis, page 412.

Vaticano (Loggia di Raffaello)

RAPHAEL, 1483–1520.
425. Frescoes. (Affreschi.) Page 135.

Vaticano (Pinacoteca)

LORENZETTI, AMBROGIO, active c.1319 – c.1348.
426. Legend of St. Stephen. (147 to 150, inc.—La leggenda di S. Stefano protomartire.) Page 141.

RAPHAEL, 1483–1520.
427. Transfiguration. (333—La Trasfigurazione.) Pages 105, 324. Analysis, page 409. Illustration, page 446.

SOSPEL

Chapelle des Pénitents Blancs

SOUTHERN FRENCH MASTER, fifteenth century.
428. Pietà. (La Vierge de Pitié—Ecole niçoise.) Pages 233, 238, 246. Illustration, page 244.

TOLEDO

Museo Parroquial de San Vincente

GRECO, EL, c.1541–1614.
429. Assumption. (La Asunción.) Page 410 n.

VENICE

Accademia

BELLINI, GIOVANNI, c.1428–1516.
430. Madonna of the Little Trees. (596—Madonna degli alberetti.) Page 145. Analysis, page 418. Illustration, page 426.

CARPACCIO, c.1455–1525.
431. Dream of St. Ursula. (578—Il sogno di Sant'Orsola.) Page 146. Analysis, page 419. Illustration, page 425.

LONGHI, PIETRO, 1702–1785.
432. Dancing Master. (465—Il maestro di ballo.) Analysis, page 432.

TINTORETTO, 1518–1594.
433. Calvary. (213—Il Calvario.) Analysis, page 431.

APPENDIX

TITIAN, c.1477–1576.
    434. Saint John the Baptist. (314—San Giovanni Battista.) Page 148.
    Analysis, page 429.

VERONESE, PAOLO, 1528–1588.
    435. Banquet in the House of Levi. (203—Cena in casa Levi.) Analysis, page 431.

VIVARINI, ALVISE, c.1447 – c.1504.
    436. Madonna Enthroned, with Saints. (607—Madonna e Santi.)
    Analysis, page 417.

I Frari

BELLINI, GIOVANNI, c.1428–1516.
    437. Madonna and Saints. (Madonna e Santi.) Page 144. Analysis,
    page 419.

TITIAN, c.1477–1576.
    438. Assumption. (L'Assunta.) Pages 43, 105, 148. Analysis, page 429.
    Illustration, page 447.

VIENNA

Kunsthistorisches Museum

BALDUNG, HANS (GRIEN), c.1475–1545.
    439. Vanity. (1423—Die drei Lebensalter des Weibes und der Tod.)
    Page 196.

DÜRER, 1471–1528.
    440. Adoration of the Trinity by All the Saints. (1445—Das Allerheiligenbild.) Page 195 n.
    441. Ten Thousand Martyrs of Nicodemia. (1446—Die Marter der Zehntausend Christen.) Page 195 n.

PATINIR, c.1480–1524.
    442. Baptism of Christ. (666—Die Taufe Christi.) Page 211.

STRIGEL, BERNHARD, 1461–1528.
    443. Kaiser Maximilian I. (1426.) Page 192 n.

INDEX

The arrangement of the preceding section—Catalogue Data—makes it serve as a supplementary index. The small n after a page number denotes a footnote reference.

A

ACADEMICISM, 27–28, 30, 42, 67, 199, 229, 240, 245
  in color, 88–89
  in space-composition, 107–108
  see also Academic criticism, and Academic painters
Academic criticism, see Criticism
Academic painters, 111, 128, 137, 140, 157, 171, 192, 207, 230, 252, 261, 262, 286, 338, 347, 357, 407, 417
African carvings, Influence of, 235
American painting, 336–347
Amiens, School of, 233
An Approach to Art, Mary Mullen, 8 n, 12 n
Andrea del Castagno, see Castagno
Andrea del Sarto, see Sarto
Angelico, Fra, 20–25, 86–87, 124–125, 137, 142, 173, 178, 185, 188, 189, 209, 394, 396, 437, 438
  "Deposition" (81), see p. 485
  "Mystical Crucifixion" (82), see p. 485
Anna Karenina, Tolstoi, 73
Antonello da Messina, see Messina
Antwerp school, 196, 211
  Influence of, 180
Appreciation
  Esthetic, 37
  Problem of, 3–7
  see also Criticism
Architecture, Space in, 106
Armory Exhibition of 1913, 356
Art
  and form, 61–62
  and instinct, 9, 12, 43–44, 48
  and interest, 11
  and intrinsic values, 9
  and medium, 31, 49–50
  and reality, 14–15, 16, 69–70, 74
  and science, 7, 13, 14, 36
  and subject-matter, 20–25
  criticism, see Criticism

Function of, 48
Mysticism in, 45–47
Roots of, 8–12
Atmosphere, 84, 84–85, 116, 300
  in Barbizon school, 286
  in Boucher, 259
  in Claude, 279
  in Isenbrant, 212
  in Velásquez, 168
  in Venetians, 144, 145
  in Watteau, 252

B

BACH, 316, 470
Background
  and foreground, 62, 123–124, 148, 179, 180, 185, 207, 213, 214, 220, 270, 333, 360, 470
  as screen, 62, 106, 124, 139, 210, 213
  in composition, 105–106
Baldovinetti, 420
Baldung, Hans (Grien), 83, 196, 449
  "Vanity" (439), see p. 504
Barbizon school, 139, 215, 219, 267, 286, 339
Barnes, Albert C., and Violette de Mazia
  The Art of Henri-Matisse, 19 n, 359 n
  The Art of Renoir, 313 n, 352 n
  The French Primitives and Their Forms, 141 n, 175 n, 177 n, 230 n
Baroque art, 18 n
Bavaria, Painting in, 172
Beethoven, 316
  Eroica (Third Symphony), 32, 33
  Fifth Symphony, 32
Bellini, Giovanni, 31, 93, 144–145, 195, 196, 205, 407, 430
  Influence of, 421, 422, 424
  "Allegory of Purgatory" (89), see p. 486
  "Doge Leonardo Loredano" (127), see p. 488
  "Madonna and Saints" (437), see p. 504

"Madonna of the Little Trees" (430), *see* p. 503
"Man's Portrait" (288), *see* p. 496
Bellotto, 157
Bellows, George, 336
Benton, Thomas, 347
Berckheyde, 217, 228–229, 339, 455
  Influence of, 257, 259
"Flower Market" (2), *see* p. 479
Berenson, Bernard, 89, 138, 139
Berlioz, 67
Böcklin, 47
Bohemian Master, active 1370–1378
  "Votive Picture of the Archbishop
    Očko v. Vlašim" (408), *see* p. 501
Bohemian Master, end of fourteenth
    century
  "Resurrection"—part of "Wittingau
    Altarpiece" (409), *see* p. 501
  "Wittingau Altarpiece" (410), *see*
    p. 502
Bohemian school, 172, 173–175, 176,
    177, 178, 179
  Influence of, 177, 179, 180, 185, 190,
    191, 246, 457
Bolognese school, 31
Bonington, 226, 272
  "Old Housekeeper" (289), *see* p. 496
Bonnard, 334–335
Bosanquet, 48, 226
Bosch, Hieronymus, 177, 186, 207, 210–
    211, 213, 410
  Influence of, 170, 212, 214, 267
Botticelli, 17, 92, 94, 127, 128, 137, 297
  Influence of, 135
  "Allegory of Spring" (90), *see* p. 486
  "Birth of Venus" (91), *see* p. 486
  "Incidents in the Life of Moses"
    (418), *see* p. 502
Boucher, 94, 250, 258–260
  Influence of, 260, 261, 315, 466
  "Bridge" (290), *see* p. 496
  "Diana at the Bath" (291), *see*
    p. 496
  "Mill" (292), *see* p. 496
  "Pastoral: Sleeping Shepherdess"
    (293), *see* p. 496
  "Rape of Europa" (161), *see* p. 490
  "Rinaldo and Armida" (294), *see*
    p. 496
Bouts, Dirk, 206, 207, 207–208, 209
  Influence of, 186, 439, 457
  "Deposition" (295), *see* p. 496
  "Entombment" (128), *see* p. 488
Braque, 355, 357
Bréa, Louis, 233
  "Pietà" (53), *see* p. 483

Bronzino, 28, 462
Brouwer, Adriaen, 218
  "Halt" (28), *see* p. 481
Brueghel, Pieter, the Elder, 177, 186,
    207, 213–214
  Influence of, 170
  "Harvesters" (269), *see* p. 495
Bruges Master of "Legend of St. Ur-
    sula"
  "Legend of St. Ursula" (48), *see*
    p. 482
Bruyn, Bartholomew, 187, 449
Buermeyer, Laurence, 35–36
The Aesthetic Experience, 45 n
Byzantine mosaics, fifth century
  "Figures of Apostles" (411), *see*
    p. 502
Byzantine mosaics, sixth century
  "Empress Theodora Makes an Offer-
    ing to Religion" (412), *see* p. 502
  "Massimiliano" (413), *see* p. 502
Byzantine tradition, 63, 111, 112, 115,
    141, 142, 143
  in subsequent painting, 113, 172, 173,
    174, 175, 176, 177, 180, 188, 200,
    230, 234, 235, 239, 245, 246, 247,
    353, 360, 365, 393, 436, 457, 458
  see also Mosaics

C

CANALETTO, ANTONIO, 157
  "Grand Canal and Church of the
    Salute" (296), *see* p. 496
Caravaggio, 225
Carpaccio, 93, 145–146, 155, 168, 198,
    199, 278, 418
  Influence of, 320, 434
  "Dream of St. Ursula" (431), *see*
    p. 503
Carraccis, The, 157, 380
Castagno, Andrea del, 91, 115, 122–123,
    123, 125, 137, 138, 140, 147, 158,
    225, 292, 397, 398, 436
  "Last Supper" (77), *see* p. 485
  "Pietà" (78), *see* p. 485
Castagno, School of Andrea del
  "Saint Eustachius" (79), *see* p. 485
Cézanne, 15, 18, 29, 30, 31, 36, 41, 47,
    64–65, 71, 82, 127, 138, 139, 153,
    159, 168, 205, 229, 266, 268, 269,
    272, 277, 292, 299, 301, 302, 303,
    305, 308, 319–324, 328 n, 351–353,
    354, 357, 373, 374, 377, 397, 454,
    467
  Drawing in, 90, 96
  Influence of, 28, 42, 314, 328, 340,
    345, 346, 356, 357, 358, 359, 360,

369, 370, 371, 372, 375, 379, 385,
477, 478
"Bathers" (175), see p. 490
"Men Bathing" (175 A), see p. 490
"Mount Ste. Victoire" (176), see
p. 491
"Nudes in Landscape" (177), see
p. 491
"Still-Life with Gray Jug" (178),
see p. 491
Chardin, 18, 229, 250, 262–264, 313,
420, 432, 442
Drawing in, 94
Influence of, 170, 261, 319, 379
"Bottle of Olives" (297), see p. 496
"Child with Teetotum" (298), see
p. 496
"Grace before Meal" (299), see p. 496
"Industrious Mother" (300), see
p. 496
"Still-Life with Fish and Eggs"
(301), see p. 496
"Still-Life with Meat" (302), see
p. 497
"Various Utensils" (303), see p. 497
Chassériau, 266
Chavannes, Puvis de, see Puvis
Chiaroscuro, 42, 62, 69, 84, 95, 102, 116,
139, 220, 225, 226, 261, 268, 298,
395, 422, 432, 452
Chinese painting, 390
Influence of, 346, 353, 358, 360
Chirico, Giorgio de, 380–385
"Alexandros" (179), see p. 491
"Horses near a Lake" (256), see
p. 494
Chopin, 39
Christus, Petrus, 205–206, 209
Influence of, 247
"Deposition from the Cross" (270),
see p. 495
"Edward Grimston" (129), see p. 488
"Marco Barbarigo" (130), see p. 488
Cimabue, 113, 141, 396
Composition in, 112
Drawing in, 91
Influence of, 436
"Virgin Enthroned"—Assisi—(16),
see p. 480
Virgin Enthroned"—Uffizi—(92),
see p. 486
Classic art, 18 n
Influence of, 158, 165, 235, 250, 258,
429, 462, 466, 467
see also Sculpture
Classicism, Nineteenth century French,
70, 81, 265–266

Claude le Lorrain, 28–30, 47, 76, 85, 94,
106, 107, 139, 140, 157, 215, 278–
279, 304, 316, 318, 324, 433
Influence of, 88, 108, 250, 251–252,
252, 259, 261, 280, 285, 286, 432,
459, 464
"Landscape" (180), see p. 491
"Seapiece" (304), see p. 497
"Village Fête" (305), see p. 497
Clouet, François, 247, 248
"Diane de Poitiers in the Bath"
(414), see p. 502
"Pierre Quthe" (306), see p. 497
Clouet, Jean, 247, 248
"François I, on Horseback" (93),
see p. 486
"François, the Dauphin" (10), see
p. 480
Clouet school, The, 230, 247–248
Clouets, The, 197, 205, 206, 247, 248
Cologne Master of beginning or middle
of fourteenth century
"Crucifixion and Four Scenes from
the Life of Christ" (58), see p. 483
Cologne Master, active c.1340
"Annunciation" (59), see p. 483
"Presentation" (60), see p. 483
Cologne Master of "Holy Kinship," 186,
193
Cologne Master of "Life of Mary," 177,
186–187, 192, 214
"Crucifixion" (61), see p. 484
"Madonna and Child, Three Saints
and Donor's Family" (29), see
p. 481
"Saint Barbara, with Donor and
Seven Daughters" (62), see p. 484
"Saint Katherine, with Donor and
Eight Sons" (63), see p. 484
"Scenes from the Life of Mary"
(257), see p. 494
Cologne Master of "Life of Mary,"
Attributed to,
"Lyversberg Passion" (64), see p. 484
Cologne Master of "Mount Calvary,"
177
Cologne Master of "Saint Veronica,"
185
"Saint Veronica" (258), see p. 494
Cologne Master of "Saint Veronica,"
Attributed to
"Madonna with Pea-Blossom" (65),
see p. 484
"Six Scenes from Christ's Passion"
(66), see p. 484
Cologne school, 172, 175, 176, 176–187,
205, 213

INDEX

Influence of, 189, 192, 194, 195, 196, 210, 214, 240, 246, 443, 457
Color, 55–56, 82–89, 297
  Academicism in, 88–89
  and form, 40–41, 65
  and light, 65, 84–85
  and mysticism, 86
  -design, 87
  in composition, 89, 102, 103–104
  in drawing, see Drawing
  in Flemish tradition, 199
  in Florentines, 137
  in French primitives, 237–239
  in Germans, 173, 174, 178
  in modeling, 85
  in space-composition, 107
  in Venetians, 155
  Structural, 65, 85
Composition, 56, 102–108
  Academicism in, 107–108
  and color, 89, 102, 103–104
  Background in, 105–106
  Definition of, 102
  Design and, 104
  in French eighteenth century, 252, 257, 260, 261
  in Germans, 174, 177–178, 187
  in impressionists, 299
  in portraiture, 105–106
  in Venetians, 106
  Light in, 104
  Line in, 103, 104
  Mass-, see Mass-composition
  Space-, see Space-composition
Constable, John, 28, 37–38, 49, 84, 85, 159, 215, 280–281, 300, 307, 316, 318, 338, 433, 461
  Influence of, 285, 286
  "Flatford Mill" (131), see p. 488
  "Hay-Wain" (132), see p. 488
  "Salisbury Cathedral" (133), see p. 488
Contemporary painting, 291, 356–385
  Transition to, 351–355
Contour, see Line and Drawing
Contrast, 62–63
Coptic textiles, Influence of, 365
Corot, 28, 85, 169, 218, 264, 266–267, 267, 269, 277, 286, 314, 378, 455
  Influence of, 303, 313, 336, 462
  "Landscape" (181), see p. 491
  "Woman in Pink Blouse" (182), see p. 491
Correggio, 75, 157, 258
  "Danaë" (415), see p. 502
  "Jupiter and Antiope" (307), see p. 497
Cosimo Rosselli, see Rosselli
Cosimo Tura, see Tura

Courbet, 28, 34, 71, 168, 169, 170, 218, 229, 264, 267, 269, 277, 286, 291, 300, 305, 306
  Drawing in, 95–96
  Influence of, 313, 317, 319, 337, 465
  "Painter's Studio" (308), see p. 497
  "Village Maidens" (271), see p. 495
  "Wounded Man" (309), see p. 497
Cousin, Jean, 230
Coypel, 261
Cranach, 186, 196, 210, 214
Criticism
  Academic, 30, 36–37, 38, 43, 89, 114, 292, 352, 358
  Art, 61, 291, 304
  see also Appreciation
Crome, John, 338
Cubism, 35, 36, 61, 104, 213, 297, 355, 356–357, 357, 370–372, 449
  Influence of, 346, 358, 375, 377, 380
Curry, John, 347

D

Daddi, Bernardo, 456
Daumier, 14, 33–34, 40, 83, 95, 96, 136, 139, 140, 153, 170, 194, 226, 267–269, 286, 300, 302, 338, 345, 378, 397, 410, 441, 454
  Influence of, 319, 374, 375, 379, 462, 472
  "Water Carrier" (183), see p. 491
David, Gerard, 208, 211, 212
  "Crucifixion" (272), see p. 495
David, Louis, 35, 40, 70–71, 81, 95, 265, 266
Davies, Arthur B., 47
Decoration, 16–19, 48
  and expression, 13–19
  and mysticism, 46
Degas, 71, 95, 96, 122, 136, 168, 269, 279, 302, 307, 318, 325–327, 345
  Influence of, 369, 375
  "Race Horses" (184), see p. 491
Delacroix, 33, 40, 49, 70–71, 73, 75, 83, 84, 85, 95, 134, 140, 157, 159, 266, 267, 269, 280, 300, 319, 356, 392, 400
  "Algerian Women" (310), see p. 497
  "Death of Sardanapalus" (311), see p. 497
  "Triumph of St. Michael" (185), see p. 491
Demuth, 213, 345–346, 449
  "Negro Dancing" (186), see p. 491
Denis, Maurice, 333
Derain, 28, 31, 379–380
Design, 14–15, 56–61, 63, 299, 304

and composition, 104
and distortion, 167–168, 292–299
and pattern
  Development of, in modern painting, 291–299
  differentiated, 56–61
  Color-, 87
  in comtemporary painting, 351
  see also Plastic form
Dewey, John, 61–62
  Experience and Nature, 62 n
Distortion, 41, 42, 167–168, 292–299
Domenico Veneziano, *see* Veneziano
Dossi, Dosso, 196
Dou, Gerard, 229
Draperies
  in Flemings, 199–200, 208, 209
  in French eighteenth century, 252, 257, 258
  in French primitives, 245–247
  in Germans, 173, 174, 176, 179, 188, 189, 190
  in Goya, 171
  in Ingres, 266
  in Poussin, 165
  in Renoir, 266, 313
  in Sienese, 142
  see also Folds *and* Textiles
Drawing, 56, 90–101
  and design, 292–297
  in mosaics, 91
  in Florentines, 137–138
  in French eighteenth century, 251
  in French primitives, 239–245
  in Germans, 173, 175, 178–179, 245
  in impressionists, 298
  in Sienese, 141, 142
  in Venetians, 90, 93, 96
Duccio di Buoninsegna, 142–143, 143
Dürer, 87, 177, 193–195, 195, 198, 200, 205, 208, 210, 213, 443
  Influence of, 196, 212
  "Adoration of the Magi" (94), *see* p. 486
  "Adoration of the Trinity by All the Saints" (440), *see* p. 504
  "Apostles John and Peter" (259), *see* p. 494
  "Apostles Paul and Mark" (260), *see* p. 494
  "Erasmus" (312), *see* p. 497
  "Girl's Portrait" (30), *see* p. 481
  "Head of Woman" (31), *see* p. 481
  "Hieronymus Holzshuher" (32), *see* p. 481
  "Jacob Muffel" (33), *see* p. 481
  "Madonna" (34), *see* p. 481

"Self-Portrait" (313), *see* p. 497
"Ten Thousand Martyrs of Nicodemia" (441), *see* p. 504
Dutch tradition, 62, 168, 206, 212, 215–229, 432, 433
  Influence of, 215, 229, 250, 251, 257, 259, 260, 261, 262, 267, 280, 286, 317, 333, 336, 338, 339
  see also Genre-painting
Dyck, van, 88, 272

E

EAKINS, THOMAS, 338
  "Dr. Agnew" (187), *see* p. 491
Egyptian art, Influence of, 235, 236, 365
Egyptian sculpture, 18 n, 354
Egyptian sculpture, 2500 B.C.
  "Statues" (314), *see* p. 497
Egyptian sculpture, XVII Dynasty, 2000 B.C.
  "Figure" (188), *see* p. 491
Egyptian textiles, Influence of, 235
Egypto-Roman portraits, Influence of, 365
El Greco, *see* Greco
Emotion
  and esthetic experience, 10
  and instinct, 10
  and interest, 10–11, 13
  and subject-matter, 35–36
English portraiture, 272
Eroica (Third Symphony), Beethoven, 32, 33
Esthetic
  experience, *see* Experience
  values of painting, 20–44
Experience, 6–7, 37–38
  and interest, 13
  Esthetic, 9–10, 13, 38, 45, 121
  Funded, 37, 38, 43
Experience and Nature, John Dewey, 62 n
Expression, 75
  and decoration, 13–19
Expressionism, 385
Eyck, Jan van, 20–25, 90, 170, 187, 199, 200, 200–205, 209, 237, 247
  Influence of, 186, 194, 196, 197, 205, 206, 207, 208, 209, 213, 247
  "Crucifixion" (35), *see* p. 481
  "Jan Arnolfini and Jeanne de Chenany, his Wife" (134), *see* p. 489
  "Man's Portrait" (135), *see* p. 489
  "Man with a Pink" (36), *see* p. 481

F

FIELDING, HENRY, 15
Fifth Symphony, Beethoven, 32

Flemish Master, fifteenth century
"Crucifixion" (189), see p. 491
Flemish Master, active c.1480
"Man's Portrait" (190), see p. 491
Flemish tradition, 157, 199–214, 235
in subsequent painting, 168, 172, 175, 177, 180, 185, 186, 187, 191, 192, 193, 196, 197, 231, 232, 237, 239, 245, 246, 433, 457, 458
see also Miniatures
Flesh painting
in Clouet school, 248
in Flemings, 205, 208, 209, 213
in French eighteenth century, 251, 257, 258, 259
in French primitives, 238, 245
in Germans, 176, 179, 188, 189–190, 192, 195, 197
in Rubens, 158, 433
in Sienese, 142
in Venetians, 147, 154
Florentine tradition, 41, 89, 115–140, 157, 292, 356, 394
compared with Sienese, 141
compared with Venetian, 137, 138, 155–156
in subsequent painting, 139–140, 158, 172, 173, 179, 185, 186, 189, 191, 193, 194, 197, 213, 245, 246, 300, 320, 417, 434, 438, 457
Subject-matter in, 137
Folds
in Giotto, 115
in Sienese, 142
in Tintoretto, 153
see also Draperies
Foreground and background, see Background
Form
and color, 40–41, 65
and matter, 38–42
and medium, 31–32
and perception, 26–27
and technique, 28–31
Expressive, 14
Nature of, 25–28, 28
Plastic, see Plastic form
Significant, 55, 61–62
Formula and form, 41–42, 67, 81
Fouquet, Jean, 188, 200
Fra Angelico, see Angelico
Fra Filippo Lippi, see Lippi
Fragonard, 94, 122, 157, 250, 257, 260–261, 262, 263, 267, 314
Influence of, 317, 466
"Bacchante Asleep" (315), see p. 497
"Bathers" (316), see p. 497

"Blindman's Buff" (317), see p. 497
"Fancy Figure" (318), see p. 497
"Gardens of the Villa d'Este, Tivoli" (162), see p. 490
"Happy Mother" (136), see p. 489
"Music Lesson" (319), see p. 497
"Schoolmistress" (163), see p. 490
"Souvenir" (164), see p. 490
"Young Woman and Child" (320), see p. 497
Francesca, Piero della, see Piero
Francesco di Giorgio
"Rape of Europa" (321), see p. 497
Franciabigio, Attributed to
"Young Man" (322), see p. 497
Franco-Flemish form, 232–234, 239
Franco-German form, 175–176, 177, 232, 238, 240, 245, 246
Franco-German Master, active first half of fifteenth century
"Holy Trinity" (137), see p. 489
Franconia, Painting in, 172
French flower-painters of seventeenth century, 259
French Italo-miniature tradition, 231–232, 238
French Master, fourteenth century
"Calvary" (74), see p. 485
"Madonna in Garden" (75), see p. 485
French Master, fourteenth century
"Crucifixion" (191), see p. 491
French Master, second half of fourteenth century
"Adoration—Crucifixion" (76), see p. 485
French Master, active c.1374
"Altar-Cloth of Narbonne" (323), see p. 497
French Master, end of fourteenth or beginning of fifteenth century
"Entombment" (324), see p. 497
French Master, active 1390–1410
"Pietà of Our Lord" (325), see p. 497
French Master, active c.1400
"Altarpiece of the Virgin" (326), see p. 498
French Master, active c.1400
"Scene in Temple" (195), see p. 491
French Master, active c.1400
"Scenes from the Life of St. Andrew" (327), see p. 498
French Master, active c.1400 or 1410
"Crowning of Mary" (37), see p. 481
French Master, fifteenth century
"Altarpiece of St. Etienne" (110), see p. 487

INDEX

French Master, fifteenth century
"Birth of the Virgin" (192), *see* p. 491
"Mary Going to the Temple" (193),
    see p. 491
French Master, fifteenth century
"Circumcision" (194), *see* p. 491
French Master, fifteenth century
"Salome" (1), *see* p. 479
French Master, active c.1480
"Saint Roch" (196), *see* p. 491
French Master, active c.1517
"Altarpiece of St. John" (47),
    see p. 482
French Master, seventeenth century
"Flowerpiece" (197), *see* p. 491
"Flowerpiece" (198), *see* p. 491
French painting of eighteenth century,
    83, 126, 159, 250–264, 432
in subsequent painting, 286, 313, 314,
    315, 316, 317, 466
French painting of nineteenth century
    prior to impressionism, 70, 81,
    265–269
see also David, Delacroix, *and* Ingres
French primitives, 17, 141, 191, 230–
    247
Color in, 237–239
Decoration in, 235–237
Draperies in, 245–247
Drawing in, 239–245
Flesh in, 238, 245
General characteristics of, 234–247
Influence of, 172, 175
Space in, 234, 235
Types of, 231–234
see also Frescoes *and* Miniatures
French school, c.1344
"Frescoes" (25), *see* p. 481
French sculpture, *see* Sculpture
French tapestry, 230, 236
Influence of, 230
French tapestry, end of fifteenth century
"Lady and Unicorn" (404), *see* p. 501
"Scenes of Seigniorial Life" (405),
    see p. 501
French tapestry, c.1500
"Concert in the Open Air" (328),
    see p. 498
Frescoes
French, 235, 236, 237, 240
Influence of, 230, 247
see also French school
Influence of, 315
see also Giotto, Masaccio, Michelan-
    gelo, Piero, Pompeian frescoes *and*
    Raphael
Fry, Roger, 89

G

GAINSBOROUGH, 272
Garber, Daniel, 28
Gauguin, 37, 38, 139, 303, 328–333,
    353, 394
Influence of, 334, 354, 358, 385
"Landscape: Haere Pape" (199),
    see p. 491
Genre-painting, 339, 466
Dutch, 215, 226–227, 443, 449
German tradition, 141, 172–198, 200,
    234, 235, 245
Contemporary, 385
Influence of, 211, 212, 213, 232, 233,
    240, 246, 457
see also Miniatures
Gerritsz, 215
Gertner, Peter, 195, 196
Ghirlandaio, Domenico del, 137
"Scenes from the Life of the Virgin
    and from That of John the Bap-
    tist" (88), *see* p. 486
Gillot, Claude
"Scene of the Two Coaches" (329),
    see p. 498
Giorgio, Francesco di, *see* Francesco
Giorgione, 18, 31, 76, 82–83, 85, 93,
    103, 133, 144, 145, 146–147, 153,
    154, 226, 278, 316, 354, 418
Influence of, 147, 424, 433, 466
"Concert in the Open Air" (330), *see*
    p. 498
"Madonna with St. Francis and
    St. Liberal" (50), *see* p. 482
"Sleeping Venus" (73), *see* p. 485
"Two Prophets" (200), *see* p. 492
Giotto, 75, 86, 91, 107, 112–114, 116,
    123, 137, 138, 139, 140, 292, 394
Influence of, 115, 124, 125, 205, 327,
    393, 400, 436
"Christ Bearing the Cross" (281),
    see p. 496
"Entry into Jerusalem" (282), *see*
    p. 496
"Flight into Egypt"—Assisi—(17),
    see p. 480
"Flight into Egypt"—Padua—(283),
    see p. 496
"Frescoes"—Assisi—(18), *see* p. 480
"Frescoes"—Padua—(284), *see* p.
    496
"Joachim's Vision" (285), *see* p. 496
"Joseph and Mary Returning after
    Their Marriage" (286), *see* p. 496
"Lamentation over Christ" (287),
    see p. 496

"Madonna Enthroned" (95), see p. 486

"Miraculous Production of a Spring of Water" (19), see p. 480

"Saint Francis Blessing the Birds" (20), see p. 480

"Saint Francis Clothing the Poor" (21), see p. 480

"Saint Francis Restores His Apparel to His Father" (22), see p. 480

"Saint Francis, Supporting the Lateran, Appears to Pope Innocent III" (23), see p. 480

Girardon, François, 250, 258

Glackens, 33–34, 96, 116, 136, 140, 269, 345

"Race Track" (201), see p. 492

Glow, see Venetian glow

Goes, Hugo van der, 209–210

Goethe, 356

Gogh, Vincent van, 63, 139, 333–334, 354

Influence of, 28, 353, 354, 358, 374, 385

"Landscape" (202), see p. 492

"Postman" (203), see p. 492

Goujon, Jean, 250, 258

Goya, 71, 116, 140, 170–171, 215, 264, 277, 410

Influence of, 267, 313, 351, 462

"Don Galos" (204), see p. 492

"Royal Family of Charles IV" (171), see p. 490

"Witches' Sabbath" (172), see p. 490

Goyen, Jan van, 215–216

Influence of, 216–217, 336, 338

"Seascape" (205), see p. 492

Greco, El, 18, 47, 74–75, 85, 94, 122, 140, 153, 157, 166–168, 193, 212, 357, 405, 410, 440

Influence of, 31, 75, 96, 154, 252, 319, 319–320, 338, 339, 369, 380, 472, 477

"Annunciation" (206), see p. 492

"Assumption" (429), see p. 503

"Vision of St. Hyacinth" (207), see p. 492

Greco-Roman sculpture, see Sculpture

Greek pottery, 500 B.C.

"Vase" (208), see p. 492

Greek sculpture, 106, 354

Influence of, 76, 127–128, 134, 135, 354, 372, 409

see also Greek tradition

Greek sculpture, 400 B.C.

"Figure of a Man" (209), see p. 492

Greek sculpture, 300 B.C.

"Standing Figure" (210), see p. 492

Greek tradition, Influence of, 133, 140, 236, 434, 467

see also Greek pottery, Greek sculpture, and Greek vases

Greek vases, Influence of, 235, 467

Greuze, 261

"Village Betrothal" (331), see p. 498

Growth, 6

Grünewald, Mathias, 20–25, 177, 187, 193

Isenheim Altarpiece

"Crucifixion" (55), see p. 483

"Entombment" (56), see p. 483

Guardi, 157, 259, 455

"Doge Embarking on the Bucentaur" (332), see p. 498

Guido Reni, see Reni

H

Hals, Frans, 220, 271–272, 320, 333

Influence of, 215, 272, 351

"Laughing Cavalier" (165), see p. 490

"Nicolas van Beresteyn" (333), see p. 498

"Wife of Paulus van Beresteyn" (334), see p. 498

Hamburg region, Painting in, 172, 190–191

Hanseatic region, Painting in, 172

Hassam, Childe, 28

Haydn, 32

Henri, Robert, 28, 336

Heyden, van der, 206, 217, 228–229, 257, 259, 455

Hindu (India) art, Influence of, 358

Hindu-Persian miniature, sixteenth-seventeenth century

"Interior with Figures" (211), see p. 492

Hindu sculpture, Kushan Empire

"Figure" (212), see p. 492

Hobbema, 216, 217, 219–220, 226, 251, 259

Influence of, 280, 463

"Water Mill" (3), see p. 479

Hofer, Carl, 385

Holbein, Hans, the Younger, 197–198

"Ambassadors" (138), see p. 489

"Anne of Clèves" (335), see p. 498

"Erasmus"—Basel—(27), see p. 481

"Erasmus"—Paris—(336), see p. 498

"Head of a Man" (337), see p. 498

"Merchant Georg Gisze" (38), see p. 481

Homer, Winslow, 337–338

Honoré, Influence of, 178

Hooch, Pieter de, 227, 228, 257, 443
Influence of, 215, 229, 262
"Court of a Dutch House" (139),
see p. 489
Huber, Wolf, 195, 196
"Man's Portrait" (213), see p. 492
Hugo, Jean
"Audierne" (214), see p. 492
Huysum, Jan van
"Fruit and Flowers" (166), see p. 490

I

ILLUMINATED manuscript, end of thirteenth century
"Roman Breviary" (24), see p. 481
Illuminated manuscripts, see Miniatures
Illustration, 25, 73–74
and plastic form, 31–38
in French eighteenth century, 251,
258
in individual painters, 134, 136, 170,
210, 214, 218, 228, 249, 269, 286,
287, 298, 327, 337, 345, 346, 347,
369, 370, 376, 393, 417, 436
in Italians, 291
Impressionism, 36, 84, 116–121, 124,
157, 159, 169–170, 217, 285, 291,
298–299, 300–304, 305, 313, 337,
357, 395, 435, 461, 463
Characteristics of, 301
Derivations of, 300
in American painting, 340–345
Influence of, 317, 319, 320, 321, 323,
325, 328, 333, 334, 340, 345, 351,
356, 358, 359, 385
Light in, 300, 301, 307
Technique in, 300, 301, 302
Ingres, 41, 73, 81, 85–86, 95, 140, 170,
265, 265–266, 285, 315, 372
Influence of, 380
"Madame Rivière" (338), see p. 498
"Spring" (339), see p. 498
"Turkish Bath" (340), see p. 498
Innes, George, 336
Instinct
and art, 9, 12, 43–44
and emotion, 10
and interest, 11
and value, 8
Interest, 10–11, 12
and art, 11
and emotion, 11, 13
and esthetic appreciation, 43–44
and experience, 13
and instinct, 11
Isenbrant, 211–212
"Nativity" (273), see p. 495

Israels, Josef, 333
Italian painting, 230, 234, 235, 237, 240,
291, 292, 346
Influence of, 172, 173, 177, 178, 180,
185, 187, 188, 189, 190, 191, 192,
193, 194, 200, 210, 211, 212, 230,
231, 232, 233, 238, 239, 246, 250,
260, 261, 262, 380, 443, 456, 457
see also Florentine tradition, Sienese
tradition, Venetian tradition, Frescoes, and Miniatures
Italo-French form, 233, 238

J

JAMES, WILLIAM, 357
Japanese art, Influence of, 28, 325, 333,
358, 360
Jongkind, 463
Jordaens, 159
Joyce, James, 15

K

KANE, JOHN, 346–347
"Farm" (215), see p. 492
Kisling, 83
Klee, Paul, 385
Kokoschka, Oskar, 385

L

LANCRET, NICOLAS, 159, 250, 251, 252–
257, 258, 259, 260, 261, 263, 264,
459
"Manhood" (140), see p. 489
Landscape painting, 155–156, 157, 165,
278–287
and form, 28–30
in Cézanne, 324
in Corot, 266–267
in Dutch, see Dutch tradition
in Flemings, 199, 205, 206, 208–209
in French eighteenth century, 250,
251–252, 259
in French primitives, 236–237
in Germans, 179–180, 185
in Innes, 336
in Italians, 278, 391, 405
in Poussin, 434
in Renoir, 315–316, 316, 318
in Utrillo, 378
see also chapter on Impressionism
Lautrec, Toulouse, see Toulouse
Lawrence, Sir Thomas, 272
Lawson, Ernest, 345
Learning to see, 5–7, 19, 53
Lehmbruck, Wilhelm, 385
Le Nain, Antoine, 248–249
Le Nain, Louis, 248–249

Le Nain, Mathieu, 248–249
Leonardo da Vinci, 41, 83, 84, 85, 87, 92, 127–128, 128–134, 135, 137, 138, 139, 145, 146, 212, 278, 297–298, 354, 418
  Influence of, 68, 75, 92, 136, 140, 157, 196, 228, 261, 262, 407, 408, 409, 430, 462
  "Adoration of the Magi" (96), see p. 486
  "Annunciation" (97), see p. 486
  "Bacchus" (341), see p. 498
  "Lucrezia Crivelli" (342), see p. 498
  "Mona Lisa" (343), see p. 498
  "Saint John the Baptist" (344), see p. 498
  "Virgin and Child" (261), see p. 494
  "Virgin of the Rocks"—London— (141), see p. 489
  "Virgin of the Rocks"—Paris— (345), see p. 498
  "Virgin, St. Anne, and the Infant Jesus" (346), see p. 498
Leonardo da Vinci (The Renaissance), Walter Pater, 134
Le Sueur, 88–89, 261
Leyden, Lucas van, 212–213
  "Adoration of the Magi" (216), see p. 492
  "Man's Portrait" (142), see p. 489
  "Saint Jerome" (39), see p. 482
Light
  and color, 65, 84–85
  and composition, 104
  and design, 297–298
  in Cologne school, 178
  in Dutch, 215–216
  in Florentines, 138
  in impressionists, 300, 301, 307
Limbourg, Pol de, 394
  and Brothers, 236–237
  "Book of Hours of the Duc de Berry" (51), see p. 483
Line
  in composition, 103, 104
  in drawing, see Drawing
  Plastic, 91, 377
Lipchitz, Jacques, 355
Lippi, Fra Filippo, 91, 123–124, 137, 138, 193, 292
  "Virgin Adoring the Child" (98), see p. 486
Liszt, 39, 67
Literature, 49, 50
  Style and subject-matter in, 30, 50
Lochner, Stefan, 178, 185–186, 187, 209, 232, 441

Influence of, 177, 189, 192, 194, 195, 196, 210, 214
"Last Judgment" (67), see p. 484
"Madonna in Paradise Garden" (68), see p. 484
"Madonna in the Garden of Roses" (69), see p. 484
Longhi, Pietro, 157
  "Dancing Master" (432), see p. 503
  "Interior Scene" (217), see p. 492
Lorenzetti, Ambrogio
  "Legend of St. Stephen" (426), see p. 503
Lorenzetti, Pietro
  "Scenes from the Life of St. Umiltà" (99), see p. 486
Lorenzetti school, Influence of, 456
Lorenzettis, The, 141
Lorenzo Monaco, see Monaco
Lower-Saxony Master, end of thirteenth century
  "Antependium from the Cloister of Wennigsen a. Deister" (124), see p. 488
Lower-Saxony Master, active c.1360 – c.1380
  "Altarpiece—Life of Jesus—from the Cologne Laurenziuskirche" (70), see p. 484
Lower-Saxony Master, active c.1360 – c.1380, Attributed to
  "Altarpiece" (268), see p. 495
Lower-Saxony Master, beginning of fifteenth century
  "Golden Panels, from Lüneburg" (125), see p. 488
Luini, 41, 73, 75
  Influence of, 261, 262
Luks, George, 339–340
Lyon, Corneille de, 197, 206, 247, 248

M

Mabuse, Influence of, 196
Madame Bovary, Flaubert, 73
Manet, 28, 29–30, 34–35, 36, 49–50, 71, 96, 105, 122, 169–170, 171, 215, 229, 269, 277, 297, 305–308, 455
  Influence of, 28, 313, 317, 323, 333, 336, 337, 339, 340, 345, 351–352, 353, 359, 360, 377, 465, 472, 477
  "Boy with Fife" (347), see p. 498
  "Boy with Sword" (274), see p. 495
  "Dead Christ with Angels" (275), see p. 495
  "Olympia" (348), see p. 498
  "Washerwoman" (218), see p. 492

"Woman with Parrot" (276), *see* p. 495

Mantegna, Andrea, 73, 76, 88, 127, 165, 196, 265, 278, 405, 418
Influence of, 70, 422
"Agony in the Garden" (143), *see* p. 489
"Parnassus" (349), *see* p. 499
"Wisdom Triumphing over the Vices" (350), *see* p. 499

Marc, Franz, 385

Marin, 347

Marmion, Simon
"Legend of St. Bertin" (40), *see* p. 482

Martini, Simone, 141, 437
"Ascent to Calvary" (351), *see* p. 499

Masaccio, 115–121, 123, 137, 138, 139, 140, 144, 147, 156, 234, 292–297, 298, 300, 380, 392, 400, 418, 434, 435
"Adam and Eve Expelled from Paradise" (83), *see* p. 485
"Frescoes" (84), *see* p. 485
"Saint Peter Healing the Sick" (85), *see* p. 485
"Saint Peter Raising Tabitha" (86), *see* p. 486
"Tribute Money" (87), *see* p. 486

Mass-composition, 102–103, 104–105
in Florentines, 137

Master Bertram, 190

Master Francke, 179, 190–191
"Adoration of the Kings" (114), *see* p. 487
"Bearing of the Cross" (115), *see* p. 487
"Birth of Christ" (116), *see* p. 488
"Christ, Man of Sorrows" (117), *see* p. 488
"Entombment" (118), *see* p. 488
"Flagellation of Christ" (119), *see* p. 488
"Flight of St. Thomas of Canterbury" (120), *see* p. 488
"Martyrdom of St. Thomas of Canterbury" (121), *see* p. 488
"Resurrection" (122), *see* p. 488
"Women of the Crucifixion" (123), *see* p. 488

Master of Flémalle, 437, 438

Master of Liesborn, 189–190

Master of Moulins, 210
"Magdalen and Donor" (352), *see* p. 499

Master Wilhelm, Attributed to
"Kaiser Karl IV, and Heads of Prophets" (71), *see* p. 484

Mather, Frank Jewett, 89

Matisse, Henri-, 17, 18, 40, 41, 62, 90, 102, 105, 111, 121–122, 124, 153, 195, 229, 234, 269, 291, 297, 308, 334, 345, 354, 355, 358, 359–368, 369, 373
Influence of, 28, 335, 358, 372, 385
"Green Dress" (219), *see* p. 492
"Joy of Life" (220), *see* p. 492
"Music Lesson" (221), *see* p. 492
"Reclining Nude" (222), *see* p. 492

Matter and form, 27, 38–42

Maupassant, 30

Mauve, Anton, 333

Mazia, Violette de, and Albert C. Barnes
The Art of Henri-Matisse, 19 n, 359 n
The Art of Renoir, 313 n, 352 n
The French Primitives and Their Forms, 141 n, 175 n, 177 n, 230 n

Medium
and art, 31, 49–50
and form, 31–33
Command of, 49–50

Meissonier, 50

Memling, 187, 188, 207, 208, 208–209, 211, 212, 439
Influence of, 192
"Duke of Cleves" (144), *see* p. 489
"Marriage of St. Catherine" (353), *see* p. 499
"Saint Benedict" (100), *see* p. 486
"Scenes from the Legend of St. Ursula" (49), *see* p. 482
"Seven Joys of Mary" (262), *see* p. 494
"Woman's Portrait" (354), *see* p. 499

Memmi, Lippo, 141
Influence of, 456

Meredith, George, *The Egoist*, 43

Messina, Antonello da
"Condottiere" (355), *see* p. 499

Metsu, 229

Metsys, Quentin, 196, 211

Michelangelo, 18 n, 76, 85, 92–93, 96, 115, 123, 128, 134–135, 138, 158, 268, 292, 324, 354, 397, 410, 411
Influence of, 140, 165, 267, 320, 323, 434
"Frescoes" (419), *see* p. 502
"Last Judgment" (420), *see* p. 502
"Moses" (417), *see* p. 502
"Original Sin and Expulsion from Eden" (421), *see* p. 502

Middle-Rhine Master, active c.1340
"Altenberg Altarpiece" (108), *see* p. 487

Middle-Rhine Master, active c.1420
"Madonna and Child, with Female
Saints" (41), see p. 482
Middle-Rhine Master, active c.1420–
1430
"Mary with Female Saints" (72),
see p. 484
Middle-Rhine region, Painting in, see
Rhine-region painting
Millet, 49, 73, 75, 286–287, 303, 333
Milton, Paradise Lost, 30
Miniatures
Influence of, 456, 457
Flemish, 187, 394
French, 141, 235, 236, 237, 240, 248,
394, 436, 437
Influence of, 177, 187, 230, 235, 237,
238, 239, 240, 245, 246, 247
German, 436
Italian, 394
Persian, 63, 111, 188, 394
see also Hindu-Persian
Modeling, 65, 85
Modern painting, 291–347
Dawn of, 111–114
Transition to, 291–299
Modigliani, 308, 353, 355, 376–377
"Girl in Sunday Clothes" (223), see
p. 492
"Red-Headed Woman" (224), see
p. 492
Monaco, Lorenzo, 83, 142, 173, 178,
438
Influence of, 124, 394
"Virgin and Child, with Four Saints"
(101), see p. 486
Monet, 28, 71, 96, 280, 291, 299,
301–302, 303, 307, 333, 334, 358,
463
"House Boat" (225), see p. 493
"Madame Monet Embroidering"
(226), see p. 493
Monticelli, 84, 226
Moorish decorations, Influence of, 235
Moreau, Louis Gabriel, 261–262
Moro, Antonio, 214
Mosaics, 91, 340
see also Byzantine mosaics and Byzan-
tine tradition
Mullen, Mary, An Approach to Art, 8 n,
12 n
Murillo, 73, 75
Music, 32–33, 39–40, 49
Mysticism
Color and, 86
Decoration and, 46
in art, 45–47

N
NATURALISM, 47, 267, 306, 313
Step toward, 115–116, 139
see also Realism
Negro sculpture, Influence of, 354, 355,
358, 370, 372, 374, 376
Negro sculpture, sixteenth century
"Figure" (227), see p. 493
Neo-classicism, 140, 285
Nolde, Emil, 385

O
O'KEEFFE, GEORGIA, 347
Orcagna, Andrea
"Coronation of the Virgin" (145),
see p. 489
Oriental art, 328
Influence of, 235, 359–360
see also Chinese painting, Japanese
art, Hindu art, Hindu sculpture,
Hindu-Persian miniature, and Per-
sian art
Originality
and use of tradition, 31
in art, 19
Ostade, van, 229
Overture 1812, Tschaikowsky, 32, 393

P
PACINO DI BONAGUIDA
"Saint Bartholomew" (228), see
p. 493
Palma Vecchio, 88, 157
Paolo Veronese, see Veronese
Paradise Lost, Milton, 30
Pascin, 33–34, 116, 122, 140, 157, 269,
375–376
"Seated Figure" (229), see p. 493
"Standing Nude" (230), see p. 493
Pater, Jean-Baptiste Joseph, 157, 250,
251, 258, 259, 261, 263, 264, 459
"Camp Scene" (167), see p. 490
"Comedians in a Park" (356),
see p. 499
"Outdoor Fête" (357), see p. 499
Pater, Walter
The Renaissance: Leonardo da Vinci,
134
Patinir, 211
"Baptism of Christ" (442), see p. 504
Pattern, 56–61
and design, see Design and pattern
Peales, The, 171, 336
Pechstein, Max, 385
"Pennsylvania Dutch" painting, 336
"Pennsylvania Dutch" painting on vel-
vet
"Still-Life with Bird" (231), see p. 493

INDEX

Perception
  and form, 26
  Psychology of, 5–7
Perrier, François, 230
Persian art, Influence of, 358, 360
  see also Miniatures
Perspective, 66, 106, 116, 121, 122, 299, 300, 393
Perugino, 69, 83, 87, 106–107, 107–108, 127, 278
  Influence of, 136
  "Christ Giving the Keys to Peter" (422), see p. 502
  "Combat of Love and Chastity" (358), see p. 499
Petrus Christus, see Christus
Photography and painting, 38–39, 40–41
Picasso, 28, 42–43, 121, 127, 136, 139, 234, 292, 308, 346, 355, 357–358, 369–373, 377, 405, 449
  Influence of, 345, 385
  "Composition" (232), see p. 493
  "Girl with Cigarette" (233), see p. 493
  "Harlequins" (234), see p. 493
  "Still-Life" (235), see p. 493
Piero della Francesca, 87, 92, 103, 115, 125–127, 137, 138, 139, 140, 156, 189, 192, 208, 238, 278, 292, 298, 394, 396, 397, 398, 458
  Influence of, 139, 327, 369
  "Baptism of Christ" (146), see p. 489
  "Discovery of the True Cross" (11), see p. 480
  "Exaltation of the Cross" (12), see p. 480
  "Nativity of Our Lord, with Angels Adoring" (147), see p. 489
  "Reception by Solomon" (13), see p. 480
  "Victory over Maxentius" (14), see p. 480
Piero della Francesca, School of
  "Marriage of St. Catherine" (15), see p. 480
Pinto, Angelo, 347
Pinto, Biagio, 269, 347
  "Checker Players" (406), see p. 501
Pinto, Salvatore, 347
Piombo, Sebastiano del, see Sebastiano
Pisanello (or Pisano)
  "Princess of the Este Family" (359), see p. 499
  "Vision of St. Eustace" (148), see p. 489
Pisano, see Pisanello

Pissarro, 31, 71, 122, 291, 301, 302, 302–303, 334
  Influence of, 320, 328
Plastic
  and other values, 31–38
  Definition of, 55
  line, 91, 377
  unity, 55, 56–61
  values, 20
Plastic form, 55–71
  and illustration, 31–38
  and reality, 64
  and subject-matter, 72–81, 121–122, 168, 291–292, 297, 356, 357
  and unity, 63
  see also Design
Poetry, Form and matter in, 39
Pointillism, 303
  Influence of, 340
Pollaiuolo, Antonio, 134, 137
  Influence of, 134
  "Hercules Crushing Antaeus" (102), see p. 487
  "Hercules Overcoming the Hydra" (103), see p. 487
Pompeian frescoes, prior to first century
  "Frescoes" (407), see p. 501
Portraiture, 270–277
  Composition in, 105, 106
  Egypto-Roman, Influence of, 36
  English school of, 272
  in Clouet school, 247–248
  in Flemings, 200, 205–206, 208, 209, 213
  in Germans, 193, 194, 195, 195–196, 196, 197–198
  in Ingres, 266
Post-impressionism, 328–335
  Influence of, 359
Potter, Paul, 218
Poussin, Nicolas, 69, 84, 87, 93, 106, 107, 139, 140, 157, 160–165, 259, 261, 298, 299, 327, 356, 380, 411, 429
  Influence of, 88, 157, 250, 258, 460
  "Arcadian Shepherds" (360), see p. 499
  "Blindmen of Jericho" (361), see p. 499
  "Cephalus and Aurora" (149), see p. 489
  "Earthly Paradise" (362), see p. 499
  "Funeral of Phocion" (363), see p. 499
  "Holy Family" (364), see p. 499
  "Summer, Ruth and Boaz" (365), see p. 499
Prendergast, Maurice, 127, 139, 340–345

"Idyl" (236), see p. 493
"Landscape" (237), see p. 493
Pre-Raphaelites, 81
Prud'hon, Paul, 261, 262
"Justice and Divine Vengeance Pursuing Crime" (366), see p. 499
Pucelle, Jean, 246
Puvis de Chavannes, 84, 327

Q

QUALITY
and color, 86
in painting, 42–44

R

RAPHAEL, 67–68, 73, 82, 84, 87–88, 88, 92, 102, 103, 106–107, 128, 134, 135–136, 138, 145, 148, 153, 158, 269, 400, 407, 410, 418
Influence of, 70, 140, 157, 165, 228, 258, 265, 433, 434
"Count Baldassare Castiglione" (367), see p. 499
"Descent from the Cross" (416), see p. 502
"Frescoes" (425), see p. 503
"Holy Family, of François I" (368), see p. 499
"Madonna, from the House of Tempi" (263), see p. 494
"Madonna: la Belle Jardinière" (369), see p. 499
"Saint Michael Crushing Satan" (370), see p. 499
"Transfiguration" (427), see p. 503
"Virgin with Blue Diadem" (371), see p. 500
"Woman with Veil" (80), see p. 485
"Young Man" (372), see p. 500
Realism, 115–116, 168, 264, 267, 298, 314
see also Naturalism
Reality, 14–15, 16, 36, 67, 69–70, 74, 84
and plastic form, 64
and space-composition, 66
Color and, 65
Space and, 63–65
Redfield, E. W., 28, 43
Rembrandt, 18, 42, 49, 62, 69, 83, 84, 86, 94, 95, 102, 116, 126, 133, 138, 159, 165, 169, 220–226, 227, 269, 272, 298, 305, 338, 367, 422, 441
Influence of, 267, 272
"Hendrickje Stoffels" (373), see p. 500
"Man with Stick" (374), see p. 500
"Old Man" (104), see p. 487

"Old Woman Cutting her Nails" (277), see p. 495
"Self-Portrait, as an Old Man" (375), see p. 500
"Unmerciful Servant" (168), see p. 490
Reni, Guido, 75, 88
"Deianeira and Nessus" (377), see p. 500
Renoir, 18, 28, 34, 40, 41, 64, 69, 71, 76, 82, 83, 84, 87, 96, 102, 107, 122, 127, 139, 140, 158, 265–266, 266, 269, 277, 299, 302, 303, 308, 313–318, 321, 322, 324, 351–353, 354, 357, 367, 373, 378
Influence of, 334, 345, 358, 375, 478
"Bathers in Forest" (238), see p. 493
"Bathing Group" (239), see p. 493
"Mademoiselle Jeanne Durand-Ruel" (240), see p. 493
"Mount Ste. Victoire" (241), see p. 493
"Noirmoutier" (242), see p. 493
Reynolds, Sir Joshua, 159, 292
Rhenish Master, active 1170–1200
"Ingeburge Psalter" (52), see p. 483
Rhenish Master, active c.1340
"Scenes from the Life of Christ: Annunciation, Nativity, Adoration, Presentation" (378), see p. 500
Rhine region, Painting in, 172, 175, 175–188
Influence of, 175–176, 177, 178
Rhythm, 62, 67
Ribera, Influence of, 319
Roman sculpture, see Sculpture
Romano, Giulio, 88
Romanticism, 70
Romney, 272
Rosselli, Cosimo
"Pharaoh's Destruction in the Red Sea" (423), see p. 503
Rouault, 269, 379
Rousseau, le douanier, 124, 346, 358, 377–378, 388, 420
"People in Sunday Clothes" (243), see p. 493
"Woman in Landscape" (244), see p. 493
Rousseau, Théodore, 88, 286, 339
"Edge of the Forest of Fontainebleau, toward Brôle" (379), see p. 500
Rubens, 17, 73, 82, 94, 122, 126, 134, 154, 157, 157–159, 165, 200, 262, 272, 279–280, 280, 299, 301, 317, 318, 324, 380, 463, 466
Influence of, 71, 83, 88, 95, 250, 251,

252, 258–259, 260–261, 262, 266, 272, 280, 317, 319, 351, 375, 376, 459, 460
"Andromeda" (42), see p. 482
"Autumn, Château de Steen" (150), see p. 489
"Baron Henri de Vicq" (380), see p. 500
"Country Fair" (381), see p. 500
"Hélène Fourment and her Children" (382), see p. 500
"Holy Family" (245), see p. 493
"Judgment of Paris" (151), see p. 489
"Landscape with Shepherd" (152), see p. 489
"Peace and War" (153), see p. 489
"Tournament" (383), see p. 500
Ruisdael, Jacob van, 216, 218–219, 219, 338
"Landscape with Water Mill" (4), see p. 479
Ruysdael, Salomon van, 212, 216, 216–218, 218, 220
"Halt" (5), see p. 479
Ryder, Albert P., 338–339
"Curfew Hour" (278), see p. 495
"Toilers of the Sea" (279), see p. 495

S

Salon d'Automne, 356
Santayana, 10
Sargent, 28, 260, 336
Sarto, Andrea del, 75
Sasaccio, Carlo, 196
Schaffner, Martin, 195–196
Schongauer, Martin, 192
"Christ's Passion" (57), see p. 483
"Madonna in the Garden of Roses" (54), see p. 483
Science and art, 7, 13, 14, 36
Sculpture
Classic, 76
Influence of, 317
see also Classic art
Egyptian, see Egyptian sculpture
French, Influence of, 250, 258
Greco-Roman, Influence of, 354
Greek, see Greek sculpture
Hindu, see Hindu sculpture
Negro, see Negro sculpture
Roman, Influence of, 76, 127
Smyrna, see Smyrna sculpture
Space in, 106
Sebastiano del Piombo, 88, 157
Sentimentalism, 10, 38
Settanni, Luigi, 347
"Russian Ballet" (246), see p. 493

Seurat, Georges, 139, 303, 328 n
"Models" (247), see p. 493
"Port of Honfleur" (248), see p. 493
Seyffert, Leopold, 336
Sienese droop, 141
in other traditions, 176, 179, 240, 456, 457
Sienese tradition, 141–143, 174 n, 394
Influence of, 172, 173, 174, 179, 185, 191, 237, 246, 417, 437, 457
Significant form, 55, 61
Signorelli, Luca, 410, 411
Influence of, 92, 158
"Four Episodes in the Life of Moses" (424), see p. 503
Simone Martini, see Martini
Sisley, 71, 301, 304, 334, 391
Smyrna sculpture, fourth century B.C.
"Grotesque Figure" (249), see p. 493
Soest, Konrad von, 188–189
"Altarpiece of Crucifixion" (26), see p. 481
"Crowning of the Virgin" (266), see p. 495
"Outpouring of the Holy Spirit" (267), see p. 495
Solario, 196
Southern French form (Pietàs), 233, 238
Southern French Master, fifteenth century
"Pietà" (428), see p. 503
Southern French Master, second half of fifteenth century
"Villeneuve Pietà" (384), see p. 500
Soutine, 87, 111, 157, 308, 355, 374–375
Influence of, 385
"Seated Woman" (250), see p. 493
Space, 63–65, 66
and reality, 63–65
-composition, 66, 105–108
in architecture, 106
in sculpture, 106
Spanish painting, 159, 166–171
Influence of, 233, 267, 336
Spanish primitives, 191, 234, 235, 238
Stained glass, 230, 235, 236, 237
Influence of, 234, 235, 239
Steen, Jan, 229
Strigel, Bernhard, 177, 186, 187, 192–193, 206
"Conrad Rehlingen and his Children" (264), see p. 495
"Kaiser Maximilian I" (443), see p. 504

INDEX

"Saint Norbert as Protector" (43),
see p. 482
"Sibylle von Freyberg" (265), see
p. 495
Stuart, Gilbert, 171, 336
Style
and form, 28
and subject-matter in literature, 30, 50
Subject-matter
and art, 20–25
and emotion, 35–36
and music, 32–33
and plastic form, 72–81, 121–122,
168, 291–292, 297, 356, 357
and reality, 70
and style, in literature, 30, 50
in Florentines, 137
in Venetians, 144
Legitimate and illegitimate use of,
31–36, 37–38
Sully, Thomas, 171, 336
Surrealism, 385
Swinburne, 67
Swirl
Compositional, 251, 431
in drawing, 93, 122, 154, 158, 258,
260, 266, 271, 317, 319, 333, 376,
379, 433, 440, 459, 466
Linear, 128, 178

T

TACTILE values, 89, 138–139
Tapestry
Influence of, 340
see also French tapestry
Technique
and form, 28–31
Command of, 49–50
Terborch, Gerard, 229, 443
Influence of, 262–263, 460
"Concert" (385), see p. 500
Textiles
Coptic, Influence of, 365
Egyptian, Influence of, 235
see also Draperies and Folds
The Aesthetic Experience, Laurence
Buermeyer, 45 n
The Art of Henri-Matisse, Barnes and
de Mazia, 19 n, 359 n
The Art of Renoir, Barnes and de Mazia,
313 n, 352 n
The Egoist, George Meredith, 43
The French Primitives and Their Forms,
Barnes and de Mazia, 141 n, 175 n,
177 n, 230 n
The Renaissance: Leonardo da Vinci,
Walter Pater, 134

Third Symphony (Eroica), Beethoven, 32
Tiepolo, 157
Influence of, 258, 260, 261
Tintoretto, 20–25, 31, 33, 49, 74–75, 83,
85, 87, 93, 133, 137, 138, 140, 144,
145, 153–154, 154, 166, 193, 212,
286, 292, 301, 418, 453, 454
Influence of, 96, 111, 157, 165, 166,
168, 251, 252, 260, 319, 320, 338,
339, 433, 455, 459, 462
"Artist's Portrait" (386), see p. 500
"Calvary" (433), see p. 503
"Origin of the Milky Way" (154),
see p. 489
"Paradise" (387), see p. 500
"Susanna at the Bath" (388), see
p. 500
"Woman of Samaria" (251), see
p. 493
Titian, 31, 40, 49, 69, 82, 83, 84, 85, 87,
93, 133, 137, 138, 144, 145, 147–148,
153, 154, 160, 169, 197, 264, 269,
278, 316, 371, 395, 397, 418, 419,
443, 478
Influence of, 154, 168, 251, 252, 433,
434, 464
"Alfonso da Ferrara and Laura di
Dianti" (389), see p. 500
"Assumption" (438), see p. 504
"Bacchus and Ariadne" (155), see
p. 489
"Christ and the Magdalen" (156),
see p. 490
"Christ Crowned with Thorns" (390),
see p. 500
"Disciples at Emmaus" (391), see
p. 500
"Entombment" (392), see p. 500
"Jupiter and Antiope" (393), see
p. 500
"Man with Glove" (394), see p. 500
"Saint John the Baptist" (434), see
p. 504
"Venus and Love" (173), see p. 490
"Venus and Music" (174), see
p. 490
"Venus and Organ Player" (44), see
p. 482
"Venus with Dog" (105), see p. 487
Tommaso da Modena, 174
Toulouse-Lautrec, 327
Influence of, 369
Tradition
Definition of, 19
Use of, 19, 31, 111
Transferred values, 18–19, 366–367
Tschaikowsky, Overture 1812, 32, 393

[520]

INDEX

Tura, Cosimo, 92, 158
"Pietà" (395), see p. 501
Turner, 73, 85, 285–286
"Calais Pier" (157), see p. 490
"Dido Building Carthage" (158),
see p. 490

U

Uccello, 91–92, 115, 121–122, 137, 139,
173, 188, 191, 193, 207, 208, 292,
299, 320, 397, 400, 411
'Rout of San Romano" (159), see
p. 490
Ugolino da Siena, 143, 437
Umbrians, 125, 173, 238, 380
Unity
and plastic form, 63
and variety, 15–16, 63
in art, 15–16, 18
Plastic, 55, 56–61, 66–67
see also chapter on Composition
Upper- or Middle-Rhine Master, active
c.1410
"Garden of Paradise" (109), see
p. 487
Upper-Rhine region, Painting in, see
Rhine-region painting
Utrillo, 378–379
"Church of St. Aignan, Chartres"
(252), see p. 494

V

Values
and instinct, 8–9
Confusion of, 3–5, 25, 54, 56, 122,
168
Esthetic, 20–44
Human, 20, 49
Plastic, 20, 31–38
Tactile, 89, 138–139
Transferred, 18–19, 366–367
van der Goes, see Goes
van der Heyden, see Heyden
van der Velde, see Velde
van der Weyden, see Weyden
van Dyck, see Dyck
van Eyck, see Eyck
van Gogh, see Gogh
van Goyen, see Goyen
van Huysum, see Huysum
van Leyden, see Leyden
van Ostade, see Ostade
van Ruisdael, Jacob, see Ruisdael
van Ruysdael, Salomon, see Ruysdael
Variety
and unity, 15–16, 63
of color, 83

Velásquez, 34, 159, 168–170, 220, 248,
272, 298, 326, 452
Influence of, 169–170, 170, 263, 267,
305, 306, 307, 313, 314, 317, 323,
337, 338, 380, 436, 455, 460, 462,
465
"Don Baltasar Carlos in the Riding
School" (169), see p. 490
"Infanta Marguerite" (396), see
p. 501
"Lady with a Fan" (170), see p. 490
Velde, van der, 215
Venetian glow, 86, 88, 144, 146, 147,
154, 155, 156, 157, 158, 197, 257,
279, 297, 300
Venetian tradition, 83, 85, 144–156, 157,
212, 214, 279, 285, 297
compared with Florentine, 137, 138,
144, 155–156
Drawing in, 93, 96
in subsequent painting, 157, 158, 165,
168, 197, 250, 252, 257, 262, 263,
266, 267, 280, 300, 316, 317, 320,
323, 339, 432, 433, 434, 459, 460
Subject-matter in, 144
Veneziano, Domenico, 192, 195, 197,
394
"Madonna and Child, with Saints"
(106), see p. 487
Vermeer, Jan, 18, 146, 206, 207, 208,
215, 227, 227–228, 228, 229, 313,
314, 420, 443
Influence of 257, 259, 262
"Cook" (6), see p. 479
"Diana at the Bath" (111), see
p. 487
"Girl Reading Letter" (7), see
p. 479
"Girl with a Pearl Necklace" (45),
see p. 482
"Girl with Turban" (112), see p. 487
"Letter" (8), see p. 479
"Little Street" (9), see p. 479
"View of Delft" (113), see p. 487
Vernet, Claude Joseph, 261, 262
"Bathers" (397), see p. 501
"Landscape" (398), see p. 501
"Port of Marseilles" (399), see
p. 501
Veronese, Paolo, 93, 147, 154–155, 157,
158, 225
Influence of, 165, 251, 258, 259, 260 n,
433, 460
"Banquet in the House of Levi"
(435), see p. 504
"Baptism of Christ" (253), see p. 494
"Burning of Sodom" (400), see p. 501

INDEX

"Jupiter Destroying the Vices" (401),
see p. 501
Verrocchio, Andrea, 397
Influence of, 133, 134, 135, 429
"Baptism of Christ, with Two
Angels" (107), *see* p. 487
Vinci, Leonardo da, *see* Leonardo
Virtuosity, 64, 67, 199, 215, 227, 229,
272
in individual men, 68, 92, 95, 128, 135,
136, 145, 198, 220, 228, 271, 286,
340, 372
Vivarini, Alvise
"Madonna Enthroned, with Saints"
(436), *see* p. 504

W

"WALL OF GALLERY, BARNES FOUNDA-
TION" (254), *see* p. 494
Watteau, 94, 157, 159, 250, 252, 257,
258, 261, 262, 263, 264, 314, 459
"Embarkation for Cythera" (402),
see p. 501
"Game of Love" (160), *see* p. 490
West, Benjamin, 336

Westphalian Master, active c.1400
"Healing of Lazarus" (255), *see*
p. 494
Westphalian Master, active c.1400
"Marienkirche Altarpiece from Göt-
tingen" (126), *see* p. 488
Westphalian painting, 172, 188–190
Weyden, van der, 206–207, 208
Influence of, 186, 209, 457
Whistler, 28, 85, 336–337
Influence of, 338
"Artist's Mother" (403), *see* p. 501
"Théodore Duret" (280), *see* p. 495
Witz, Konrad, 191–192
"Christ on the Cross" (46), *see*
p. 482
Wood, Grant, 347
Woodcuts, German, 141, 240
Influence of, 177, 178
Work of art
Nature of, 13, 16
Purpose of, 3

Z

ZOLA, EMILE, 15

10.2.91

1ST chapter pg 3

pg. 111 Dawn of Modern Ptg

Pg 141-142

10.9.91
1. Giotto 112-114
2. Masaccio 115-117
3. Uccello 121-122
4. Andrea del Castagno 122-123
5. Piero della Francesca - 125.127

Plastic-form

10.23.91
1. Fra Angelico pp.124-25
2. Botticelli   128
                    128-134
3. Leonardo   134-135
4. Michelangelo   135-136
5. Raphael
6. Summary of Florentine form 136-140

1. FRENCH TRADITION   P. 234-235
2. FLEMISH   P. 199-200
3. GERMAN   P. 172-173
4. MAKE CHART - TRAD SUBJECT COLOR LT. LINE SPACE FOLD
                                                  FACES